Life as a Novel

ALSO BY PHILIP TEMPLE

Novels
The Explorer
Stations
Beak of the Moon
Sam
Dark of the Moon
To Each His Own
White Shadows
I Am Always With You
The Mantis
MiStory

History and Biography
Castles in the Air
New Zealand Explorers
Presenting New Zealand
A Sort of Conscience: The Wakefields
Chance is a Fine Thing

Travel and Adventure
Nawok!
The Sea and the Snow
The World At Their Feet
The Last True Explorer

Nature and Environment
Ways to the Wilderness
The Book of the Kea
Milford Superguide
Lake, Mountain, Tree (ed.)

Photographic
Mantle of the Skies
Christchurch
Patterns of Water
Philip Temple's South Island
New Zealand from the Air

Political
Making Your Vote Count: A Guide to Electoral Reform
Manifesto Aotearoa: 101 Political Poems (ed. with Emma Neale)

Life as a Novel

A biography of Maurice Shadbolt

Volume One: 1932–1973

Philip Temple

David Ling Publishing Limited
PO Box 401106 Mangawhai Heads
Mangawhai, Northland, New Zealand
www.davidling.co.nz

ISBN 978-1-927305-44-7

First Published 2018

© 2018 Philip Temple

The moral rights of the author have been asserted.

This book is copyright. Apart from any fair dealing for the purpose of private study, research, criticism, or review as permitted under the Copyright Act, no part may be reproduced by any process without the prior written permission of the Publisher.

Typeset by Express Communications Limited
Printed in Taiwan

Front cover photo: Maurice Shadbolt in the early 1960s.
Back cover photo: Maurice (at left) with Lois McIvor, Colin McCahon, Anne and Garth Tapper at Garth Tapper's house in Titirangi. (Both Sean Shadbolt collection.) Author photo: Reg Graham.
The koru on pages 1, 15, 145 and 281 was designed by Colin McCahon for Maurice Shadbolt's use as a letterhead.

Published with the assistance of a grant from Creative New Zealand.

CONTENTS

Prologue		9
Part One Finding a Genre		15
1	Insurrections	17
2	The country boy	30
3	Disruptions	41
4	Sex and socialism	47
5	Someone to watch over me	55
6	Thinking visually	67
7	Opening shots	72
8	Opo	78
9	Maurice and Maurice	84
10	A few flowers blooming	95
11	A comprehensible country	105
12	Thank you goodbye	110
13	A smoking ruin	122
14	London glowed	130
15	Departures	137

Part Two Telling Stories	145
16 A strange unexpected land	147
17 Threesomes	160
18 Summer fires	169
19 Full of the warm south	179
20 At the edge of the sky	194
21 Hot coals	204
22 Coming apart	218
23 Wild colonial boys	226
24 Swimming with dolphins	231
25 Buttercup fields forever	236
26 A self-confessed adulterer	244
27 Perfect and imperfect	259
28 In the zone	271
Postscript	280
Acknowledgements	283
Bibliography	285
Notes	290
Index	312

'We spent a happy night conjuring pictures of you gorged on Kolenko [sic] and vodka in your palace on a hill overlooking the proles' tenements. 'That's the sort of feeling I've always imagined would make a writer feel pretty happy with his lot and ensure he would make a novel of his life'.[1]

Louis Johnson to Maurice Shadbolt, 27 October 1957.

PROLOGUE

Maurice and Bridget (Armstrong) had been invited to an early evening party at Pat and Gil Hanly's villa in Epsom. They said I should go too, and meet some new people while I was up for a few days. But on that mild April evening in 1984 few seemed interested in talking with a stranger from the south who wrote mostly about mountains and the outdoors. Crevasses and kea lay on a distant continent for painters, writers and theatre people catching up with Auckland artworld goss or fencing with old foes and friends. With the exception of Don Binney: we both had an enthusiasm for birds.

Bridget could see my discomfort and, after a while, she said she would go back home to Titirangi and put on a chicken for dinner. She had had enough too, tired after days of rehearsing for a production of Chekhov's *Three Sisters* that opened the following week. She left, saying we should follow an hour later. I was looking forward to another evening of drinking, smoking and talking about books.

When we pulled up at 35 Arapito Road, it was dark but still warm enough for cicadas to zing through the Titirangi bush. Maurice had planted banana palms on the front boundary, and the atmosphere was thick, heavy with impending rain, and it all seemed semi-tropical and exotic for someone accustomed to the sharper, cleaner climate of Banks Peninsula. The house appeared to have sunk among the trees, its dark green weatherboards and grey roof planted and grown from the steep section that ran down to the shores of the Manukau Harbour.

I followed Maurice into the porch and I was close behind him as he opened the door into the long narrow kitchen. When he stepped inside, something flew through the air and hit him on the chest. It was a half-broiled chicken, which then fell to the floor. Instinctively, prompted by the five-second rule, I bent to pick it up but then realised that, on this particular floor, even one second would have been too long.

The flying chicken was the cymbal clash for the most impressive performance of outrage I had ever witnessed. Bridget railed at Maurice for his deceit, his dishonesty, themes with variations that filled the air with a fury and invective that allowed no opening for response. Maurice, in any case, had nothing to say, nothing in defence. As Bridget moved up and down the stage of the kitchen, he shuffled past her and slumped into a chair in the corner of the lounge. He began sucking on his pipe, watching her with a hang-dog look as the diatribe continued. I put the chicken on a plate and stood to the side, no actor in this, but acutely aware I was an audience of one, a witness perhaps, as I often seemed to be when I visited Titirangi. Bridget had recently performed the part of Deborah in Harold Pinter's play *A Kind of Alaska*. Deborah had been in a comatose state for thirty years and awoken to discover shocking revelations about the world and the people about her. And here was a live reprise for, when Bridget had returned home to put the chicken on, she had seen the answerphone light blinking, a cue to the next episode in her personal drama. From the torrent of angry words directed at Maurice, I deduced that the message on the answerphone had been meant for him: from Fleur Adcock [*] in London, as she had mentioned a recent trip she and Maurice had made to Dublin. He had told me about this, *sans Fleur*, the evening before. It had been an enjoyable assignment for *Reader's Digest*, all expenses paid. We could exchange notes on the process because I, too, had undertaken European assignments for the *Digest*. But I had never taken girlfriends.

I lived too far away from the Shadbolts to know all the twists and turns of their relationship and I was not anxious to learn more. But from the tenor and detail of Bridget's disquisition, it was clear this was not the first evidence of Maurice's infidelity. Seven years before, I had witnessed more closely the end of another of his relationships and sensed what was to come, though it proved more drawn out than I would have expected.

Bridget suddenly stopped and ran out of the house. Slowly the sound of the cicadas penetrated the deep silence that followed, until Maurice got up and muttered something about attending to the dinner. I could think of nothing to say as he cleaned the chicken and put it on to cook again. He did not seem in the least agitated. But, after a while, I could stand the tension no longer and said, 'Don't you think we should go and look for Bridget? Where do you think she's gone?' There had been no sound of a car departing.

Maurice seemed content to follow my lead when I suggested that he search

[*] No. It was from Beverly Bergen.

around the house while I went down to the end of the road and the track to the beach. Not even a stray cat was to be seen there and when I returned he said he had been unable to find her, too. The situation had now become bizarre as Maurice continued to prepare the chicken dinner as if nothing had happened.

Some time later, we heard sounds outside and we went out to find Bridget standing against the wall of the carport. He moved to say something to her but she rushed past us both, into the house and bedroom and slammed the door. I do not remember the rest of the evening, but presumably the chicken was eaten.

The next day, Bridget disappeared early into town, to the theatre, and Maurice and I went on a tramp in the Waitakeres. It rained so hard we soon returned home to dry out and the following day I flew south, home to Banks Peninsula and a domestic environment that seemed as solid and unchanging as the peninsula's grand hills and headlands, compared to the volcanic chaos I had left behind.

I had a story to tell my wife; but I had no inkling that, more than thirty years later, it would be the opening for a much longer story, about a writer who always had trouble separating fact from fiction, who lived to write novels but whose life was lived as a novel, and of which, in April 1984, I had seen just one paragraph.

I first met Maurice Shadbolt in 1967, at the Christchurch home of David Lawson, the publisher for Whitcombe & Tombs. Maurice was completing work for Whitcombe's on his *Shell Guide to New Zealand*, and I was working on my first book for them. At the time, he had published two collections of short stories and one novel, *Among the Cinders*. But he had become best known for his phenomenally successful 'coffee table' book, *Gift of the Sea*, created with photographer Brian Brake, following their *National Geographic* magazine article on New Zealand. Published in 1963, the book went on to sell towards 100,000 copies. It was both a record breaker in New Zealand publishing and set a new standard for photographic books.

I was impressed by what Maurice, then thirty-five, had achieved as a freelance author, the only one in the country who made a living from books, with some supporting international journalism. His model was one I tried to emulate when I went freelance myself five years later.

During the twenty years that followed, we met at regular intervals. He stayed with us on Banks Peninsula and I went with him to various sites around Akaroa Harbour as he searched for evidence of Shadbolt ancestors. I stayed with him in Titirangi when I was up north on book or article projects. I took all the key photographs for the revised edition of his *Shell Guide*, and he ushered me into the local and international world of *Reader's Digest*. But differences in age, background, literary goals and simple geographical distance, meant that close encounters of the intimate kind coincided only with these widely separated visits; yet none of them was without emotional incident or stress. The effect of these became cumulative, so that when he broke with Bridget Armstrong at the end of the 1980s, I broke with him too, as did others who had known him for much longer. I saw him once or twice during the 1990s and paid a final, distressing visit to see him at the Avonlea Rest Home in Taumarunui, eighteen months before his death.

After he died in 2004, the English *Guardian* newspaper asked poet Kevin Ireland, his oldest friend, to write an obituary. He was so disaffected with Maurice that he could not bring himself to do it and passed the task on to me. I had mixed feelings, but I retained some affection for the best times we had had together, and gratitude for the help he had given me in my career. Whatever one thought about his writing or personal life, I wrote he had 'believed that New Zealanders should tell their own stories, cherish their own myths and believe in their own big lies before they could stand upright in a post-colonial world … Many literary critics in New Zealand considered his writing to be either flawed or populist — or both [*and still do*] — but neither his readers at home and abroad, nor book award judges, cared much.'[1] And the *Guardian* had considered his passing worth marking, for his books were often better regarded abroad. When a friend looked around a Philadelphia bookshop recently for New Zealand titles, all she found was Maurice Shadbolt's *Season of the Jew*.

Over the years following his death, several people suggested that I would be the best person to write his biography, although some thought he was 'not worth it', referring to both the mixed quality of his writing and his reprehensible behaviour towards the women in his life. From my own reading of his work and personal experience of him, I tended to agree.

But my inherent scepticism towards the 'received' views of others' character and work kept the idea alive. My large biography of the Wakefield family[2] had been partly prompted by scepticism that neither their early heroic status as the 'founders of New Zealand' nor their later post-colonial status as the villains of early European settlement could be valid; the truth lay somewhere between. In a similar way, the truth of the value of Maurice Shadbolt's writing could not lie at either pole of opinion; especially when he usually claimed to be no more than a storyteller. And was he only a villain in his personal life? I spoke to one woman who had known him and who described Maurice as a 'malignant philanderer' but who then followed this statement with the comment, 'I would have put my slippers under his bed', if she had been given the opportunity. The paradox in this suggested something else.

I finally decided to tackle a Shadbolt biography when I realised that, no matter what critical opinion maintained, he had been arguably the most well-known New Zealand writer of the second half of the twentieth century. He was a major contributor to the flowering of a New Zealand literature during that time and played a leading role, as a popular novelist, non-fiction author and journalist, in exploring and defining New Zealand identity as the country emerged from the semi-colonial condition of the 1950s into something like independent nationhood by the 1990s. The diversity of his work and his exploration of New Zealand history and life also meant that he had been associated with not only most other writers of his time, but also many of the visual artists — including such luminaries as Colin McCahon and Michael Smither — as well as notable New Zealanders across all walks of life. More than any other writer of his time, his work took New Zealand to the world.

A biography of Maurice Shadbolt would, therefore, also be a biography of a time of great change and growth in New Zealand literature, culture and society. As a participant and an observer of this from the late 1960s, it could also be an examination of my own experience and understanding of all this and of the many writers, artists, editors, publishers and friends that Shadbolt and I had both known. Above all, it would allow me to reach a true appreciation of his work and to discover who this 'malignant philanderer' really was. Were his novels the most memorable, or the novel he made of his life?

PART ONE

FINDING A GENRE

CHAPTER 1

INSURRECTIONS

In the beginning, 'I am walking along a riverbank with my mother. I am, possibly, five years old. There is sunset in the sky; the river still has faint colour in the smoky dusk. The stretch of river we are passing is shallow, and used as ford by trucks and horses. Pale stones glimmer under the fast current; willows and large ferns overhang the river. Some way upstream a trout-fisherman, on the edge of a pool, is casting a fly. Downstream a Maori woman is washing and beating clothes on stones at the water's edge. Otherwise the world is quiet. A whitened log, with twisted branches, juts out into the river. My mother and I climb out on to this log, bend down, cup our hands and drink from the cold river, which races out of high limestone bluffs in the bush country beyond the town. The water tastes of those places beyond'.[1]

This is Maurice Shadbolt's seminal early memory, a vignette of childhood in Te Kuiti that, he wrote in 1970, was his first experience of beauty and so important to him that he practised remembering it in the years that followed. 'It was really the discovery of memory, the capacity to make a personal myth. I had begun to stock a storehouse of personal mythology.'[2] A later version, in 1981, had it that he had begun to 'furnish a small mansion' and the 'decor has proved durable'.[3] A decade later still, in his memoir *One of Ben's*, it had shrunk back to a 'small storehouse' but 'I may even have been composing my first fiction'.[4] In his Author's Note to that memoir, he advised the reader 'that a novelist is at work in these pages'.[5]

In the writings of Maurice Shadbolt nothing is quite what it seems, fiction or non-fiction, and a biographer's task is one of finding truths somewhere among the shelves of private mythology in his small storehouse, or even mansion. But then, don't we all conjure myths about ourselves, construct a story of our lives that supports who we think we are; one that provides us with a security of identity that allows us to find a place in our world? In this conjuring and constructing, writers are the worst (or best) of all.

By 1981 Shadbolt had pushed memory back even further, to 1934 and the age of just two, to the Coromandel township of Waikino where his father Frank had found work in the Golden Dawn gold mine. Water, ferns and, by 1993, his mother Violet figure again as she takes a bucket out to the spring behind their decrepit cottage to collect water for cooking and washing.[6] Mother, water, ferns, the 'taste' of the bush and the hills.

At the height of the Great Depression, men went wherever there was work and when Frank Shadbolt's brother, Arthur, wrote to say there was a job at Waikino for a man with his blasting skills, he did not hesitate. Frank, at age twenty-eight, and Vi Kearon, ten years younger, had married in 1929, just after the Wall Street crash, and he had soon been laid off from his West Auckland quarry job, forcing the couple to move in with Vi's widowed mother Louisa. For the previous ten years, Louisa had raised Vi and her older brother Joseph, alone; supplementing her widow's pension by charring for Auckland's wealthy. Her property on the West Coast Road, just down from the Waikumete cemetery and on the boundary between town and country, was large enough to grow some sustaining vegetables and fruit; but it could not sustain hope or paid work. Frank found hope in the political activities of brother-in-law Joe, a card-carrying member of the Communist Party; as well as unpaid work in distributing propaganda pamphlets and taking a seat on the executive of the Unemployed Workers' Movement.

Joe Kearon had inherited the considerable library of his father, also Joseph, a seafarer, socialist and raconteur from Arklow in County Wicklow. Young Joe had been forced to leave school at fourteen and work in a footwear factory; but his father's legacy was priceless for an auto-didact who was to prove the political and philosophical father of Frank's family.

By 1932, with about 80,000 people unemployed in a New Zealand population of only one and a half million, despair queued at the soup kitchens and revolution brewed in working-class meeting rooms. The Soviet Union was a beacon to the most radical, the nirvana of socialism to the likes of Joe Kearon. Abject poverty fuelled a rising anger that culminated in riots across the country in April, most notably in Auckland's Queen Street. Joe and Frank were in the thick of it when unprovoked baton work by police turned a 15,000-strong, peaceful demonstration into a fighting and looting mob. The two became separated in the mayhem and, according to family legend, Frank returned home to Glen Eden at midnight with a pocketful of watches he had picked up near a looted shop; whereupon Vi insisted he was no thief and should bury them under a plum tree.[7] Maybe they are still there.

Seven months pregnant, Violet did not need the stress. She had lost her first child — 'Marie Louise' — stillborn eighteen months before, following the trauma of a car accident. She was no doubt terrified that, if the police came looking for leaders of the unemployed in Glen Eden, a watch on every wrist would be just the evidence they needed. There was no raid, but Joe appeared in court to give evidence of unprovoked police action; this was denied by a battery of police witnesses who prevailed in the judgement.

At the beginning of that winter of deep discontent, on 4 June, Violet gave birth without incident, thankful for a healthy boy they christened Maurice Francis Richard. Triple Christian names were common among the Shadbolts but there was no Maurice in the family lineage. Vi might have fancied a Gallic version of her mother's maiden name, Morris. More likely he was named for cabaret and movie star Maurice Chevalier whose biggest hit song, 'Louise', from the talkie *Innocents of Paris*, had been a best-selling record during the months she and Frank had courted in 1929. She had a 'bit of a crush on him'.[8]

Maurice's second name, Francis was his father's first, and his grandfather Ernest's second. Richard may have been for an uncle, Dick (Seddon) Shadbolt. But from the beginning he was always (little) Maurie.

Maurice was a fourth generation New Zealander, part of a rapidly expanding clan of Shadbolts, descended from Hertfordshire brothers, Benjamin and Peter. Ben arrived on Banks Peninsula from Hobart in April 1859. Aged thirty-four, he had spent most of the previous dozen years either in the penal colony of Norfolk Island or in Tasmania's Port Arthur prison as a recidivist petty criminal. In 1845, along with his brother, cousin and uncle, he had been convicted of burglary and theft at the Hertfordshire Assizes and sentenced to transportation. While many New Zealanders routinely disparage Australians as descendants of convicts, for Maurice Shadbolt his convict ancestors were heroes, adding a nice rub of colour and notoriety to family history.

Maurice created more romance for his story by suggesting that, after Ben arrived in Akaroa Harbour, a strange access of supposed sudden wealth could have been down to either gambling or a mysterious English legacy; but more likely a spot of bush-ranging in Tasmania.[9] The answer was more prosaic: years of back-breaking labour, something Ben had become inured to during his years of penal servitude.

In absences from prison in Tasmania, Benjamin Shadbolt impregnated Somerset-born Elizabeth Perham, at first when she was fifteen. They arrived in Banks Peninsula's Duvauchelle with two girls under the age of four but had left behind their first-born, a boy aged seven, with upright cousin George. Ben and Eliza were unmarried because he had also left behind a wife and child in Hertfordshire fourteen years before. Canterbury settlers around them assumed they were married, and Ben and Elizabeth did not disabuse them; but in 1866 the pair regularised matters in a discreet Christchurch registry wedding, bigamously or not. By then, they had also registered four more children with another eight to come.

Ben made his pile by milling most of the timber over and across the hills at the head of Akaroa Harbour; by taking over the local pub where he recouped much of the money he paid his mill hands; and by farming, when his stock won prizes at the local A&P shows. He built a fine house for his increasing brood and moved into the road transport business. A bit of a gambler, he bred and raced horses, enthusiasms he was to pass on to at least one grandson.

'In perhaps the most piquant twist of all, he became the arm of the law in his neck of Banks Peninsula. As a condition of holding the licence of The Travellers' Rest, he was sworn in as a local constable, obliged to assist magistrates and police, and responsible for keeping the peace and bringing burglars, rustlers and other undesirables to book.' Employ a thief to catch a thief. 'The Hertfordshire housebreaker and Hobart horse-thief was not only a pillar of propriety in his rough-cast colonial community; he was squire of Duvauchelle too.'[10] Ben was the rags (and crime) to riches success that figured in one kind of archetypal colonial tale.

He encouraged his brother Peter to immigrate from Hertfordshire, too, and he arrived in 1864 with his wife and seven children. The more God-fearing Peter wanted not pub or racehorses but just land to call his own, something impossible in the class-ridden county he had left behind. Ben helped him on to land at French Farm where his descendants continued to farm until recent times, a century longer than any one of Ben's. 'Benjamin's were the wild Shadbolts; Peter's were the sober. Benjamin's people were improvident, reckless with land and money; Peter's were frugal and canny.'[11] With nearly thirty children between them, it was inevitable that the several thousands of Ben's and Peter's progeny would help to populate most parts of the country.

Benjamin Shadbolt died in April 1882 aged (probably) fifty-seven by which time his horses had stopped winning, the timber was all cut and the price of cocksfoot seed, which had overtaken it as a rural earner, had fallen. There was still money in booze, and his estate, for all that, was £11,000, worth about $2 million today. Four hundred mourners followed his coffin to the small cemetery above Duvauchelle. He would be missed, not least by wife Elizabeth who rebuilt the pub which had been attacked by a mystery wowser arsonist who torched several of Banks Peninsula's licensed premises in the 1880s. Daily, Eliza climbed the hill to visit Ben's grave before fortifying herself with a bottle of brandy. She died, aged sixty-six, in 1903 from cirrhosis of the liver. Yet she had not drunk all of Ben's fortune away: her estate amounted to £13,000; but inflation had eaten away at relative value, making it worth half of Ben's.

Maurice's father Frank — Francis Clement William — was two years old when Elizabeth's estate was split among the ten surviving children, a thousand pounds or so going to Frank's father, thirty-year-old Ernest Francis, Elizabeth's thirteenth born. Ernest was a chip off the old Ben block, a strapping colonial outdoorsman and athlete. He captained rugby and cricket teams at Christchurch Boys' High, boxed and rowed, was an axeman, runner and rifleman and a stalwart member of the Canterbury Yeoman Cavalry. His cavalry record was distinguished enough that he was one of four men chosen to be bodyguard to the Duke of Cornwall and York, later King George V, when he visited New Zealand in 1901. The occasion was to prove the highlight of Ernest's life, and he recounted the honour of riding alongside the future King of England when it helped him to exert authority over ungrateful children, or to advertise his sterling character to judges and juries in the many court cases he was to become engaged in.

Frank was born two months after this event and must have proved a disappointment to his father. Tapping family lore, Maurice wrote, 'It seems agreed that he was born premature, less than three pounds in weight; that he was abandoned for dead by a doctor and revived miraculously by a midwife; that he was christened within five days of his birth [on 12 August 1901]; and that he remained a sickly infant'.[12] What was not entirely agreed, according to Maurice ninety years later, was whether Ernest's wife Ada, then aged twenty-two, or Ben's 42-year-old spinster daughter, Frank's Aunt Amelia, was his mother. Rumour, rumour.

Ada Shadbolt had arrived in Christchurch with her parents, William and Annie Shaw, in the 1890s but the family had shifted to Duvauchelle and a climate that seemed more congenial to William's frail constitution. What proved most damaging to the health of both of these bookish and devout Anglicans, however, was the declaration of their only daughter, a water-colourist and versifier, that she was determined to marry a hunting, shooting and boxing yeoman cavalryman who was the son of a publican and gambler. Annie is said to have dropped dead from the stress, whereupon William, fearing the same fate, allowed the marriage to go ahead to save himself.

Ernest and Ada shifted over the hill to Little River in 1906, and spinster

Amelia was the only one of Ben's line to remain in Duvauchelle. Ernest expected to prosper there, investing all the money he had in an accommodation house and general store at the junction of the railway terminus from Christchurch with the coaching service to Akaroa. But the railway had been built in boom times for timber milling and cocksfoot seed to sow the new broken-in pastures of the North Island. By the late 1900s it was the end of the line for both; Prime Minister Dick Seddon's promise to build a railway tunnel from Little River to Akaroa Harbour was buried with him.

Ernest's fortunes dissolved in a swamp of faeces. Outfall from public toilets at Little River railway station did not drain away through pipes but soaked Ernest's property, causing dysentery and diarrhoea, not only among his family but also among those who stayed at the accommodation house. When his doctor declared the property dangerous, Ada and the children fled back to Duvauchelle while Ernest sued the Crown, as owner of the railway station, for damages. Juries found for him but the judge did not, twice, and only after petitioning Parliament did Ernest receive a mere £100 of public monies, leaving him well out of pocket.

Disillusioned with Canterbury and short of the wherewithal, Ernest put his name into a government ballot for central North Island bush country and, according to Maurice, won 268 acres. Exactly how and when this occurred is unclear; but he had no idea what he faced as he journeyed north and up the Whanganui River to find his block, with Ada and six young children in tow. The seventh and eldest, Frank, still sickly and delicate, had been left behind with his Aunt Amelia. He was lucky that his holiday visits to the roughly cleared, stump-ridden farm downstream from Taumarunui, with no road access, were few and far between. Frank was to tell young Maurie what it had been like. 'His muddy brothers and sisters made his visits torment. This Little Lord Fauntleroy in fashionable check cap and knickerbockers was a freak from a far planet. They circled him menacingly, teased him, tugged off his cap, messed his hair, and dumped him in deep puddles. When he tried to woo them by judiciously handing out sweets from a bag, they grabbed the entire bag away. It was as dizzying and dismaying as a collision with a rogue tribe in dark Africa.'[13]

The 'novelist at work' in Maurice's memoir of his father's and grandfather's generations would have taken stories, fact or myth, detailed or half-forgotten, not only from his father's accounts but from his numerous aunts and uncles. Four more were born up the Whanganui, ordeals for Ada who had to be transported to the hospital at Taumarunui by horseback and boat, once arriving with only minutes to spare. Infant Stanley died of pneumonia in a storm and, when that was over, Ernest roped the body to his back and rode into Taumarunui for the inquest and burial.

It seems as if Ada survived the privations of primitive farm life by withdrawing into her own world. Maurice's cousin Tim recalled that 'She loved Greek and Latin and was rather cultured. She loathed the harsh, brutal life on New Zealand's bush-clad farms and escaped that reality through books. I remember her when I was a child, always with her nose in a book, but kind enough to give us threepence if we sat with her but didn't talk.'[14]

For Maurice, his grandmother was an enigma. 'Wispy, gentle and intelligent, she followed her headlong husband — with no audible complaint — from one faulty farm to another; from one legendary litigation to the next. In harness to a perambulating fumarole, her serenity was astonishing'[15] as she took refuge in books, in worlds far beyond her own.

'With Ada almost always sick, emotionally detached or bailing her husband out of trouble, it was Aunt Sis [Renee] who, as the eldest daughter, raised most of the children.'[16] Aged twelve when they arrived in the Whanganui, Sis grew proficient at household management and child nursing in a farmhouse that was a conglomeration of sods, timber and corrugated iron. 'The fireplace was virtually a room in itself. Logs glowed there yearlong, an iron kettle steamed, and clothes hung to dry. Pigeon, duck and wild pork comprised much of the family diet … there were eels boiled in a billy-can.'[17] Sis came out of it a tough, self-reliant no-nonsense woman who, aptly, was to fashion a distinguished nursing career. 'She had a huge influence over the family'[18] and sorted the disputes of her younger siblings in later life with the kind of brutally honest judgements that were also to put Maurice in his place.

The Whanganui hinterland was wicked, bloody country, the land of the Bridge to Nowhere, where government promised roads that never materialised or, if they did, were soon washed away. It broke and bullied the people who tried to make farming a go on land that was fit only for forest and which, in the end, was mostly abandoned to it.

In 1917, Ernest moved his family from the original farm to another better situated upstream, and later to another, each time appearing to make a profit. But if he did, it was not used to pay mounting unpaid bills due to the Taumarunui Hospital Board. He disputed these, honing his skills as a bush lawyer in order to take on river shipping operators, stock and station agents and anyone else he viewed as failing to fulfil their contractual obligations. 'For the next thirty years, almost literally to his last breath, law was the unrequited passion of his life … he was to fight more than forty actions before he died … Most were theatrical rather than judicial events; he played to full houses, with spectators having ridden in from miles around, and standing room only at the rear of the court.'[19] Ernest passed on his sense of theatre to his grandson.

The law caught up with Ernest after he left the black hills of the Whanganui for a farm outside the Waikato's Matamata. By now Ernest and Ada had their full complement of ten children with them. Their Aunt Amelia had died in 1920 and Frank, now nineteen, was required to leave his cosseted life in Duvauchelle and join his father with the £200 legacy she had left him. This was appropriated by Ernest as fast as the sweets he had earlier brought for his siblings. Here, one must ask why Frank went north, despite Ernest declaring it was time to make a man of him. Aged nineteen, with £200, could he have not been his own man, made his own life on Banks Peninsula? It seems he did not have the necessary self-reliance and practical resourcefulness. Maurice wrote: 'Pampered to the last, he was never to recover from Amelia's maternal attentions.'[20] This failing may have been Frank's most telling and unwonted legacy to his son.

The Taumarunui Hospital Board debts caught up with Ernest in the winter of 1921 in the shape of police who arrested him on his Waikato farm and transported him to serve a two-week sentence in the Victorian fortress of Auckland's Mount Eden Prison. The arrest cost the authorities more than it was worth. The hospital board, the police and the prison service were to rue the day as Ernest never let up with his petitions for a royal enquiry into the circumstances surrounding his arrest and imprisonment.

Yet this was the least of Ernest's worries as he pursued the crooked farmer and fraudulent land agent from whom he had purchased his Matamata farm. The quality dairy herd promised as part of the deal had been replaced with animals fit only for dog tucker; and after £3000 had changed hands, it turned out that Ernest and Ada still did not have clear title. The consequent court work preoccupied Ernest throughout the 1920s. 'The land agent went to prison, in the end, but that was no help to Ernest and Ada. This time they were ruined.'[21]

After all this, Ernest abandoned farming and shifted the family to a patch of land on the western edge of Auckland between New Lynn and Green Bay.* Now in his fifties, he cleared the scrub, dug a large vegetable garden, raised chooks, milked a couple of cows and sometimes grazed racehorses. The kids helped to meet grocery bills by collecting stray golf balls from the course across the road, which Ernest would then sell back to players at the clubhouse. The younger children were able to get some real schooling for the first time and if the older ones were unemployed, Ernest told them to get on with work somewhere on the section.

Disputes among the boys were settled by handing them boxing gloves,

---

*Now Sister Renee Shadbolt Park, Portage Road, Green Bay.

which led to both Jack and Johnnie becoming proficient enough to engage in professional fights with a purse attached. They were said to have to walked all the way down the railway line to Huntly — about 60 miles — to take part in a fight, returning to west Auckland the next day.

Family disputes at the breakfast or dinner table were fixed by Ernest launching lumps of firewood at the child he found most offensive. One of his granddaughters found him a 'gruff and difficult man. He had no way of dealing with children, to make them feel happy, or better informed or liked by him.' As a small girl, she thought him a 'cruel, cruel man' for the way he 'threw the chooks over the high fence into the chook run'.[22]

All his life, Ernest Shadbolt was at war with the world and almost everyone in it. He was an 'insurrection of one'.[23] As he grew older, he took to writing tracts about his court cases, the condition of society and mankind and a chronicle titled 'Shadbolts by Land and Sea'. He rented empty shops during the Depression and used their windows to display his manuscripts, changing chapters daily. Maurice wrote that they called for most 'human institutions to be levelled, and society to be shaped as Ernest saw fit' but 'paid no dues to the art of the possible'. He concluded, 'For the life of me, I should like to find him an endearing rogue … He may have been a rogue. He was never endearing.'[24]

In the mid-1920s, Frank Shadbolt queued up for a quarry job and was taken on to be trained in the use of explosives; he 'soon won a ticket attesting to his competence with hazardous substances'.[25] He had had no formal schooling after primary school and this was his only educational certificate. The job brought some money into the family home but Frank had little left over from his wage packet after he had paid his share of board and placed his bets on the Saturday races. Although his father could not abide such newfangled things in the house as electricity, Ernest relented when he realised that, with it, he could listen to race commentaries on the radio. Passed down from Ben Shadbolt, both father and son had this gambling gene in common, if not much else. For Frank, and many others of his generation, a big win at the races was his only chance of a fortune, his only chance to get the money to go back to Banks Peninsula, to return to the idyllic days of his childhood and youth. It was a dream he never lost — even after he died. According to Maurice, during a seance, his father exhorted him to go back and recover the family's Duvauchelle land.

To celebrate his rare wins, or forget his more frequent losses, Frank walked down with his younger siblings to the Saturday night dances in the Blockhouse Bay hall. He was a good dancer and could play the piano; his growing-up years with musical Aunt Amelia had not been wasted. He may have taken stock of eligible girls at the dances earlier, but nothing had come of this until, in the summer of 1929 he spotted eighteen-year-old Violet Kearon. She and her girlfriend were not impressed with the quarryman ten years her senior, dressed in a crumpled suit and with his shirt tail hanging out. But he was a 'charmer' and once he had her foxtrotting across the dance floor, there was no going back. Maurice wrote that Frank took over the dance hall piano, playing by ear, and sang hits such as 'Ramona' and 'If You Were the Only Girl in the World'.

They made an unlikely couple, the quarryman and legal secretary whose widowed mother had supported her to stay at school so that she might learn shorthand, typing and filing to secure a better job than her own wearying work as a charlady. Physically, Frank and Vi were very different, too. 'He was tall and fairly slim which contrasted with my mother who was short and rounded.'[26] This is shown in their wedding photograph, Frank in double-breasted suit and tie looking pleased with himself and Violet less certain in her wide shadowing hat and layered silk dress. They were also a contrasting couple in personality. Frank was outgoing and friendly, to the point where he would exasperate Vi by bringing home strangers he had met on the bus to 'meet the wife'. Vi was much quieter and reserved and 'would stay on the margins of a social group, often busying herself in the kitchen'.[27] But this behaviour was prompted by the conductive hearing loss she had suffered since birth, and which was not remedied until she was fifty.

So little Maurie inherited his 'rounded' physical build from his mother, although he grew to be taller. From the Kearon side he also inherited colour blindness from his late grandfather 'Arklow Joe', and perhaps his later short-sightedness. Maurice also thought he may have inherited a depressive gene more likely from the 'reflective' Kearons than the 'extrovert' Shadbolts. Grandma Ada was the most introvert of those and exerted a bookish influence; but even there, Arklow Joe and his son trumped any Shadbolt literary and political heritage. Although Maurice revelled in the rumbustious and volatile characters decorating the Shadbolt family tree, whose adventures he narrated, often romantically, in *One of Ben's*, he was more of a Kearon than he liked to admit.

The Kearons were master mariners, generations old, out of Arklow on the east coast of Ireland. Their bones were scattered among sailing ship wrecks all over the world; but young Joe Kearon in the 1880s 'loved the tall ships leaning into the wind' that took him to ports on every continent. 'Good-looking, lively and loveable Joseph had lady friends in most.'[28] This 'blue-eyed beguiler ... never had difficulty finding an excuse to fall into conversation with a likely lady'.[29] Arklow Joe 'swallowed the anchor' in New Zealand around 1900 and, after he had won and married the dark-eyed Welsh beauty Louisa Morris, she discovered a photograph album of Joe's girl in every port, sometimes two or three. 'What kind of Irish philanderer had she wed? Had her parents been right?' But Joe 'did the decent thing. He heaved the incriminating album into the fireplace and put a match to it … He again managed to convince her that he worshipped the ground she walked on.'[30] Maurice, a later 'blue-eyed beguiler', was a Kearon indeed.

Arklow Joe Kearon found work in the 1900s navvying on the new North Island main trunk railway line. The sweethearts album was not the only volume Louisa had to cope with in their rough and cramped railway quarters. There was the huge collection of books which Joe had carted round from ship to ship, from Arklow and London to San Francisco, Sydney and Auckland. A Protestant turned atheist turned socialist, Joseph's literary tastes ranged from Thomas Paine's *Rights of Man* and socialist prophet Edward Bellamy's *Looking Backward* to Shakespeare, Byron and Shelley. There was a complete five-volume set of Edward Gibbon's *The History of the Decline and Fall of the Roman Empire* as well as the novels and essays of that bestselling radical socialist of the time, Jack London.

Maurice wrote that his earliest memories were of his mother filling buckets from a spring to wash and cook in a ramshackle Waikino cottage that constantly vibrated from passing mine trains. He also recounts that in 1935, at just three years old, he met his father as he came off shift at the Golden Dawn mine and walked with him to the local pub where he was placed on a high stool with a raspberry drink. He 'marvelled at so many men with filthy faces' and remembers one saying, '"You starting your boy off early, Frank?"' and then the 'conversation became incomprehensibly political'.[31] If this memory was more Frank's than little Maurie's, it has an authentic ring from a year when everything changed in New Zealand politics. The election of the first Labour government brought the progressive introduction of a welfare state, housing and infrastructure development and, for working men, compulsory unionism and the introduction of a 40-hour, five-day working week. The Labour Party's efforts were not radical enough for their Communist comrades but they were reforming and worker-friendly enough for Frank and brother Arthur. 'If it wasn't socialism, at least it was an end to misery.'[32]

Maurice remembered, 'We moved from the cottage to a small farm back in the Waikino hills, and I had a pet pig'; and his younger cousin, Arthur's daughter Yvonne, to play with. But the Golden Dawn soon faded and the Shadbolt family, now four with the arrival of Shadbolt's brother Peter in 1935, moved five miles down the road to Waihi. Frank had found work at the Martha

Mine, the most lucrative gold and silver mine in New Zealand and one of the richest in the world.

The 1905 Cornish pumphouse still stands today as a monument not only to the old underground workings, but also to one of the most notorious strikes in union history. In 1912, the British-owned Waihi Gold Mining Company cut production and laid off Federation of Labour affiliated workers. Protest and strike action against the use of 'scab' labour culminated in the fatal events of 'Black Tuesday', 12 November, when eighty police, ten per cent of the entire New Zealand force, were used to attack and round up strikers, one of whom was killed. This, and other strike events in the years before the outbreak of World War I, were the founding causes of the Labour Party.

Memories of 'Black Tuesday' remained strong in Waihi when Frank Shadbolt was approached by old Communist Party comrades to become more active in the union. According to Party doctrine, the Labour Party would sell out the workers and they needed to be radicalised. After he had earlier passed out pamphlets at Waikino, Frank had been keeping his head down, pleading the responsibility of a wife and two children. Whether Frank agreed to speak at union meetings or not, whether he handed out pamphlets again or not, his Communist sympathies became known and he lost his job. On the move again, the family went back to the Kearon house in Glen Eden.

Even in 1937, with the first Labour government's reforms in full swing, jobs were hard to come by for a man with such limited educational qualifications as Frank Shadbolt. As his niece recalled, he and her father Arthur went wherever any good job was offering.[33] Frank heard there was something down south in the heart of the King Country and went by train to have a look around. He returned to announce that the family was off again: he had found a blasting job in the Te Kuiti limeworks quarry.

The family with its baggage and pots and pans were squeezed into Maurice's Uncle Johnnie's Model T Ford, ten years old at the very least, and a vehicle that was 'given to hysterics, with gusts of blinding fog from the engine and evil emissions from the exhaust … Mile by mile we laboured into the heart of the North Island, lurching in and out of ruts and potholes, crockery clinking, pots and pans crashing, suitcases bouncing on the roof.'[34] 'I read Steinbeck's *Grapes of Wrath* before the age of ten; and recalled how we had arrived in Te Kuiti, much like Arkies and Oakies … True we had nothing like the tragedy of Tom Joad. But otherwise it did seem all most familiar.'[35]

Uncle Johnnie drove them steaming down the main street, past the schools, past the railway station, out the other side, past the stockyards on a road that wound up the Mangaokewa valley to the vicinity of the limestone quarry. Frank called on Johnnie to stop when they arrived at a cross between a shed and a shack that made the Waikino cottage seem palatial. 'It had two bedrooms, a living room, a water tank and an outdoor privy. The floor creaked and one wall had a sinister lean.'[36] But it was shelter for now and work for Frank was just a walk down the road. School for Maurice was a mile's walk into town, and for Vi it meant more backbreaking housework with two boys under six and the only washing facility the Mangaokewa riverbed which she shared with wahine from the nearby pa. This was the place where Vi took little Maurie for summer evening walks, where he experienced his childhood epiphany.

CHAPTER 2

THE COUNTRY BOY

To the newly arrived Shadbolts, Te Kuiti reflected its beginnings. 'Grey pioneers still walked the streets. So too did more than a few Maoris who remembered the King Country when it was territory forbidden to white men. Their children and grandchildren now rode horses noisily down the main street. One side of that street was dedicated to the railway … The other side was given over to a ramshackle line of shops. There were still hitching rails and horse troughs, and some shops retained boardwalk frontages….'[1]

Te Kuiti first became a settlement of note at the end of the New Zealand Wars. Following defeat at the hands of government troops in 1864, Waikato chief, and second Maori king, Tawhiao, retreated south into the Ngati Maniapoto rohe with about 2000 followers and established pa in the basin of Te Kuiti(tanga), the 'valley' or 'narrowing in'. Tawhiao's presence attracted leading Maniapoto chiefs to settle. The wider region had already become known as the 'King Country'. As legend has it, a chief at a hui in Taupo, gathered to choose Tawhiao's father as the first Maori king, had thrown his hat on to a survey map of the area and marked a line around its circumference. The King Movement declared this an aukati (border) beyond which no European would be allowed.

Consequently, the King Country, with Te Kuiti as its 'capital', and beyond the reach of missionary, surveyor or armed constabulary, became a place of refuge for Maori opposing the colonial government. The most prominent refugee was Te Kooti Rikirangi, the Poverty Bay rebel military leader, prophet and founder of the Ringatu religion who was pursued by government forces into the King Country in 1872. But Tawhiao would not accept Te Kooti's presence until he agreed to adhere to the king's pacifist philosophy. Te Kooti gave up militant action in September 1873 and supervised the carving of a new meeting house which he gifted to Maniapoto leaders. It became known as Te Tokanga-nui-a-noho ('the large food basket of the settled'), and still stands. Young Maurie often went to the meeting house with his parents for 'hangis and tangis; I gazed, without much comprehension, at fierce ancestral figures.'[2] But by the time he was ten, Maurice had heard enough Te Kooti tales to play 'Te Kooti wars' with Maori mates in limestone caves near the town.

For twenty years the King Country remained self-governing behind the aukati but settler pressure to open up more country for farming, and especially to build the main trunk railway, brought about negotiations between government ministers, Tawhiao and Maniapoto chiefs. Three key events eventually prompted agreement: the symbolic laying down of arms by both pakeha and Maori at Pirongia in 1882; the Amnesty Act of 1882 which pardoned anyone who had committed 'political offences', including Te Kooti; and, finally, the 'Sacred Pact' of 1884 when Maniapoto chiefs agreed to allow the building of the railway, provided no licensed premises were allowed throughout the King Country. A dozen years later, the King Country Maori leaders were gone, the population shrunk to dozens and the aukati a memory.

Work on the mile-long Poro-o-tarao tunnel south of Te Kuiti began in 1885, two years before the railway from the north reached the 'town', a boarding house and two stores. The tunnel was not fit for service until 1903 and settlement was slow. In 1901, a newspaper correspondent complained, 'Our shops and houses … are illegally rented from the natives, and in most cases at exorbitant rents … We have a railway station but no station master … no township except a Maori pa with streets knee deep with mud and alive with Maori dogs and pigs.'[3]

The population began to grow as more and more settlers arrived to clear the bush for farms, and with the completion of the railway Te Kuiti became a service centre for the district with a population of more than 4000. But by the time the Shadbolt family rolled into town thirty years later, its population had halved. Farmland had become afflicted with 'bush sickness', a collapse in soil fertility that was not identified as cobalt deficiency until 1935. But by then, hundreds of farmers had walked off the land and the general effects of the worldwide Depression had also hit the town.

The Shadbolts moved right into town in 1938, renting a marginally better house in Nettie Street that was Maori-owned. The Waikai family were neighbours, their backyard filled with 'cars in disrepair and empty beer bottles, evidence of prosperity. My parents were never to own a car, and beer was for birthdays and Christmas. We were among the least affluent families in a neighbourhood of poor whites and moneyed Maori … By our modest measure families like the Waikais were wildly wealthy; they were still living off the largesse of land sales early in the century.'4 But Bill Waikai, the local taxi driver, was generous, not always charging for a ride to the railway station or the hospital; and the Waikais took the Shadbolts down to Te Kooti's meeting house for the 'hangis and tangis'.

Prompted by Vi's anxieties, Frank had left the dangers of quarry shot-blasting for a linesman's job with the Post and Telegraph Department (P&T). But after the outbreak of war, the Shadbolt household came under suspicion, with its Left Book Club meetings and Frank's known opposition to the war on Communist ideological grounds. Dissidents and pacifists were declared unpatriotic and Frank was mysteriously laid off his P&T job. Maurice was beaten up at school because his father was a 'fifth columnist' and a traitor.

So for Frank it was back to the quarry and when he continued to distribute Communist anti-war pamphlets — reluctantly because he wanted to see Hitler beaten — the threats were enough for him to keep a couple of sticks of gelignite on a high shelf in the kitchen. Maurice had no idea what his father planned to do with them if the house was attacked.

Then Frank was nearly killed when blasting went wrong and he was caught under a rockfall. Young Maurie had been there too, on a day his mother had sent him off with a packed lunch to see his dad at work. Frank had missed the worst of the rockfall but Maurice was terrified at the sight of blood pouring down his father's face as Bill Waikai whisked him away to hospital. Frank was lucky to get away with a badly grazed forehead and a battered but not broken leg. That was it. Vi insisted he would work with gelignite no more.

Maurice had begun school in Glen Eden, not long before the shift to Te Kuiti where he was at primary school until 1945, with breaks from time to time in Auckland. Te Kuiti Primary burned down in March 1939, a notably disruptive event that seems to have evaded Maurice's memory, and school attendance records went up in smoke. But later records show that his biggest break and months-long return to Glen Eden occurred after the end of the 1941 school year — and was caused by Frank's shocking kiss at the garden gate.

It was hard enough for Vi to make ends meet and to put up with Frank losing his hard-earned money on bets with local bookies. Bookies were illegal; but with no phone or telegraph betting possible on the totalisator, they thrived all over the country.* When another loss on the horses, or Frank bringing

---

*By the end of WWII it was estimated £24 million (about $2 billion in today's money) was being spent annually. Source: nzhistory.net.nz

another stray home for tea, brought Vi to the edge of fury, he turned on the charm and soothed her anger with a sweet popular song. The technique worked until Party member Doris came to visit.

Frank may have hoped that he was now far enough away from Auckland to be free of Communist Party activism, especially living in conservative Te Kuiti, and after Stalin had made a deal with Hitler just before the start of the war. But the Shadbolt house became a meeting place for the Left Book Club and attracted left-leaning railwaymen, timber workers and teachers. One of these, Doris, a committed Marxist-Leninist, saw she had to bring Frank and the others back to the true path from which they had strayed. These others included 'a tattooed Norwegian ex-seaman and anarchist, a Trotskyite Maori, a Fabian beekeeper, and a one-legged Jewish second-hand dealer and Social Crediter'.[5] Long-haired, chain-smoking Doris came often; Frank agreed with her more and more until one night Vi came upon them kissing at the gate, and heard Frank call Doris 'Darling'. There followed nine year-old Maurie's first experience of domestic drama, emotional conflict with sexual underpinnings. 'Darling' indeed! None of Frank's usual placatory techniques worked this time. The next day, Vi was on the train with the boys, back to her mother's house in Glen Eden.

Frank now did it hard, no cook or housekeeper himself, and just when he thought his work and life had settled down and he had become more accepted in the community. He navvied on the railway for a while before getting back his linesman's job with the P&T. For in the meantime Hitler had invaded the Soviet Union and supporting the Communists was now patriotic. Locals began to ask Frank for his opinion on Soviet matters and invited him to play poker at the Cosmopolitan Club. Life had become easier and smoother for him in that conservative town; but then he had lingered too long with Doris at the garden gate.

Back in Glen Eden, Vi and Grandmother Kearon took the boys to visit the relatives. The Morris and Shadbolt households could scarcely have been more different. For Maurice, visits to the inner city Morris clan, 'little apologetic people', were 'occasions of agonising inertia' in 'gloomy parlours' behind lace curtains where there was 'never ice cream', only 'tea and lumpy fruit cake'. The Shadbolt household down at Green Bay, on the other hand, was 'loud and bewildering' where Maurice seemed to have 'a score of burly uncles' at 'rowdy Sunday dinners' which comprised 'roast beef and Yorkshire pudding in a huge pile'. Feuds were 'settled with boxing gloves on the back lawn' and 'unattended grandchildren were liable to be trodden underfoot'.[6]

In late-life hindsight, however, Maurice thought that both families had a good deal in common. Behind both was a 'history of lost chances, lost land, and dimmed hope. Their forebears had travelled twelve thousand miles — the Shadbolts in shackles, the Morrises in steerage — to begin again in a land that promised affluence and freedom. They were also-rans, the residue of the nineteenth century's pioneer heroics. The unhumbled Shadbolts made enough din not to notice. The self-effacing Morrises went to church.'[7]

Most rewarding for Maurice at Glen Eden was the chance to dive into Arklow Joe's library. His most 'damaging boyhood fight' was with his brother Peter over a volume of Byron's poetry. He also took to 'making my favourite books my own by copying them out in juvenile scribble. The exercise was useful. I discovered that such as Rider Haggard and Edgar Rice Burroughs — and sometimes, so help me, Jack London — could be improved on.' Life as a novelist began at nine years old.

Violet had found work in an army boot factory and Maurice also did not see as much of his beloved Uncle Joe as he would have liked. He had been conscripted into the army and was only in Glen Eden on weekend leaves. Like Frank, he too had been released from the dilemma of having to follow the Communist Party line against the war on Hitler by the invasion of the Soviet Union. Joe was training for service in North Africa when news came of the Japanese attack on Pearl Harbor in December 1941; early in 1942 he departed to Fiji with the New Zealand troop reinforcements.

For months, Frank wrote and sometimes rang Vi, trying to persuade her to return to Te Kuiti with the boys; but she was happy where she was; until a telegram arrived in April 1942 advising her that Frank was in hospital with broken ribs, a punctured lung and concussion after falling from a telegraph pole he had been wiring.

Vi and the boys returned to Te Kuiti to the 'first passably conventional house my brother and I had inhabited', on Esplanade, close to the treelined banks of the Mangaokewa Stream. 'Walls didn't lean; floors didn't shake; windows were where they should be.'[8] There were no more Left Book Club meetings, no more Trotskyite Maori, above all no more visits from long-haired, chain-smoking schoolteachers.

But socialist beliefs were firmly rooted in the Shadbolt household and when the established Protestant churches launched the Campaign for Christian Order in 1942, Violet felt compelled to speak out. The churches were concerned at the repercussions of the war on home and family, especially with women being 'manpowered' for the war effort. 'Implicit also was the conviction that most women could expect to marry and leave the paid workforce and that the majority of women were best employed in the home.' The National Council of Churches even issued a pamphlet advocating a 'system of community service to socialise young women into domesticity'.[9]

In the columns of the *King Country Chronicle* Vi wrote stridently about the pros and cons of the Campaign, as a 'humble socialist'. Although she took on those who argued both for and against the Campaign, her main message was for the churches and their support of 'Capitalism as ordained by God in his wisdom for the purification of our souls from any unholy desires for a fair share in the good things of life.

'Who will dare say one child is less eligible than another to benefits and opportunities of education and when manhood or womanhood is attained and in return for its labours who will dare say it should not receive a fair and equitable share of the good things in life … If the Church refuses to be concerned with politics, then how are they going to give material help to the world's teeming millions, since politics are part and parcel of our daily lives?

'Perhaps if less idealism and a great deal more realism were infused into the campaign the chances of its success would be immeasurably greater.'[10] Her letter demonstrates that the propagation of socialist ideals should not be attributed solely to the Shadbolt men.

Frank had been too young to take part in World War I and was now too old to be conscripted for World War II, so he had joined the Home Guard. Although the Battle of the Coral Sea in May 1942 stopped the Japanese advance into the south-west Pacific, the threat of invasion seemed real enough for most New Zealanders until the end of that year. Maurice's account of Te Kuiti's Home Guard defence preparations in *One of Ben's*[11] was both colourful and distorted. Te Kuiti's older men were poorly armed and commanded, like all Home Guard units, and some of the training manoeuvres were reminiscent of the best of *Dad's Army:* 'On a weekend exercise two platoons were sent out to familiarise themselves with the region's forest. It took most of a week to find them again. This suggested that the forest might war with the Japanese more efficiently…'

Equally colourful was ten-year-old Maurie's creation of the 'Home Guard Assistance Corps', which he commanded as 'major-general' with his friends holding lesser ranks. 'We wrote to the Prime Minister asking for two dozen .303 rifles, Bren guns and a tank or two. The Prime Minister failed to acknowledge our patriotic plea' so that the Assistance Corps was reduced to ambushing real Home Guardsmen with catapults and acorns. A few found their target, whereupon 'unfriendly adults then put our column to flight'.[12]

Maurice's recollections of school and teachers serve to either reveal the springs for his future writings or to mark him as precocious. He wrote of a Miss Graham, an early teacher and a bitter spinster who had lost her fiancé at Gallipoli. As she pursued her 'seven-year-olds vengefully around the classroom, lashing at our bare legs with her cane, she screamed that we would never be worthy of the men who gave their lives at Gallipoli'. It was a 'history lesson of sorts' and Maurice had 'Miss Graham to thank for my fascination with the infamous Gallipoli campaign',[13] although this 'fascination' would not emerge in his writing until he was middle-aged.

To distract attackers when he was being bullied for Frank's role as a 'fifth columnist', Maurice developed a technique of telling stories drawn from local gossip and rumours and fabrications of teachers' sexual lives: a regular Te Kuiti Scheherazade. This defensive technique later developed into rainy day storytelling for its own sake, thrillers borrowed from the likes of Rider Haggard.

A later neighbour and teacher, Mabel Wilson, took an interest in Maurice's literary education and asked him what he had been reading. When he said Hemingway's *For Whom the Bell Tolls* and Steinbeck's *Of Mice and Men*, she thought those too advanced for an eleven-year-old and steered him towards *David Copperfield* and *Huckleberry Finn*. 'I was fourteen before she thought me enlightened enough to take on Olive Schreiner's *Story of a South African Farm*.'[14]

In election year 1943, he and a classmate stole some chalk and went around town writing 'Vote Labour' on telegraph poles and fences. A National Party official reported them to their high school headmaster, 'Bully' Howes, who strapped their hands with six of the best. When Maurice returned to Mabel Wilson's class, fighting back tears, she whispered in his ear, 'Consider yourself a martyr to the cause'. Mabel was a Labour Party activist and reforming Rationalist; but Maurice was honest enough to admit to himself that chalking up the occasional 'Vote National' might have avoided the pain.

Brutality at school, whether teacher on pupil or pupil on pupil was commonplace at the time, especially in country schools. Maurice moved to the secondary division of Te Kuiti District High School in January 1946, and 'The first day of the secondary school year was designed as a nightmare for newcomers. In the lunch break senior pupils formed two lines. New boys were then obliged to run the initiation gauntlet twice over. They were kicked and punched back and forward, reeling from fist and boot to boot and fist. Bullies became more so, stripping their belts and using them to leave long weals on bare legs.'[15] One lad was 'daily inverted over the high pressure drinking fountain and then dispatched over the escalonia hedge onto the football ground beyond to dry out'.[16] After an inquiry into a near fatality a few years later, teachers disingenuously declared ignorance of this annual first-day ceremony. Maurice was to detect the legacy of this* thirty-five years later in the 'same unlovely faces' and behaviour of Waikato rugby supporters baying for the blood of anti-apartheid demonstrators who succeeded in stopping the game in Hamilton during the 1981 Springbok tour.

Inevitably, Maurice introduced an element of fantasy to his own rugby story. Conspicuous among that Hamilton rugby crowd, he wrote in 1993, was 'my onetime tackler, with the nasty knuckles'. In 1970, he first described how he learned to play rugby and 'I remember once, in some scratch game, playing alongside a skinny child, a friend of my brother's',[17] and four years younger than Maurice, who went on to become one of the greatest of All Blacks, Colin Meads. Later, the story changed to 'I once played against a skinny kid called Colin Meads',[18] and at last to the 'skinny youngster who brought me down in a cruel tackle once. When I protested that I didn't have the ball, and was therefore no target for a tackler, he rubbed his knuckles in my face.'[19] Colin Meads remembered nothing of the Shadbolt family in Te Kuiti.[20]

Among the few who do remember, Maurice was 'not a sporting person' when at school; but he was 'a bit different' and would have 'a go at everything' which included professional bike racing until he crashed during a race at Otorohanga. He also declared he could ride a school friend's horse before it promptly threw him.[21] Another remembers Maurice as a 'quiet, reserved boy', the only one in her academic/commercial class when all the other boys were in the agricultural/practical stream.[22] Learning to begin writing his way into a life real or imagined.

The later Maurice did not publicly mention it, perhaps embarrassed by its juvenile gaucheness; but his first surviving short story comes from his first year at high school. Entitled 'Saved from the Hau-Haus'[23] it tells of a boy his own age who witnesses the killing of his family by Te Kooti's warriors at Matawhero (1868) and then rides off, despite being wounded, to warn settlers at the next village of Ngatapa. Perhaps this was the only one of Maurice's 'Scheherazade' stories to be recorded; it was certainly the seed to larger stories written forty or more years later.

Teacher and neighbour Mabel Wilson enabled the Shadbolts' final shift in Te Kuiti, to a farmlet at the western end of King Street and the first property Frank and Vi owned. Here, Frank could talk politics to Mabel; place a bet with her husband Norman, a much decorated WWI soldier who did a bit

---

*Violent initiations occur to this day in New Zealand secondary schools, especially those with boarding establishments.

of bookmaking on the side; and Maurice could get to know the three Wilson girls. The farmlet also had enough pasture to graze a couple of cows and keep chooks so that, apart from learning to type, Maurice contributed to the war effort by milking cows Bluey and blind Helen Keller night and morning. He separated the cream and carried this each day, about a gallon, to a dairy factory depot on his way to school so that this could be churned into *Butter for Britain!* 'Consumption of cream was illegal' under wartime rationing regulations and 'We pilfered a little of our own only for Christmas strawberries.'[24]

So Maurice milked cows, fed chickens and raked hay, presumably with some help from younger brother Peter, Mum and Dad. Later, he wrote: 'I still find it difficult to visualise a childhood without a haybarn. A hideout from parents, a place to sulk, or read; a gang den; an arena, when cleared of hay, for a boxing match. At the edge of adolescence it also functioned as a site for sexual experiment. I lay naked with our neighbour's daughter in the hay … but in the end couldn't find anything more exciting to do than smoke some American cigarettes I had stolen from an uncle just back from the war.'[25] Uncles on leave and aunts came down from Auckland to visit, and there were Christmas family gatherings. Cousin Yvonne remembers games were played according to Maurice's direction, in the hay barn or elsewhere, because it was his place.[26]

Maurice's Te Kuiti childhood was 'never short on rumour, terror, and death in sorry form'. At times he and his mates explored caves that were everywhere in the Waitomo district. 'Some were rumoured to be ancient burial places heaped with old Maori bones. I began bypassing likely caves when I learned of the fatal consequence of violating tapu … Your hair went white overnight; your teeth fell out; you went mad and were dead in a week.'[27] In Te Kuiti, Maurice absorbed not only country matters but also an enduring sense of superstition, of the supernatural.

As he grew older, Maurice ventured further afield and during school holidays spent many days with his father in the P&T truck. Frank installed telephone lines linking remote hill farms whose paddocks at the edge of the bush were still littered with charred stumps and already riven with erosion in country never meant for pasture. No good place for families, the farms were often inhabited by 'Bachelors wedded to half-tamed hill country [who] no longer knew why they were there … human beings dying of loneliness'. For Maurice, the 'land whispered around me. A land still often unknown, more ample than maps of the world showed, and mine. I was comfortable with its silences; I knew them in myself.'[28]

At night there were the steam locomotives and wagons, the 'lingering reverberation of freight and passenger trains hurtling out of the dark island

and into the dark again'. On Friday and Saturday nights, before going to a movie musical at the State or a western at the Empress, folk would wander down to the station as the Auckland-Wellington Express arrived at 7.15 p.m. There they watched passengers rush off during the quarter-hour halt to buy a meat pie or piece of fruit cake and wash it down with tea from the unbreakable railway china cups. After the movies at 11 p.m. moviegoers went to watch the Limited go through. These occasions were when 'Te Kuiti viewed the outside world, if only as faces at passing windows'. They had a 'mystery which local faces never had'.[29]

The world came to Te Kuiti once a year with the A&P Winter Show. Travelling sideshow men set up their tents to brighten and enliven the stands of agricultural equipment; the rows of stalls with the cakes and preserves produced by farming wives; the yards and ring with paraded prize livestock; and the damp hall displaying the best of local children's schoolwork. 'Most parents seemed to give unlimited leave of absence to their offspring, and excited home-coming children could be heard late into the night … Whether it was screwing up enough courage to link up with a jerking mate attached to a demonstration electric fence or rashly expending 6d to control a car on the sparking steel clad Dodgem circuit, the Winter Show was not to be missed.'[30]

At the 1944 Winter Show a banner above one sideshow tent announced *The Mistress of Mystery,* Ranee, a beautiful and alluring Indian woman with whom twelve year-old Maurice fell in love in 'fewer than five minutes'. Her barker husband declared that Ranee had 'bewitched presidents, prime ministers and monarchs' with her magical powers and for just one shilling (sixpence for children) these would be revealed to anyone who ventured inside the tent. As a teaser, Ranee would make an egg appear and disappear in the clothing of a volunteer from the crowd outside. For as long as the winter show lasted, Maurice became the most fervent volunteer both outside and inside the tent where Ranee 'did extraordinary things with doves, rabbits, silver rings, billiard balls, coins, razor blades and playing cards'. Maurice tried to make himself 'indispensable; I wanted to run away with Ranee in a coloured caravan'.[31] But then the winter show ended and Ranee and her caravan vanished overnight. Te Kuiti was a 'morose country town again. If my heart didn't break, there must at least have been a hairline fracture.' Ranee never returned to Te Kuiti, but her presence had been so intoxicating that Maurice was determined to become a conjuror himself.

In 1947, as Maurice turned fifteen, Frank secured a transfer within the P&T department and got a job as a line foreman in West Auckland. He had been trying to move for some time because he and Vi had decided the social climate in Te Kuiti was 'unhealthy' and no place for their sons to grow up, to become 'local louts'. In the early hours of a frosty August morning, Bill Waikai drove the Shadbolt family to the station to catch the express to Auckland. 'We peered out as the lights of the town trickled away. We were suddenly faces in the window ourselves.'[32]

Maurie the country boy was going to town; and whether Te Kuiti was unhealthy or not, he had done most of his growing up there. He had grown roots in the land and had become 'comfortable with its silences', comfortable with its stories, its myths and its heroes. And, towards the end, something startling had occurred: an exotic flower had sprung from that 'morose' country town's showgrounds, prompting him to become a conjuror in more ways than one. In the big smoke, he was to become a 'professional magician, a precocious boy wonder in top hat and silk scarf, and make a modest income — after swearing an oath upon a phosphorescent skull in a darkened room among members of a notionally ancient international brotherhood'. Of all Maurice's early occupations, this was the one he valued 'most highly … it taught me that nothing is ever quite what it seems; that reality could be reshaped, and in any case only resides in the eye of the beholder … it also taught me that cunning and craft can go a long way.'[33] Further than he could have imagined

CHAPTER 3

DISRUPTIONS

Auckland in 1947 was an overgrown country town of quarter of a million people with its port servicing a dairy and agricultural hinterland beginning just a few miles from the city centre. Its side streets still harboured cottages and pubs that spoke of its colonial origins a century before; and beneath the verandahs of the three- and four-storey buildings lining Queen Street, white lines told you to keep left on pavements that were deserted after the pubs closed at six. There was no need for parking meters because private cars were mostly luxury leftovers from the 1930s and wartime petrol rationing remained in force. Commuting city workers lived in wooden bungalow communities which mushroomed close to the tram and railway lines that snaked across town before petering out in the rural margins of town-supply dairy farms, orchards, market gardens and vineyards. With food rationing also still in force, renting a house in an Oratia apple orchard, with room for a veggie garden, was an ideal first port of call for the migrating Shadbolt family.

Frank and Vi's migrations were not to end there. They had already lived in nine homes and west Auckland's Oratia would be the first of fifteen over the next fifteen years; by the end of their married life, the tally came close to forty. For Maurice, 'Upheavals known as "shifting Saturdays"' marked his childhood and youth. 'The radio, relaying racetrack commentaries, was always last out of the old house and first in the new. My father refused to be detained long by such worldly business as carrying furniture.' For Maurice this reflected some kind of 'manic-depressive cycle'. 'Before a move there was optimism: a many-coloured future was about to begin. Soon there was obscure melancholy. The kitchen was too small, or neighbours unfriendly, or the roof needed repair. My mother was moody, my father dour. Then they were house-hunting again. Was it the dynamic of their marriage?'[1]

Moving more or less every year did not help Maurice settle into his new high school, co-educational Avondale College. The complex off Rosebank Road had been built in 1943 as a US Navy hospital but with the intention it would be converted into a school after the war. It had been opened as Avondale Technical High School in 1945 but upgraded to academic college status two years later. Maurice not only faced the difficulties of a broken fourth academic year by the shift from Te Kuiti; in November, less than three months after he started at Avondale, all schools in Auckland were closed because of a major polio epidemic. At home in the Oratia orchard, Vi supervised his and brother Peter's correspondence lessons, but they finished them 'fast and filled our days fishing, hiking and reading'. They biked around the Waitakere hills, discovering the ruins of gumdiggers' and sawyers' huts in the bush and the graves of pioneers: 'Again, as in the King Country, I had a sense of unsung lives lost in the land: old hopes, old despairs.'[2]

That summer seemed to go on for ever and did not end until after Easter 1948 when schools were reopened a full term late. Scarcely had Maurice's fifth high school year begun than he suffered his own personal health setback. At the bottom of ruck in a school rugby match, a stray boot found its way into his crotch, causing damage that needed medical attention. Examination of his bruised scrotum produced a surprise for both doctor and patient: Maurice had only one descended testicle. So he was off on another holiday from school, this time to a hospital bed. A surgeon retrieved the missing testicle from his lower abdomen and fastened both scrotum and testicle to his upper leg where they remained for nearly three months during the healing process.

Rugby was out of the question when Maurice was allowed to return to school but he had to somehow cover up exactly what had happened to his nether parts. He did not like the 'idea of being called "One Ball" or "Oddball"' for the rest of his school days so 'did nothing to dampen the rumour that I had just been cured of venereal disease. I was seen with awe by intimates. There were sympathetic smiles from girls I had thought frosty.'[3] The effect of being surgically provided with his full genital equipment at the age of sixteen was to accelerate Maurice's delayed puberty: 'My voice broke in weeks; a beard began to bristle; I grew an inch or two in height; I woke from my first racy dream.'[4]

About the time of his hospital holiday, the reason for mother Vi's most recent bout of moodiness was confirmed: it was not related to house unhappiness. She was unexpectedly pregnant, and in the same December week Shadbolt returned to hospital to have his scrotum unhitched, she gave birth to Julia Louise. It had been an eventful year for the family.

Despite the disruptions to Maurice's 1948 school year, he passed School Certificate without difficulty and was praised by his English teacher, 'Froggy' Martin, for getting 83 out of 100 for English. Martin, and Maurice's sixth form English teacher, Maurice Hutchinson, had also taught another promising young student of English, Maurice 'Moss' Gee who was a year ahead and, in 1949, an Avondale prefect and vice-captain of the First XV. Maurice continued to play rugby, too, and claimed friendship with Moss Gee, a 'quiet boy, who also liked his rugby, and was useful with boxing gloves … he had a radical background, also leavened with grandparental eccentricity, not dissimilar to my own … Not that we ever had a conversation then which might pass as literary …'[5] It is unlikely Maurice knew much about Moss Gee's family at the time and, in the class hierarchy of high schools, where the lower class members are aware, and sometimes in awe, of those above them, juniors rarely figure in the landscapes of senior students. Although they were both on library and school magazine committees, Moss Gee has no clear memories of Maurice at school other than being 'aware of a very bright, rather smallish, a little bit tubby, cheerful fellow … he seemed always to be laughing …'[6] By the sixth form, he was 'boldly confident and when approaching people his cheerful, friendly manner won them over. He was good company and when amused had a particular way of chuckling through his teeth.'[7] A kind of 'gurgling' laugh.

All of this was, perhaps, a reflection of the self-confidence he had developed during his increasingly competent conjuring performances. These could only have been achieved after many hours spent practising both his skills and his audience presentation. He was spurred on by his mother, who bought him his silk top hat and magic wand. Both mother and son would have been glad that his public performances began to earn some useful money.

The image of a 'cheerful fellow' does not accord with Maurice's later statement that, 'For some reason I loathed every hour of my schooldays.'[8] He failed to achieve to the extent that, in his sixth form year, his maths was so poor his teacher excused him from classes and suggested he would be better off in the school library. This fitted well with 'Froggy' Martin's frequent exhortations to his pupils to 'Soak yourselves in literature!'.[9] The Avondale curriculum covered Shakespeare, Dickens and nineteenth century English poets, especially Robert Browning and Gerard Manley Hopkins and, later, included T.S. Eliot. The course was partially based on E.G. Biaggini's *The Reading and Writing of English*. This Cambridge Leavisite textbook included a variety of contrasting prose extracts designed to assist sixth formers evaluate what made good or bad writing through the 'practical criticism' method: a piece of D.H. Lawrence, for example, was contrasted with an advertisement text for lipstick.

In the school library, Maurice discovered Rabelais from whom he quoted to reinforce his spurious reputation as a 'sexual desperado'. But he was also expanding his knowledge and enthusiasm for modern American novelists that had begun with Steinbeck and Hemingway in Te Kuiti. In these late teenage years, he discovered John dos Passos, James T. Farrell, Erskine Caldwell, Upton Sinclair, Nathanael West: all the great social literary evangelists of the post-World War I period and the 1930s Great Depression with their 'grand, barnstorming American style'.[10] By the time he reached university, Theodore Dreiser was 'his literary god',[11] but novelist Thomas Wolfe was to become his hero. Maurice loved 'his spread and scope and piling on and putting in, everything in, and he tried to make that his way'.[12] But in his sixth form year, and even at university, he still had no developed ambition to become a writer.

Maurice did not find books about New Zealand in the school library. 'What was missing was the land in which I lived … There was seldom a paragraph in a history textbook of New Zealand; there was never a line of New Zealand verse in the literature we studied.'[13] When he did discover a volume of verse by Eileen Duggan, he had a 'sense of forbidden fruit'.

But in a country where Britain was still routinely called 'Home'; where the major sporting event held in Auckland in 1950 was still the British Empire Games; where institutions such as the State Literary Fund and the literary quarterly *Landfall* had only recently been established, the English tradition still ruled. A few years earlier, Janet Frame had undergone a similar experience to Maurice until she discovered *Speaking for Ourselves*, a collection of short stories edited by Frank Sargeson, and *A Book of New Zealand Verse*, edited by Allen Curnow, both published in 1945. They gave her 'hope for my own writing while wakening in me an awareness of New Zealand as a place of writers who understood how I had felt…'[14] Some years would pass before Maurice would 'identify the lack', understand the cultural servitude. In 1949 he could not have imagined there would come a time when he might become part of the solution.

The disruptions to Maurice's 1947 and 1948 school years were a major contribution to his failure to make lasting friendships. But he was to see in his generation of schoolmates a greyness, a lack of distinction that would mark their entire lives. 'Born in the depression, reared in war, ours was a submissive generation … Security was a national religion. We were destined for dependable jobs and inoffensive opinions.'[15] In 1949, a geography class trip he organised to Henderson's Corban's Vineyard did nothing for his school relationships. The trip ended with 'fighting drunk' and vomiting classmates arriving late back to school. A threat of suspension was not carried out because it would have been difficult to expel a third of the sixth form.

But in his last year at Avondale College, and after the family had shifted closer to the school, Maurice often found himself walking up Rosebank and Great North roads to his new home in Walsall Street with a 'black-haired, gangly, earnest, and Jewish' classmate, Carl Freeman. Freeman had Marxist parents; his mother had stood for Parliament as a Communist. Maurice's upbringing with activist socialist parents and Uncle Joe's unwavering communist beliefs meant they usually saw eye to eye in classroom debates. Freeman took Maurice along to the Young People's Club located in a Customs Street attic on the Auckland waterfront. The walls were covered with revolutionary posters and Marxist slogans and was a fertile recruiting base for the Communist Party; but Maurice either did not know or did not care. It was more to the point that the club included 'unattached and lively-eyed girls' and that its members were literate, read poetry and novels and discussed movies. 'It was a rousing climate for a teenager fresh from a rural town, one who had never talked more than rugby to contemporaries.'[16]

Equally rousing for Maurice was the government's announcement in May 1949 that a referendum would be held on the reintroduction of compulsory military training (CMT) for all males on reaching the age of eighteen. Labour Prime Minister Peter Fraser, who had been a conscientious objector in World War I, was now in the grip of Cold War anti-communist paranoia. With the aid of the National Party, Fraser worked hard to suppress protest and opposition to the proposal, going as far as newspaper and radio censorship, and flooded the nation with pro-conscription propaganda. No doubt with a tad of self-interest — the new law would come into force just as he turned eighteen — Maurice joined Young People's Club, trades union and church members in a street march protest. Frank and Vi thought he should keep his head down and concentrate on becoming a teacher, and when Maurice pointed to their own activism, they told him that had been different. Fighting for a cause was necessary during depression and war, but he did not need to: 'You have your own life to live'. But for the succeeding decade, 'I was to live theirs before I lived my own.'[17] On a low turnout in August 1949, the country voted to reintroduce CMT by 78 per cent to 21 per cent. It did Fraser's electoral chances no good. Labour was voted out at the end of November after fourteen years in office, and National became government with Sidney Holland as Prime Minister. Reducing the power of the unions was one of his policy platforms.

In October 1949, Maurice returned home from school to find father Frank on his knees, sobbing over a page of the *Auckland Star* with the headline 'Man Who Fought Injustice Dies'. In September, 76-year-old Grandfather Ernest had had a bit of a turn and fallen out of his armchair. Wife Ada had turned off the blare of the radio before reviving him with brandy; whereupon he had sat up, pointed at the radio and shouted, 'Who turned off that bloody machine?'. Then, on the morning of 6 October he sat down to breakfast, declaring, 'It's going to be a great day today!' before his head dropped, face first into his cereal. 'Neither a full card of winners nor a barrel of brandy could have revived him this time.'[18]

Six sons came to carry Ernest's coffin, including the youngest, Donald, who was called Tim; Arthur who had long been nicknamed Bill; and boxer Jack, christened 'Dardy' when, a few years old, this had been his childish pronunciation of 'darling'. But Jack was no darling. He had been convicted of running a seedy massage parlour and was out on a two-hour pass from jail to attend his father's funeral. Being caught as a pimp was a real comedown after years of evading conviction for following a profitable line of self-employment as an arsonist. 'When an inner city landlord or householder thought to dispose of a derelict property to advantage, Jack was called in. There was never a trace of accelerant found in the ashes; Jack could be trusted to do a clean job and insurance companies paid up …'[19] For Dardy, post-war life had also been a comedown after a life of drama and footloose violence fighting in Greece and North Africa as one of Bernard Freyberg's 'Forty Thousand Thieves', the New Zealand Second Division. Sometimes he was a sergeant and sometimes he was not, depending on current disciplinary events.

Grandmother Ada did not attend Ernest's funeral, stating she did not believe in goodbyes; but maybe she had said goodbye to Ernest long before, withdrawn into her own world of books and versifying. In the rowdy family wake that followed, she came to sit beside seventeen year-old Maurice and said, 'I believe you're going to be a writer'. Maurice was not so sure; he would not know where to begin. But Ada said he had the creative makings, she had seen how he listened and watched. 'We need a writer,' she said, 'to make sense of all this'. Back home, Maurice wrote in his diary, in red ink, *Write about the Shadbolts!* He was to manage it in fiction long before actual family memoir more than four decades later; because Aunt Evelyn threatened to sue him if he did, and Dardy even worse.

CHAPTER 4

SEX AND SOCIALISM

To his surprise, Maurice was credited with his University Entrance and, rather than stay on for the upper sixth at Avondale like Carl Freeman and, a year earlier, Moss Gee, he enrolled at Auckland University College in February 1950. He chose law 'by way of elimination' because he had no wish to be a schoolteacher and could not afford medical school, at least not on the proceeds of legerdemain'.[1] Conjuring had its limits as an income earner and he took odd jobs in a wool store and labouring to put some savings together. Academically, Maurice achieved nothing at Auckland University, failing English 1 three times. All his energies were poured into political activities, sexual 'endeavour' and, with Grandma Ada's words niggling at the back of his mind, his first attempts at writing.

In history and English lectures, Maurice sat with Don Wolf whom he had met at the Young People's Club (YPC), an active Communist Party member who 'talked a persuasive Marxism in my ear'[2] and together they joined the university's Labour Club. Sid Holland's new National government had not taken long to start removing pieces of Labour's welfare state. When food subsidies were removed in mid-1950, 10,000 unionists marched up Queen Street in protest and, in Myers Park, Maurice took his turn on the stepladder to make an 'incendiary contribution to the national debate'[3] on behalf of New Zealand student socialists. Soon afterwards, just turned eighteen, he left a philosophy lecture and walked up to the Communist Party office in Karangahape Road to join up. He was expected: they had had their eye on him for some time; but he was told that he would be of more use to the Party as a sympathising non-member, a kind of socialist mole attending and agitating at university gatherings, spreading the word without the Party label.

Unable to seriously engage with university studies and frustrated with his first attempts at seduction, Maurice found distraction with the left-wingers of the YPC and the drifting young who 'lived on the fringe of Auckland's semi-urban society'.[4] Their club rooms were Somervell's coffee bar and Chinatown's Golden Dragon café. Somervell's was a 'lone island of light and warmth the chilly length of Queen Street. Inside were the disaffected, the disenchanted, and the merely lonely.' Among them were 'unpublished novelists, biding their time as newspaper proofreaders, impoverished painters producing portraits for tobacco money, corduroy-trousered actors in search of a theatre and architects desperate for clients'.[5] Twenty years later, Maurice would write, 'The landscapes of bohemia are trackless if well-trodden, but I do wonder what I might otherwise have been without this territory … it was to provide shade and shelter when I dropped out of university, then out of politics; it was a sanctuary — if largely of slum rooms, unmade beds, cheap wine and impromptu parties — in a dull, colourless, post-colonial city with a distinctly empty and abandoned air'.[6] In reality, for much of the time, Maurice was still comfortable enough living at home, looked after by Mum; and weekends brought healthy YPC tramps and camps and 'revolutionary songs around log fires in bush huts'.[7]

Vi became alarmed at Maurice's casual approach to his university studies and urged him to think about going to teacher's college instead. He got as far as the steps of the Auckland Education Board before fleeing to the refuge of his Queen Street bohemia. By the end of 1950, 'My savings were depleted; my engagements as a conjuror few. I took work which clashed with lectures and tutorials.'[8] And he did not let up on his extracurricular pursuits. Something had to give and he 'had a small collapse which precluded both belated cramming and the passing of examinations.'[9]

When he had recovered, he took a job on the railways and became involved speaking and on the picket line when the railways union called a national strike just before Christmas. This lasted only a fortnight but by the time Maurice planned to go back to university in February 1951, the most socially and politically damaging industrial dispute of the twentieth century had begun.

Waterfront workers had worked long hours during the crisis times of World War II, and later as the nation recovered. In January, the Arbitration Court awarded all workers a 15 per cent wage rise, but this did not include watersiders who were controlled by a separate commission; and they were offered only 9 per cent by their (British) shipping company employers. In protest, the watersiders refused to work overtime to make up the difference, whereupon the companies locked them out.

Prime Minister Holland labelled the lockout a strike, 'industrial anarchy', and passed draconian emergency regulations on 21 February that 'imposed rigid censorship, gave police sweeping powers of search and arrest and made it an offence for citizens to assist strikers – even giving food to their children was outlawed'.[10] Declaring that the country was at war, Holland sent in troops at Auckland and Wellington to load and unload ships. The lockout and associated strikes were to last 151 days but the emergency regulations remained in force until the end of the year. Although as many as 22,000 workers were involved in the dispute, these made up only 8 per cent of the country's work force; allowing the government to isolate the watersiders and break up their union. As soon as the dispute was over, Holland called a general election and increased National's majority, taking fifty of Parliament's eighty seats.

The watersiders had called on other unions to strike in support. Railway union militants urged fellow workers not to handle cargo coming from the wharves and Maurice spoke in favour of a ban. But the vote was against striking and 'A number of old-time unionists walked off the job rather than handle black cargo'. Maurice walked off, too, but 'as much for convenience as conviction' and walked into the 'headquarters of black reaction ... the *New Zealand Herald*, and asked for a job. I had seen journalism as a way out of my impasse over a career.'[11] His Communist Party comrades were not impressed; he should have stayed to fight the cause.

Back at university, Maurice did. He got himself elected president of the Labour Club and saw its name changed to the Socialist Club, disaffiliating from the Labour Party which was declared no longer socialist because of its pusillanimous role in the waterfront dispute. With the suppression of civil liberties, club membership increased. Maurice, Carl Freeman and other club activists called rowdy meetings at university, defying the ban on public debate. When it was proposed students join a 'scab' union to work on the waterfront, they leafleted lecture rooms with a broadsheet version of Jack London's 1903 anti-strike-breaking polemic *The Scab*.

Activism on campus came to a head when Maurice and the Socialist Club called for a special general meeting of the Auckland University College Students Association on 4 July and put forward a motion calling for the immediate repeal of the government's emergency regulations. This caused an uproar: right-wing opponents put up posters declaring 'Shun Shadbolt and his Mobsters' and at the meeting the students voted overwhelmingly to actually *support* the emergency regulations.

At this time, the beginning of the Cold War and the Korean War, anti-Communist 'Reds Under the Bed' McCarthyism was rampant in the United States and the student magazine *Craccum* had already labelled the Socialist

Club a 'tool for Moscow'. Now its editor, Gerald Utting, in the 13 July issue,[12] viciously attacked Maurice and the club, provoking letters from non-members shocked at Utting's behaviour. Maurice wrote to accuse him of 'scurrilous journalism' and of being 'out to get' the club. But now the police took a serious interest and, according to the September issue of *Craccum*, there was a 'Police Search — Socialist Club probed'. Socialist activism on campus was quelled amid the environment of New Zealand's most repressive ever political regime. Carl Freeman left university to go to teachers' college, and it was the beginning of the end for Maurice's studies.

He took a more passive role from the reading room of the *New Zealand Herald*. As Grandmother Ada observed, he listened and watched. 'If I leaned far enough from the window … above Queen Street, I could see fists at work, fallen men, and strikers led away in police hammerlocks.'[13] At the beginning of June, he used a fictitious dental appointment to leave the building and witness a protest march against the emergency regulations. When he reached upper Queen Street, he found that 'Two or three hundred police had halted the march and given strikers five minutes to disperse … they were still leaving quietly … when the first baton charge was launched. The second was even more stunning. I found bleeding men and bruised women still sitting dazed on the footpath, others being helped to hospital.' A *Herald* journalist, under police supervision, reported that the strikers had tried to break through the police cordon and that batons had been used 'in reply to attacks with sticks and bottles'.[14] After this false reporting, Maurice handed in his notice and took a job with a back street publisher, proofreading business directories. 'The money was better. So were my spirits.'

Maurice's time at the *Herald* was not entirely wasted. He was able to pass on information gleaned from edited copy or in-house comment for strikers to use in their clandestine bulletins and pamphlets. He also learned some valuable journalistic rules from a retired British army colonel who spent most of his time, not reading proofs, but writing freelance articles. He told Maurice there were four rules to writing: 'First you don't talk about it. Second, you park your bum on your seat. Third, you place paper on your desk. Fourth, you pick up your pen.'[15] And write. The colonel wrote several travel and eye-witness articles a week, about places he had never visited, events he had never seen, plagiarising the pages of *Encyclopaedia Britannica*. 'Though they posed as robustly factual, most were undiluted fantasy. I had met my first professional storyteller.'[16] The colonel's rules and example were never to leave him.

On a more literary level, Maurice wrote poetry and shared it with his admired Avondale College senior, Moss Gee. Despite his family's left-wing history, Gee did not take part in any of the Socialist Club activities but, rather, worked hard in the library to achieve a good master's degree in English. Sometimes Maurice and Moss would take their lunches across to the Albert Park Gardens and, as Gee recalls, they would read their latest poems to each other, echoing Avondale English classes. 'I seem to remember that [Maurie's] great enthusiasm was for T.S. Eliot … while I was fascinated by Gerard Manley Hopkins's sprung rhythm … neither of us were destined to be poets.'[17] But the pair did end up as the characters Jack Skeat and Rex Petley in Moss Gee's 1993 novel, *Going West*.

In 1951, Shadbolt also began to share his poems with a seventeen-year-old first-year student, someone who would endure as a friend and mentor until the end of his life. 'Among the Socialist Club's new members … was a gangling young freshman, with cadaverous face named Kevin Jowsey [later, Ireland*]; he had some literary aspiration.' Ireland *was* destined to be a poet. 'His father was a striking watersider and his radicalism, like mine, to some extent an inherited garment … He was to become, and remain, my literary conscience.'[18]

Ireland became one of the Socialist Club's keen activists and was present at the special general meeting 'when the students actually voted in favour of the emergency regulations — can you imagine, "Take away our liberty please". This was a centre of learning.'[19]

Maurice and Ireland went along to the Young People's Club to read their, often sexually charged, poetry. It was not appreciated by the Communist cadre. One asked where had the 'leading role of the Communist Party' been acknowledged. Asked another, 'Of what value is writing like this to the working class?'. What about the workers indeed? Ireland went along with Maurice to a Party meeting: 'It was a cell, they called it, but it was a "sell-out" as far as I was concerned … where people just talked Marxist gibberish … Maurie found an excuse for leaving and we all went up to the university field club hut for a weekend … we went to a Dally vineyard, bought some piss and all got very drunk and a fight broke out over some imaginary slight and it all ended in a dustup which showed how fragile these political nests were as soon as there was a bit of personal stress. The unity of purpose and workers solidarity didn't provide enough glue … Everything just collapsed and Maurie found it a good excuse, good timing, to say I resign and he left everything.'[20]

By 1952, they both lived on Auckland's North Shore: Ireland at home in Rewhiti Avenue, Takapuna while the Shadbolt family had moved from Avondale to a P&T flat in Preston Avenue, Belmont. Kevin would often go by

---

*Several years later, Jowsey changed his name to Ireland and will be referred to as that throughout this book.

to accompany Maurice on his way into town; they would also go home together on the ferry and catch a bus from the Bayswater terminal, or sometimes walk the mile or so up Bayswater Avenue to the Shadbolts'. Kevin Ireland recalls, 'His mother doted on him … it was open and shameless and embarrassing to watch … Maurie playing the grown-up infant and his Mum acting the part of the bustling, indulgent young servant of her little babe'.[21] He did not lift a finger. From the beginning he had been her special boy; her gift.

But Maurice was no longer a 'little babe' sexually. After a few unsatisfactory encounters, and fruitless lusting after a lecturer's daughter, he had his 'first regular mistress: a psychiatric nurse, red-haired and willowy, some years my senior. We made love in a variety of borrowed rooms and flats; I also grew to know Auckland's parkland intimately.'[22] Maurice threw himself into the affair to the point of 'carnal exhaustion', into a summery oblivion that marked his divorce from political activism, from university, from journalistic ambition, even from conjuring. Ireland had witnessed his last public performance in Pitt Street's Oddfellows Hall. He had gone along ready to sneer but was 'actually impressed' by Maurice's skills and performance. But he was not impressed by being on the outer during Maurice's all-consuming sexual affair. According to Maurice, Ireland told him, 'Man had to rise above lust … man, in the long run, was more than a perambulating penis.'[23] Maurice, who put this down to Ireland's jealousy, was always open to his friend's literary advice, but rarely to anything concerning his perambulations.

Maurice was working as a builder's labourer early in 1952 when he heard that there was to be a Communist-inspired Youth Carnival for Peace and Friendship in Sydney. Despite strong opposition from the conservative Menzies government and right-wing media, around 30,000 young people attended from around Australia and New Zealand. Included among a variety of sporting and cultural events was a literary competition with prize money of £300 for various forms of writing, including the short story. Up to that time, Maurice had written only bad poetry, left-wing polemic and student essays. Why he decided to enter the competition with a short story is unclear: perhaps it was the chance of payment and a trip to Sydney, which would be his first outside New Zealand, even the upper North Island. And he still believed in the socialist dream. So Maurice 'set aside a Saturday, bought a bottle of sherry and a packet of cigarettes, and wrote a short story — about a young soldier dying on a battlefield — in four hours, and revised it in one; a girlfriend typed the manuscript on Sunday and I mailed it to Australia on the Monday'.[24]

The story won a minor prize and Maurice travelled over to Sydney in March, joined by other New Zealand prize-winners. Among them were Noel

Hilliard, a 22-year-old short story writer and journalist from Wellington who had worked on the recently defunct Labour Party newspaper, the *Southern Cross*; 29-year-old Hone Tuwhare, a boilermaker from the Far North who, with Hilliard's encouragement, had begun to write poetry: both were Communist Party members. Also in company were twenty-year-old journalist Gordon Dryden, who had been blacklisted after printing a censored article during the waterfront dispute; and student radical Conrad Bollinger who was soon to write *Grog's Own Country*, an exposé of the liquor industry's influence in national politics.

In hindsight, Maurice wrote that the carnival had been one of a number of 'proliferating Communist-backed peace fronts' and that he and the others had arrived on the scene at the 'sputtering fag-end of the international Communist movement'.[25] But in March 1952 Maurice, along with Hilliard and Tuwhare, was still far from abandoning the cause. In New Zealand, he considered that the Communist Party 'provided almost the only visible avenue for social dissent in the stagnant fifties and attracted many on that score alone'.[26]

On his return to New Zealand, Maurice drifted, taking casual jobs in freezing chambers, wool stores and warehouses; he wrote bad, pessimistic verse and fell out with political friends. He had avoided four months of CMT because of his colour blindness and short-sightedness which would soon require him to wear glasses. Maurice had also begun to drift away from his father. Frank had persuaded Vi into an Akaroa Harbour holiday in early 1952, a major journey by train, ferry and bus, taking three-year-old Julia to be christened before his Aunt Amelia's memorial at the church in Duvauchelle. Frank eulogised the derelict Shadbolt family homestead and its associations in an article for the *Akaroa Mail*. He was nostalgic for the idyllic childhood and youth he had left behind more than thirty years before, and concluded with, 'I can think of no lovelier place to retire'. Fruitlessly, he tried to persuade Vi of the truth of this.

Trying to make sense of his world, of where he belonged, of where he should be heading, Maurice went to stay more and more often with Uncle Joe in his simple cottage in the Waitakere hills. By now Joe Kearon had become 'far more my father than my father; his tiny house more my home than any my footloose parents owned or rented. His was a place to take problems, woes and confidences.'[27] A survivor of depression and war, bachelor Joe worked on the roads, as a gardener, and as a gravedigger at Waikumete Cemetery. He was a literate and introspective man with whom Maurice could discuss all manner of literary questions as he began to scribble away at more short stories. Politically, Maurice had hidden his Communist Party connections from Frank and Vi, but with Joe, a dyed-in-the-wool Stalinist, there was no need and they could argue the ideological pros and cons. Although he was a declared atheist, Joe had the resources of the King James Bible, as well as Shakespeare, on hand to score philosophical points.

Maurice turned again to the prospect of journalism as a career and, soon after his twentieth birthday, applied for a cadet reporter's job on the *Taranaki Daily News* in New Plymouth. But when he was offered it, he prevaricated and asked, not Joe's, but Kevin Ireland's advice. Ireland remembers 'We sat outside, on the lower deck of the ferry and went backwards and forwards from Auckland to Bayswater, while I argued for him to take a chance and go, and he kept counting over and over again all the things he'd be losing … There were the friends and parties and pubs and politics and good times he would have to sacrifice.' On the third harbour crossing, Ireland simply said, "Do you really want to be a writer?" "Yes," he said. "Well, forget the friends and the parties, and go and learn the trade – at least for a year or two"'.[28]

CHAPTER 5

SOMEONE TO WATCH OVER ME

Maurice had been hired, not to learn the trade and progress up the New Plymouth head office ladder, but to be thrown in the deep end — writing lead stories after three days — to see if he could survive exile to the *Daily News* branch office in South Taranaki's Hawera. This was the 'New Zealand version of Siberia' where journalists were lucky to last more than a few months. The problem was not only the stress of small town politics, personal and public, and the hours of work, but also the alcoholic lubrication that went with it. Maurice started in the Hawera office with George Koea, later editor of the *Daily News*, but he was soon in sole charge with a sub-office just down the road, in the back bar of the White Hart Hotel. There he met with his mentor and collaborator, 'Geoffrey', an alcoholic veteran reporter for the opposition newspaper, the *Taranaki Herald*. Geoffrey assembled most of his stories between drinks, interviewing local policemen, council officials and firemen from his bar stool, anyone who had a story, which he would then dictate over the phone to his New Plymouth office. 'He was at home in Hawera's effervescent sub-culture of betting and booze.'[1] He spotted a willing ingenué in Maurice and proposed the pair could cut down their work by sharing stories without their head offices catching on. It was a provincial newspaper convention. In practice, this meant Maurice did the typing while Geoffrey snored off the booze. He typed reports of accidents, court cases, scandals, crimes, fires, rugby matches; reviews of plays and light opera; interviews with visiting celebrities such as Yorkshire brass band composer and conductor, Harry Mortimer and Australia's Queen of Song, Gladys Moncrieff. When news was in short supply, Maurice took to interviewing his typewriter, practising his skills at fiction.

Sometimes the intrepid reporters had to leave pub and office and chase stories in Geoffrey's car which he contrived to overturn when 'pursuing police, who in turn were chasing a pair of joy-riding prison escapers'. Bruised and dishevelled, they had to hitch-hike back with no story and when they returned to collect the car found that the 'backtracking fugitives had … bounced it on to its wheels again'[2] and taken off. Maurice and Geoffrey ended up in a ditch once more while careering around the countryside at night in pursuit of reported flying saucers.

The apotheosis of the pair's collaborative reporting came when, as Hawera's racecourse grandstand burned down, they found themselves inside. Brushing sparks from their shoulders, they emerged to the awe of waiting fireman with an exclusive eye-witness account. Maurice pounded his typewriter with the story of the 'hottest event in Hawera since Titokowaru heaped the legendary Major von Tempsky … on a funeral pyre'. He also wrote Geoffrey's account for the *Taranaki Herald*. 'As I began to flag, my prose became blowsier, freer with adjectives than facts.' The next day, the story under Geoffrey's name was judged superior to Maurice's. '"What the hell happened to you?" asked my chief reporter. "Did you sleep through it?"'[3]

Hawera was famous only for its water tower and for briefly acting as a republic in 1879 when locals considered the government dilatory in providing troops to defend them against Maori 'invasion' of their land and so set up their own militia. With a population of about 6000, the town serviced dairy farms sweeping down from the mountain, Taranaki, twenty miles to the north, and south towards Patea. As a country and small-town boy himself, Maurice had an instinctive feel for the lives of the townsfolk and farmers around him. Writing about this, day after day, soberly or creatively, in every mundane or bizarre detail, helped to establish a work ethic and gave him a wealth of knowledge of the human condition that he was able to draw on to imaginative effect in the years to come. What he did not know at the time was that another habitué of the White Hart, and every other pub in town, Ronald Hugh Morrieson, was writing his own imaginative takes on Hawera's seedy 'sub-culture of betting and booze', sex and violence, that was to find its hilarious expression in such novels as *Came a Hot Friday* and *The Scarecrow*.

Maurice also got to know the only other reporter in town, 23-year-old Gillian Heming, who worked for the *Hawera Star*. They soon became an item. Gill was an Australian journalist who had learned the ropes on Sydney tabloids, and had come over to New Zealand in search of snow and skiing.

Gill's father Ray had emigrated from Gloucestershire to Queensland after fighting in World War I, wishing to put the horrors of the Western Front well behind him, and went on to manage W.R. Carpenter coconut plantations in New Ireland. In 1928 his Devon sweetheart, Minnie 'Bunty' Weymouth, sailed out to meet him in Sydney for their marriage; and the following year she returned there from New Ireland to give birth to Gillian Eve Muriel on her first wedding anniversary, 21 April 1929.'While Mum was in Sydney Dad built her a large comfortable chair on which we would be carried by natives the eighty miles home to Karu plantation.'[4]

Gill spent her childhood barefoot free, swimming naked in the equatorial heat from the long golden beaches that fringed the plantation coasts. She rode her ponies Christmas and Sailor and took correspondence lessons with her mother on the wide verandahs of the 'masta's' house, attended by servants. The outside world only called in with the rare visits of sailing ships or steamers. With her younger brother Robin*, she was once paddled out by their 'meri' (nanny) to a schooner manned by a single Japanese sailor whom, she realised much later, was almost certainly one of the Japanese naval officers who voyaged around the Pacific in the 1930s collecting navigational information for future military operations.

Gill was sent to board at a Catholic mission school in New Britain's Rabaul; until her father became manager of Kurudui plantation, twenty miles out of the town, enabling both Heming children to attend from home. But in 1937 most of the town was destroyed by the cataclysmic eruption of two volcanoes on the Rabaul caldera that killed more than 500 people. The Hemings survived injury but the damage and disruption prompted a move back to New Ireland. On the verge of her teens, Gill accepted that her father would remain a New Ireland plantation manager until he retired, perhaps in 1945 when he reached sixty. But Japan's invasion of the Philippines and Malaya in December 1941 ensured that Ray Heming would never enjoy his anticipated retirement in Queensland.

Bunty Heming, with twelve-year-old Gill and nine-year-old Rob, along with hundreds of other European women and children, were evacuated from the New Guinea islands not long before the Japanese invaded New Britain in January 1942. Ready for embarkation at the Rabaul Hotel, Gill remembers to her mortification an Australian soldier asking her — clad in shirt and shorts — to dance but lasting only a few steps before dashing away in embarrassment to bury her face in her mother's shoulder. Of the 1400 Australian soldiers sent to defend Rabaul, only 300 escaped death or capture. 'Everyone was down at the docks the next morning ... Rob held my hand as we waved goodbye to Dad and

*Rob Heming was born in December 1932. In the 1960s he played as an outstanding lock forward for the Australian rugby union team.

those on the wharf — some of whom we had known as uncles all our lives.'[5]

Bunty and her children were disembarked in Sydney. Robin Heming recounts: 'When we landed, we had the clothes we arrived in and no money ... For quite a while the three of us lived in one room. It was a terrible battle for a long time: how my mother managed was amazing. She was never anything but positive. Somehow we survived.'[6] Survived the move from the tropical isolation and a 'masta's' plantation life in New Ireland to a precarious existence in wartime Sydney.

By the end of the Pacific war in 1945, Gill had finished her schooling, decided she wanted to write, and began to think about a career in journalism. The war officially ended on 15 August, but another month passed before an Australian warship arrived in New Ireland to take the surrender of the Japanese forces there; and to pick up the estimated eighty-seven European civilians who had remained on the island at the beginning of 1942. They found only seven and Ray Heming was not among them.

The family had to wait until May 1947 before receiving the inevitable: a Certificate of Death issued by the Department of External Territories. It stated, 'Horace Ray HEMING became missing on the Eighteenth day of February, 1944, and is for official purposes presumed to be dead.'[7] But the date given was false, taken from the testimony of the perpetrators of what came to be known as the 'Kavieng Massacre' when they tried to disguise their actions. Later in 1947, at a war crimes trial in Hong Kong, it was revealed that in March 1944 the Japanese military at Kavieng, erroneously expecting an imminent invasion by allied forces, executed the thirty or more European men they had been holding in an internment camp. They took them down to the port's wharf, blindfolded them, garrotted them one by one, and pushed their bodies into a barge below. The barge was then taken to sea and the bodies, including that of Ray Heming, were weighted with concrete and thrown overboard. The admiral who gave the execution order was hanged and his officers sentenced to long prison sentences. None of this was of much comfort to Gill, Bunty and Rob who had lived with the certainty, after September 1945, that Ray was gone. But Gill always held on to the belief that her father had done the right thing by staying on in New Ireland. She was certain there was 'no way' he would have deserted his plantation workers and left them to the mercies of the invading Japanese; he had paid with his own life in his efforts to protect them.

Maurice and Gill do not seem to have been a natural match. Gill the tall, well-built girl with English parentage and a New Ireland and Sydney city background; the 'rounded', full-lipped Shadbolt, a fourth-generation New

Zealander with a provincial upbringing. Maurice was the member of a large and complex clan while Gill had only a mother and brother to call on as family. But they had writing and journalism in common and were lonely outsiders in a small town which, for both, could only be a staging post. Maurice found her 'lively' and she, no doubt, was open to his self-assured manner, his gurgling laugh and air of sexual worldliness. Gill would have Maurice round for tea and listen to him talk about the autobiographical novel he was struggling with, a 'treasure box' constructed from the styles of the writers that most impressed him at the time — Hemingway, Wolfe and Faulkner. Apart from tea, she provided sympathy for the increasing woes of his job with its excess boozing, his real doubts about the worth of what he was doing, even about whether he should be a writer at all. Three years his senior in years, she was ten in maturity, offering him comfort and reassurance, with food and sex at the weekends.

But Maurice missed the company of Kevin Ireland, his literary talk, and like-minded people in Auckland and, when he could on weekends off, hitch-hiked up and back, 200 miles each way. In January 1953, Ireland and Carl Freeman decided to hitch-hike the other way for a holiday in Hawera and were surprised to find that the relationship with Gill, which Maurice had earlier only mentioned, was a 'romance in full blossom'. Gill had two friends over from Sydney for a holiday, too, and one evening all six squeezed into her little Morris 8 and headed out of town, singing songs such as 'Swing Low Sweet Chariot', driving into an episode worthy of a Ronald Hugh Morrieson novel. Kevin Ireland recalls: 'Gill was teaching Maurie to drive … so he had the wheel, and it was his first experience of driving overloaded and at night … Maurie couldn't resist showing off, so he did wheelies on a rough patch of parkland. Several local desperadoes came hurtling out of the scrub surrounding it and they tried to force our doors open. Maurie drove off, with Gill very calmly instructing him not to accelerate too hard and stall the bloody engine. He did so and we only just got away, though a couple of toughies held on to a door handle and the rear bumper and got dragged quite a distance.'[8] Later, Maurice wrote to Freeman to say that learning to drive had given him a 'sense of freedom'.

Despite Gill's ministrations and the enlivening visit of his two closest friends, the stress of the *Daily News* job was becoming too much and, one day, he walked out of the Hawera office and took a casual job with a road gang: his Uncle Joe's prescription for stress had always been fresh air and hard physical labour. But George Koea came down from New Plymouth and persuaded him back behind his typewriter.[9] By this time, 'Geoffrey' had been sent to dry out in a sanatorium and Maurice had begun to notice the tremble in his own hand when he reached out for his first beer of the day.

Then he was put on the mat, called up to head office in New Plymouth to explain himself. He had been shut out of a Patea Hospital Board meeting considering letters of complaint, but managed to obtain these which he then quoted in a report. There was clear evidence of malpractice and incompetence at the hospital under the medical management of two octogenarian doctors, one of whom had been there almost fifty years. Patea worthies complained to the *Daily News* editor that there was a left-wing journalist upsetting the community (reds under the bed). Editor A.B. Scanlan quizzed Maurice on his political leanings and told him, '"We rake no muck on the *News* … Leave Patea alone".'[10] But Maurice had a side job as a stringer for *Truth*, who certainly were interested in 'muck', and he slipped them a story that brought about an investigation leading to resignations, and better health care, in Patea.

By March, Maurice was on the verge of a nervous collapse. He took sick leave and went to stay with Uncle Joe on Forest Hill Road, up the hill from Henderson, from where he went on long walks in the Waitakeres. He told Gill that these had done him 'the world of good'. From his parents' home in Preston Avenue he wrote, 'I am feeling really up to par now … but I am not keen on coming down to Hawera and squandering all my new-found fitness away again in the Daily News office'. He said the doctor agreed with him — 'He is not keen on me staying in the job and advised me to take it easy'.[11] He also gave him some more 'nerve dope'. This was the second or third depressive collapse that Maurice had experienced since leaving school, but the first time he had taken prescription medicine to combat the effects of the 'depression gene' he considered he inherited from the Kearons.

Maurice went back to Hawera by train on 23 March but was already planning to leave again. In Auckland he had tried to find a job on either the *New Zealand Herald* or *Auckland Star*, without luck, but then applied successfully for a job on a Christchurch newspaper. In early May he travelled south to stay with Con Bollinger in Wellington before he caught the ferry to Lyttelton. This coincided with Victoria University Capping Weekend and he had just finished partying with Bollinger and others when he received a telegram to tell him that Grandmother Kearon had just died in Glen Eden; she had been in and out of hospital for months.

Maurice made it to the funeral just in time and, for him, the event was not only farewell to Louisa but also to the Morris family: 'Who were they? What had they been? And who would ever know? … Near anonymous, they said goodbye and vanished.'[12] He never made the effort to find them again.

After the funeral, Maurice went to live with Uncle Joe again. He joined him working as a roadman and, although he applied for jobs on the Auckland papers, he was soon to abandon, for good, a career in daily journalism. The nine months on the *Taranaki Daily News* had trained him in interviewing, observational and reporting skills across an immense range of topics, all of which was to prove valuable in a more lucrative kind of journalism to come.

After three months on the roads, he also put his skills to immediate use in a part-time job as the editor and sole reporter of the *Waitakere Gazette*. He soon uncovered more scandal. To keep commercial property rates down the local council allowed its sewage to drain 'downhill into low-cost housing and fouling a stream in which local children swam'.[13] The *Gazette* proprietor blanched at running the story, so Maurice fed it to the *Auckland Star*, which caused an uproar among aggrieved Waitakere residents, and consequent action. Maurice ended his *Gazette* career by capriciously suggesting in his editorial column that something different be done to mark the procession of Queen Elizabeth II and the Duke of Edinburgh through the West Auckland district during their grand Commonwealth tour — a Walter Raleigh-style cloak of flowers on the road. To Maurice's amazement, the idea was picked up. 'On December 28, 1953, the royal entourage hurtled through West Auckland and passed over, without slowing, or Her Majesty knowing, a shimmering rug of summer flowers thirty feet long and eighteen wide.'[14]

The only other mention of queen and coronation in any of Maurice's memoirs or letters is his strong objection to seeing the coronation movie, despite Kevin Ireland's argument that it was the 'last one they're going to have so we might as well put all that mumbo jumbo under a microscope and analyse it'.[15] His four-and-half-year-old sister Julia finally wheedled him into going but he wrote that 'she was as bored as I was. I am sorry, but I can't help seeing the slums of London when I see a picture like that … as far as doing anything to contribute towards world peace goes, the coronation's effect was nil as far as I could see.'[16]*

Parallel to developing journalistic skills, he continued to plug away at fiction: the doomed tyro novel and short stories that he spilled out after roadman's work with Uncle Joe. 'The roads we repaired and the verges we trimmed lay among Dalmatian vineyards and orchards … We tidied their drives on the side; and bicycled unsteadily home with gifts of apples and dubious sherry.'[17] The other men who worked on the roads were 'depression-weary or war-weary men seeing out the last of their working lives'.

---

*Curiously, there is no reference anywhere in Shadbolt's writings of that time to Ed Hillary's first ascent of Everest which was announced on Coronation Day, 2 June 1953, and just before Shadbolt's 21st birthday.

In the evenings, Maurice offered up his stories for Joe's advice. A purist versed in Shakespeare and Milton, Joe thought that trying to write the way people spoke was a big mistake: it was not literature. Apart from talking literature, they discussed philosophy and politics. The Soviet Union's 'Uncle Joe' Stalin had died a few months before and stories of his regime's atrocities had begun to circulate. These caused Maurice's Uncle Joe to be uncharacteristically quiet on the subject of the socialist dream. 'Joe held out against the bad news longer. "Socialism might come right, one day," he sighed, and lit his pipe. "There has to be a better world than this."'[18]

Left-wing journalist Gordon Dryden, whom he had met at the Sydney Youth Carnival a year before, had joined the staff of the Communist weekly *The People's Voice*, and asked Maurice for reviews, articles, even verse, all of which he provided under a *nom-de-plume*. Dryden also ran a short story competition, judged blindly by an independent academic, and Maurice took first, second and third prizes. He maintained that he wrote all three in one afternoon and, probably correctly, were better forgotten. Despite this facility and success, he remained unconvinced that short fiction was his métier.

The Party cadre were not convinced for different reasons and protested to Dryden and the editor that Shadbolt was a renegade, not one of the Party faithful. Had they seen the letter that Maurice wrote to Gill around this time they may have retracted their complaints. Gill had said to Maurice that she thought his political ideas 'funny' and 'dangerous'. On a visit to Auckland, he recalled, 'You come into my room at home. You see a book, pick it up. Suddenly you realise that it touches on Communism, and you drop it like a hot potato.' He accused her of believing a 'great deal of the propaganda churned out about Russia' and in a six-page typed letter,[19] which took him all day to write — and which he hoped had not become a political pamphlet but which had — he strove to convince her of the socialist cause.

Maurice's passionate exposition of the history and virtues of the Communist cause was prompted by the electrocution in the United States the day before of Julius and Ethel Rosenberg. They had been convicted as spies for passing on atomic and electronic secrets that enabled the Soviet Union to keep up with United States' weapons technology. Many prominent figures around the world, from the Pope to Einstein, considered the Rosenbergs innocent and that the trial was driven by McCarthyite hysteria.* Maurice wrote to Gill:

---

*The 'unjust' conviction and execution of the Rosenbergs was a cornerstone of left-wing dialectic in the United States for decades. But in 2008 a colleague of the Rosenbergs finally revealed that they had all been spies and had passed on much vital defence information to the Soviet Union.

'The swinish ruling class of the U.S. added two more victims, a loving mother and father, to the list of those they have slain'. This statement could have come directly from a Soviet propaganda sheet.

He told Gill that he was willing to lay down his life for the 'cause in which I believe … Am I a communist for my own gain? Or am I just a deluded idealist?' An idealist certainly and, as he was to discover later, deluded indeed: 'I am a communist because I love life and hate death. Because I reject war, and love peace. Because I love progress, and hate sterile reaction. Because I believe … logical thought. Because I was born among the working class'. Most of the letter was a lecture in political science, and its tone mostly strident. But there was a pressing reason why he felt it essential, whether Gill was willing to join the cause or not, that she should know where he stood. 'It would be better for you to appreciate my point of view, and me yours, before we marry … my ideas influence the whole of my life; they cannot help but do that.'

By the time Maurice left Hawera in May, his relationship with Gill had developed beyond a romance, beyond a mutually rewarding affair between two young outsiders in a conservative country town. Soon after Maurice's 21st birthday in June, it had become time for Gill to travel up to Auckland to meet his parents. Wisely, he had not invited her to the party on 6 June because 'The whole Shadbolt clan was there, and it finished with the uncles slugging it out across the back lawn. There was blood everywhere'.[20]

Vi and Frank took a shine to Gill and after she had returned to Hawera, Maurice 'told Mum today how old you were, and she didn't turn a hair, just saying "I don't think it matters at all because you're both very well suited"'.[21] Gill wrote to her mother; Vi and Bunty wrote to each other, both approving of the match, and it was not long before Maurice told his mother that he and Gill were getting engaged. 'She was very pleased and said I was lucky to have found such a nice girl. I think so too.'[22] In another letter he confirmed, 'Kev and Carl, by the way, and for what it's worth, have given their approval to our relationship "as long as they see us once in a while"'.[23]

In his 1953 letters to Gill, his affection and longing for her are strongly expressed. Each one begins, 'My darling' and ends 'Good bye for now my darling' or 'All my love' or 'Your sweetheart'. After Gill had left Auckland on one occasion, he wrote: 'I had the most terrible feeling after you had gone, and I was quite miserable for some time after … I felt part of my mind and body had gone last night, and I know it will never be the same until we are together again.'[24] He wrote execrable love poems for her:

> We built our dreams
> As the sanddrifts build from rock
> Slowly, with time, grain by grain
> The dream made itself.
> It had many parts
> But the main ingredients were just
> You and I.

Maurice's page after page of letters arguing his dedication to communism are evidence of how serious he took his relationship with Gill. Not to persuade her into the same beliefs or to restrict her freedom of decision, or even her freedom to apply for journalistic jobs wherever she saw fit; but to feel secure that the grounds for their relationship would not be compromised. 'You seem sure that it will all come right in the end … And inside yourself, I feel that you think that perhaps one day I will drop my ideas, or something like that. I may be wrong. But it is just as well to bring these things out in the open.'[25]

The time of engagement brought conflict. Maurice objected to Gill's inference that his 'family were pigs. I am aware that my family may not have the best manners in the world, that they may be a little confused at times, that they have a lot of faults. But they are hard-working, honest people who have had to struggle hard all the lives. And I owe a lot to them.'[26] But he had also behaved like 'a heel' to her and was anxious to justify himself. 'I am in the worst mental state of my life. My mind is a sense whirl of contradictory thoughts. It would not take a great deal more to put [me] into a madhouse … considering some of the fits of temper and periods of depression that I have.' He put this down to uncertainty about the future and about her: 'Will you really appreciate what I do, or rather what I try to do?' He was also a 'victim of a terrible disease: the artistic temperament. That would be very hard for any woman to stand.' Especially when she had a 'tendency … to be unable to make the distinction between good writing and trash.'[27]

Gill seems to have taken Maurice's mixture of priggishness, self-importance, insult and appeals for understanding in her stride; to have tacitly accepted his 'artistic temperament', and claims to know what was best. Perhaps she did feel it would 'all come right in the end', that he would change as he grew up, when they lived together. It was a common, often fatal, female condescension. And whatever her literary judgement, she supported his writing, typed his stories, sent them off for possible publication, recognising that there was more than simply a journalist in him.

None of his friends had pursued it, or seemed likely to pursue it at the time, but Maurice's need for marriage as soon as he turned twenty-one* revealed his emotional insecurity and inability to cope with the uncertainty he felt about his future. The sexual relationship with Gill was good but that was not the priority; he now had little difficulty finding sexual partners. But none of these could offer what Gill had shown: a propensity to look after him. She had the ability to cope with his periods of depression, and to help manage his practical affairs. Reaching the 'age of majority' appears to have prompted, whether he was aware of it or not, a need to move from the uncritical support and love of his mother to the care and understanding love of a wife. Maurice had never lived independently. In Hawera he boarded and had weekends with Gill. In Auckland, he lived and worked with Uncle Joe during the week and went home to Mum on the weekends.

Then there were practical imperatives to marriage. In the conformist climate of the early 1950s, 'living in sin' was frowned upon. If Maurice and Gill were to avoid problems travelling together, of finding rented accommodation together, they needed genuine rings on their fingers. Obtaining jobs was easier for a man when a husband was expected to be the sole breadwinner for his family. Having children out of wedlock was an even greater social sin, as well as a practical mistake: only a married woman could claim the Family Benefit, for example.

Little sister Julie asked Maurice why people got married and he said, '"To have babies." "Many babies?" "Lots and lots of them." We'll show her — won't we?'[28] He seemed more enthusiastic about having children than Gill and wrote, with a touch of joshing bravado, 'Don't be frightened to have children — we going [sic] to have ten — aren't we?'.[29] Gill was more circumspect.

Maurice was anxious to be married sooner rather than later and, after many attempts by both to secure new jobs, an offer from Wellington added more urgency to his pleas to fix the date. Both had applied for the same position as a trainee director and scriptwriter for the National Film Unit (NFU), although Maurice had not been aware of Gill's application. The NFU had been formed in 1941 to produce information and propaganda films in support of the war effort, in particular through the agency of the ten-minute newsreel *Weekly Review* distributed free to all cinemas. After the war, its focus shifted to an educational role and the production of documentaries that promoted New Zealand to the world in the cause of tourism, investment and produce marketing. *Weekly Review* had been abolished in 1950 by the National government, partly because several of the NFU film-makers did not see eye to eye with its policies. Earlier,

---

*Still the legal age of majority in 1953.

in 1948, a leading NFU director had been sacked after Acting Labour Prime Minister Walter Nash had, scandalously, used the contents of the man's stolen brief case to expose him as a member of the Communist Party.

Maurice was aware of the politics surrounding the NFU when he went for his first job interview in Auckland and was asked what books he read, what libraries and organisations he belonged to, where he had travelled. He inferred his trip to Sydney in 1952 was related to his Australian fiancée. But the public service did not take his word for it. His former boss in the *New Zealand Herald* reading room was contacted by the Security Intelligence Service (SIS) and asked if he had ever uttered 'sentiments of a subversive or inflammatory nature'. The *Herald* man replied, 'With respect — weren't you ever young?'.[30] It seems unlikely (though possible) that the SIS were ignorant of the *Craccum* affair and Maurice's connections with the Communist Party. If they were not, the cue from Maurice's old boss may have caused them to decide it was all down to youthful impetuosity. He was called down to Wellington for a final interview, and got the job.

The wedding was set for 21 November at Auckland's St Matthew-in-the-City, Hobson Street. Maurice and his father wore pinstriped suits and Gill a two-piece cream costume with a floral appliqué collar. Gill's mother had been unable to make the trip from Sydney but Maurice was able to invite some people to the wedding who had missed his 21st birthday party; and probably did not invite some who had. His best man was Gordon Dryden because he 'had the best suit. A second consideration, and almost as important, was that he could rely on Gordon to make a sound and sober speech; he couldn't rely on any other friend not to drink too much Dally plonk and tell terrible, hearty jokes about getting married.'[31] The marriage certificate recorded that Maurice's profession was 'Journalist' but Gill was listed as having none.

Julia, almost five, was the flower girl. As the reception drew on, she went round and drank the dregs from all the beer glasses, undetected until she began whirling around and fell over.[32] She was the only one who had to be carried home as Maurice and Gill went off on their honeymoon to Rotorua.

CHAPTER 6

THINKING VISUALLY

When Maurice Shadbolt arrived at the National Film Unit in Miramar in May 1954 he was given the empty office of a producer on leave. The best producers had left altogether, frustrated by an increasing level of bureaucratic intervention. Nothing now could be produced that did anything other than show New Zealand as a progressive modern society living in a scenic wonderland and with the best race relations in the world. The music tracks were jaunty or inspiring, the commentaries in accents that would do credit to British Movietone News.

Maurice had scarcely met cameraman and director Brian Brake before he also quit and went to Europe where he was soon accepted as a photographer with Magnum, the Paris agency founded by Henri Cartier-Bresson in 1947. After he left the NFU, Brake's recent documentary *The Snows of Aorangi* was good enough to be nominated for an Academy Award. John Feeney, who had produced *Legend of the Wanganui River*, was leaving to take up an award-winning career with the National Film Board of Canada. Much earlier, another NFU director, Roger Mirams, had left to found Pacific Films and, with John O'Shea, had produced New Zealand's first post-war feature film, *Broken Barrier*, in 1952. Two years later this was still the talk of local film-making. Inspiration was outside, not inside, the NFU.

According to Maurice, he was given no training and left alone in his little office for weeks, even months. Occasionally, a senior executive would put his head around the door, once to find Maurice reading a Norman Mailer novel. Maurice wrote that, during this time, he managed to read 'most of the novels in the Wellington Public Library'.[1] The executive reminded him that film was a visual medium and that good writers did not necessarily make good film-makers. 'Think visually,' he said and, on another occasion, asked 'Still thinking visually?'. Maurice wrote, 'That was my apprenticeship in movies.'[2]

Contradicting this, he wrote elsewhere: 'Since the training was minimal, I immediately began directing short documentaries.'[3] In fact, when Maurice was not reading novels, he visited the film labs, talked to technicians about film processing and editing; chatted to cameramen; dropped into the offices of working producers; and viewed past editions of *Pictorial Parade*. This had become the staple NFU product, a monthly 10-12 minute newsreel free to cinemas, comprising two or three items that covered everything from royal tours to washing machine manufacture.

A senior NFU director, James Harris, also took young Maurice under his wing. 'When I was still in a very junior position at the Unit, I was assigned to go along with him on a project in the South Island. His position was director-cameraman; I was strictly an assistant. The film — eventually released as *Inventor in the Mackenzie Country* —was the story of Bill Hamilton, the industrialist and inventor of the jet-boat. Time after time, in the course of shooting this film, Mr Harris stood to one side, and allowed me to direct scenes … in order that I should get the experience of directing films that I still needed …'[4]

As his skills developed, it became easy enough for Maurice to pick up on a new or neglected topic, find a willing cameraman and head off to shoot enough useable footage for a three- to four-minute segment; and this is what he did for the next two or three years. 'There was felicity in the travel: I found my own country. I rode out on high country musters in the South Island [Molesworth]; I journeyed with fishermen through muddy Northland tidal estuaries; I bounced across Lake Ohau in Bill Hamilton's prototype jet-boat while he explained that he had invented it so he could enjoy New Zealand more.'[5] It was not just the travel. He was researching and experiencing a New Zealand he had never encountered before, building a store of character and story. Despite his aspersions about his NFU boss, he also learned to see New Zealand, to think visually.

Sometimes his projects fell foul of the censorious government policy directives. Drawing on his high school and Young People's Club experiences, he started filming an item about Dalmatian vineyards in West Auckland. On seeing the rushes, his producer telegrammed, 'TOO MUCH DRINKING IN THIS FILM. ALSO TOO MANY DALMATIANS SOME ARE SAID TO BE COMMUNIST. IT MUST NOT BE THOUGHT THAT NEW ZEALANDERS ARE ALL DRUNKS AND DALMATIANS. THE PROJECT IS CANCELLED.'[6]

From time to time, Maurice scratched away at his Wolfeian novel and wrote bad poetry but, despite the bureaucratic frustrations, his main ambition now was to develop his career as a film-maker; Mirams and O'Shea were showing what could be done. The NFU job was also his most secure so far, with about £10* a week guaranteed by the Public Service Association union at its strongest. Paid travel for work also allowed him to catch up with friends and family in Auckland from time to time.

Maurice sometimes wrote book reviews for the *Evening Post* where Gill had a reporting job and earned about £7 a week. Their combined income allowed them to rent a cottage at 370a The Terrace, near its junction with Abel Smith Street, where they were able to follow a modestly comfortable lifestyle and host friends who were not so well off. They 'lived a rackety, if now marginally more respectable life'.[7]

Not far away, Kevin Ireland shared a flat with John Kasmin who recalled, 'It was often the case that Kevin and I were very hard up … Gill remembers me turning up famished and skinny and eating potatoes with them because they had a bit more money than we ever had, there'd always be a bit of a meal. [Maurice] had a wife at the stove.' To 'Kas', Gill did not seem 'sexually such a catch, a docile placid sort of lady … although she was a sweetie, she was lovely'.[8] Ireland remembered differently: 'I was sleeping in the next room … when Maurice and his newly married wife … actually broke their double bed in the middle of the night'.[9]

Aged seventeen, Kas had arrived in New Zealand from England in 1952 with some Bar Mitzvah money in his pocket. He had come to escape National Service, and his father who wanted him to work in his pressed steel factory when, 'All I wanted to do was write poetry and get away and live a different life'. For a London East End Jew and Oxford classical scholar, New Zealand seems an unlikely place at the time to pursue that ambition. But there was a family connection** and he soon met up with Ireland in Auckland where booze eventually got the better of him, 'being a wild boy', and he shifted to Wellington. There he met Maurice, 'one of the first older, successful writing people that I knew'. Kas did write poetry, including some published in *New Zealand Poetry Yearbook*, but he was better known around town for his risky fraternisations with members of the criminal community. 'In the wake of a crime, to which he might have been witness, two bulky detectives questioned him vigorously. They examined his possessions, taking particular note of his dog-eared copies of *Ulysses* and *Finnegan's Wake*. They carried these suspect volumes off for further study. "It looks to us like you're in the pornography

---

*Worth about $NZ750 a week today.
**An aunt and uncle for whom he babysat his nephew, John Barnett, later the film producer.

business," they judged. "Who are your associates?"

"'Dostoyevsky and Proust,' he informed them.

"'Dostoyevsky? He'd be Russian, would he? A Commo?'

"'Proust is French,' Kas said helpfully.

"'And we know about *them*, don't we?' they said. "How would you describe yourself?"

"'As a poet,' Kas said.

'They shook their heads and warned him, "We don't need your sort here".'[10] When things grew too hot for him in Wellington, Kas worked his passage back to London in 1956.

The Shadbolts went up to Auckland at the end of 1954 to spend Christmas with Grandmother Ada and other members of the family at Green Bay. Now aged about seventy-five, Ada was becoming increasingly vague about the past but more prescient about the future. Almost three years before, she had burst into a grandson's bedroom in the early hours of the morning to announce that her youngest son Timmy (Donald) was dead. Timmy had flown with the Fleet Air Arm during World War II, married, had two sons, Tim and Rod, and had become a schoolteacher when the call came on the outbreak of the Korean War for ex-FAA pilots to retrain for the conflict. Timmy volunteered, took his young family to England; and then was killed when he flew his Blackburn Firebrand torpedo fighter into a Sussex hillside while training with his Royal Naval Air Squadron: at just about that moment Ada burst tearfully into her grandson's bedroom.

Over Christmas dinner, Ada chatted with Maurice about his work and told him she had enjoyed reading his story in the latest issue of the literary quarterly *Landfall*. But Maurice had never sent a story to *Landfall* and Ada could not find her copy to point it out. Ada died a year later on 13 December 1955, soon after *that* quarter's *Landfall* had appeared with Maurice's story 'Sing Again Tomorrow'. Maurice was deeply influenced by these demonstrations of his grandmother's psychic powers and was later to claim a kind of inheritance.

Maurice was becoming disillusioned with the 'propaganda' regime at the National Film Unit and continued to pick away at the novel and his verse. Talking with Ireland one day, he admitted he was not much good at poetry. Ireland responded, 'Yes, your talent is for bloody stories, you've written one or two little sketches, why don't you do more of that? Maurice, I would say, It's too clunky … It's just terrible stuff. For Maurice a poem was just a way of saying, I'm the unhappiest man in the world, I'm full of brotherly love, and I would say to him if you want to say that, say it in a story for God's sake. This [poetry] is just preposterous rhetoric.'[11] Maurice took this to heart. Grandmother Ada had also prodded him again in the direction of writing and, after all, in Wellington 'Everyone else seemed to be writing. It was the thing to do in Wellington in the mid-fifties, like playing a guitar in coffee shops in the mid-sixties.'[12] Ireland considered Wellington the most 'dynamic' of the four main centres at the time, 'the magic pumpkin'.

But in March and April of 1955 Maurice was away from Wellington for weeks on end, on the road for a variety of NFU assignments in the north: filming navy divers; the first logging train out of the Kawerau pulp and paper mill; plant research at Mount Albert; shark fishing in the Kaipara. Gill complained about him being away for so long, and his boring letters which were all about him and his work. He responded, 'Why the hell does this bitching have to go on every time we're apart. It's always been the same … All right, so I'm self-centred and my letters boring … But, God, darling, I just can't go through this again if it's going to happen every time I'm away from home. I'd sooner throw in the job, much as I like it, and be with you in our home and be content with my writing.'[13] He felt he was 'going mad' with the stress she was putting him under. It had taken him a couple of weeks to write the letter, and he had torn up earlier drafts. He laid out his love for her — a page of kisses at the end — and wrote, 'If you want me to change, I probably could, but I wouldn't be worth a tin of fish to you or anyone else … I know I am terribly weak in lots of things, useless in a lot of day to day things, I'm anti-social, perhaps too harsh in judgement of people etc … But if I didn't have certain attitudes to life and human beings, what the hell would I write about?' Much as he liked the job, much as he sometimes fantasised to Ireland and others about becoming a famous film director, his underlying drive was to think fictionally, not visually.

Soon after he came home again, early in May 1955, Maurice put Ireland's advice into practice, made a 'bonfire' of his novel, put aside poetry for good, and wrote four short stories in four weeks. All were accepted for publication. He also began to read New Zealand writing more seriously, beyond Katherine Mansfield whose stories had revealed to him, after his arrival in Wellington, that there could be a literature from his own country. The poets excited him most: A.R.D. Fairburn, Denis Glover, Charles Brasch, James K. Baxter, Allen Curnow. 'They wrote of first things, tribal things of the homeland I had haphazardly begun to glimpse.'[14] The world of New Zealand fiction writing was to prove more hostile to the 23-year-old tyro.

CHAPTER 7

OPENING SHOTS

Maurice's first published story, other than his short pieces in Communist periodicals, was 'Annual Holiday' in the 10 June 1955 issue of the *New Zealand Listener*. The *Listener*, under the editorship of Monte Holcroft since 1949, had become more than the radio times of the New Zealand Broadcasting Service; it was also the unofficial weekly journal of literature, arts and culture. Its brief was reflective of the wide range of topics covered by NZBS programmes. Holcroft, a 53-year-old prize-winning essayist and published novelist, as well as experienced editor, included as many short stories and poems as magazine space would allow. He also paid for the most informed book reviews in the country, especially of New Zealand work. Holcroft made all the selections himself, which gave him an unparalleled influence over the presentation of New Zealand writing to a wide public. The weekly circulation of the *Listener* which, at the time, had exclusive rights to forward radio programme listings, was more than 80,000. It was read by four times that number and found in households across the country. This compared to the sub-1000 copies quarterly of *Landfall*, which were bought only by libraries and the literary cognoscenti. Holcroft was also a member of the NZ Literary Fund panel for fifteen years, influencing who received state writing grants. Holcroft's roles and selections attracted both praise and fury, often sparking controversy in the letters pages of the magazine. 'But, acutely aware of the *Listener*'s importance as a national forum, Holcroft strove for balance and fairness in representing correspondents' views, even when attacked personally (though he was unable to resist occasional waspish footnote comments).'[1] As Maurice was about to discover.

'Annual Holiday' was a story told by a university student who had made friends with 'Shorty', old enough to be his father, while working at a summertime job in a wool store. Shorty's main vocation was as a fisherman; he had a launch on the Kaipara and had invited the student out fishing every year he had been at university. The story told of the student's last fishing trip with Shorty before he moved on in life, perhaps to write. 'In the morning the tide was out and the launch was touching bottom. We jumped into the shallow water and plucked the scallops from the sand, later frying them in butter for breakfast. It was the memory of this kind of thing, together with Shorty himself, that had taken me back year after year to the Kaipara to live a strangely different kind of life.' The two men spoke little, and did not reveal themselves emotionally, in the inarticulate way of the male world of the 1950s. Even at the end the men could say little more than, 'Look after yourself', stretching as far as 'I hope you find what you want to find'. The story was without frills, technically imperfect but with poignancy, and owed much to Maurice's readings of American fiction by the likes of Hemingway and Farrell. He drew the material from his own life: as the university student who worked in a wool store; Uncle Joe for 'Shorty'; the location and action from filming Kaipara shark fishing.

Three weeks after the story's publication, a letter to the editor appeared over the signature of 'K' of Henderson: 'So many ill-formed judgements of local writing — especially in verse — appear in your correspondence columns that one hesitates to make adverse comment. But when a short story is printed that seems to indicate a complete suspension of critical taste on the part of an editor for the sake of a theme which is congenial to him, it is difficult to remain silent.

'The clichés and bad grammar of Maurice Shadbolt's story "Annual Holiday", the sentimentality, the confusion of subject matter, the self-conscious university attitudes, and above all the prolixity, must be apparent to the kindest of readers. The handling of the theme of friendship is unsubtle (one thinks by contrast of Frank Sargeson's brilliant compression), and the elaborate detail about shark catching belongs to a journalist's report or perhaps a school essay.

'I do not mean to be uncharitable towards Mr. Shadbolt. The fault belongs entirely to the editor, who does even greater disservice to the writer than to readers when he prints poor work.'

Holcroft added one of his 'waspish' footnotes: 'If it is true that "many ill-formed judgments of local writing" appear in these columns, we can scarcely refuse to print another; but our correspondent should not suppose that anonymity entitles him to be offensive. The last sentence of his letter has been deleted.'[2]

This was the opening shot of a feud that was to last all of Maurice's life. With his first published story, an 'apprentice work' that Maurice never chose to anthologise later, he had been caught in the crossfire between Holcroft, the influential national literary editor, and New Zealand's most respected fiction writer of the time, Frank Sargeson.

Sargeson was regarded by the literary community as the finest short-story writer since Katherine Mansfield. During the late 1930s and 1940s, after committing himself to a life as an essentially New Zealand writer — as distinct from a colonial writer in the English literary tradition — he published many short stories in which his 'major achievement was to introduce the rhythms and idiom of everyday New Zealand speech to literature, although his technical sophistication makes even the short stories of the 1930s and 1940s much more than the mere transcription of reality for which they were sometimes mistaken. While his first stories were about the constricting effects of a puritan and materialistic society, many of his later writings celebrated the freedom of those who had escaped from it.'[3]

Sargeson's almost monk-like devotion to the cause of a New Zealand literature had led to his position as guru and mentor to many younger writers. His modest bach at 14 Esmonde Road, Takapuna — then a no-exit road to mangrove swamp — was a gathering place for literati; and the army hut he erected on his property had become a refuge for younger writers such as Maurice Duggan and, most notably, Janet Frame, who came to stay in the year of the *Listener* dispute, and who would write there her first novel *Owls Do Cry*.

But the writer Sargeson and the editor Holcroft did not get on, from their very first meeting in the *Listener* office in 1950, when Sargeson commented, 'I suppose, Holcroft, you only need to come down in the afternoons'. Sargeson 'sat in my office and we talked for an hour without making any deep impression on each other'.[4] Although acknowledging that his own negative judgement of Sargeson's work was probably a failure of his own critical insight, Holcroft felt that Sargeson in his 'private vision' of the New Zealander was 'preoccupied with his essential loneliness and his struggle against Puritanism. Yet I could not believe that he saw his countrymen in the round: they were incomplete or lamed; a larger and richer humanity remained undiscovered outside them.'[5]

For his part, Sargeson seemed to consider the *Listener* an inferior vehicle for his work, submitting mediocre short stories under a pseudonym. When Holcroft tried to give him some income and a platform with a regular column, but under his own name, not a pseudonym, Sargeson's response was: 'One surely has the right to reserve one's name for what has been most deeply felt and thoroughly worked out, and the *Listener* is only occasionally the medium for that sort of work.'[6]

Kevin Ireland and Gill wrote letters to the editor in support of Maurice and 'Annual Holiday', and he received personal letters of support from poets

James K. Baxter and Louis Johnson and fiction writer Phillip Wilson. Maurice met Holcroft a little later when he went to be interviewed for a job on the *Listener*. His boss at the NFU, on reading 'Annual Holiday', had said, 'I hope this doesn't mean you're using your time here to write'. Maurice assured him he was thinking visually but the acceptance of other stories by literary magazines, and another by the *Listener*, had begun to steer him away from the film director dream. Holcroft found Maurice 'nervous and shy' (and not suitable for the job) but tried to console him over the letter controversy by telling him that 'young writers who find themselves under attack at the beginning of their careers … is at least a hint that [they] are being taken seriously'.[7] Maurice was not convinced and wondered who his anonymous attacker might be. To that point he had not read much of Sargeson's work but decided it was probably about time he did — and the fiction work of other New Zealand writers such as Dan Davin, John Mulgan and Maurice Duggan whom he came to admire most of all.

Maurice's second *Listener* story, 'On the County', appeared in the 4 November issue. It attracted no letters to the editor although 'K's' criticisms of 'Annual Holiday' might have been better applied to it. 'On the County' is a mediocre tale about a road gang replacing a road culvert, and the tensions between the foreman and an older new chum. The emotional responses are not well handled and the story suffers from adverbial overload. Again, the sources for the story — Maurice's own work on road gangs, and his father's betting habits — are clear.

More convincing and accomplished was a shorter story, 'Twosome', that appeared in the Wellington literary magazine *Numbers* in October. A young man picks up a young woman at a dance and walks her home, intending to make out. Awkward and inept, the young man thinks he's going to miss out yet again but aggressively persists. She strongly resists, but also acknowledges to herself that she has found herself in this situation too often, ever since she was at school; she has been with too many men, has been too easy. He is obsessive. There is a struggle but she gives in again, and it ends in emptiness for both. The transition from 'no' to 'yes' is not adequately rendered but the story is redolent of the dance hall culture of the 1950s.

That fourth edition of *Numbers* was edited by James K. Baxter. *Numbers* had been launched the year before by poets Baxter, Louis Johnson and Charles Doyle with the intent of providing an outlet for work that was experimental or with a 'forthrightness' that would not find a home in more conventional magazines. Maurice's 'Twosome' met the latter criterion in a climate of moral panic that had prompted the September 1954 Mazengarb Report. Although this was focused on 'Moral Delinquency in Children and Adolescents', a number of its recommendations impinged on general questions of public morality, including tighter censorship of print publications, movies and radio programmes. 'Twosome' would never have been countenanced by Holcroft for the *Listener* whereas Johnson, Baxter and Doyle intended to be actively provocative.

These three were the core of a Wellington school of poets who dominated literary discourse in the capital during the 1950s and into the 1960s.* Johnson in particular vigorously opposed what he saw as the nationalism school of poetry promoted by anthologist Allen Curnow and Charles Brasch's *Landfall*. Johnson was concerned with the urban, the domestic, the universal role of poetry in everyday life, less with landscape and national identity. Now in his thirties, Johnson had been publishing poetry since the end of World War II. He had worked as a journalist, editor and teacher and was currently editor of *NZ Parent and Child*. As well as establishing *Numbers* in 1954, he had also set up Capricorn Press to publish volumes of poetry. A large, expansive and generous man, he gave much of his time to fostering the talents of young writers; and was aggressive in challenging the received truths and sermons handed down by literary mandarins such as Curnow. The dispute between the two camps became bitter and acrimonious. 'In retrospect the dispute was personal, regional and intergenerational rather than ideological'.[8] Old versus new, Wellington versus Auckland, Johnson and Baxter versus Curnow and his acolytes.**

Kevin Ireland had gone back to Auckland but, through his connection with Johnson, Maurice began to mix with other Wellington poets. Johnson believed he would amount to something as a fiction writer but in a Thorndon pub, Denis Glover told him he would not, 'unless I wrote more like Jack London. New Zealand prose, he insisted, was too precious. The country deserved a bigger, bawdier literature. ("All those imitation Hemingways," he said, "Why don't they go out and catch a fish?")'[9] From 1937 to 1952 Glover had been publisher at Caxton Press and co-founder of *Landfall* in 1947, so had seen into print most of New Zealand's leading fiction writers. But he had been dismissed from Caxton for alcoholism and by 1955 had developed a jaundiced view of local literature.

---

*Doyle left New Zealand in 1968 to pursue an academic career in British Columbia.
**Probably Johnson's most lasting contribution was his founding of *New Zealand Poetry Yearbook* in 1951 and which ran its course until 1964, when he fell foul of the Literary Fund committee who refused to support its publication because six of the poems he had chosen were deemed obscene. The *Yearbook* had also been under attack from the Curnow camp for Johnson's eclectic choice of contributors, including unknowns as well as established poets, thus supposedly lowering literary standards. The 1964 *Yearbook* was published with private funding but it was the end of the line.

Maurice's first story in *Landfall*, long foretold by grandmother Ada, appeared soon after this and fitted Glover's view. 'Sing Again Tomorrow', a simple and spare story, with telling dialogue, conjured up the humiliating experience of a sixteen-year-old girl's first Saturday night dance in a farm and country town setting (not far from the Hawera Maurice had recently left behind. It even included a crowded Morris 8). It garnered praise from Moss Gee, with whom he had re-established contact after a lapse of more than two years. From Paeroa District High School, Gee wrote: 'The Numbers & Landfall stories I liked particularly. Your writing is much better controlled than mine at present.'[10] But Maurice's approach to his writing had already begun to shift.

CHAPTER 8

O P O

By the end of 1955, Maurice had accumulated four weeks' leave from the NFU and decided that he would find a bolthole in the north to start another novel. He wrote to his Aunt Sis, matron of Rawene Hospital in the Hokianga, for her suggestions. She replied, '*War and Peace* has already been written … There is now no point in writing anything less. Nevertheless, if you mean to persist with your mad plan of adding to the world's store of mediocre novels, I can find you a cottage up here.'[1] Aunt Sis always blew a refreshing blast of cold air through Maurice's literary pretensions. After bringing up most of her siblings amid the privations of Ernest and Ada's primitive farms up the Whanganui, she recognised a spade when she saw one.

Sis had left Ernest and Ada and her younger siblings to their own devices in the early 1920s and trained to be a nurse. By the time of the Queen Street riots in 1932 she was at Auckland Hospital treating head wounds inflicted by police batons. She was astonished at the extent of the injuries and more so at the number of doctors and nurses who refused to treat them, prompting her politically to move 'as far to the left as her lifelong suspicion of fellow human beings allowed'. But she joined no party, believing that no manifesto had a 'remedy for human suffering', that the 'destiny of the human race was to dwell in cruel muddle. No cause was worthwhile unless based in compassion.'[2]

Sis found her cause in 1937 when a Spanish Medical Aid Committee was established by left-wing supporters of the republican International Brigade fighting in the Spanish Civil War. Money was raised to send 34-year-old Sis and two other nurses to work with the wounded and dying.

First they went to a hospital in central Spain. 'The wounded came in daily by the truckload; ambulances were few … Each day began with decisions on who should be allowed to perish. Amputation was the favoured method of treatment for those selected to live … until limbs needing removal exceeded the supply of sterile instruments.'[3]

In 1938, Sis helped set up a new military hospital in Barcelona. The republican movement had begun to split and there was internecine warfare in the city's streets. Under suspicion by the Stalinists, her letters were heavily censored or destroyed. Sis kept her head down politically, so that she could continue her humanitarian work but believed that the fight for a democratic Spain was a just one. It was a war against the 'creeping monster of fascism'.

By now, she had a personal stake in the war. She had fallen in love with and married Willi Remmel, a German officer in the Communist Ernst Thaelmann battalion. 'They may have spent a night or two together; there was nothing in the nature of a honeymoon. Sis went back to patching up people, and Willi back to battle … she was discreet to the last. Her New Zealand sponsors were never to learn of her marriage … Her family knew only the little she saw fit to confide.'[4]

At the end of 1938, the International Brigade was disbanded; the republican movement declared it could stand alone against the fascists. Sis returned home to an Auckland mayoral reception and then went on an exhausting lecture tour to raise funds and medical supplies for the republicans. To no avail: they were decisively defeated by Franco's nationalists six months later.

When the brigade disbanded, its members returned to their home countries, except for the likes of Communist Willi who faced only a concentration camp if he returned to Germany. He crossed the Pyrenees to the relative safety of France where he was placed in an internment camp. Sis managed to maintain a correspondence with Willi and send him money. She did everything in her power to get him asylum in New Zealand. But in August 1939 her application for his immigration permit was refused and weeks later Europe was at war. 'He sent me one or two pictures of his camp and said as they look over the barbed wire they think how long, how long before we are free.'[5] She never heard from him again.

Aunt Sis had found them a cottage at Opononi, near the mouth of the Hokianga Harbour. On their way, at New Year 1956, Maurice and Gill stayed with Kevin Ireland in Takapuna. He took them to a party at printer Bob Lowry's place where they met Maurice Duggan. 'Shadbolt was in awe of Duggan, who to a younger generation was already a writer of some achievement.' Duggan had read a story by Maurice and 'opened the conversation by remarking that there were a number of people who thought Shadbolt was a pseudonym. This left Shadbolt uncertain whether Duggan was really being friendly ... such hesitancy was long to remain a feature of their relationship.'[6] Duggan drove them home and, since Frank Sargeson lived just five minutes' walk away from Ireland's place, Duggan suggested they all go and visit him the next evening. Duggan had been a protégé of Sargeson's since 1944 and had been a resident in his army hut in 1950. Ireland was reluctant because he had fallen foul of Sargeson as a schoolboy while on his paper run down Esmonde Road. For Maurice, the letter to the *Listener* from 'K' of Henderson continued to rankle but he still had no idea who had written it. In the past months he had taken the trouble to read Sargeson's work but had not warmed to it, inclining to *Listener* editor Monte Holcroft's view.

But Maurice and Ireland did go round and Ireland experienced his 'first true literary conversation. Real writers: Frank, the two Maurices — book talk, no coffee-bar humbug'.[7] Maurice wrote in 1970: 'I sat, rather awed and inarticulate, in his tiny Takapuna cottage, clogged with books and sweet with the scent of drying peppers; and made attempt to understand all he said. His long and solitary perseverance with the craft of fiction made my own raw effort seem thin; I realised I should never have the strength of character, or the self confidence, to survive as he had. The truth was that each literary encounter like this left me with large doubt not just about my literary ability, but also about my right to enter fairly into the company of other New Zealand writers. They all seemed alarmingly (or inspiringly) dedicated and embattled men. Where were my credentials? I had begun to write, not because it seemed the best thing to do with my life, but because I could find nothing better to do. If anything, I had begun to write out of frustration — first, with my own life and its untidiness; then out of my mounting dismay with my employment at the film unit. Given the right circumstances, I could just as easily have gone on to make films, and forgotten fiction.'[8]

Kevin Ireland's recollection of the evening was very different. 'Though [Maurie] was young and little published at the time he had decided already that he would become a major writer and ... he could get very uptight and pompous about both his work and his ambitions.'[9] 'He gave notice that he most certainly *was* the next generation, that, think of him what you would, there was more room than anyone had taken into account, and he would occupy it. Strong stuff, and accurate.'[10]

Ireland's account is consistent with his experience of Maurice's behaviour in other literary, or sub-literary, company. Maurice's 1970 account was written with publication in mind (and while Sargeson was still active) for Robin Dudding's *Landfall* series of writers recounting their early literary careers. This was shelved on Dudding's dismissal as editor; and when Maurice's 'Beginnings' essay was finally published in Dudding's journal *Islands* in 1981[11] he chose to omit this account and other reflections on starting out. Maurice's ambitious declarations in the mid-1950s almost certainly masked uncertainty about his choice of career and whether he could indeed foot it with the likes of Sargeson as a 'major writer', an uncertainty at least partly sponsored by the anonymous letter to the *Listener*. At the time of his meeting with the 52-year-old guru, Maurice was only twenty-three, still wet about the ears in the matter of career options. Even Sargeson had been twenty-eight before he saw his way clear to becoming a writer; and film-making was to preoccupy Maurice again in an unexpected way.

Opononi was a place where 'Dwellings were few, wooden and modest. There was a pub, post office and store, linked by rickety boardwalk. Gillian and I could pick mussels and pull in fish a dozen yards from our door.'[12] But Opononi was no haven of peaceful isolation

A dolphin, christened Opo, had been interacting with local people since the winter before and by December had become confident enough to swim with anyone who went into the water. 'It allowed bathers to caress it; small children to mount its back. Soon it was clowning with a rubber ball, or balancing beer bottles empty or full on its nose.'[13]

By the time the Shadbolts arrived in Opononi, reports and features on Opo had appeared in newspapers in New Zealand and around the world. A banal pop song, 'Opo the Friendly Dolphin', was annoying radio listeners. Opononi became a 'roaring town of thousands. There was a religious aura to the event. People travelled hundreds of miles merely to touch the miraculous dolphin.'[14] 'The road beside our cottage grumbled with traffic: with buses, trucks, and queues of cars trying to park ... So much for romantic isolation. I was trying to write in New Zealand's noisiest square mile.'[15] Maurice gave up and swam with Opo instead. After three weeks, as they packed to leave, he had not completed a page of his novel. '"Fate," Aunt Sis judged with satisfaction. "It wasn't meant to be."'[16] But Opo was fate enough.

Maurice returned to Wellington and the NFU, 'only to be sent speeding back to Opononi with a cameraman.'[17] 'There was standing room only on the shore ... The cameraman and I bunked among empty bottles in the Opononi publican's back shed.'[18] Despite the logistical difficulties, they captured the only professional movie footage of a rare historical event that was to take up two-thirds of one edition of a *Pictorial Parade*, screened at Easter 1956.[19]

Maurice directed, edited and scripted the film just in time. The local community had become concerned for Opo's welfare as hordes of visitors fought for her attention, grabbing her and poking her with oars. They formed the Opononi Gay Dolphin Protection Committee and petitioned the government to take action. An order in council came into effect at midnight on 8 March, making it an offence, subject to a £50 fine, to 'take or molest' any dolphin in the Hokianga. The next morning Opo was found dead, jammed between rocks.

The cause of her death was never properly established. But there had been much disruption to Opononi community life, and some believe that the order in council, protecting all dolphins, was seen by local fishermen as a threat to their livelihood; and a stick of gelignite was thrown her way. There was a parallel in ancient history. A similar event had occurred at the Roman town of Hippo in North Africa and the disruption and stress caused by thousands of visitors wishing to commune with a magical dolphin prompted its citizens to destroy it. At Opononi, 'Maoris ritually mourned, children wept, and old soldiers dug Opo's grave six feet deep on the waterfront. Through New Zealand flags flew at half-mast. I had another novel, if I could fortify myself to write it.'[20] Such fortification took time.

Maurice was to spend much of the summer in the Hokianga. 'Rather deviously, I persuaded my producer to allow me to direct a film on the painter Eric Lee-Johnson, who had made the ragged shore, dramatic churches and dilapidated homesteads of the Hokianga his own.' It was an influential moment in Maurice's development as a writer. 'It was the first time I had been intimate with a painter. Lee-Johnson, gentle and dedicated, gave me eyes to see not only his Hokianga, but an entire country. In Klee's phrase, he didn't just render the visible; he rendered visible. At the least he gave me good reason to look again, and then again ... that friendship of the fifties, in a most formative year, might go some way towards explaining why painters so often inhabit my fictions. In the Hokianga, too, I discovered a setting which suited my more parochial preoccupations; the idiosyncratic colours of the place were to tint a dozen stories.'[21]

Lee-Johnson's paintings and drawings of early wooden buildings in the north had sparked a romantic movement in New Zealand art. In 1956 he was the first New Zealand painter of his generation to be the subject of a published monograph and Maurice's short documentary greatly increased public awareness of his work. Lee-Johnson was approving: 'All of my friends think you have done me proud, and say that the whole thing is very well done.'[22]

Maurice's NFU producer had not been so approving. The first rushes of the Lee-Johnson film showed derelict or rundown farmhouses in the background.

He telegrammed Maurice: 'SHOW NEW HOUSES. IF THIS FILM IS SHOWN OUTSIDE NEW ZEALAND THERE MAY BE A SCANDAL. IT COULD BE THOUGHT NEW ZEALANDERS LIVE IN SLUMS.'[23] Maurice added footage of Lee-Johnson driving past the only new house in the district.

Perspicaciously, Lee-Johnson had seen another value in Maurice's film work: 'I suppose you realize how the experience in films adds strength to your elbow? I mean the clear visualization of situations — a pictorial visualization — a faculty not every writer is able to develop.'[24]

CHAPTER 9

MAURICE AND MAURICE

Maurice's 'most formative year' continued when he returned to Wellington. A fresh winter was coming on and the crowd of young writers and hangers-on congregated again in the Willis Street pubs, taking their turns to shout with milk bottle crates of six or eight ounce beers, hosed into the glasses, smoking and arguing their way out at 6.15 with the avalanche of boozers carrying flagons in bowling bags, on their way home to tea with the missus on the clanging trams that swerved and jerked out to the cold weatherboard suburbs. Maurice and mates, looking for a feed, squeezed on to Te Aro or Brooklyn trams to the top of Upper Willis Street and then walked up steepening Abel Smith Street to the cottage at the end of The Terrace, where Gill was home from work. Gill rarely went to the pub with the boys because public bars were off limits to women; so Maurice might take a bottle or flagon or two home to go with the evening meal or to start off a party at the weekend. Some weeks he was not there at all, away on NFU assignments when Gill grumped at his absences and having to cope with unannounced visitors. But there was not too much to grump about: they both had jobs, Maurice had his ambitions and Gill had faith in them, wherever they might lead. His ambitions as a film-maker continued to be frustrated by the deadening hand of the NFU bureaucracy. His ambitions as a writer remained steady but were undercut by continuing doubts about his ability. Which way to go?

Maurice's story 'And then there were two', an inconsequential sketch, was published in *Numbers* in May 1956 in conjunction with another by poet and co-editor James K. Baxter.[1] Around March, they met for the first time, and Baxter, usually clad in his grubby gabardine raincoat, came to make the Shadbolts' 'small inner-city cottage … a home for his monologues on life, death, sex and poetry. He had just given up the drink, following the death of Dylan Thomas*, and in its place used talk and tobacco. He was the first writer, apart from Kevin Ireland, to whom I showed my work in unfinished state; his criticism was always pertinent. Above all, he didn't seem frighteningly dedicated as a writer; he just loved life and language. With other writers I could never relax or become articulate. With Jim it was different. I have reason to think that he coaxed the best out of me; and that I might never have written a great deal without his friendship.'[2]

Maurice was not having much success with more stories he sent to the *Listener*. Editor Holcroft, when he turned down one titled 'Conversation', wrote, 'I am sorry to have to disappoint you again, but I feel that this story does not quite come off, in spite of a good idea. Your work seems to me to be in a difficult stage ... I hope this does not depress you: it has happened to many other writers, and simply means that your work is developing — perhaps, for a while, in the wrong direction.'[3] Maurice went in Holcroft's right direction a few months later with 'The Gloves'.[4] This morality tale follows two young boys' enthusiasm for boxing, approved of by father but not mother. The denouement follows one boy's horrified realisation of what boxing might lead to, after they go for instruction under the mentorship of an old punch-drunk boxer. A story with a heavy message signalled early, but adequate for a 1950s family magazine.

With Baxter's encouragement, Maurice was working on something much more substantial, what he described as a 'novella', a long short story of about 15,000 words which he sent to *Landfall*. Editor Charles Brasch responded in June: 'I do want to print the story. But when? This year if I possibly can; but it might just have to wait ...'[5] One of the problems was that 'End of Season' would take up nearly half of a *Landfall* issue. In the meantime, Brasch made several suggestions for revisions that Maurice could work on. To keep him going, Brasch added, 'All my readers, by the way, were very taken with the story'.

Two months later, Brasch could tell Maurice, 'You've made a lot of improvements in the story, and strengthened it at several weak places,'[6] before going on to recommend even more detailed cuts to reduce over-writing and to improve the pace of the story. Maurice responded well to Brasch's editorial guidance and was rewarded with its publication in the December issue of *Landfall*.[7]

'End of Season' marked Maurice's arrival as a fiction writer to be taken seriously. His earlier published stories were all deficient in form or style

---

*Poet Dylan Thomas died from alcoholic poisoning in November 1953, more than two years before Maurice and Baxter first met. Baxter had joined Alcoholics Anonymous in 1954.

or adequate characterisation or in their capacity to carry cogent meaning. Although later stories by Maurice continued to owe something to the Sargeson (and Hemingway) tradition, 'End of Season' owed nothing to it. It is marred by the occasional choice of flashy adjective and an over-dramatic treatment of a rugby game fatality, revealing traits that were to mark his entire published work. But these do not diminish the impact of a novella which showed that Maurice was moving into a larger world of subject matter, expression and scale for New Zealand writing. Orbiting around an end-of-season rugby final in a place not unlike Te Kuiti, the story examines the nature of friendship between young rural men, and their girls, and the attractions of another life in the city. There are memorable portrayals of the natural and social environments of the mid-1950s and a sensitive examination of the situation of Maori within them.

Maurice had been working on another long short story which he sent to Kevin Ireland who had moved back to Takapuna. Ireland's excited response was, '"Night of the Chariot" is a brilliant piece of work and puts you in the first rank of NZ prosofists (my word = prose writers) along with Sargeson, Duggan, Frame …' He claimed it was second only to Sargeson's story 'I for One' and, that 'For the first time too Maurice you have made me jealous of your achievement…'[8] For Ireland, the story also came as a relief: 'Those evenings that I spent on The Terrace, in your house, listening (sometimes as first audience) to the baby-heart beat in some of those stories, meant a certain dishonesty on my part. I could hear the heart-beat in some of those stories, feebly in some stories, boyishly in others, growing-right-up in others, but I never heard the heart beat of the man in any, save the long Landfall story.* So I criticised with a certain restraint …' But he now felt free to open up about Maurice's earlier work. 'And then there were two' in *Numbers* 5, for example, was a 'parody of frontier writing'.

Maurice had sent him the new story for the anthology of new writing that Ireland and he had been attempting to put together since the beginning of the year, and designed to be a modern version of 1945's seminal *Speaking for Ourselves*. Ireland did all the legwork, and numerous letters from him during 1956 describe the difficulty of finding acceptable material to include from the scores of stories and poems submitted. He also resented Maurice's criticisms from a distance that bordered on the offensive. By August, the anthology had taken shape, with fiction from such as Maurice Gee, Terry Sturm, Brian Bell and Noel Hilliard; and poetry from Con Bollinger, Karl Stead, John Kasmin,

---

* 'Sing Again Tomorrow'.

Alan Roddick and Peter Bland among others. Plus a poem from Ireland and Maurice's 'Night of the Chariot'. Printer Bob Lowry, who had been responsible for producing numerous significant New Zealand literary works, including *Speaking for Ourselves*, had agreed to print 250-300 copies of a 70-80 page anthology for £70-£80. But Lowry was constantly in financial trouble and also had an alcohol problem. By September, it seemed as if the arrangement with Lowry was collapsing. Ireland wrote to Maurice: 'He was down on the beam ends at one stage & I helped him as much as I could in return for the promise that he do the book. I can only hope to God that he's able to. As a matter of fact it's £100 — small enough for some, but a good deal for me — and I only mention this now because you should know exactly what the position is.'[9] A couple of weeks later, Ireland had reached crisis point with both the anthology and Maurice's behaviour: 'Let's not go through all this drama — you threaten to resign, I'll threaten to commit suicide … For God's sake let's see you soon — I'm just about off my nut with all this'.[10] Maurice did soon see Ireland but this did not help to solve the Lowry problem. The crisis reached a stalemate that lasted into the next year. In the end, Lowry did not deliver and Ireland lost his money. It had been his savings for a trip to England he had been planning for 1957.

Maurice travelled up to Auckland at Labour Weekend 1956 on NFU assignments and persuaded Ireland to go north with him to take a break in the 'backblocks' of the Hokianga, and to meet Aunt Sis. One of the *Pictorial Parade* assignments was to film the daily 'milk run', accompanying a local launch as it delivered mail, milk and freight to farms and villages around the harbour. When he wrote to Gill from the Masonic Hotel in Rawene, he complained that Ireland, his cameraman Brian Cross and the launchmen were 'shickered as newts' and making so much noise he could barely concentrate on writing the letter — let alone listen at the same time to the latest episode of 'Journey into Space', a radio science fiction serial that had much of the nation in its grip. He told Gill that 'even he [Frank Sargeson] listened to it!'. On the way north he had been around to Esmonde Road again and spent a pleasant evening with Sargeson, Duggan and historian and poet Keith Sinclair. He had also caught up with his family in Glen Eden — 'Dad had two radios going for the Labour Day races, which damn near drove me silly'.[11]

Back in Wellington, Gill kept the domestic and social scene together. She lent a sympathetic ear and a bed to a woman friend for whom 'some sort of crisis is about to be reached but it's taken a long time and may last a long time yet'.[12] One night James K. Baxter turned up, after his Alcoholics Anonymous meeting and when Gill was half undressed for bed. 'He is terribly worried about his relationship with Jacquie … and got a terrific lot off his chest. Things are not at all happy there and they are certainly not helped by his guilt complex for things done in the past and her nervousness and "work obsession."'[13]

More cheerfully, she noted Gordon Dryden's wedding in Auckland. 'You may have gone … I know he was going to try and get hold of you …' He did not and Gill decided, 'in view of all our past associations' to send them a set of Chinese bowls.[14]

Gill took care of the finances and her accounting sheds light on the practicalities of this working couple's life in late 1956: 'Our finances are going fine. I have managed to pay our electricity bill, Meanjin*, your doctor's bill, the 30/- I still owed on my typewriter, the florist and bought myself a pair of shoes. I hope to get it up to £300 before you get back but it really seems pretty hopeless unless I get a cheque for two stories I had in Parent and Child last month'. There was the Dryden's wedding present, 'And this week I simply had to buy two pairs of stockings. Last week I got the gas bill which just about knocked me and also my journalist's union bill so I'll try and get these cleared up next week — or rather I'll get the gas paid and the £1 I still owe my doctor'.

But there had to be enough money for theatre: a disastrous New Zealand Players production, 'The Solid Gold Cadillac'; and visits to the pictures: 'Can Can' with Jacquie Baxter, and 'Richard III' — 'There is certainly no doubt about Larry [Olivier]. He sure can act.' But despite full-time work on the *Evening Post*, her domestic distractions, reading new novels and evening entertainment, Gill still concluded: 'There's something missing in my life at the moment'. 'I love you madly.'[15]

Just before Labour Weekend, Maurice had visited Moss Gee in Henderson and, on his way back through Auckland, en route to Rotorua, he and Ireland took Gee along with Brian Cross and writer Dave Walsh to see Sargeson. The evening ended with Maurice, Ireland and Gee 'quaffing ale down on Takapuna beach at 4 in the morning and discussing literature of all things!'[16] Gee had left his teaching job in Paeroa and returned home to write, but the words were not coming. He had written a confessional letter to Maurice earlier: 'I'm very disappointed in myself. To tell you the truth I've made a real mess of this full-time writing business …' But he was 'quite determined to go on to better things … I'll have to take myself in hand, and work.' His despair even went so far as lamenting 'I'm beginning to lose my hair, a real tragedy for an unmarried

*An Australian literary journal.

man'.[17] Maurice suggested that it might be better if he left home, 'cut the apron strings' from mother Lyndahl, a published writer, and shifted into the 'company of like-minded fellows' — in Wellington.

Gee was not so sure but in December, when he learned that Maurice and Gill were travelling to Auckland for Christmas, he wrote that not only was he looking forward to meeting Gill but was also 'really very keen to come down to Wellington so we'll talk about that soon'. Gee had begun to think, 'Well, why not, it's about time I started doing something real ...' and agreed to hitch-hike back to Wellington with Maurice.

Gee relates how they 'got a couple of rides out of Auckland, then we were picked up by a guy going down the other side of the Bombay Hills and ... he was a crazy driver and he terrified both of us and when we suggested he drive a little more slowly, he got very irate and angry with us for criticising his driving. So we were pleased to see the last of him at Hamilton'.[18] They reached Hawera the same day, where they stayed with Maurice's friends from his reporting days, and Wellington the day following.

For Maurice, the hitch-hike helped to forge a strong bond with Gee. 'We both had grandfathers filled with cosmic discontent ... we both had fathers with a feeling for racehorses, mothers addicted to poetry; we both had parents who made Marxism their faith in the sullen thirties and whose lives cried out for chroniclers. There was a pact of sorts between us. We were going to tell their stories.'[19] Maurice's view of Gee's parents was off centre and, as Gee recalls: 'There was not any solemn pact or understanding that I remember, just lots of talk — lots of fun, too'. But, like Maurice, Gee did want to write his family's 'stories about the Depression and their faith in Labour'. Forty years on, Maurice constructed a shared beginning, and claimed a hand in Gee's literary journey, too. But they *had* begun together, Gee said, 'just young guys starting off and we were going to write about what we and our parents knew'.[20]

At this time, Moss Gee considered Maurice to be 'far ahead' of him in his writing career. He was 'very impressed by Maurice, not so much Maurice, but the idea of Maurice ... of someone who had gone out and started to live, and ... had started to produce and write which ... I was trying to do on a much lower level ...'[21]

Arriving in Wellington, Gee slept on a couch in the Shadbolts' The Terrace living room for four weeks, 'wide-eyed with wonder at the life he wrongly imagined we lived'.[22] Maurice introduced Moss 'to all sorts of people. He knew all the major writers ... The first night I was there, absolutely exhausted from the trip, Baxter walked in ... and he talked and talked and talked and I went to sleep with my head on the table ... I met all these people and I branched out enormously and I thank Maurice for that still.'[23] Afterwards, Maurice wrote to Frank Sargeson, 'I don't think he realised we were just entertaining him, taking him to meet people … our existence down here for nearly three years now has really been very hermit-like.'[24]

Maurice announced to Sargeson that he had just left the NFU to spend two months writing full time. He had never before given up all work to write, and now felt 'very empty of inspiration … the thought that now, for a while, I won't have to squeeze my writing between other activities is really quite terrifying.'[25] He was full of praise for Moss Gee's work and told Sargeson that he seemed to 'have had a wonderfully good influence on [Kevin Ireland], stimulating his poetic activity; something I could never do'.

Maurice outlined to Sargeson the short stories he was working on, and another novel; and felt 'End of Season' was his best so far. He was bolstered by the widespread praise he had received for it; and by a Wellington visit from Charles Brasch the day before who had told him that his story 'Play the Fife Lowly', which he had entered in a *Landfall* competition, would be published in either the March or June issue. There is a sense in this February letter that Maurice was not only ingratiating himself with Sargeson but also, despite all his words of self-deprecation, reinforcing Ireland's view he was giving 'notice that he most certainly *was* the next generation'.

Maurice had begun to stake out his position as a young writer with some literary authority in a newspaper article, 'The Value of the N.Z. Short Story', published in December in the *Evening Post*,[26] and facilitated by Gill's position and contacts on the 'paper. He used a largely praiseworthy review of Maurice Duggan's new collection of stories, *Immanuel's Land*, to pronounce that 'most of New Zealand's best prose-writing has so far been in the short story'. One reason was the 'difficulty of getting publication of the serious novel here or overseas; though it would appear that the prejudice of overseas publishers against New Zealand work is, to some extent, being broken down'. He does not argue for more local publishing. The other chief reason was that writing a novel needs time, 'which in this country is too often a rare and expensive commodity for the young writer' with job and family. This supported the move by the Literary Fund to establish a Scholarship in Letters worth £500 just three months before and for which Maurice had applied.

Maurice did not win the first Scholarship in Letters but in March he was the co-winner of the *Landfall* prose competition for 'Play the Fife Lowly'.[27] This had its origins in the story 'Night of the Chariot' which Ireland had deemed 'a brilliant piece of work', while also warning that some of the characters were a little too close to life for comfort. Maurice had become aware of this problem:

'In trying to avoid the strongly autobiographical tradition (and sometimes crudely confessional) in New Zealand fiction … I fed off lives other than my own, sometimes unforgivably'.[28] He moved to find a denser filter for his fiction; but the journalist and documentary maker would always remain with him. To the end, the resemblance of his fictional characters to the real often lay only in a change of clothes and a name.

Maurice had told Gee about 'Night of the Chariot' who had commented, 'I can't recall that anyone has tried that sort of thing in this country yet — virgin soil'.[29] Yet Maurice had already begun to turn over this 'virgin soil' with his 1955 *Numbers* story 'Twosome', poking a finger into the 'rackety' Saturday nights of 1950s Wellington. In 'Play the Fife Lowly' he portrays the lives of young men and women driven by the social expectations of coupledom, of marriage, yet unable to understand each other, to clarify their feelings, to perceive the real relationships around them.

'End of Season' captured the character of contemporary provincial New Zealand; 'Play the Fife Lowly' was its city sequel. It revealed the consequences of a conformist, repressive culture that saw women but not men gain a 'reputation' for having sex before marriage; when this was dangerous for women in a society of 'randy bastards and chemists' shops' a decade before oral contraceptives; where homosexuality was alluded to and practised but never openly admitted. Even consensual homosexual acts were regarded as 'sexual assault' and could lead to imprisonment. Penalties were to be reduced in 1961, but 30 years passed before full homosexual law reform. 'Play the Fife Lowly' was a brave story for 1957.

There were parties still at 370a The Terrace, perhaps to mark his winning the *Landfall* prize, or finishing at the NFU, Maurice holding court, pontificating on the state of New Zealand literature or the future of film. Others found him good company, his gurgling laugh infectious, but he still thought of himself as socially inept. At other parties he often perched in a corner, beer in one hand, dwindling cigarette in the other, listening and watching — as his grandmother Ada had noted — playing his fife lowly while he gathered new tunes.

Maurice's literary confidence was dented in May when he was told that C.K. Stead was the notorious 'K of Henderson', the letter writer to the *Listener* two years before. The March issue of *Landfall* had contained not only Maurice's prize-winning story but also his letter criticising Stead's earlier review of poetry by Maurice's Wellington friends Charles Doyle and Alistair Campbell.[30] Charles Brasch had rejected Maurice's first letter, citing some questionable arguments about Stead's intentions. Brasch wrote: 'Where I do think you have a case is that Stead's tone suggests … a rather grudging admiration of Campbell's poetry instead of the whole-hearted admiration you'd like him to accord it.'[31] Maurice revised his letter accordingly; but its publication, which had improved his standing with Doyle and Campbell, and others in the Wellington literary community, now threw him into a panic.

Maurice hardly knew Stead. They had exchanged greetings at university in the early 1950s, maybe been part of groups at Somervell's, talking politics. Over the previous three years, Stead had published some well-received poems and short stories; he was highly regarded by Sargeson and was an acolyte of Allen Curnow's in the noxious Auckland-Wellington literary disputes. He was clearly destined for a distinguished academic career and was currently holding a lectureship at the University of New England in New South Wales.

Since Maurice could claim no friendship, he must have felt threatened when he wrote to Frank Sargeson at the end of May that he was upset Stead might take his *Landfall* letter the wrong way: 'The thing which really horrifies me … and which has caused me to write two letters to Carl [sic], both of which I have torn up in despair, is that this business of personal animosity can be read into it.'[32] He was 'horrified' that Stead would think Maurice had known about 'K. of Henderson' when he wrote to *Landfall*. He asked Sargeson if, when next writing to Stead, he would 'give him some idea what I've said to you. It might stop a molehill growing into a mountain, and ill-feeling festering. These things are all rather silly, I know, but since I've met writers I realised how enormously silly small things can become.' Sargeson did not pass this on, for reasons which only became clear later. In any case, Stead had put the business behind him, something 'best forgotten.'[33]*

But this 'silly small thing' festered among the doubts Maurice had about himself as a writer, stirring up the unease and vulnerability he felt at the judgement of others in the literary and academic world. In December, Moss Gee had written to say that the £15 Maurice had received for 'End of Season' meant 'you are now a real professional.'[34] An older Maurice was to write of the *Landfall* prize: 'There was a cheque for £25 in my pocket to say I might be a professional writer.'[35] This could turn out to be real but Maurice always declared ambivalence. He 'had no intention of becoming a professional writer. Writing was no more than an indulgence, and never could be more. A defence against boredom. Therapy possibly. Relief, certainly. My trade was film.'[36] Earlier, he had written, 'I considered my prize-winning story a possible swan-song. If I was going to make a life for myself, and find any kind of stability

---

*There was a 'K of Henderson' in fact — Stead's wife Kay (née Roberts) — and his letter was sent from her family's Henderson address.

in a profession, it had to be in film. With this in mind I resigned from the National Film Unit, and planned to journey to England and find film work there …[37]

There is a sense in all of this that the author 'doth protest too much'. There is no evidence that Maurice made any real attempt to find film work when he did finally arrive in England. Resignation from the NFU was resignation from his film career. If a career in film really had been a deep-seated ambition, and not just a glamorous mirage, why was he always struggling with a new novel, writing new stories, reviews and letters, trying to ingratiate himself with Sargeson and others? His plea to Sargeson about the Stead letter reveals that he knew his career probably lay in writing and did not need enemies as he set about it. Moss Gee equally lacked confidence but could not escape being a writer, the need to keep working away at his craft. Nigel Cook who, with his wife Julie, moved into 370a The Terrace after Maurice and Gill went overseas, had met both Maurices after he moved from Auckland to Wellington the year before. He and others of the literary pub and party crowd had no doubt that Moss Gee 'was born to it' but Maurice was not and had to work hard to 'construct himself' as a writer.[38] The excuse that all he ever really wanted to be was a film-maker, and had fallen into writing by chance, was a shield against criticism.

Gill and Maurice had been saving hard for their big OE and, to add to their few hundred pounds, he abandoned full-time writing and took a job in a textile factory. They booked sea passages to London for early June and had intended travelling together with Kevin Ireland until printer Bob Lowry made off with his savings. A few weeks before the sailing date, Maurice bumped into a friend from Communist Party days who told him that there was a youth festival in Moscow and New Zealand participants* could travel there via China and the Trans-Siberian Railway.

At first, Maurice and Gill were in two minds. Any attachment Maurice may still have had to the Communist dream had been severely damaged by two events in 1956. In February, Nikita Kruschev, in his 'secret' speech to the 20th Congress of the Soviet Communist Party, had denounced Stalin for his abuse of power during the Great Purge of the 1930s; his failings as a leader during World War II; and for the personality cult he had promoted. This condemnation of Stalinism led to the Hungarian revolt of October when students and workers fought successfully for the removal of Stalinist leaders and set up a new government promising free elections and the withdrawal of

---

*Gill became a New Zealand citizen on 24 May.

Soviet forces. At first, Moscow agreed to negotiate with the new government but then, at the prospect of a domino effect across Eastern Europe, weakening Soviet control, a large armed force was sent into Hungary and authoritarian control re-established. More than 2500 Hungarians and 700 Soviet troops were killed; 200,000 fled as refugees and thousands persecuted, imprisoned and executed in the years that followed.

Maurice claimed that Kruschev's speech had given him 'the chance to remind old comrades I had told them so'[39]; but even after this 'they had clung on to their faith by their fingertips'. The suppression of the Hungarian revolution was, however, the last straw for most, including Sid Scott, who had been a founding member of the Auckland Branch of the Communist Party in 1921 and who, with his wife Nellie, had devoted most of forty years to the Marxist-Leninist cause. Scott resigned from the Party in January 1957 and, soon after this, Maurice and Gill had him as a guest. 'Some thirty or more of his old friends and ex-comrades crowded into our cottage to hear him confess his life a lie … This is not what his audience wished to hear. They still hoped for a new, purer Party; a new refurbished Soviet Union … Someone protested that Sid was too bitter … "I have earned the right to be," he announced.' Maurice wrote that the 'Party to which my parents had given their hopes and often their happiness was as good as gone'.

But now, three months later, the chance of a fabulous free trip across two continents, visiting the two great beasts of Communism, was really too hard to turn down. Maurice went to the Soviet Legation. At least he and Gill could see Communism for themselves and, as he told Frank Sargeson, he hoped to meet Chinese and Soviet writers and film-makers, and perhaps visit other Eastern Bloc countries.

On 16 June, they flew out of Auckland: 'We had our last view of New Zealand between drifts of cloud … For the next three years I talismanically recalled that scrap of New Zealand again and again: the hills of fern, the tangle of tidal channels, the salty mangroves. They were telling me something … I had the powerful fear that I might never be back,'[40] like all the expatriate writers and artists who had gone before him.

CHAPTER 10

A FEW FLOWERS BLOOMING

There was the simple excitement of their first overseas trip beyond Australia, one that would take them on a journey behind the Cold War curtains of Mao's China, the Soviet Union and eastern Europe and on to the 'Home' of England; and there were no planned conclusions, the future lay open. There was even the novelty of air travel, all the way to Hong Kong: 'Lunch at 12,000 feet above the Tasman was very nice; crumbed cutlet and peaches and cream. I kept the menu and will post it to Julie as the first souvinir (sic) of our trip.'[1]

In Sydney, Maurice and Gill stayed with her mother in Manly, met up with brother Peter Shadbolt, who had taken a teaching job there; and on 17 June they all went to see Gill's nineteen year-old brother Rob Heming play for the Australian Barbarians against the All Blacks.*

After a week in Sydney they flew via Darwin and Manila to Hong Kong. Maurice was appalled at the poverty there, the sweatshops producing cheap clothing and the heat, the heat, the heat. There were fifteen others, including Maori, in the congregated New Zealand party travelling to the festival; fourteen more would travel to Moscow from London. In a 'circular' letter intended for wider family and friends, Gill wrote, 'We are travelling with a very good crowd of people, including the Southern Cross Jazz Band from Australia.'[2]

At their hotel there was a message for Maurice from Brian Brake, the former National Film Unit cameraman whom he had met briefly before Brake's departure three years before. Brake had been accepted as a nominee

---

*Marking Rob Heming at lock was the star 21-year-old All Black flanker from Te Kuiti, Colin Meads.

by the world's top photo agency, Magnum, after meeting Ernst Haas and Henri Cartier-Bresson in Paris in 1955. He achieved almost instant status as a photographer with his pictures of Pablo Picasso at a bullfight that same year and by 1957 was a full member of Magnum. His photographs had appeared in many of the leading magazines at a time when photo-journalism was booming. Brake had just returned to Hong Kong after being granted unprecedented access to China on a photo shoot for *Life* magazine: he had been allowed to take close-up portraits of Mao Tse-Tung walking in Beijing's Forbidden City. At barely thirty, he was the 'most successful expatriate New Zealander of his generation'.[3] Gill wrote that 'Brian was terribly enthusiastic about what is being achieved in China'.[4] More serendipitous for Maurice was Brake's declared enthusiasm for photographing New Zealand, once he had finished 'photographing the world', and working with Maurice on the project — as a writer. Brake already judged that Maurice would make it with words and not behind a camera.

The New Zealand and Australian delegations were met in Canton (Guangzhou) by members of the All-China League of Democratic Youth, who sang them on the way to their 'huge' hotel, built in colonial days. At the formal reception, Maurice was 'trapped by young girls, most of them factory workers, who almost smothered me with kindness and hospitality. Believe me, I didn't escape until the end of the evening! I think Gill thought she had lost me for good.'[5]

Gill wrote about events at the reception where the New Zealanders sang two songs and 'then the boys got up and did a haka, which they had devised out of two to make it look like a battle and stole the show for the night'.[6] Most of their time was taken up with the entertainments, visits to recreational parks, a swimming pool capable of 'seating 23,000', or official tours to factories and the memorial hall to Dr Sun Yat-sen, the revolutionary who helped overthrow Imperial rule fifty years before.

Gill's 'circular' letter was mostly a detailed travelogue of life and scenes from a city not long free of the ravages of war and revolution. A New Zealand woman she met in Canton revealed the realities of life behind the waving of banners and singing of songs. There was food rationing, 'called controlled consumption by the Government. She said life was very hard' but even so, restaurants were 'always packed … no-one starved! as they do in Hong Kong — we saw them'.[7]

Affected by the hospitality, the stimulation of the exotic, and her political sympathies, Gill described her experiences in a positive light. Maurice also put an optimistic leftist slant on his news: 'Nationalist saboteurs operate at irregular intervals. Last October there were a dozen bombs planted around the city ... When I went out to a paper-mill we passed a grim-looking detachment marching with tommy-guns ...

'... What I have most enjoyed is the very frank discussions I have had with our interpreters ... about international affairs, Soviet Communism, and Hungary. They are, to a certain extent, reserved; but that is only natural ... They are eager, however, to learn of the better features of the West; you sense that they are hungry for knowledge and that Mao Tse-tung's policy of liberalisation and letting a "hundred flowers bloom" is opening up vast frontiers for Communism in China. There is a growing ferment of intellectual dispute.'[8] At first, he may have genuinely believed all this; although Maurice would have been conscious that his Uncle Joe would read the letter.

If he did, Maurice was soon disabused, and later recorded that his Chinese comrades were not so eager for knowledge after all, let alone intellectual dispute. In Canton he asked to meet writers and eventually a couple were produced in the presence of a 'cultural commissar'. Maurice asked about the hundred flowers, '"Were a hundred schools of thought contending? Were poets writing love lyrics again, novelists freely telling their tales?"' Conscious of the commissar, one finally replied, '"It is difficult for comrades of the West to understand ... There is no gap between theory and practice here. Nor is there room for idealist philosophy".'[9]

In Peking (Beijing), Maurice was taken on a tour of a film studio and told, 'We welcome criticism from comrades of the West'. He found the studio's documentary work both 'hysterically propagandist' and 'technically abysmal' and made a passing comment that understatement was a good quality in documentary work: messages 'were best left to look after themselves'. That brought the studio visit to an abrupt halt. Maurice's interpreter, when pressed, told him that the studio people had declared him an enemy of the Chinese people, 'an agent of reactionaries'. Maurice's opinion was not sought again. He had misread the Communist Chinese way: to politely offer the opportunity of criticism which should be, equally politely, avoided: then no one loses face.

Maurice and Gill travelled for two days by train from Canton to Shanghai, first class in a compartment of four bunks separate from the corridor; second class was four bunks open to the corridor; third class, upholstered seats; fourth class wooden benches with spittoons at each end. Maurice wrote that the heat was still 'terrific. I am sitting in the guard's van writing this stripped to the waist, sitting in a cool draught, and yet the sweat is still flooding off me.' They had both lost pounds in weight. Despite this, 'I'm afraid China has captured me altogether. If I could, I'd love to get a job and live here for a year or two ... we're having the most wonderful time of our lives.'

On arrival at Shanghai, a city of 'six million people — the fourth largest in the world'* they were greeted by hundreds of young people. 'Flowers & Chinese bands & handshakes everywhere' and they were lodged in a luxury room at the famed Cathay Hotel on The Bund. The city became flooded from four days of continuous rain during their stay but their schedule was still packed with meetings and receptions. Then, on again to Nanking at the end of the first week in July, 'Remember the wartime stories on the "rape of Nanking"? It is mostly rebuilt now … Methods of work are still very primitive … men and women still haul enormously heavy carts up and down the streets.'[10] Then another day's travel and on to Peking, everywhere parks, everywhere children, donkey carts, a whole morning in the Forbidden City but, alas, no time to visit the Great Wall.

In Peking, Maurice and Gill stayed on 'Embassy Row', were entertained by the Reuter correspondent, and met the Chinese General Secretary of Foreign Affairs to do their bit in promoting trade, handing on official literature they had carried from New Zealand. By now, Maurice was beginning to express uncertainties in his letters home: 'I have seen many things I like, some I don't like; I appreciate that the problem here is a tremendous one, and that amazing advances have been made. But I would not like, till we have left, to sum up a conclusion.'[11] He was helped in his summing up by meeting an old Communist colleague from Wellington: New Zealand-born Chinese Alex Young, who had gone to China in 1955 to throw in his lot with the revolution. In his letter home, Maurice simply wrote that Young told him there was a 'lot of dissatisfaction in the universities; and there has been a great letting-off of steam in the past few months.'[12] But Young had not been welcomed with open arms. Foreigners were treated with distrust, especially the university-educated, and many were exiled to remote provinces to rid themselves of reactionary ideas by undertaking menial work. Young had had his 'share of cleaning latrines and humbling himself before sadistic commissars'. He told Maurice that he dreamed of New Zealand beaches but woke to find himself 'in this strange and cruel country called China again.'[13]

After stays in Mukden (Shenyang) and Harbin, Maurice and Gill crossed the border to the Soviet Union and the Trans-Siberian Railway on about 20 July. The 'faces were suddenly and dourly Russian. Moscow was now a mere six-day journey. Lovely Lake Baikal floated past at sunset. There were knives and forks instead of chopsticks … and caviar too. Siberia, a name rich with

---

*Shanghai now has 25 million people and is the third largest in the world.

misery, was colourful in summer … forests, sparkling rivers, candy-coloured villages' but which were seldom 'innocent of Marxist icons. Even the humblest whistle-stop had its statue of Lenin, and banners and slogans riding the breeze off tundra and taiga.[14]

'But it was the people we saw most of — at every station hundreds and thousands, with flowers and gifts and badges for the Indonesians, Viet-Namese, Australian, New Zealand, and Chinese people on the festival train.'[15]

It was wonderful travelling with such a mixture of nationalities. 'At nights we would clear out a dining-car and have international concerts. The Indonesians always stole the show with their singing.'[16] They stole many people's health, too, bringing the Asian 'flu* with them to which Maurice succumbed; and Gill but less so. Four of the New Zealand delegation were taken to hospital when they arrived in Moscow.

In Moscow the delegations were given a 'film-star reception' but had to endure long speeches before they were bussed to a hotel. Although new, this had no lifts and Maurice and Gill had to climb to the fourth floor. For meals, the New Zealanders, along with the Australians, Irish and Nepalese were bussed to the 'Children's Café' in the Agricultural Exhibition Hall.

The Sixth World Festival of Youth and Students was organised by the socialist World Federation of Democratic Youth and the International Union of Students.[17] The Moscow event was the biggest ever, 34,000 young people gathering from 131 countries in the period of the 'Khrushchev Thaw' when First Secretary of the Soviet Communist Party, Nikita Khrushchev, allowed a measure of cultural liberalisation in the USSR. He was half opening the doors of the USSR to the world, and ordered his officials to 'smother foreign guests in our embrace'. Three million Moscovites joined with the tens of thousands of young visitors in events that ranged from discussion groups to events in the Kremlin.

Gill reported that they left their hotel on the opening day of the festival, 28 July, at ten in the morning, riding in specially decorated trucks. The Lenin Stadium, the new national stadium of the USSR, was about ten miles away but the crowds en route were dense from the start. Red Army soldiers struggled to keep the road open and at 'places along the route the crowd was completely out of control', calling out '"mere mere" [mir] and "droosbah droosbah" [druzhba] which means peace, peace and friendship, friendship', the slogan for the festival. It became an almost 'meaningless chant with special chant leaders here and there

---

*The 1957 Asian 'flu (influenza A subtype H2N2) was the second major 'flu pandemic of the 20th century and killed between one and two million people worldwide.

... we were amazed that in the huge crowd some people were so considerate that they passed ice-creams up to us.'[18] It took five hours for them to reach the stadium where they then had to take part in the nations' march past before Khrushchev, other Soviet leaders and a crowd of 100,000. Curiously, neither Maurice nor Gill wrote anything about the opening spectacle at Lenin Stadium except to comment that 'it was a day never to be forgotten' and other events were 'something of an anti-climax after the magnificence of the opening.'[19]

The other events included concerts, opera, circus, an international art exhibition, and official, tiring meetings with other delegations. Soon after arrival, Maurice was interviewed about New Zealand writing for *Literaturnaya Gazeta*. He explained the 'salient differences between the literature of Australia and New Zealand; pointed out that, because of the development of our society, our writers were, on the whole, less politically conscious than the militant Australians … Our social conflicts revealed themselves more in quiet internal situations, rather than in dramatic externals …' But New Zealand writers 'did work within the humanist, socially critical tradition of world literature.'[20]

Maurice avoided most formal programmes as he endeavoured to meet Soviet writers. 'Literary occasions were fiascos.'[21] One was advertised as an opportunity for the world's youth to meet Soviet writers of distinction but the panel presented were 'middle-aged mediocrities', none of them of the stature of someone like Ilya Ehrenburg whose novel *The Thaw* had given its name to the Khrushchev liberalisation. The event was taken as an insult to many of the young people there and hundreds left in disgust.

But the next night, at a less formal event at Moscow University, 65-year-old Ehrenburg took the platform. In the same way as composer Dmitri Shostakovich, he was 'one of the few Soviet writers to have survived Stalin's purges, if not without compromise'. His World War II journalism had put his patriotism beyond doubt and his memoirs, as well as works on the German invasion of the Soviet Union and the Holocaust, had achieved international resonance. 'Many distinguished dead seemed to keep him company … the likes of Osip Mandelstam and Isaac Babel long in unmarked graves.* Quietly, sanely, Ehrenburg led his audience through the Soviet maze and, in the end, offered light and a little hope. "We have to learn to be critical of ourselves … Be patient"'. When a student in the audience asked for how long, he answered, 'You will live to see the day'; his demeanour showed he did not expect to see it himself.**

*Writers Mandelstam and Babel were arrested during the Stalin purges of the late 1930s. Mandelstam died in a Siberian transit camp and Babel was shot.
**Ehrenburg died in August 1967.

Maurice was shocked to find that Ehrenburg's 'masterly performance' was not even mentioned in the Soviet press and thought to put the record straight when he was asked to write an article for the journal *Druzhba Naradov* (The People's Friendship). In an otherwise bland account, Maurice 'praised Ehrenburg for not treating foreign visitors as fools.'[22] Its editor seemed pleased with the article; but when he was asked to write another for the English-language *Moscow News*, he was told it was 'not convenient' to write about Ehrenburg. When his *Druzhba Naradov* article appeared, all reference to Ehrenburg had been removed.

On a boat excursion on the Moscow-Volga canal Maurice met writers who approved of what Ehrenburg had said, writers such as Samuil Marshak, an essayist and translator of Shakespeare and Burns who had managed 'perhaps by deft evasion ... to outlast the Stalin years with serenity.'[23] Another was Korney Chukovsky, one of the most popular children's writers. He warmly recounted his meetings with New Zealand soldiers in World War I and wished to return their hospitality by inviting Maurice and Gill to his dacha at Peredelkino, southwest of Moscow. He said they might be interested in meeting his neighbour, Boris Pasternak. Maurice tried to take up Chukovsky's invitation but when he asked his guide to arrange a visit, this was also 'not convenient' and he was diverted by a visit to Tolstoy's Yasnaya Polyana.

After the festival was over, and the peace and friendship banners taken down, Maurice and Gill were housed as guests of the Soviet Writers' Union in the Hotel Leningradskaya, a Stalinist monstrosity outside the city centre. Maurice loathed the modern Moscow architecture, 'giant buildings like wedding-cakes ... a corruption of good taste.'[24] In his letter of 15 August he also spelt out to the family back home, Frank and Joe in particular, the kind of monstrous persecutions that had taken place during the Stalinist era.

Carl Freeman had asked Maurice if he could find out what had happened to forty Jewish cultural figures arrested during Stalin's 'anti-cosmopolitan' purge of 1948, 'Cosmopolitan' being a Soviet euphemism for 'Jewish'. As guests of the Writers' Union, Maurice and Gill had guides (minders), interpreters and a limousine on call. They used this one evening to pick up Esther Markish, widow of Peretz Markish, a Yiddish poet among the forty arrested, and take her to a union meeting.

Earlier in the day, Maurice had evaded his minders and, with the help of some Soviet 'friends', visited Esther in her small Moscow flat. It was a shrine to her husband of photographs, paintings and books; and she told him how the KGB had arrested Peretz without warning nine years before and thrown her out of her flat. After four years in Lubyanka Prison, Peretz had been shot after an orchestrated trial, but Esther did not learn of this until 1955. His name and work were rehabilitated in the 'Khruschev Thaw', and Esther was given a new apartment and compensation. She and her sons Shimon and David had worked hard to bring new editions of Peretz's poetry into print. But the evil could not be undone. 'The arrests and executions had torn the heart out of Jewish culture … Yiddish literature had literally been destroyed. Some called it a literature of manuscripts. She called it a literature of the dead.'[25]*

Despite his experiences, Maurice reassured the folks back home, telling them the USSR had been through a terrible war, the living standards were tough, but the post-Stalinist generation were well aware of the sins of their fathers. 'Let's not think that Russia has changed overnight. Many bad — and, yes, evil — features remain. But all of them are being questioned by the young people … Eventually they will have their say, and build a socialist society worthy of the name.' Although it was still possible to hold that hope, did Maurice simply want to mollify Uncle Joe and father Frank; or did he suspect the letter would be opened before it left Moscow?

One of the 'bad features' of the regime was the phone call that Maurice or Gill received each evening about 6.30, consisting of a few words of muffled Russian and then silence: a KGB operative, whom they nicknamed 'Charlie', just checking. A more subtle KGB presence was a friendly journalist named Misha who admitted having once worked for both the NKVD and the KGB overseas. He said he had been dismissed for refusing to work against his own citizens and had then experienced a rough, jobless time until the 'thaw'. It was only when Misha began talking about the 'Family', about settling differences from within, and 'Family friends', that Maurice began to realise he was being recruited. The KGB 'liked outside friends, desirably recruited young, who might at some point become prominent in their own societies. Loyal friends. Family friends … agents of influence.'[26] After several convivial meetings, Misha must have decided that Maurice would not be a reliable recruit. But as a 'parting gift', he gave Maurice unpublished information about the state of Stalin's apartment after he died: a bare, bookless 'dwelling place of a hermit, a recluse, a terrified man.'** Misha said,

---

*Esther Markish continued to be brave in restoring Peretz's reputation and promoting his work. But the 'thaw' was only provisional; the persecutions of both her writer son, David, and herself continued. When they applied for exit visas to Israel in 1970, David was thrown out of the Writers Union and forced to work as a porter and baker to support them both. When they finally made it to Israel in 1972, Esther declared, 'I feel as if I am re-born … I can say what I have not said for so many years, I am happy'. She went on to publish a successful memoir in 1978, *The Long Return*, in which she told the full Markish story.

**At his death, Stalin had a library of about 25,000 books spread across his Kremlin apartment and his dachas at Sochi and Kuntsevo (where he died).

'Write it down somewhere, print it anywhere, so that one day it can be found and not forgotten.' Maurice retold the story in *One of Ben's* (p.230) as evidence of 'what writers were for', to collect, keep and tell stories, no matter how long untold. The delicious irony is that this story was entirely false. Maurice had been duped, even thirty-six years later, into repeating anti-Stalinist propaganda.

Maurice continued to request a visit to Peredelkino to see Korney Chukovsky and his neighbour. First it was 'not convenient' and then 'impossible'. After being diverted to Tolstoy's estate, they were then diverted on a visit to Leningrad and, when they returned from there, with a trip to Georgia. Later, Maurice was able to put the clues together: there had been the Italian journalist at breakfast in the hotel who told him he was there to check on a translation of the new novel by Boris Pasternak, about to be published in the USSR. Then there was Maurice's broken appointment with Alexei Surkov, secretary of the Writers Union. He was eager to ask Surkov about the Pasternak novel; but Surkov could not see him; he had flown to Milan on 'something urgent'. Publication of the novel had been halted in the USSR and Surkov had flown off to try and stop it in Italy. He failed and soon *Dr Zhivago* was in print everywhere in the world except the Soviet Union.

In Moscow, the Shadbolts were told their next, and final, excursion would be to Uzbekistan which was transformed, after many delays, into Georgia. With time on their hands, they went to museums and the ballet, read and listened to the radio. At the end of August, Gill wrote home that listening to the BBC European Service, 'makes you realise how panicky the "free world" is; and reading statements by John Foster Dulles about China and so on seems like reading a child's fairy tale'.[27] In the bubble of their seventeenth-floor suite at the Leningradskaya Hotel, they were able to read recent copies of London 'papers and magazines borrowed from the Ceylon Embassy, situated on another floor.

After camping at Moscow airport all night, waiting for a 'plane, Maurice and Gill took off for Georgia on 1 September with 'leftovers from the festival', young writers from Pakistan, Bolivia, Peru, Chile, Venezuela and Persia. The flight was a rough ride of eight hours with four stops en route before a lurching landing at Tbilisi. Met by officials of the Georgian Writers Union, the clutch of literary leftovers were whisked away on an exhausting three-day tour. They visited quaint villages on hilltops; the mountain where Prometheus had been bound for 30,000 years; and the great 1500-year-old Orthodox church where Georgian kings were interred and where, in spite of the Soviet Union's formal atheism, an active congregation worshipped. Rather more were required to worship at Stalin's birthplace in Gori. This was a humble two-roomed cottage but, next door, despite Kruschev's denunciation of the Stalin personality cult, a marble Stalin Museum was being built. Gill wrote that it was a 'monstrosity of a place … Honestly, I was so depressed when I left … I felt like demanding why they didn't use the money to improve the roads … build a Stalin hospital — anything but a museum.'[28] Or maybe modern plumbing — the Great Stalin Sewer — as she, and the rest of the party, reeled back at the often noisome toilet facilities.

Maurice later portrayed the Georgia trip as a bizarre, drunken riot[29] where every day was a 'recipe for delirium tremens'. In her contemporary letter home, Gill was more restrained, describing how Maurice was fussed over as the first ever New Zealand writer to visit Georgia. He gave a talk on New Zealand literature; and they watched a local movie, a 'Robin Hood type of thing set in the days when the Persians invaded Georgia'. But she did admit to a final party at a hillside vineyard where 'Everyone got very merry: the Latins danced; Maurie did a haka; the Russians sang and everyone drank including me'. Hangovers the next day made the endless flight back to Moscow harrowing. But when the 'plane stopped for refuelling at Sokhumi on the Black Sea coast, the writers went off in a bus for a swim, and took the pilot and crew with them so they would not be left behind. Back at their Moscow hotel exhausted, the Russian party finally over, Maurice and Gill waited for tickets to Bulgaria.

CHAPTER 11

A COMPREHENSIBLE COUNTRY

They had been thinking of Czechoslovakia, Yugoslavia, even Poland, but in Moscow Maurice had met Vasil Popov, a crop-headed young Bulgarian writer, who was open in his contempt for the Soviet Union and its time-serving writers and assured Maurice that things were much better in Bulgaria. With Popov he also met Peter Tempest, a London publisher's editor and his Bulgarian wife, Brigita Tempest-Yossifova, who worked as the London correspondent for the official government newspaper. Popov warned Maurice against the Tempests: Yossifova's father was a prominent figure in the Communist regime, she was more than a journalist, and he wanted the Shadbolts to stay with him in Sofia and meet real Bulgarian writers. But Maurice and Gill succumbed to the 'overpoweringly friendly' Tempests who travelled ahead at mid-September and were on hand to meet them after another gruelling flight via Kiev, Rostov and Bucharest. They whisked them off in a flash car to the Slavyanska Hotel in downtown Sofia and could not have been more hospitable and attentive. Gill developed a nasty cold on arrival and, 'Brigita, when she heard about it, thoughtfully arranged for a big glass of cognac to be sent up to me with a huge lemon and an equally huge pot of tea. Honestly, she is a wonder.'[1]

The Tempests began introducing them to prominent writers and artists and to find a place for Maurice to write in peace. Popov made sure they were not under the exclusive oversight of the Tempests and took them on a tour of Sofia before inviting them to a gathering of writers at his home. Compared to the Soviet Union, that was 'one thing different in Bulgaria. People have been inviting us to their homes ever since we arrived.'[2] Bulgaria was 'comprehensible in a way that the Soviet Union could never be. It was a small country' and

Maurice felt more at home in a place that was, on first sight, 'as gentle, modest and egalitarian as New Zealand'.[3] Bulgaria was undergoing its own post-Stalinist 'thaw' and Communist dictator Todor Zhivkov, in the first years of his 45-year rule, was still entrenching his authority. 'We seemed to be in Europe at last. The autumn weather was warm; there were outdoor cafes with colourful umbrellas.' In the Writers Union restaurant where they ate most days, 'the wine was good, company lively, and conversation seemingly unfettered'.[4] But Popov warned Maurice not to believe all he heard there, appearances could be deceptive, it was still a one-party state.

Although they ate at its restaurant, the Writers Union had not sponsored their five-week visit to Bulgaria and, while the Tempests and Popov provided generous hospitality, there was no charity. They had to pay their own way. This proved easy enough. Maurice and Gill were said to be the first New Zealanders to visit Bulgaria since World War II and Maurice was certainly the first New Zealand writer. There was an instant demand from local 'papers and magazines for articles about New Zealand and even for his short stories. 'Twosome', which had first appeared in *Numbers*, and for which he received no payment, earned him the equivalent of £20. In room 418 of the Slavyanska Hotel, Maurice hammered out articles on the one portable typewriter he and Gill used between them, and a short story, 'A Beer for Old Johnny', which became popular in Bulgaria a year or more before it was published in New Zealand.

In his last article, Maurice compared the life and customs of Bulgaria and New Zealand and when he sent a clipping of this home, he wrote, 'You really have to come to Europe to appreciate just how uncivilised we are in New Zealand'. He wished he could take his folks along the tree-lined, yellow-cobbled Russian Boulevard to enjoy an evening glass of cognac or slivovitz at one of the open-air cafés. 'No drunkenness, no brawling; just people relaxing, talking, playing chess, passing the time.'[5] Altogether he earned Bulgarian leva worth £200 during their month-long stay. They had to spend it all, too, in those open-air cafés: leva were worthless anywhere else.

Maurice and Gill's warm reception in Sofia, the good food and wine, home hospitality, the demand and pay for his work, all prompted him to write home, after just ten days, a paean to socialism in a small country. He gave an account of Bulgaria's recent history, how 'In 1949 things became really terror stricken and chaotic. There was not enough to eat' and fake trials and purges followed. But now everything was greatly improved, the standard of living was rising rapidly. 'There is quite a free atmosphere; young people are frank and vigorous, earnest in their desire to build a good socialist country.' Maurice was on an idealistic roll, concluding, 'As a socialist, I must always face the truth. And if the truth is that bad things have been done, then I must face that. But the <u>real</u> truth is that socialism — whatever may have been done wrongly in its name — is a superior system of life for human beings. And that we must never forget. Socialism will always overcome its mistakes; but capitalism will never.'[6] There were the makings here of a fifth verse to 'The Internationale' and the words and tone echoed those of the letters he had sent to Gill in 1953, to convince her of his belief in the eternal values of socialism. There is a sense that the person he was really trying to convince was himself — or, rather, to convince Frank and Joe he still believed — in order to rationalise the 'bad things' Communism had been up to during the previous twenty years. It was his last recorded attempt.

Despite Maurice's praise of Bulgaria's version of socialism, he was still a young man a long way from home. He told family: 'You can't imagine how isolated and lonely you begin to feel in foreign countries without news from home.'[7] Despite the attractions of Bulgaria, 'You have no idea what letters mean and it is the little things that are so important because they show that things are going on in the same way as when we left.'[8]

Gill rarely reported to the Shadbolt family on her own condition, feelings or activities. There are a few signs of tensions with Maurice, such as when she writes he is 'screaming' at her as she types wrong instructions about how Vi should keep yoghurt! She seems mostly grateful for the trip of a lifetime which is really down to Maurice, his connections and his work. She reassures mother Vi about his physical welfare and state of mind and that she is adequately fulfilling the role she has taken over from her. She reports that Maurice is upset with the need to share a bathroom at the Slavyanska, occupied when he needs to use it; that he has a bad cold but he is getting over it. Gill began one letter with the comment that Maurice was not very well, but soon added, 'you will start to worry but it is only a slight tummy upset and will, no doubt, be alright tomorrow. He has been working very hard ... Bulgarian food, too, is very rich ... they cook peppers in everything ... you can imagine Maurice's reaction to them, though he has done his best to eat them.'[9] He came right later with a plate of steak and eggs.

Gill's letters were filled with descriptions of Bulgarian everyday life, food and clothing prices, shops and the urban landscape. But, where Maurice wrote of the socialist dream, Gill reported realities. Educated people might be multilingual but there was a high level of illiteracy and an old man she encountered could not even tell the time from her watch. Maurice waxed lyrical about the amount of apartment building taking place. Gill wrote: 'there is a shortage here ... and everyone is allocated two to a room but a hallway, or middle room, can be extra'. Most people she had met, however, had flats with their own bathrooms and kitchens, and 'If you are an artist — painter, singer or writer — you are entitled to an extra room for your work.'[10] Locals were astounded at how much rent was paid in New Zealand when people in Bulgaria worked on average only two days a month to pay for accommodation.

Maurice began to notice that critical dissent from Bulgaria's writers was countered, not so much by the direct censorship, imprisonment or exile tactics of the Soviet Union but by corrupting them with privileges, provided they stayed inside the regime's tent. 'The opulent life of Bulgarian writers, even of the mediocre, made even the wealthiest of Western authors seem down at heel. In this devious manner, with considerable personal charm, Zhivkov silenced two generations of Bulgarian writers; and all but levelled a literature … it made for a literary history even sadder than the Soviet Union's.'[11] Vasil Popov stayed outside the tent and Maurice wrote that, consequently, he never did write and publish the great Bulgarian novel he had in mind before he died of heart failure in 1980 aged fifty.*

Brigita Tempest-Yossifova did not approve of Maurice associating with Popov and friends and, as the 'Queen Bee' in Sofia on her visits from London, expected Maurice to pay her court, along with other admirers, rather than spending time talking to other women with dubious connections. In particular Eugenia 'Jenny' Bojilova, an editor and translator who had interviewed Maurice for the literary press and translated one of his stories. In *One of Ben's* (p.246), Maurice described her as having 'high Slavic cheekbones, a touch of Turkish in her complexion, eloquent eyes and a bewitching Bulgarian smile' and was easy to fall in love with. 'Most men did, and I was no exception. She had just ended a long affair with a French philosopher who wanted her to live in Paris. ("He was too much a Marxist for me," she explained wryly. "I have enough ideology at home"). Our encounters were affectionate but chaste. They remained so.'

To Yossifova, Jenny Bojilova was not only a rival for Maurice's attentions but also had too many connections to people of the old régime. Yossifova exerted her political influence by booking Maurice and Gill into an artists' retreat at the Bistritsa Palace, high in the Rila Mountains, well away from the heady distractions of Sofia. 'She looked at Gillian, then at me. "Also," she added, "you can walk in the woods and by mountain streams. You may even see that there is more to Bulgaria than beautiful women."'[12]

Gill described the 'adventure' of the journey forty miles south in an ancient bus to Borovets and then by horse and cart up the mountain to the palace

---

*In fact, Popov had two novels published in Sofia in the 1970s, with themes acceptable to the regime, and wrote the screenplays for movies based on them.

retreat. Bistritsa 'palace' was a grand hunting lodge built in the years before World War I for Tsar Ferdinand and his son Boris, and had been 'nationalised' in 1945. Gill wrote about the heavily decorated rooms, the carved wooden ceilings, the lines of trophy heads on the walls. She and Maurice had a room in the same wing as the royal suite and took 'very great delight in using the royal toilet — which in itself is built like a blinking throne!'.[13]

The entrance to the palace was guarded by an armed sentry, which perplexed Gill as local peasants from nearby Borovets appeared to wander in and out at will. Maurice spent some time talking and walking with 'Anton', a writer who found it politically expedient to spend more time at Bistritsa than in Sofia, and came to the conclusion that those same peasants resented writers and artists living luxuriously on the back of their hard labour and might just decide to take matters into their own hands. The sentry with the sub-machine gun might be needed.

There was also an elderly longer-term resident, a children's book illustrator named 'Sonia'. She told Maurice about the past show trials, the executions, the people who returned, if they were lucky, 'skeletal' from gulags. It was still going on, she told him. Recently her cousin had been sent to the Danube island concentration camp of Belene for speaking his mind too publicly. Maurice did not have the chance to speak to 'Sonia' again; she 'disappeared' from one day to the next without saying goodbye.

During their fortnight's stay, visitors came and went, including the Tempests to see how they were faring; and, despite Yossifova's manoeuvre, Jenny Bojilova made a discreet visit, too. Maurice and Gill ate their meals at the long royal table in the cavernous dining hall, often alone, and walked in the vast pine forests as the air became chill with deepening autumn. Most days, Maurice commandeered the typewriter and tapped out the first chapter of a new novel.

Back in Sofia by 14 October, after their little exile, Maurice wrote home that they were 'much refreshed after our wonderful holiday' and sent little sister Julie a postcard of Bistritsa 'to illustrate her geography lesson about Bulgaria'.[14] A few days later they left by train for London via Belgrade, Vienna, Munich and a short stay in Paris. Jenny Bojilova, Vasil Popov and other literary friends were at the station to see them off, even the Tempests, but keeping their distance. In an emotional farewell, they were showered with gifts and told to come back soon.

CHAPTER 12

THANK YOU GOODBYE

Maurice and Gill arrived in England at the end of October and he soon wrote to Kevin Ireland: 'So now we have come to a bleak rainy autumn London: it is, of course, a bloody dreadful anti-climax, but one must make the best of things. The best thing about England, it seems just now, is that the people speak English. The worst thing is that the people are bloody English.'[1] It could only be an anti-climax after four months of exotic travel when they had been treated continuously as honoured guests, where money had been no problem, and where Maurice had been fêted as that rare bird of passage, a New Zealand author. Ending up in a flat in Ealing with no welcoming party, winter coming on, money running out and no job prospects was a nose dive into cold reality that would have made the idea of returning to the socialist dream something worth considering. He told Ireland that he had fallen in love with Bulgaria and its people and 'I can almost certainly go back if I want, on a scholarship to Sofia university; or into the film industry'.[2] Even at the age of sixty, he would write, 'It has never been fashionable to celebrate Bulgaria and its people. But a little of both would live in me for the rest of my life. It was as if I had found another homeland. I still go into retreat there, in my imagination, and sometimes in dream.'[3]

Why did those feelings linger after he had spent little more than a month in Bulgaria, half of that in the isolation of Bistritsa which soon became no retreat of dreams but the private lodge of dictator Todor Zhivkov? He recorded that he had fallen in love with Jenny Bojilova. But she had also fallen in love with him; the Bistritsa isolation had been less than complete; their relationship had been more than 'chaste'. He told Ireland nothing of this, but the prospect of life without her was the ultimate anti-climax.

Maurice had fallen in love not only with a beautiful, intelligent and accomplished Sofian woman, but also probably with the *idea* of falling in love with someone like her, in that place and under those circumstances. Throughout the long journey leading to Sofia he had been drawn to women from cultures unknown to him, and was especially drawn to those who were both physically attractive and intellectually sophisticated and who lived in environments with ancient political and cultural traditions and conflicts. Even at the beginning, there had been the young girls in Canton; there had been visions of women sighted from trains; in Georgia; there had been the 'most beautiful woman' he had ever met in Esther Markish. Jenny Bojilova was the apotheosis of his emotional and sexual dreams. Their affair would not only live with him for the rest of his life; its excitement and powerful emotions were to prompt him to try and repeat it again and again, with disregard for the distress he inflicted on many of the women he encountered.

Maurice and Jenny wrote to each other frequently over the six months after he left Sofia. At the end of November, she wrote in response to his question: 'My darling, Why are you not here? Why can't I tell you all I want to tell you lying near you? Why are we such idiots? Why did you leave the country? And knowing that I love you so very much why do you feel helpless and miserable?'[4] Probably because after the passionate play he had made for Jenny's affections, declaring she was the woman he had been looking for all his life; after his promises of eternal love, of returning to Sofia as soon as he could sort matters out with Gill, the prosaic demands of real life in damp London began to tell him that a romantic return to a life with Jenny would be almost impossible. But for months he could not accept this reality. Jenny's exhortations and reassurances kept him suspended in hope; but his final commitment lay always just beyond reach. 'Dear, dear Maurice, What I feel is something so big and so warm and so consoling … it is impossible to say it in a letter, in English.' She was in daily discussions with Vasil Popov and her other friends about finding him a job in Sofia; they made an appointment with a leading figure in the film industry. 'If that does not work we'll try something else. I promise you we will do it, my darling, and you'll come here because I want you to be here and you want to be here, and I tell you again — there is nothing impossible if two people want something so strongly.'[5] When Maurice wrote about being depressed, Jenny responded, 'Smile to me, my dear, and say you feel a little better now. Please, Maurie, darling. You know how beautiful you are when you smile, don't you?'[6]

Somehow, Maurice kept his correspondence with Jenny away from Gill. At the end of December, when their future in London was still uncertain, Gill wrote to the Shadbolt family: 'Maurie is even thinking seriously about going back to Bulgaria … He is having a terrible time with his first Russian lessons. He wants to be prepared for Bulgaria* if he decides to go.'[7] The operative word here is 'he'. Yet, at some point, Gill must have seen letters from Jenny and discovered or deduced that they contained more than discussions about translations and literature. Maurice probably insisted there was nothing going on. But tensions between them increased and Maurice described his marriage as 'faltering'.[8] By Christmas, Gill may have sent home the subtle signal of 'he' to suggest all was not well on the marital front; but there is no clear evidence. When he wrote to Jenny about his difficulties, she replied, 'Yes, dearest, I know how you feel about Gill. Maybe that is why I worry so much about you. But I tell you — it will pass. And it will be much better for you two when you don't live together any more, because you do torture each other. The less you want to do it, the more it comes so. I know.'[9]

As passion and conflict bubbled under the surface, and sometimes burst out in complaints and arguments, day-to-day life continued. When Maurice and Gill first arrived, they stayed for some days with a friend in Barons Court. Maurice described him in *One of Ben's* as 'Howard', an ex-pat Wellingtonian who had secured a good job on a Sunday 'paper, had literary ambitions, and considered New Zealand to be 'on the dark side of the moon'. He assured Maurice that he, too, would become a permanent ex-pat in London, joining the 'cultural chameleons' who had settled in London from all over the Commonwealth, shaking the rough colonial dust from their feet. 'Howard' told Maurice that, after his travels behind the Iron Curtain, he should write a Cold War spy thriller; that would 'go down big'. Maurice demurred; he continued to write New Zealand stories.

But who was 'Howard'? Was he really a composite character, an archetype that Maurice constructed to demonstrate the failure that awaited ex-pat New Zealand writers, even to the point of drunken suicide, while he cast himself, in contrast, as becoming a successful writer by remaining true to his origins and native experience?[10]

Within a week they found a two-roomed flat in a three-storey Edwardian house in Ealing, down the road from Ealing Film Studios and within easy walking distance of Piccadilly Line Tube stations. It was small, with the stove in the living room but it was 'nicely furnished with good carpets, silver and crockery'. Ex-pat friends they had round for dinner were 'amazed at our good luck' and the only problem was that it cost them three shillings every time they wanted to travel into town.[11] It was 'good luck' because although London and

---

*The Russian and Bulgarian alphabets were the same and many Bulgarians spoke Russian.

(Top left) Ben Shadbolt, ancestor extraordinary on Banks Peninsula, c.1875.
(Top right) Ada Shadbolt, wife of Ernest, Maurice's paternal grandmother and psychic prompt, before becoming mother of ten.
(Above) Ernest and Ada with most of their children on one of their Whanganui River farms, about 1920. Renee (Sis) stands tall at the rear.

(Top left) 'Arklow Joe' Kearon and Louisa Morris on their 1905 wedding day.
(Top right) Maurice's Uncle Joe in late 1930s.
(Above left) Quarryman Frank Shadbolt and secretary Violet Kearon on their wedding day in 1929.
(Above right) Little Maurie, first portrait, c.1934.

(Top left) The Shadbolt family at Te Kuiti: Peter, mother Vi and Maurie at back; father Frank bottom right, others unknown.
(Top right) Frank Shadbolt and his P&T truck.
(Above) Te Kuiti Primary School 1938: Maurie at end of back row, right.

(Top) Maurie at Te Kuiti District High School 1946, third from left back row.
(Above) Young People's Club tramping party at Simla Hut in the Waitakeres, 1951. Maurice is at centre back row, Carl Freeman bottom left.
(Left) The conjuror. 'Cunning and craft can go a long way.'

(Left) Carl Freeman (left) and Kevin Ireland at Maurice and Gill's wedding, November 1953.

(Above) Wedding breakfast 21 November 1953. Best man Gordon Dryden with Maurice and Gill, Julia bottom right corner.
(Left) Frank and Vi Shadbolt at the 1953 wedding.

(Top) Hawera, New Year 1953. Passengers in the Morris 8: Kevin Ireland at left with Maurice, Carl Freeman, Gill Heming (upper centre) and her two friends from Sydney.
(Above left) Frank Shadbolt with race book and radios.
(Above right) Aunt Sis, Spanish Civil War hero and matron of Rawene Hospital.

(Above left) Maurice, with Don Oakley on camera, filming Eric Lee-Johnson at Waimamaku, Hokianga, 1956. ERIC LEE-JOHNSON COLLECTION, TE PAPA TONGAREWA.
(Above right) Maurice's literary mentor James K. Baxter, late 1950s.

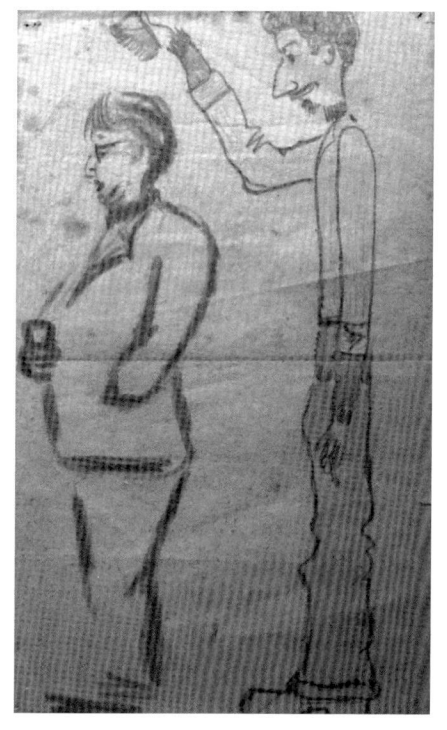

(Above left) Poet and Landfall editor Charles Brasch at home on Heriot Row, Dunedin, 1960. ZELDA LOUISE PHOTOGRAPH: S18-524A, CHARLES BRASCH PAPERS, MS-0996-012/094/009, HOCKEN COLLECTIONS, UNIVERSITY OF OTAGO.
(Above right) Party time sketch by Kevin Ireland, c.1957. Notes on back state, 'Shadbolt talking, Ireland assisting, Gee collecting'. COURTESY MAURICE GEE.

The State Literary Fund Committee in 1958. L-R: Prof. John Garrett, Prof. Ian Gordon, *Listener* editor M.H. 'Monte' Holcroft and Sir Leon Gotz. COURTESY ANTHONY HOLCROFT.

The only photograph of Maurice Shadbolt together with Maurice Gee (at left); Dave Walsh and Kevin Ireland at right. Parnell, Auckland, 1956. BRIAN BELL COLLECTION, ATL PACOLL-9389.

The Shadbolt family at Glen Eden, new year 1957. L-R: Vi, Julia, Frank, Maurice, Gill and Joe.

Maurice in Canton crowd, 1957.

(Top) Delegates on their way to the opening of the Sixth World Festival of Youth in Moscow, 1957.
(Above) Maurice and Gill at tea with festival friends in Moscow.
(Right) Maurice (far right) and Gill (bottom left) with Soviet essayist Samuil Marshak on Moscow-Volga Canal.

(Above) Maurice with
Jenny Bojilova at Bistritsa,
Bulgaria, October 1957.
(Left) On Chelsea
Embankment, 1959.
'London glowed.'

Kay and Karl Stead, 1957.
COURTESY C.K. STEAD.

Maurice and Gill, at left, on CND protest march with Conrad Bollinger and family behind, London 1958.

England were emerging from the tough post-war austerity period — Britain had now 'never had it so good' Prime Minister Harold Macmillan declared — good quality accommodation in the city was still hard to find. They had money to get by after spending on essentials for the flat, and they received a little from home at Christmas, but they still had to find sources of income.

Maurice's only complaint about the flat, Gill wrote, was that he found it 'difficult working with me moving round the place all the time but that will be remedied when I go out to work'.[12] While Maurice wrestled with articles and fiction, practical reporter Gill tried newspaper after newspaper for a job or commissions. She even considered a factory job but the wages were 'terrible' and not enough to pay the rent. Maurice did apply for a sub-editor's job but she hoped he would not get it. 'I would much rather he stayed at home and did his work. He has so much to do'[13] — while she kept looking for work, shopping, cooking, cleaning, putting up with his moods.

Gill wrote articles about their travels for New Zealand newspapers, undertook a reporting commission for the *Sunday Express* and, to make ends meet, took a job as a 'nippy', a waitress at a Lyons tea shop, earning overtime by working on Boxing Day. But at the middle of January 1958, after months of pounding pavements, she was finally interviewed for two jobs, and on 27 January started as the publicity officer for the National Union of Students (NUS) in Bloomsbury. She thought she would have needed a tertiary degree but her journalistic experience in Wellington, which included some work at Victoria University, and her recent socialist credentials, saw her through.

She soon settled in but her workload was heavy and she had board meetings to cope with, too. The first went late into the evening when 'amateur student journalists had a wonderful time picking a professional to pieces'. It took her a couple of days to recover from this: 'I've had the feeling of hating everyone, particularly men'. But she soon began 'to order people around again'[14] and became responsible for the production of an impressive stream of NUS publications. These ranged from the monthly 'Student News' to the substantial *Student Guide to London* (price 3/-). The £12 10s or more she earned each week was just enough to support them both.

Maurice's 'much to do' involved hammering away at the novel he had started at Bistritsa and a series of articles for both the *NZ Listener* and *Landfall*. He wrote to Charles Brasch soon after arriving in London who responded with, 'Dear wandering Sputnik,* So you've come to earth at last!' Brasch was interested in a piece about Soviet writers as well as John Feeney and the

---

*The first earth satellite, launched by the Soviet Union on 4 October 1957.

National Film Unit[15] and Maurice responded immediately. He completed the first piece, 'China, Russia, Bulgaria. A Journey' on 27 November, but Christmas mail delays meant that Brasch had to hold over this 10,000-word 'letter' for the June issue of *Landfall*.[16]

Despite its title, only half a dozen of the article's twenty pages covered China and Bulgaria. It is notable for its detailed discussion of the state of Soviet literature in the mid-1950s, recording Ilya Ehrenburg's responses to audience questions after the lecture Maurice had found so memorable. Maurice recounted an extended interview with Alexei Surkov, secretary of the Soviet Writers' Union whom he found 'frank' when he said that the Stalinist 'purges went through my heart and through my conscience' and had caused him 'many doubts'. Now, 'more than many of his compatriots, he felt a responsibility for the Stalin cult. Now that it was cut from so many hearts, cynicism was, he admitted, beginning to show itself among many young people. This was a problem.' Maurice became more and more 'aware of Surkov the wily politician rather than Surkov the poet'.

In the Bulgarian coda to his article, Maurice referred to the 'thaw' in cultural matters there, the increased scope for writers to produce literature at least obliquely critical of the regime. But his main focus was on film: 'In cinema, Bulgaria, a small, largely peasant country of eight million people never blessed by prosperity, must put both Australia and New Zealand to shame'. Bulgaria had produced seven feature films in 1957 and numerous documentaries.

Bulgarians were 'able to see themselves and their own life portrayed imaginatively on screen, while New Zealanders might see a National Film Unit documentary once a year, a piece of commercial advertising from Pacific Films, and perhaps an odd revival of *Broken Barrier* or *Rewi's Last Stand*'. It was a theme he returned to in his next article.

In the same package as the 'letter', Maurice sent Brasch his 6000-word article on director John Feeney and the National Film Unit.[17] Maurice described and extolled Feeney's film-making with the NFU over the seven years from 1947 when he produced outstanding documentaries such as *Kotuku, Pumicelands* and *Legend of the Wanganui River* which won an award at the Edinburgh Festival. He then went on to describe how the bureaucratic strictures of Public Service management led to Feeney leaving the NFU, and New Zealand, for good and joining the National Film Board of Canada at three times his New Zealand salary. The dead hand of the Public Service, including the Unit's 'unfortunate tie with the Tourist and Publicity Department', had also led to the departure of other leading directors and cameramen, such as Brian Brake and Michael Forlong, who went on to outstanding international careers.

Maurice wrote that his article was 'simply a brief attempt to underline the tragic … situation which happens to exist in the field of government film-making'. The 'only clear answer' was to free the NFU from 'direct political control' and place it 'under board control as a public corporation, like the BBC' and its Canadian counterpart. It was a brave call for action but governments of the 1950s and 1960s had no interest in creating an entity that might cost money and would be beyond their direct political control.

Charles Brasch had encouraged Maurice to 'meet the English', not just New Zealand ex-pats, and 'don't be put off easily by different manners and the like, as some N.Zers are; the English in general, writers and others, are quite prepared to be friendly and interested'.[18] Despite this advice, Maurice and Gill's social life during the first months revolved around New Zealand ex-pats whose contacts they had had before leaving home. At one Kensington party 'they could have been in Lower Hutt or Parnell'.[19] Christmas prompted spasms of homesickness, especially for Gill, but they iced the cake Vi had sent over from New Zealand and ate their way through a large roast lamb meal which, after other friends could not join them, they shared with the Venezuelan writer, Pedro Duno, whom they had met in Georgia. Maurice gave Gill a pair of stockings and *Teach Yourself Russian*, while she gave him a small diary for 1958.

They had little money to spare for entertainment but soon after arriving in London they went to see John Osborne's *Look Back in Anger*, which was ending its run of more than a year at the Royal Court Theatre. Osborne's play had caused a tectonic shift in English theatre, kicking for touch drawing-room plays with its excoriating contempt and angry disillusionment with the state of post-war end-of-Empire England and its failed promises for the working class. Apart from Gill's complaint at having to pay 10/6d for a seat, their letters are silent on the play. Except when Maurice wrote to Jenny. She replied: 'If you know how much this letter of yours upset me, you'll become more optimistic and confident. No, you are not the hero of that play! You are not so angry with yourself and everybody as this Jimmy Porter. Why, of course not. Don't you want to live a more beautiful life?'[20]

Look Back in Anger was a useful prop for Maurice's disjointed mood. The play fitted with an urban landscape of cramped bed-sits smelling of gas and baked beans; Tube trains with worn-out pre-war carriages; double-decker buses that rumbled down the streets in convoys; army surplus duffle coats; pubs with warm frothless beer, dense cigarette smoke inside and fog outside that blurred the boundaries of day and night at four in the afternoon; snow that turned to a grey slush with the soot that grimed the face of every public building.

Gill plugged in to London and English life more easily through the agency of her work with the NUS; but Maurice, in emotion and imagination, still lived in either New Zealand or Sofia. There is no reference in his letters or writing to the cultural life or events of that place and time. He and Gill went to the National Film Theatre to see Eisenstein's films and other classics; but did they go and see Henry Fonda in *Twelve Angry Men* or the Oscar-winning *Bridge Over the River Kwai*? And 1957 was not only the year of John Osborne with *Look Back in Anger* and *The Entertainer*, but also of John Braine's novel *Room At the Top*, Jack Kerouac's *On the Road*, Nevil Shute's *On the Beach*, and Ian Fleming's *From Russia With Love*. The aspirations of Joe Lampton, the peripatetic Beat generation, the end of the world after nuclear holocaust, James Bond, none of these appeared to impinge on Maurice's discontented view of the world.

The new year arrived with a bleakness caused by more than London's frosty midwinter darkness. Maurice faced hospital treatment for a medical problem that had begun to cause him increasing discomfort and which had not been dealt with adequately in New Zealand. After consulting National Health Service (NHS) specialists he was listed for a major operation which would involve an extended stay in Hammersmith Hospital. For a short break before this, Pedro Duno persuaded Maurice to join him for a few February days in Paris and celebrate with his fellow exiles as they prepared to return home to Caracas after a coup d'état had restored democracy in Venezuela.

After Maurice left, Gill wrote to the family, 'I can't write such an honest letter to you about him while he is here … you must not mention anything I say in this letter directly when you write'. She told them that the operation was serious but likely to be 100 per cent successful. 'The whole thing is caused by a cluster of hairs at the base of the spine' and their growth 'causes the formation of a little cyst which fills with pus … and is very painful just before it bursts which is about every fortnight'. The NHS doctors planned to undertake more radical surgery than had been attempted in Wellington but there was nothing to worry about; although 'Maurie, in fits of deep depression (and he has had a lot lately) is sometimes inclined to think it is something that is going to kill him and he talks about dying on the operating table and all that but you know him as well as I do …'

Gill wrote that Maurice's chief problem was isolation, going out to the pub only on Friday nights to meet the odd New Zealand friend and he did not 'come into direct contact with English people at all'. She blamed herself for discouraging him from getting a job so that he could concentrate on his writing. 'He is inclined to feel at present that this flat is a prison and that I am warder No.1.' He had finished his novel but was not sure it was any good, and had also put some New Zealand short stories together for Russian translation. Yet, 'Everything seems to go wrong for him and he raises such tremendous obstacles for himself'. Gill thought that once the operation was over, it would do him good if he went away for a week or two. 'He may go back to Bulgaria we still have some money there …'.[21] She seems still to have been ignorant of Jenny's siren call.

While Gill managed three snowy days off with second cousins in Brixham, where her mother was born, Maurice frequented the cafés and bars of the Left Bank with Pedro and his friends as they were 'busy packing stowing canvases and manuscripts into trunks, stripping their dim little hotel rooms in the Latin Quarter'.[22] There was one painter in exile that Pedro was determined to find, a revolutionary comrade who was 'crazy but great' and whom Venezuela needed; but they could not find him among the bars of Pigalle. Maurice would later say that this search gave him a 'new opening chapter' for the novel he would eventually call *Strangers and Journeys*:[23]

> The cab dropped him at the Place Pigalle. The air was mild with September. Rain, earlier that evening, had left a melancholy shine on street and pavement. Lights flashing and jiggling advertised strip-tease cellars, hamburgers, Cinzano. The noisy crowd rippled sluggish each side of the street. Prostitutes formed ranks up side alleys … He floundered along with the crowd for a time, without an idea of how or where he should begin his search.[24]

The novel's genesis lay, perhaps, in the uneven manuscript he had been struggling with at Bistritsa and Byron House. When Maurice told Moss Gee about it, he replied, 'sounds intriguing. From your description, I should think its appeal should be pretty wide. We need something that really spills and overflows. And moves — we've been parked on our farmyard behinds too long.'[25]

Maurice's operation on 13 March left a 'hole as big as his fist' at the base of his spine. The radical surgery was successful but he faced an extended period of healing that involved skin grafts. This was initially thought to take three to four weeks, then five, but Maurice finally spent almost two months in hospital as the grafting process proved more complicated than expected. Gill wrote home that he was 'being treated very royally and has a room to himself' and, while England's March winds blasted outside, his was 'as warm as toast'.[26] The nursing staff called him 'the intellectual' but the ward sister disapproved of him reading the *Observer* rather than the *Sunday Times* because she considered it too left-wing. The nursing staff were attentive, and the room may have been comfortable but the pain and soreness from continual redressing, salt baths and more minor surgery were not.

Gill visited him almost every evening, bringing news, magazines and letters. They were both unhappy with the Ealing flat and she was continually searching for somewhere closer to town at no more than £4 a week. She kept the family better informed of his progress than he did but, at times, Maurice treated her like a dumb minion. To cheer him up, Gill had asked his Uncle Joe to send Maurice some New Zealand tobacco. 'What I had to go through … I was abused up hill and down dale. I was the biggest dim wit in the world … it would cost us a fortune in customs …' But it arrived marked 'Gift' and cost nothing and then Maurice took 'great pride in showing his New Zealand friends his packets of Greys'.[27]

After only a week in hospital, Gill brought him the best post-op news he could have asked for: the Literary Fund had granted him £200. Before leaving Sydney, Maurice had applied again for the £500 Scholarship in Letters and, although this had gone to novelist Phillip Wilson, £200 was a sizeable boost to both Maurice's ego and bank balance. A couple of months later, a tax refund of £99, consequent on the introduction of PAYE in New Zealand, plus article fees, meant that Maurice and Gill's income for the year had increased by 50 per cent.

The good news, and time on his hands in hospital, prompted him to write more letters home and both Moss Gee — with much goss — and Louis Johnson responded. Maurice had thought that his grant had been down to the influence of Denis Glover and Monte Holcroft on the Literary Fund committee. Holcroft had welcomed his article 'Evening in Moscow' for the *NZ Listener* and used it with alacrity. Johnson told Maurice that he had been 'consulted' about the grant but 'Put down your consolation prize to "conscience money" rather than anything else'. He was referring to PEN's past dissatisfaction with the awards system and Johnson was PEN secretary. Maurice planned to use the money to finish putting together a collection of his own short stories. Johnson said he would publish these under his own Capricorn Press imprint, but saw his main function was 'to put things into print that others won't take on, & frankly I don't think you're in that category'.[28]

In mid-March, Vi Shadbolt wrote to say that the family was moving from Glen Eden to Waihi. This provoked a despairing and almost vitriolic response from Maurice: 'Are you <u>sure</u> this is the right thing? You have made these shifts from Auckland so often, yet always you have come back … And Waihi? Are you sure it has so very much to offer?' He was concerned about Julia's secondary education and, 'At your time of life it is often difficult to begin all over again'. If they eventually decided to leave there, 'Waihi is a dying town … you would be lucky to get much of your money back or even to re-sell the property at all'. He hoped this would not be 'another fiasco … some idea scratched up on the spur of the moment'.[29]

Vi wrote back to say how upset she had been at receiving Maurice's letter and Gill tried to smooth things over, wife writing to mother about the behaviour of their boy. Gill wrote that, as Vi knew, 'He is liable to go off at the deep end now and then … he says all sorts of things on the spur of the moment he could cut out his tongue for afterwards'. Gill wrote that Maurice cared deeply for his family, worried when he did not hear from them, and the move to Waihi was a 'challenge to his mental security and his initial reaction is to fight against it … like a furious child protesting at some injustice and quite often he acts on this initial reaction. He is very like Pop [Frank] in so many ways.' She considered that Maurice's behaviour was 'something we have to accept in his make-up. I think really it is all this that gives him something that we haven't got and will never have and he has got terrific talent although he is still groping desperately with it.'

This letter more than any other reveals how thoroughly Gill had taken over his mothering from Vi Shadbolt; and hard-working Gill kept Maurice afloat in a time of physical stress, emotional volatility and the strains of everyday living. But now he was talking of going back to New Zealand and this had begun to stretch her endless patience. She was sure he could make a go of it in England but he needed to stop wasting his energy on such things as the state of the flat or whether he had the right clothes, 'everything in fact rather than getting down to tin tacks and waking up to the fact that we are in England and should make the best of it … It is a terribly trying time but we are getting over it.'[30]

The 'trying time' probably now included knowledge of Maurice's liaison with Jenny Bojilova. As she was writing to Vi and family in Auckland, Jenny in Sofia was becoming desperate to hear from him. 'I am terribly worried about you. How are you? Are you so very ill that you can't drop just a line? … Oh, Maurie, what is it?

'How shall I go on like this? This is a torture — a torture that seems to me endless, unless you come here and take care of me.'[31]

Maurice was discharged from hospital on 5 May, soon after he would have received this letter. So — would it be London, Wellington or Sofia? His first letter home after leaving hospital was full of the joys of spring that buried thoughts of returning to New Zealand: 'Bright gardens, astonishingly green trees, showers of falling blossoms; and the old, old buildings, the red pillar-boxes, the little pubs, and the mixed-up streets. England, for the first time, has come alive for me; and I love it.'[32]

But what to do about Jenny, about Gill? Maurice would later fudge the truth: 'My marriage was faltering. Late in the day, I tried to behave honourably, as people then did. I wrote to Jenny to say that I couldn't come; that I might be a liability to Bulgarian friends. I would certainly find it difficult to keep quiet in Eastern Europe about such events as the execution of Imre Nagy and Pal Maleter.

'Was this genuine? Though it sounded a serviceable excuse, it possibly was. A day or two after writing to Jenny I tried to get it down in a story.'[33]

The execution of the leaders of the 1956 Hungarian Revolution on 16 June could well have been the 'serviceable excuse' Maurice needed for breaking with Jenny. Her letters up to that time show she still hoped, wanted, to have him return, to go on holiday with her to the Black Sea coast. She had not been well herself, struggling with a stomach ulcer, although life had been enlivened by the books he sent her and later by the gift of book-ends that arrived from Vi in New Zealand. But Maurice's sporadic, ambiguous letters led her to write at the end of May: 'I wonder whether you still think of me as you did some time ago? I do not know. And if this is over for you, will you please let me know?'[34] In an earlier letter she had written, 'P.S. I would like to read the short story about Bulg[aria]. May I?'[35] Maurice had 'got down' his story soon after leaving hospital; but Jenny was kept in suspense.

'Thank You Goodbye' is one of the few stories that Maurice set outside New Zealand. With strong echoes of Ernest Hemingway's 'Hills Like White Elephants', it is equally short, equally deals with a couple at a point of departure both physically and emotionally and who, equally, are not named. But where Hemingway's locale is unspecifically Spanish, Maurice's is explicitly Sofia. His description of the girl is largely a description of Jenny: 'She was petite, lightly built, with smooth brown slender limbs and an expressive, delicately-boned Slavic face of dark complexion. Her hair was black and short cropped; she wore a light grey skirt and a black short-sleeved sweater with a thin white peasant motif woven about the neck.'

The New Zealander and the Bulgarian girl are having a last cognac before he must leave to catch a train, on a journey that will end in London; they have come to the café after making love for the last time. They argue about what is necessary and what is possible and the difficulties caused by the politics of the place. The man does not evince any flexibility, any strong desire to remain and he accuses her of becoming cold because she does not understand his position. She gives up and will not go with him to the station. She will pay the bill. After he has left, she finishes her drink and eats some peppers in oil. Earlier, the elderly waiter had proudly demonstrated his small store of English words to the man and, after he has left, he repeats them with satisfaction: "'How you do. I love you. Thank you goodbye'". A telling précis of the couple's time together and their separation.

'Thank You Goodbye'[36] is one of Maurice's stories that endures and, despite its debt to Hemingway, is drawn from felt experience. It does not reflect the romance by letter that continued for months between Maurice and Jenny Bojilova; it is a fiction after all. But the story does reflect the conclusion that Maurice had come to about their relationship. It was over for him but he could not bring himself to make the break until late June, after he had decided to take a recuperative holiday in Ibiza. Earlier, when he told her he was thinking of this, she exhorted him to somehow divert to Sofia on the way. She was still writing: 'Tell me … whether you still love me because I love you terribly and I need you now, as much as I never did before'.[37]

By this time, Gill was well aware of the *billets-doux* and he had confessed the brief affair in Sofia, prompting acrimony and what Maurice described as Gill's sexual jealousy. On 13 July,[38] Jenny wrote to Gill, not for the first time. She knew Gill would be 'astonished' but thought she should write and 'explain things once more' after she had received a 'terrific letter' from Maurice. 'He has decided to stay with you, because he loves you and you are his best friend and he has made you unhappy with this whole story of ours. This was a good, sane and fine letter. It made me glad and unhappy at the same time.' There had been letters sent and lost, misunderstood cables, so his letter was 'full of hard words'. But Jenny thought the break had to happen and she had told him not to come to Sofia: 'Don't you see how hopeless and dreadful his coming here would have been for me?' And 'What was between him and me was so hopeless and all'. She had written to Maurice, saying 'he must stay really with you, because you've proven your love to him … We've been just cruel with you and I know how much you've suffered …' Jenny ended, 'I do not know why, but I think of you as for a little girl. I feel myself much older'.

CHAPTER 13

A SMOKING RUIN

The break with Jenny had been made and the simmering discontent between Maurice and Gill was suppressed beneath the excitement of moving, in early June, from the grey surburbia of Ealing to a Tite Street flat in the 'arty' quarter of Chelsea. Oscar Wilde had lived a few doors up, Sargent and Whistler had painted across the road and Olivier and Leigh lived not far. It was a five-minute walk to busy King's Road and the Chelsea Potter pub. Although the flat was in a basement, dark and with no outlook, it had two large rooms and a kitchen (with bath) and was altogether in a much-improved locality for the aspiring author. A photo of the Hokianga on the mantelshelf and a Lee-Johnson drawing on the wall kept Maurice's heart in the right place. He still required two saline baths a day and Gill to change dressings for his operation wound. But they did not deter him from taking in New Zealand-England test cricket at Lord's and going on a CND march with Gill, Con Bollinger, writer David Ballantyne* and wife, and other expatriate New Zealanders.

Ibiza, long isolated from mainland Spain since the civil war, had attracted a small bohemian expat community. The cheap rural lifestyle allowed long stays on minimum funds; time to knock out the next *The Sun Also Rises* or to demonstrate radical colour techniques under the noonday glare. 'Most of those writing and painting on Ibiza that summer were discovering that they were not writers and painters.'[1] Although Jackson Pollock and Willem de Kooning discovered that they were and New Zealanders were among them. By the time

---

*David Ballantyne had published his novel *The Cunninghams* in the USA in 1948 but had difficulty placing his fiction subsequently. He had been in London since 1954 working as a journalist.

Maurice arrived in July 1958, Janet Frame had been and gone away pregnant, and Auckland painter Pat Hanly was in situ with wife Gil.* They were to keep close company there and over the years ahead.

Six weeks in the eternal Ibizan sun completed Maurice's convalescence and generated a tan and a new moustache that became a permanent feature. Maurice and Gill continued bickering and arguing via aerogrammes. He complained about the heat, the mosquitoes, the primitive plumbing and sewerage while Gill resented his absence and having to deal with the last pangs of the Jenny affair. He told her that her complaints and indecision about joining him were upsetting his writing: 'I'm just about ready to give up. How do you think you would feel, flung down in a strange place, trying desperately to get your life into gear, and getting from me the letters I've been receiving from you? … Do you think it would be conducive to any bloody thing except defeat and frustration?'

He then wrote: 'The last month before I left London, I imagined, perhaps foolishly, we were happy … I thought we might have got out of the forest into the light again. It seems I am wrong. I'm certainly still in the forest; like a wounded animal, with a spear twisting in my gut. I'm good for nothing: and perhaps I knew that a long, long time ago. If you want to book a passage home, as you say you felt like doing, then perhaps you'd better do it.'[2] Self dramatisation as the misunderstood victim of an artistic temperament seamed his letters. The tone swung from self-pity to self-justification to the shifting of responsibility: he exhorted Gill to write to Jenny, because 'it would be stupid and ridiculous for us to end that friendship, just because we had, the three of us, become involved in a situation that was too much for our emotions.'[3]

Before Gill joined him in his fishermen's quarter casa, using her fortnight of annual holidays, Maurice worked on a collection of stories that might amount to a publishable manuscript. The novel had been put aside, sections of it used as seeds for stories. In retrospect, he wrote: 'Trying to master my manuscript and counting my pounds, I puritanically kept my head down while others banged on in cafes about their destined place in literary history … After tea and an Ibizan pastry, I worked through the cool hours, lunched with the Hanlys, then took a siesta and swam.'[4] In the evenings he hobnobbed with wannabe US and UK writers and artists; although he was drawn more to the tales of an Italian partisan turned artist and the Republican songs of a guitarist who turned out to be a spy for the Franco régime.

Back in Tite Street by the end of August, Maurice continued working away at

---

*Frances Hodgkins had also stayed and painted there in the 1930s.

his collection. His six weeks of sun and sea had not only completed the healing of his operation wound. Maurice and Gill's Ibizan fortnight of swimming and love-making had at least changed the dressing on the wounds in their relationship. Gill, back in the NUS office, was surprised and gratified when she came home to find Maurice had often cleaned the flat and done the washing at the local launderette.

Friends from Ibiza or New Zealand passed through on their way to work or study, fame or oblivion; the Shadbolts went to the theatre, frequented pubs, joined protests, mined their journeys in travel articles for the *NZ Listener* and *Evening Post*. Maurice went to a socialist camp at Kessingland on the Suffolk coast and then told the folks back home he had decided to join the Labour Party to help stiffen its left wing; he also told them he was perfecting his Spanish and Russian.

In the middle of October, Maurice accepted the invitation of a Scots 'mariner friend', Alistair Couper, to stay with him in his home town of Aberdeen. Maurice had met Couper on Ibiza and was attracted to the idea of hiking with him before Couper began his studies as a marine geographer. Hill-walking in the highlands with a sympathetic friend might help clear his confusion, not only about what he should do with the manuscript, but also what he should do with his life and his domicile. Was he good enough to persist as a writer? Should he stay in Britain? He was entertained and stimulated by the theatre, the galleries, the pub dialectic, the depth of old culture. He even sometimes admired the landscape, if not the weather. But he knew he did not belong, that he could not turn himself into an English writer. All of this was entangled with continuing agonies about his relationship with Gill; they blew hot and cold; reconciliation was only skin deep.

Hill-walking and the cold North Sea easterlies promoted a kind of clarity in the form of a five-page typed letter to Gill, transcribed from a twelve-page handwritten draft. It was a brutal assault on their marriage and on his own worth in a sustained expression of self-loathing. It was an emotional battery to test Gill to the limits of her understanding and forgiveness; a cry, almost a scream, for help; an attempt to find some explanation, some justification, for his behaviour.

'I am going back now … England — and London — is death to me. I only wish I had finished my book before this final and total collapse.'[5] He did not know what to do but he was more likely to find the answers 'at home than here; among sights and sounds known and familiar. You might as well face it now — my emotional landscape is one vast, devastated, smoking ruin. I am entirely incapable of what you call love. It is no good running away from that fact ... I'm pretty damn sick, sicker than I've ever been, and I'm getting worse ... If only we could talk ... but communication is altogether impossible in that way, as we discovered.'

Maurice went on to question the 'artificial construct' of marriage: 'It is the human relationship that is important. I don't believe in marriage; I don't believe in love ... the most abused word in the language.'

Jenny Bojilova had been the catalyst. He told Gill that she 'persisted in forcing the image of Jenny into a cliché, that of a deceitful, dishonest woman'. She did not realise that the world was not entirely 'made up of Anglo-Saxons' and that elsewhere people 'think that barriers between people are artificial and do not matter'. But the 'cruel irony' of it all was that 'when I signed the letter which told Jenny I wouldn't come to Bulgaria to live, I also — unknowingly at the time — signed my way out of marriage'. He not only killed what had existed between him and Jenny, 'I also somehow killed our own relationship.'

Maurice continued, 'I no longer have the power or strength to give you happiness; nothing is more certain than that you will never find it with me. You must recognise that.' He expressed fear that Gill was making a prison for herself by 'trying to tie yourself to me absolutely'. He described his condition as a 'sickness of discontent which makes me incapable of building any enduring relationship'. Tellingly, he wrote that he was not sure he wanted to find a cure for this, 'to be a different person. I would much sooner go through life, for better or worse, knowing what I am, than not knowing.'

Maurice could not guarantee Gill there would not be another Jenny and then, as if to shock her into recognition, he revealed he had had another affair at Kessingland with a young Jewish woman whose own marriage was collapsing. He declared that this showed the 'sincerity of what I have been trying to tell you'. He was 'not a Jim Baxter who can toy with sincerity; nor are you a Jackie Baxter who can tolerate insincerity. The thought of another woman, or another man, is a terrible one: and that is what I am trying to save us from.'

Ever the martyr to his own inadequacies, he had decided that the 'best thing is for me to go home', that they should separate, because it was now too late 'to examine ourselves together'. And yet, and yet, after five pages and 3000 words, he concluded, 'One can only explain things up to a point; beyond that is intuition. And I have the intuition that, unless I do something soon and break the vicious circle that both of us are in, something terrible will happen to us ... try, darling, to understand'.

It is not known exactly how Gill replied to this letter except by Maurice's response to it. He was 'overcome by the fact of my having hurt you ... I feel as though I had sinned finally & unforgivably against some fundamental code of human existence … betrayed the hope & trust of another human being.'[6] Gill had written that he must hate her but he protested, 'I can't hate you. I feel helpless trying to wonder how you could think that.' He had now discovered, twice, that he could not leave her for another woman but now he has to leave her, for her own good: 'I can't go on shredding your emotions and dessicating your life'.

Gill wrote two more 'wonderful letters'[7] in response to this. He replied, 'You observe many things perceptively and penetratingly … but then you know me too well not to be shrewd in your observations'. Gill had probably recognised much of Maurice's first letter as having some equivalence to his fear of dying on the operating table, his cyclic bouts of depression and a cry for maternal reassurance.

Maurice decided he would not reply to all she had written; that could wait until his return to London. His second five-page letter focused partly on his writing but mostly on the nature of his relationship with the Kessingland 'girl', Pam. Whether wittingly or not, he used the age-old argument that she, Jenny and Gill were all of the type he was attracted to; that Gill would really like Pam and maybe he should invite her round to the flat, although he could not promise 'I will not be a lover to her again'. Did Gill not understand the reality that he had been able to love both Jenny and her at the same time but social convention did not allow for that, and this engendered dishonesty all round; because no matter what happened with other women, 'it in no way alters my affection or attachment to you'. That is, he wished to have his emotional and sexual cake and eat it, too.

Writing to the Shadbolts in Waihi, Gill revealed none of the drama, although she said that Maurice had been on the verge of going home rather than face another smoggy English winter. They were staying put for the time being, but would definitely be on their way back before the end of 1959. She was sick of the NUS job, it did not pay enough to properly support them both, and she was applying for a variety of new positions. Both of them would like to find work in Europe, especially Yugoslavia, because they enjoyed the Slav character and culture. In the meantime, Maurice was typing out the last pages of his story collection and needed to get it bound properly before he sent it off to a publisher in the new year. She painted scenes of domestic harmony. Maurice's letters home were similarly bland and positive. Behind the facade, they had patched things up. Gill, John Kasmin's 'docile, placid sort of lady … a sweetie', had again given Maurice the understanding, the comfort and support he craved and demanded. For a time, at least, they were again a couple and not an incipient threesome.

In Aberdeen, Alistair Couper had taken Maurice to dinner with Jean Cockburn, a lifelong Communist who had been married to Claud Cockburn, editor of the Soviet-funded *The Week* in the 1930s. During table talk, Cockburn referred to writers she had got to know as a consequence, including W.H. Auden and Christopher Isherwood.* When she learned of Maurice's hopes as a writer and his languishing manuscript of stories, she encouraged him to try them with Victor Gollancz, well-known for the publication of socialist literature in Left Book Club editions. She said, 'Victor has an eye for fresh writing. He might be the answer to your prayers.'[8]

This meeting and Gill's 'wonderful letters' stirred him to write back to her with more confidence about his writing. Of the fifteen stories he had put together for his collection, he knew 'damn well' that 'they are better, more real more important than almost everything else written in my country: with one or two things of Duggan's perhaps excepted'.[9] He would not say this to anyone else, and also acknowledged his debt to others, like Frank Sargeson: 'They made the garden; I grew in it'. He considered that, if he had written nothing else, some of the collected stories, such as 'End of Season' and 'After the Depression',[10] 'would justify the agony that produced them'. He admitted he had a long way to go, was full of self doubt, but had 'scented the rarefied air that the great ones breathed'. He did not want to compare himself to James Joyce and his own short story collection to *The Dubliners*; but there was a 'surface similarity in that I am a regional writer, too — my book could be called, quite easily and with truth "The New Zealanders"'. If Maurice was aware of his shortcomings as a writer, he also believed he was working towards greatness. As Kevin Ireland had witnessed nearly three years before, 'He had decided already that he would become a major writer'.[11]

Apart from preparing his story collection, Maurice had become engaged in commenting on Boris Pasternak's *Dr Zhivago*. At the end of October, Pasternak had been awarded the Nobel Prize for Literature and Stephen Murray-Smith, editor of the Australian left-wing periodical *Overland*, asked Maurice to write a commentary on the novel, thinking he would receive a piece similar to Maurice's broad-ranging *Landfall* article on literature in the Soviet Union and Bulgaria. But the furore over the novel had set off international debate on the role of the artist and their responsibility and commitment to the nature of truth and reality in the polarised world of the Cold War. The violent Stalinist-style attacks on

---

*Maurice did not realise until much later than she was Jean Ross, the cabaret singer in Berlin who had inspired the character of Sally Bowles, the heroine of Isherwood's novel *Goodbye to Berlin* and the musical *Cabaret*.

Pasternak from the Soviet literary establishment, as well as their international camp followers, and the cooked-up political campaign to have him driven from the country,* prompted Maurice to write in his defence. Pasternak, he wrote, 'is not a Communist; not strictly a Marxist ... not a social realist. He is a humanist, imaginatively tied to the best in the socialist tradition; a Russian, as passages in "Doctor Zhivago" so movingly reveal, who loves his country and his people and feels for them in suffering and triumph.'[12] The article proved a problem for Murray-Smith because *Overland* was heavily subvened by the Australian Communist Party and its associated bookshops and he was only able to publish it the following March by including a counter argument by the 75-year-old literary doyenne and founding member of the ACP, Katharine Susannah Prichard. She needed 'no introduction' but Maurice was described as an 'NZ Literary Fund Fellow now working in London'. Prichard took the current anti-Pasternak Soviet line but Maurice proved to be firmly on the side of history.**

Christmas 1958 was again roast lamb with all the trimmings plus a fruit cake sent by mother Vi and iced by Maurice. Gill was grateful for gift money which would keep her 'stocked up with undies' and Maurice was delighted with his new Kaiapoi woollen shirt, just days after he had put an elbow through the sleeve of his old one. They shared Christmas dinner with New Zealand and Indian friends but, on Boxing Day, Karl and Kay Stead came over from Kensington and they all went to the Ballantynes in South London.

Until early December, Stead had been at the University of Bristol working on his doctoral thesis which later yielded his seminal academic work, *The New Poetic*, a study of modernist poetry. After their move to London, the two couples became close, visiting each others' flats for dinner, going to galleries and plays together. Although Maurice knew Stead was the author of the 'K of Henderson' letter, with its denigration of his first published story, neither of them wished to reveal their unpleasant little secrets. Stead continued to be ambivalent about the literary quality of Maurice's writing. Nevertheless, Stead

---

*Nikita Kruschev dictated a speech for the head of the Young Communist League which included the statement that Pasternak 'went and spat in the face of the people' and 'If you compare Pasternak to a pig, a pig would not do what he did ... shits where it eats'.
**Boris Pasternak was forced to decline the Nobel Prize, expelled from the Soviet Writers' Union and moves were made to have him exiled. Top level international intervention saved him from imprisonment, but the stress of persecution contributed to his death only two years later. The persecution of Pasternak was driven partly because the KGB discovered that the CIA was buying huge quantities of each new edition of *Dr Zhivago* and distributing them far and wide as an anti-Soviet propaganda tool. The CIA sponsored the first Russian language edition.

wrote to Sargeson: '"You'll laugh at this but I really like Shadbolt, we get on really well"'. Stead was to liken it to a 'love affair with us seeing each other … two or three times a week'. Although they got on well, they also 'clashed terribly, we disagreed on virtually everything and we got very passionate arguing … I liked being with him, but also I found him maddening and obviously he found me maddening'.[13] When Maurice wrote to Charles Brasch about his times with Stead, Brasch replied, 'It intrigues me to think of you and Karl Stead planning the future as my friends and I did twenty-five years ago at our flat on Primrose Hill … all power to you both!'.[14]

CHAPTER 14

LONDON GLOWED

Early in the new year of 1959, Maurice made two firm decisions: to send off his manuscript to Gollancz and apply for the new Robert Burns Fellowship at the University of Otago. Charles Brasch had written to Maurice about this in December, an indication that he thought him a likely candidate.* But Brasch had written to him again in January with a pitiless critique of 'The Waters of the Moon', a story he had submitted for *Landfall* and which he had included in 'The New Zealanders'. Brasch began by saying that the opening section 'seems to me rather badly over-written, keyed altogether too high, even bordering on the hysterical, here and there, in the descriptive passages … In general, it seems to me, there's rather too much violence in the language.'[1] Brasch's editorial guidance had been crucial to the successful completion of Maurice's earlier *Landfall* stories and his general development as a writer. Brasch's trenchant comments must have deepened Maurice's doubt about the chances of being accepted by Gollancz.

Just before he sent off the manuscript in February, Maurice showed it to Karl Stead for his comments. Perhaps, perversely, he was now challenging his judgement. The seven pages of Stead's notes[2] reveal a conscientious reading of the 350-page manuscript; but a comparison of his suggested corrections with the published work show that Maurice took heed of only a few. Stead's suggestion of replacing the phrases 'might of' and 'could of' with 'might've' and

---

*This literary fellowship had been established with an endowment from a group of Dunedin benefactors, of whom Brasch was the most prominent, and allowed for a writer to work unhindered for a year on a lecturer's salary. The Burns Fellowship, after 60 years, remains the most secure and richest literary fellowship in New Zealand. Even now, the actual identity of the benefactors and the original endowment sums involved remain confidential.

'could've' in 'After the Depression' indicate that he did not have Maurice's ear for the appropriate vernacular. 'After the Depression' and 'Thank you goodbye' are the only stories that Stead gave the higher pass mark of 'Good' and they remain 'Good' today.

'After the Depression' is the narrative of a man trudging the road in search of work in the 1930s, dragging wife and child behind him, and being turned away because of his Communist sympathies, his reputation as a propagandist preceding him like a malevolent ghost. 'You're the Morrison,' the mine manager says, 'who was gaoled for sedition three years ago, aren't you … everywhere you've been there seems to have been trouble.'[3] Turned down for work yet again, Morrison and his wife wait for the miners to come up from their shift to hand out leaflets: 'Get the truth, comrades'. Some turn away, some take the leaflets to crumple them up but 'One or two stopped to talk briefly with the gaunt man in black; one pressed money into his hand. And then they were gone, all of them, into their square ugly homes …'[4] The family walks back down the road into the darkness and the boy asks '"Why Daddy taking us?"' The man picks up the tired '"Poor kid."' and the story ends with, '"Why?" the child said, stubbornly'.[5] This last line carries the harrowing resonance of all that has gone before, underscoring what was to become the archetypal New Zealand story of the bleak 1930s.

'After the Depression' owes its authenticity to Maurice's deep-felt rendering of his father's and uncles' experience, especially that of Uncle Joe. It was both a memorial and an expression of gratitude that was to be repeated in his later fiction; for both Bill Morrison as Bill Freeman, and his son Ian, were to appear in the novel *Strangers and Journeys* a dozen years later; they had almost certainly been drawn from the nascent form of this novel that Maurice had been struggling with over the previous year.

Jean Cockburn had told him, 'Most good writing is local' and that 'some localities are more fashionable than others' to which Maurice had supposedly replied, 'New Zealand's day hasn't come'.[6] Yet the previous eighteen months had seen the publication of a clutch of novels that marked a coming of age for New Zealand fiction. Janet Frame's *Owls Do Cry*, Ian Cross's *The God Boy* and Sylvia Ashton-Warner's *Spinster* had all been published since Maurice and Gill left New Zealand and were achieving international publication. New Zealand's own 'regional' experience was being heard. Maurice's absence from the country may partially explain his failure to refer to these novels; but both he and Gill were in regular touch with New Zealand writers and publications and must have read reviews if not the books themselves. In January 1959, Gill told the family that they had both just read Keith Sinclair's new book,

A History of New Zealand. Perhaps Maurice felt overawed, even threatened, by the success of those novels and, after Brasch's letter, doubtful that his own ambitions would be realised.

On the Saturday morning of 7 March Maurice received a letter from Gollancz. Certain it was a rejection, he took his time opening it. When he did, he read, 'Dear Mr. Shadbolt, We are delighted with THE NEW ZEALANDERS and would very much like to publish it. It is a long time since we've come across stories of this quality.'[7] The letter was from Victor Gollancz's nephew, Hilary Rubinstein, a director of the company, who went on to say that the collection was 'rather on the long side' and some stories would have to be dropped. He suggested an advance of £75* against a royalty of 10 per cent on the first 2500 copies with an escalation rate thereafter. He apologised for the small advance, 'but the truth is that short stories sell notoriously less well than full-length novels'.

Shock, disbelief, doubt, euphoria, all of this would have run through him and Gill as he read out the letter to convince himself it was true. A young painter friend, Dennis Chesworth, ran off to buy champagne and, later, Maurice walked with him down the Chelsea Embankment to recruit friends for a party at the World's End pub: 'Each paving stone seemed remarkable and distinct in itself; London glowed. If I remember my delight precisely, it is because I will never know it again.'[8] He was exploding to share the news: he sent a cable to the family in Waihi; he rang everyone he knew, despite the sudden panic that maybe it was all a mistake. Almost everyone was glad for him, save those for whom his success merely underlined their own failure. Karl Stead only revealed his true feelings in a letter to Frank Sargeson who replied that Stead was just jealous of Maurice's success and the two would never get on because Stead was a poet and Shadbolt a journalist. Stead wrote back, 'You are right about Maurice. Also no doubt there was a fair whack of jealousy in my bitchiness. After all he has had the courage to sit in Chelsea writing his own work while I have been preparing for my future by engaging in an elaborate piece of critical hackwork.'[9]

The one person with whom Maurice most wanted to share the news was beyond the reach of a cable or phone call. Kevin Ireland's mother had written to say that, in the wake of an unhappy love affair, he had disappeared in the direction of the Australian outback.

In his letter of acceptance, Hilary Rubinstein wrote that Gollancz would like to drop both 'End of Season' and 'Night of the Chariot'. He thought the former too drawn out and a 'bit sentimental' and the latter 'less effective than

---

*Worth about £1300 today.

the rest'. A week later, he apologised for his miscalculation, but another story or two would have to go to make the book an economic proposition. Although he would have been sad to drop 'End of Season', Maurice did not argue and also took out 'Twosome' and a story titled 'Sing Again Tomorrow'. The book's title was not queried and the subtitle to *The New Zealanders*, 'A Sequence of Stories', signalled the grouping of the final eleven stories into three discrete sections. Maurice drew the titles for these from an epigraph taken from his mentor James K. Baxter's poem 'Homage to Lost Friends'.

> Cloud riders, companion
> Shakers of morning all,
> Rope coiled on saddle horn
> At the sun's funeral,
> Sleep in the blind canyon
> Of a dream's rock …
>
> Wave walkers, at the edge
> Of dark …

The first section, 'Wave Walkers', included four stories from his parents' generation, and touching on his own childhood; the three in 'Cloud Riders' portrayed the young in the urban world of 1950s New Zealand; and four 'In the Blind Canyon' were redolent of the ex-pat New Zealander at large. Only 'After the Depression' ('Wave Walkers') and 'Play the Fife Lowly' ('Cloud Riders') had been published before; but the collection included stories he had been working on over two or three years — such as 'The Strangers'('Wave Walkers') — as well as more recent writing such as 'Thank you goodbye'('In the Blind Canyon').

'The Strangers' joins those other three stories as one that has weathered the years best. A hard-working widowed farmer struggles to keep his farm going and bring up a sensitive son to whom he does not feel close. He takes on an itinerant Maori farmhand who does a good job and also takes the son fishing, showing him ways of living in the bush that do not accord with his father's puritan ethic. The father wants to keep the farmhand on but the Maori tells the boy he has still has 'lots of things I want to do. Like a bit of shooting. I need a good new rifle,' and he is working for the money he needs. The boy wonders if 'he might stay long enough for me to leave school and go away with him. But then I thought of Father lonely by himself on the farm: and I didn't know.'[10] When he has earned enough, the Maori announces he is leaving. The farmer is uncomprehending; surely he wanted to keep his job and all that money he had been saving was so he could get married. 'There were the two of them there, neither understanding the other, and I stood between, only knowing that of all the strange and terrible things in life the strangest and most terrible was that of two people not understanding each other.'[11]

The story drew directly on Maurice's youthful years in Te Kuiti and was an affecting portrayal of the incomprehension that figured the conflicting worlds of Maori and pakeha, 'The Strangers' to each other. Father and son were named Ned and Tim Livingstone. Like Bill Morrison and son Ian in 'After the Depression', they were nascent characters for *Strangers and Journeys*.

Maurice withdrew 'Waters of the Moon' from *Landfall* because he could not accept Brasch's criticisms. He did, nevertheless, revise this story for *The New Zealanders* in accordance with his suggestions. Brasch had also commented on the book: 'May I say I am not altogether happy about its title; but I think it will be criticized for that, as sounding rather exclusive, or prescriptive.'[12] Brasch saw the trouble in store but Maurice, riding his wave, replied, 'I doubt if Henry James' titles ('The American' 'The Bostonians' 'The Europeans' etc) were ever criticised for sounding exclusive or prescriptive; but, on the other hand, we do have a national thin skin; and some of our vast army of illiterates, academics and journalists alike, do have the habit of ignoring the contents of a book. Anyway, everyone who's seen it thinks its a fine title, for the kind of book it is; so I'm not terribly worried.'[13]

In the same letter, Brasch also turned down Maurice's latest story which he thought should be titled 'The Negative New Zealander'. Although it was an 'interesting picture of the man who never acts, but only reacts ... typical of some NZers', this character had been described before and Maurice had not explored the inner man.

Maurice wrote to Karl Stead, saying he was withdrawing this story, too: 'I've a feeling it probably means the end of my fiction in LF'. This also meant he might publish very little new work again, because most of his stories were too long for other magazines. 'Who cares, anyway? Certainly I'm not going to endure all this cross-examination again.'[14]

Maurice's rejection of Brasch, his mentor, in the hubris of his success was ungrateful, especially when Brasch had been among the first to congratulate him on his acceptance by Gollancz: 'Well, your journey has been a success. I'm really delighted.'[15] But what would stuffy old Charles Brasch know when, Gill told the family, the blurb on *The New Zealanders* dust jacket declared that the book 'will undoubtedly be acclaimed on both sides of the globe; that he is a born writer and that he will ... prove to be one of the most important writers of our time.'[16] Gill said these comments nearly made Maurice 'crawl under the table' but 'You should be very proud of your son'.

Maurice had dedicated the book to Gill, acknowledging her unflinching support for his work and wellbeing over the previous six years. In the flush of success it was also, perhaps, a sign that, despite the immense stresses on their relationship during 1958, they had made it through. In the months to come, as good news followed good news, as Maurice began to earn and financial pressures eased, there is no evidence of conflict between them, of intimate distractions to upset their life as a couple. They took part together in the second anti-nuclear march at Easter 1959, when they were among the fifteen thousand who walked the fifty miles from the Atomic Weapons Establishment in Berkshire's Aldermaston to central London.

Gill continued to impress in her own work. She organised a student journalists conference in Hull, incorporating a *Daily Mirror* award, which prompted accolades from NUS management; and had an article accepted by *Woman's Own*, the leading women's magazine of the time. Later, an article on the Hokianga appeared in the hallowed pages of *The Times*. But in letters to Waihi the emphasis remained on what Maurice was doing, including the play that he was trying hard, and ultimately failed, to place with Joan Littlewood's Theatre Royal or the Royal Court.

Later in the year, they worked together to collect 2000 signatures for a petition protesting the exclusion of Maori from the All Black team to tour South Africa in 1960. 'You've no idea what a terrible effect this decision is having outside NZ', he told his mother.[17] To Stead he wrote, 'So the All Blacks are to be All White ... I thought for a while of chucking a brick through the window of NZ House.'[18] The *New Statesman* of 11 July included a letter 'Apartheid in Sport' over the signatures of Conrad Bollinger, David Ballantyne, Wellington poet John Boyd, Maurice and Kevin Ireland, 'isolated New Zealand writers in London'. They deplored the exclusion of Maori as well as Prime Minister Walter Nash's pusillanimous attitude and exhorted people to send cables and letters of protest. But real change would have to wait for the end of the apartheid régime itself.

The proofs for *The New Zealanders* arrived at the end of April. After he had corrected and revised these, Maurice went north to stay with Denis Chesworth near Manchester. Together they walked in the Peak District, visited Brontë country and later Wordsworth's Grasmere in the Lake District. On return, he was in time to catch film-maker John Feeney on his way from Canada to Russia and then, without any warning, Kevin Ireland turned up on the Tite Street doorstep. He had travelled from Australia in a 'rust bucket' of a ship that broke down in the Red Sea and ran out of beer, causing some Australians on board to become violent, one of whom 'clocked' him for no reason.[19] At last, Maurice could share his good news with the friend who meant most to him, the 'literary shoulder' he most wished to lean on.

All the while he had been away, Maurice would have recalled some of the sentiments in a letter Ireland had written to him not long before he left New Zealand. Despite the arguments and tensions that had arisen between them over the doomed 'Chapter and Verse' project, Ireland had praised Maurice's writing, saying that he was 'breaking in new lands for the mind of man to inhabit'. Further, 'I accept the fact that our friendship is beyond words, and … that we deserve each other by some depraved trick of fate'. He ended the letter: 'So much for these words — what's important is that I should tell you of my love for yourself and Gill'.[20]

Ireland bolstered Maurice's ego by saying *The New Zealanders* would be a 'surefire success' but, more bluntly than Charles Brasch, told him the title 'is going to piss people off'. But Maurice was 'totally oblivious that it was going to be a red rag to a lot of people, as if he was the person who was going to define the national character'.[21]

Maurice insisted that Ireland not only stay until he had found work and a place for himself, but also that now was the time for him to complete his own first collection, of poems. While Maurice worked in the basement bedroom, Ireland used the cover on the bath for a desk. Maurice had him 'working week after week there until I got all the manuscripts together to rough out a book. I'll always thank Maurice for that.'[22]

John Kasmin 'materialised benevolently in our lives again. First he found Kevin a job as a handyman in Soho's lively Gallery One. Then he took us to parties and gallery openings to demonstrate that his police-ridden past was behind him …'[23] * 'Kas' had arrived back in London after being 'rescued' from a 'bohemian' life in France by Jane Nicholson, the niece of leading British painter Ben Nicholson. Kas wanted to marry her but her mother strongly disapproved of 'this bohemian Soho denizen with loose behaviour and curious ambition'.[24] Kas recruited Maurice, the new London writing star, as one of his two 'relatively honourable references' to help persuade Mrs Nicholson. Maurice met her several times in Bloomsbury restaurants. A 'woman of much charm', Mrs Nicholson paid most of the bills, and 'She was not averse to being courted'.[25] 'She took a shine to him', Kas recalled and Maurice's 'very winning way with ladies'[26] did the trick. Jane was soon Mrs Kasmin.

*Kasmin went on to open his own gallery in the 1960s, tripled Francis Bacon's worth, discovered David Hockney and promoted Anthony Caro and Frank Stella.

CHAPTER 15

DEPARTURES

Armed with a commission to write a report for the *Times Educational Supplement*, Maurice set off for the Seventh World Youth Festival, held in Vienna from 26 July to 4 August. Despite the commission, and the boosting news that Victor Gollancz had just sold 'The Strangers' to the *New Yorker*, Maurice panicked about not having enough money for the trip. 'He is so frightened that he might run short!'[1] Gill reported because, although his post-Vienna plans were loose, they might include Yugoslavia and certainly Bulgaria: Vasil Popov had pressed him to return to Sofia after the festival and Maurice had pressed Kevin Ireland to join him there.

There were both physical and ideological clashes at the successor festival to Moscow's 1957 event. Democratic 'Westerners found themselves shouting into a sour void. The Chinese were preoccupied with the perfidy of the Russians. The Russians were being made miserable by prickly Poles' and at a literary seminar 'Soviet apologists presented the case against *Dr Zhivago*'.[2] Maurice could not let this pass. Not long before leaving for Vienna, he had received a letter from *Overland* editor Steven Murray-Smith, telling of the far-reaching fallout from Maurice's Zhivago article in the March issue. It had 'touched off one of the most virulent and unprincipled attacks on an individual (in this case me) that I have ever seen in any press' — the Australian Communist press, that is. 'Unpleasant while it lasted but educational for all.' Murray-Smith said he had 'stuck firmly to my guns'[3] and now Maurice had to stick to his. He stood up and asked the Soviet delegation if they were really writers and, if so, how could they approve of Pasternak being hounded and *Dr Zhivago* being banned. This was 'helpfully melodramatic'[4] and cleared the way for a more considered attack from the Americans.

Afterwards, he was invited to Poland by Jerzy Szkup, a translator engaged in a doctoral thesis on Katherine Mansfield. Spending time with Maurice was a rare opportunity to talk with a New Zealand writer. Szkup took Maurice to Poznan, Auschwitz and Warsaw where he told of his experience as a twelve year-old when Soviet forces outside the city left its citizens to their fate when they rose against their Nazi occupiers and were then destroyed.

Maurice wrote in *One of Ben's* that two experiences in Poland provoked his sense of identity as a New Zealander. In a Poznan war cemetery, among thousands of Red Army graves, he saw a cluster of headstones marked by the silver fern. He had no idea who these fallen men were but, 'All that mattered was that they were dust of my tribe; clay of my clan.'[5] Later, Szkup told him that he had not taken the opportunity to defect to the West on visits to England and France, 'Because I am Warsaw ... Warsaw is me'. For Maurice, London and Europe remained seductive; he was thinking of soon spending six months in Spain to write. There was *The New Zealanders* to promote and follow up and publication had been delayed until the autumn by a printers' strike. But then ...

Maurice stayed in Poland for a fortnight and then endured a gruelling train journey through Czechoslovakia and Hungary to Belgrade. Here he discovered that his Bulgarian visa had expired. At the Bulgarian embassy he found French and Americans had been waiting days for visas and he despaired of catching his onward train. Then he was taken in hand by an Italian who had grown up in Sofia and who made some kind of deal with the embassy officials who produced visas for them both. Then he persuaded Maurice to forget the train and go to Sofia in his 1935 Ford, which was loaded to the gunwales with suitcases and bags. 'Fred' was carrying contraband American cigarettes, nylons, instant coffee and other goodies in demand on the Bulgarian black market. Maurice was more worried about the contraband books *he* was carrying: *Animal Farm*, *Darkness at Noon* and, of course, *Dr Zhivago*. 'Fred' tactically chose to cross the frontier in the middle of the night when the guards were sleepy and disposed to be distracted by free packets of cigarettes. They examined everything except the baggage and in the early hours 'Fred' tipped his treasures on to the floor of his brother's flat in Sofia. Later, Vasil Popov began hiding Maurice's gifts of forbidden books.

Kevin Ireland arrived by train soon afterwards and brought news from Gill: 'K says I'm likely to be a Daddy, well, well, well — this is news indeed. Really I take the news so calmly; I'm surprised at myself.'[6] He might well have been, given his thoughts on the matter of children in his Aberdeen crisis letter. Children, he had written, 'are altogether out of the question. It is hardly even worth discussing ... How, in this state of mind, could I go through with it?'[7]

Gill had begun to broach the question of having children after Maurice left Hammersmith Hospital. Her biological clock had begun ticking, even louder when she turned thirty on 21 April.* The questions of having children and going home became intertwined and increasingly influenced their thinking. Maurice told the family that, on her birthday, they planned on returning to New Zealand by the end of the year but, as late as September, Gill told them the delay in publication of *The New Zealanders* might mean them staying in London another year. By the time of her birthday, their relationship had also become strong enough for them to begin trying for a child. Around the time she first suspected she was pregnant, Gill wrote, 'Somehow life doesn't seem to be worth living when you haven't got the main reason for living it around, even if he is bad tempered and inclined to live in a dream world at times.'[8] On receiving the good news in Sofia, Maurice reassured her, 'Don't worry, darling; all is fine,'[9] knowing that, inevitably, she knew he would be seeing Jenny Bojilova again.

Maurice met her in the same café where they had parted nearly a year before, the setting for 'Thank you goodbye'. 'Lunch was quiet and introspective. We didn't dwell on the details of our fiasco. They were in the story.'[10] Jenny had moved on, knowing that, realistically, Maurice could not have lived in Bulgaria and it was unlikely she could have lived in New Zealand. She was about to 'share her life' with Nikolai Haytov, a prominent novelist, and with whom she was to remain married until his death in 2002. Kevin Ireland observed that Vasil Popov and others who had befriended Maurice on his first visit, and tried to find him work for his anticipated return to Jenny, were distinctly cool towards him: he carried the odour of betrayal.

Maurice took Ireland around Sofia to show him the sights. Along the Russian Boulevard, Maurice waved to acquaintances in a café who invited them in for coffee. 'Among them was a woman called Donna Marinova, who could have been a double for the actress Ingrid Bergman.' Ireland asked who she was, Maurice asked why, and Ireland replied, '"I'm in love with her"'. Maurice was distraught: '"Don't you think we've already had enough international poetic near-disasters without you starting one of your own?"' Ireland said, '"I can't help it … I'm going to marry her"'. He proposed and, 'She was so astonished she keeled over with some sort of cramp and had to be taken to hospital'.[11] Despite him having no Bulgarian and only bad French — Marinova's second language — they were married a few weeks later.

Perhaps Ireland's quixotic proposal was a consequence of having drunk too much slivovitz during the 'poetic near-disaster' of the evening before. Maurice

---

*Only about a quarter of women at that time had their first child after the age of 30.

and he had both been at a literary dinner for the cantankerous Scots socialist poet Hugh McDiarmid who was on an east European tour to mark the 200th anniversary of Robbie Burns's birth. McDiarmid had been commissioned to translate the work of nineteenth century Bulgarian poet and hero Hristo Botev, in order to secure him a 'place in the pantheon of the world's best poets'.[12] At the dinner McDiarmid, half drunk, announced that Botev's work was 'sub-Byronic' and banal. This caused Vasil Popov, sitting between Maurice and Ireland, to turn puce. When an official asked if he would, nevertheless, fulfil his commission, McDiarmid declared he was 'too old to waste his time on rubbish', whereupon Popov stood up and announced that he had both insulted a great poet and the hero of the nation and would now knock his block off. Maurice and Kevin rose together and pinned Popov between them while Ireland raised his glass to propose a toast to Bulgarian and Scottish friendship. Following this, McDiarmid shouted that, just in case anyone had missed his meaning, Botev's poetry was crap. Immediately, Ireland rose again and proposed a toast to the friendship of the peoples of New Zealand and Bulgaria and then he and Maurice grabbed Popov and propelled him through the door. Botev's poetry did get translated into good English, by Ireland himself when he found work in Sofia after his marriage as a 'translation polisher' in a state publishing house.

Maurice began his journey back to London in mid-September, using the return segment of Ireland's train ticket. He told Jenny he had dedicated to her the last story in *The New Zealanders*, one whose characters would resonate between them,[13] and then said thank you and goodbye forever. Maurice also said goodbye to Ireland for, not just a couple of years this time, but for more than a decade. Ireland later wrote: '... he then remembered more than fifteen years ago an express train hauling Shadders out of Sofia station — leaving him abandoned to private ridicule and conflict'.[14]

Maurice wrote to him: 'I fear already we may have said the great farewell of our lives'. In London, increasingly anxious, Maurice packed up Ireland's belongings and sent them off to Sofia: 'More & more I wonder if you're doing the right thing. Are you, for Christ's sake? ... Is your poetry worth a woman? ... Is Donka [sic] really ... the kind of girl who will share the life you want to lead? Do you really think so? This is one question you must face before it is too late.'[15] But neither was any good at taking the advice of the other in matters of the heart or gonads.

In Tite Street Maurice found Gill's pregnancy confirmed, the baby due in late April, and *The New Zealanders* due on 26 October. He was on a high: 'Life seems so very wonderful & good just now ... Gill is looking very beautiful. I'm so happy about everything.'[16] Apart from the baby and the book, a cheque worth the huge sum of £325* had arrived from the *New Yorker* for 'The Strangers'. With this in hand, Maurice and Gill could make the firm decision to sail home. Although booking at fairly short notice, they managed to find berths on the Orient Line's SS *Oronsay*, sailing from Tilbury on 26/27 November. Their last two months in England would be a whirl.

Gollancz had sent out proof copies of *The New Zealanders* to garner pre-publication promotion and copy for the cover blurb. Shelagh Delaney, whose play *A Taste of Honey* was a current hit in the West End, wrote that Maurice had 'peopled New Zealand — for me a hitherto uninhabited country — with characters at once alive and kicking, sensitive and suffering'.[17] The Shadbolts came to know well the twenty-year-old working class playwright from Salford, partying with her and attending her twenty-first when they asked her to be their first child's godmother: 'It's the best birthday present I've had. Although we have known each other such a short time you must indulge me while I shed a few tears at your departure.'[18] Towards the other end of the age spectrum, 54-year-old distinguished novelist and biographer Elizabeth Jenkins wrote that she had never read modern short stories that had impressed her more. They told of 'men and women we know, in a life we don't know ... haunting, like a glimpse of another world.'[19] Immediately on his return, Maurice was interviewed for *The Bookman* which also planned to print one of his stories; and he was told that *The New Zealanders* was to be a Book Society recommendation.

The book was published in New Zealand three weeks before the London launch. This may have been the prompt for Maurice to write his first letter to Frank Sargeson since he left New Zealand. Maurice wrote that the immediate purpose of his letter was to let Sargeson know of Kevin Ireland's marriage in Bulgaria. But this served as a friendly prelude to telling Sargeson about the London critical interest in *The New Zealanders*, its possible translation into German and French and the fat fee he had received from the *New Yorker*.[20] For Sargeson, who had struggled for decades to have his own work published widely overseas, let alone earn good money, Maurice's letter would have provoked an almost unreasonable envy.

James K. Baxter wrote from Wellington a few days after the book's appearance. He took it as a 'genuine honour' that Maurice had used his poem for an epigraph. He found 'great delicacy' in the book and 'force as well: a vigorous

---

*Worth about £6000 today. Hilary Rubinstein wrote to MS saying that, although it may not have been clear, under the terms of the contract, Gollancz was due 10% of this, especially since Gollancz himself had sold the story to the *New Yorker*. Generously, he did not ask for reimbursement but would expect 10% on any other of the stories sold.

outpouring of the interior life. You have managed to piss higher over the wall than any of the other boys. It takes some generosity of spirit to make a good writer, an ability to see through the moral categories for the sake of something better, and I think you've brought it off.' In several of the stories Maurice saw 'things so well from a woman's point of view'.[21]

The New Zealanders had been published in New Zealand under the imprint of Whitcombe & Tombs, Christchurch publisher and the main chain bookshop. The book sold out within a couple of weeks and Maurice discovered to his horror that they had imported only 500 copies. An independent bookseller told him he could have sold 150 himself but Whitcombe's controlled the supply. Just as reviews began to appear, none were for sale. Maurice wrote to the London manager for Whitcombe's, fuming at their incompetence: 'I can only regard the fresh orders of the book (200, 50, 137) as jokes in bad taste.'[22] He promised to complain to Gollancz and PEN New Zealand. To no effect: Whitcombe's lack of faith in New Zealand fiction was generational.

On Monday morning, 26 October, Maurice walked up to the King's Road and saw in the bookshops that, 'No longer a collection of coffee-flecked pages, *The New Zealanders* was now magically virginal in yellow jacket … Rites of passage were past: I was a neophyte in the largely reclusive calling of letters.'[23]

Reviews seemed painfully slow in appearing. Doubts set in: would these be any good, would the book sell, would they really have enough money to go home? Gill reported that she was having terrible trouble persuading Maurice to buy a new (first) suit and a sports jacket. To distract himself from the fate of *The New Zealanders*, he began writing new stories. But he became 'very tense and nervy' from working too hard on these. This was exacerbated by too many late nights out with friends like the Bollingers and Ballantynes, catching up with theatre, even attending their first concert at the Royal Festival Hall. Then there was the pressure of packing, of the 'rooting up of our home once again'. Gill enjoined his parents not to talk to Maurice about '"security" he doesn't want anyone to talk about his responsibilities and the need for security. He is terribly touchy about it.'[24]

Maurice was reassured by a night out with the *Express* newspapers' books editor Robert Pitman,[25] and *The Outsider* author, Colin Wilson, which resulted in Maurice being the subject one of Pitman's *Sunday Express* full-page features. The first short but favourable reviews appeared. Poet Stevie Smith in the *Daily Telegraph* wrote that Maurice had 'immense talent and gusto'. Alan Sillitoe,*

---

*Sillitoe's novel *Saturday Night and Sunday Morning* had been published in 1958 and his story *The Loneliness of the Long Distance Runner* in 1959. Both were made into memorable films.

then at the peak of his fame, wrote in *The Bookman*: 'Most of these stories are set out with a loose ease that draws one in with hypnotic effect ... you want to write off to the author and ask for more'. Maurice's self-confidence rebounded and he wrote to Kevin Ireland: 'I plan, by the way, three novels and two more collections of stories by the time I'm thirty-two; that's my five year plan'. The first novel was well under way (again) but he had been distracted from this by writing a new story 'The Room' 'which is taking my heart's blood. You'll read it one day, don't worry; everyone will.'[26]

As sailing day approached, there was an increasing round of farewell parties and visits, including a trip to Oxford where he dined at the high table in Pembroke College and enjoyed a convivial evening with expatriate New Zealand author, and Oxford Clarendon Press publisher, Dan Davin and his wife Winifred. The increasing success of *The New Zealanders* meant that 'Doors had begun opening in England; doors on which I had never knocked'.[27] He was, for example, asked to review for the *Sunday Times*. Gill and he continued to vacillate: had they made the right decision to go home? Maurice had no job to go back to and a letter from Karl Stead in early November was hardly encouraging. From Auckland, he wrote: 'Arriving back here after nearly 4 years away was like running slap into a brick wall when one is expecting boundless space in front'. He was not sure if, returning to New Zealand after adjusting to another world, 'makes us a blighted race, or fortunate for having such intensity forced upon us at intervals.'[28]

At the same time, Maurice had received the wonderful letter of praise from Jim Baxter and just read a complimentary review in the *NZ Listener*. David Hall had written that 'foreign travel has evidently served primarily to allow him to see his own country with a new sharpness and a new wholeness'. The earlier *Landfall* stories had given 'some foretaste of Shadbolt's quality. But the strength and authority of this book could scarcely have been predicted. As we put it down, we realise Shadbolt had good right to speak *for* all of us, as he speaks to us all, in his proud title.'[29] This may have prompted Maurice to recall the words of Jerzy Szkup: 'I am Warsaw, Warsaw is me'. Did he really have a choice?

As the *Oronsay* steamed slowly down the Thames, Maurice opened up the latest issue of the *Times Literary Supplement* which he had bought just before boarding and read its review of *The New Zealanders*. 'Mr. Shadbolt is a find indeed. His publishers declare themselves convinced that he is most likely to become "one of the most widely acclaimed writers of the present time" ... their enthusiasm is understandable. Certainly, even on the strength of this volume, he can be described as probably the most promising author produced by New

Zealand since the war — perhaps since Katherine Mansfield — a figure already to be spoken of in the same breath as Mr. Patrick White of Australia.'[30] Gill said, "'What if you'd read it a month sooner? Would you have wanted to stay?' … But England was gone.'[31]

PART TWO

TELLING STORIES

CHAPTER 16

A STRANGE UNEXPLORED LAND

Sailing through the tropics should have been transition enough from London's November gloom but, from the deck of the *Oronsay*, Maurice found Auckland a 'strange sunny tropical city, with palm trees, spiky pines, and pale houses'.[1] At New Year, 'Summer's lethargy was thick on the land, difficult to accommodate after the liveliness of London'.[2] Vi and Frank were at the wharf to meet them and there was a family welcome home party with his uncles Joe and Dick. They were less interested in his writing success than what he had to tell them about the glories of the Soviet Union. Maurice thought he had already made it clear in his letters but repeated, 'Worse than my worse expectation … A monstrosity. A perversion … New Zealand was more authentically socialist.'[3] This was too much for these old communists; they suggested he had been 'bewitched by Trotskyites'. So Maurice softened his tone, withdrew, left them to the beliefs they needed.

Frank and Vi soon took Maurice and Gill off home to Waihi; but before they left Auckland, Maurice rang round a few old friends. There had been a story about his arrival home in the *Auckland Star*, WRITER RETURNS, written by a journalist who had boarded the *Oronsay* from the pilot boat, prompted by advance news items of the glowing London reviews of *The New Zealanders*. But the news Maurice picked up over the 'phone was less glowing. One writer friend told him he had been making enemies; few were anxious to see him before he went south. Maurice and Gill did go to see Robin Dudding, a close friend of Kevin Ireland's with whom he had established the literary magazine *Mate*. Maurice told Ireland that Dudding seemed to have 'lost all the freshness and vigour he once had … Something dead about him, Gill observed.'[4] Perhaps Dudding's demeanour was related to the hostile review of *The New Zealanders* he was soon to publish. He told Maurice it was coming but, as some kind of amelioration, asked him to write a 'credo' essay about his writing life for the same issue. What was this all about?

Maurice countered his anxiety by revisiting the scenes of his early childhood. 'If I was to make sense of New Zealand, where better to begin than where my recall reached? Memory offered more nourishment than literary envy.'[5] At Waikino, the cottage they had lived in when Frank worked for the Golden Dawn mine in 1934 was abandoned, roof red with rust, windows broken. Waihi was more to his liking, a place it seemed Frank and Vi had settled on for their retirement once Frank finished work for the P&T Department the following year. While Gill and he cogitated on where to settle, Maurice could enjoy a beer with Frank in the Rob Roy pub, beach walks with Gill and renew his friendship with artist Eric Lee-Johnson who had just moved down from the Hokianga with his third wife, Elizabeth. Lee-Johnson's devotion to 'native imagery' found him many subjects among the 'lonely townships, humble dwellings, ravaged hills, and slain forest'[6] of the Coromandel region. He helped bring Maurice home to where he belonged, to look at his 'land afresh'.

Another who helped Maurice come home was Barry Mitcalfe, teacher and writer, whom Maurice had got to know at pubs and parties in Wellington. The ebullient Mitcalfe had written to Maurice in London from Ahipara, at the bottom of Ninety Mile Beach. He was teaching English and Social Studies at Kaitaia College and he said Maurice should come up to stay. His and Barbara's place was small but Alistair Campbell and family were coming, so why not him? 'I hear you know the Hokianga. Well, this place is better, wilder, more ringworm, T.b. and ticks.' There were 'Pubs, shellfish, netting & congenial (albeit not intellectual) company'. He had been 'Glad to hear about "The New Zealanders" — bloody good title for the self-conscious kiwi — and sales point of view.'[7] When Mitcalfe rang him in Waihi, Maurice could not resist, and he hitchhiked his way north, leaving six-months pregnant Gill to the security of the family home.

With Mitcalfe, Maurice claimed he 'heard all that was good in my country in his joky and generous voice'. When Mitcalfe praised *The New Zealanders* and said, 'A couple of your stories gave me an erection', it was the kind of blokey reassurance Maurice needed and 'Those edgy Auckland voices ceased to matter.'[8] Walking the surf-edge of the misted beach that seemed to have no end, watching Maori children riding bareback, and collecting shellfish, Maurice agreed with Mitcalfe that he had been too long away from all of this. Mitcalfe had begun to translate Maori waiata and karakia into English which was to be his lasting legacy: 'You dart like the shag beneath/ The dark waters of the stream,/ Dive like a gannet to a death/ In the deep where small fish gleam.'[9]

They went on an expedition with four other Maori and pakeha friends to Cape Reinga, eighty miles along a notional State Highway One of shingle and sand into which their car sank down to the axles; it took half a day with a last chance to fill up at Te Kao. Here they were joined by Maori elder Joe Conrad who filled them up with the history and myths of the Far North. When Maurice climbed down to the legendary pohutukawa tree growing from the last rocky promontory of the cape, from which Maori spirits of the dead leap to the sea below and into the underworld, Maurice experienced 'an unfamiliar rejoicing. Was some passing spirit at work in me?'[10] He told Kevin Ireland that it was 'impossible to convey the vivid quality of the scene and the complex of things I felt when I got up there.'[11] He had felt at home with the Maori but their stories had stirred in him the need to tell the stories and myths of his own people.

Two messages awaited him back at Waihi that were to govern the course of the next year. First, Jim and Jacquie Baxter had found them an 'eccentric' place to live in Upper Hutt while its owner, anthropologist and editor of the magazine for Maori, *Te Ao Hou*,[12] Erik Schwimmer, went off to Canada for a year. Before he left London, Maurice had applied for the State Literary Fund's Scholarship in Letters and at Colombo, on the voyage home, he learned he had been successful in being awarded its £500. In Upper Hutt, he could get down to finishing his novel. But this was scarcely enough to see them through the year, especially with Gill's confinement due at the end of April. The second message solved this problem. Photographer Brian Brake was making good on his promise in Hong Kong two and half years before. He wanted to work on a New Zealand project with Maurice as the writer and now had an assignment from *National Geographic* magazine: was he still interested?

Brake came down from Auckland in a new Jaguar and picked up Maurice before driving on to Christchurch for a setup meeting with the *Geographic*'s editor. Brake's endorsement and the reviews of *The New Zealanders* were enough: Maurice was offered $US2000 for a text plus $US500 for expenses. This was more than double the fee he had received from the *New Yorker* for 'The Strangers'. But the assignment would have to be finished before Gill was due on 18 April. Maurice also heard that *The New Zealanders* had already sold 3300 copies. Victor Gollancz told him it was a wonderful result for a first book, especially of short stories. Now they would have enough money to keep them going for a couple of years. He could not have been aware of it at the time, but he had become the first full-time professional author in New Zealand.

In late January they flew down to Wellington where, to their surprise, the Baxters picked them up in their own car. Jim Baxter currently had a well-paid job as an editor at School Publications which, at the time, was something of a refuge for impecunious poets and fiction writers. Baxter drove them out of town; past the Lower Hutt housing estates, through Upper Hutt to the last signs of settlement at Te Marua. It was a frightening drive as Baxter 'frequently and unnervingly took his eyes off the road to ensure I wasn't missing the point of his current monologue'.[13] The house at 46 Valley Road was a picturesque and airy relief. An A-frame structure, on one side of a stream patrolled by ducks, housed a living and bedroom area that was connected by a footbridge to a kitchen and guest room which Maurice commandeered as his study.

Brake's photo schedule was tough and tight. First, they drove to the Bay of Islands for scenery and big game fishing where Maurice assisted Brake, a student of available light photographer Cartier Bresson, with his first and rare use of a flash gun. Driving back south they located champion sheep-shearer Godfrey Bowen in a back country shed training youngsters with the machine shearing technique pioneered with his brother, Ivan.* At Ngaruawahia, their arrival coincided with the annual waka regatta on the Waikato River. Maurice continued to marvel at Brake's 'capacity to remain unobtrusive with two or three cameras swinging round his neck. He came and went before his subjects knew he had been there.'[14] On the banks of the Waikato, a Maori elder related legends of the river to Maurice but said, '"I can tell you one, two and three. But I can never tell you four. That is mine. Four is what makes me Maori"'.

They drove down the South Island's West Coast as far as the glaciers and a goldfields festival at Hokitika complete with the Kokatahi miners band. Licensing laws still required that pubs close at six and, as guests at the City Hotel, Maurice and Brake were expected to 'cover' for all the other 'guests' in the crowded bar. When Maurice retired from rowdy boozing to his room he found someone already in his bed. There was no mistake: the publican had told the intruder Maurice was a 'decent joker and wouldn't mind'.[15]

They encountered a different kind of hospitality when they drove over the alps to Arthur's Pass. Brake had grown up as the son of the storekeeper, and taken his first photographs there with a Box Brownie. People crowded round to shake the hand of the now famous local boy. Down the road, they stayed at Grasmere Station, but it was on the Rangitata's Mount Possession

---

*Godfrey Bowen set a world record in 1953 by shearing 456 sheep in nine hours. The Bowen Technique became the standard.

that Brake shot his famous high country portfolio. They were in time for the autumn muster. After several days of hard work with the musterers, Brake on upper beats, Maurice on the lower, about 20,000 merinos had been brought on to the slopes of Mount Guy, above Lake Clearwater. Brake and Maurice went ahead of the mob to find the best position for photographs with the lake and mountains of the Two Thumb Range in the background. As ever, the sheep did not co-operate and began to veer uphill. To save the day, Maurice ran and scrambled behind a ridge, diverting the merinos back towards the lake by bleating and distracting them on all fours. Brake was able to take the photograph that became emblematic not only of Mount Possession but of all high country musters, a picture that has seen the flattery of endless imitations.

Maurice also took credit for the Brake photograph that became the recurring image of Arrowtown: old miners' cottages by poplars with piles of autumn leaves beneath. At first, Brake did not know what to make of it, until Maurice pulled out matches and set the leaves smoking, prompting a local to come out and rake up more. 'Brian had to concede that writers might have their uses.'[16]

Dunedin was the last stop on the *Geographic* tour before Brake flew off to Paris and London where he attended and recorded the marriage of his photographer friend Antony Armstrong-Jones to Princess Margaret. His next major assignment was an Indian Monsoon essay for *Life* magazine. Despite his heavy international schedule, Brake told Maurice there was a book to be made from their *Geographic* assignment and he would look into it when he had the chance.

In Dunedin, Maurice took the opportunity to meet Maurice Duggan again; he was currently the Robert Burns Fellow at Otago University. Maurice greatly admired Duggan's writing but had always found him difficult company. Poet Fleur Adcock was present. She had separated from Alistair Campbell and was now working in the university library and in the midst of an affair with Duggan. Maurice wrote that Adcock 'wore her familiar feline expression', familiar from earlier social times in Wellington. 'She said little, smoked and drank quietly … and seemed to have everyone in the room summed up sexually and socially.'[17] Maurice described Duggan taking offence at his statement that, on coming back to New Zealand and undertaking the *Geographic* assignment, he had discovered the country was more 'wildly diverse' than the particular landscapes he had carried in memory, and Duggan took this as criticism of a lack of diversity in his own writing. But Adcock recounts that Maurice was 'full of himself' after his overseas trip, 'going on about all his travels, and customs and borders, all this drama and showing off'. Duggan 'was jealous … and contemptuous [of] this young whippersnapper,[18] twenty-seven years old with a book called *The New Zealanders* ... Duggan was a little square ivory man with perfect style, had taken two years to write a short story while [Maurie] was pumping them all out ... no two people could have been more incompatible.'[19]

Maurice stayed with Charles Brasch at his Heriot Row home. He acknowledged Brasch's sensitivity and generosity but thought him remote from ordinary New Zealanders, deploring the kiwi accent, and part of a small and beleaguered cultural elite. He also criticised Brasch's literary preferences, yet his stringent editing had been crucial to Maurice's early success. On this occasion, Brasch gave Maurice a copy of the latest issue of *Landfall* which included a review of *The New Zealanders* which he said would go some way to compensating for the 'disagreeable' ones.

The most disagreeable had recently appeared in *Mate*. Robin Dudding had told Maurice a harsh review was coming. It seems also as if someone had given Maurice a clue to its content because he withdrew his 'credo' essay. The pair engaged in an acrimonious correspondence in which Dudding tried to convince Maurice that the forthcoming review was not personally directed. Yet four pages of the small journal had been given over to a withering attack, headed 'The Amazing Mr Shadbolt', not only on *The New Zealanders* but also Maurice and the *Listener* reviewer David Hall. Its author was Ian Hamilton a 54-year-old 'wealthy and debonair socialist' who had come to New Zealand from England via South Africa thirty years before. A pacifist playwright, he had been imprisoned as a conscientious objector in World War II, and had become a 'stimulating' friend of Frank Sargeson. Yet he behaved as something of a womanising and 'glamorous remittance man' and often held 'rabid opinions'[20] which were now vented in *Mate*.

Hamilton wrote that Maurice's stories 'suffer from almost every fault ... to which the writer in this most difficult medium is subject ... there is no reason why the reader of any of them, like David Hall and the blurb-writer, should mistake energy for genius, slick writing for style and stereotyped patterns for "extraordinary intuition into the complexities of the human mind"'. (Jacket blurb.) He accused Maurice of being of a type with 'Leftish, so-called free thinking, nibbling at pacifism, keen on art and psychology, but with a kind of pseudo-Lawrentian feeling for nature, children and people of another colour ... on the other side of this coin, lie the beats, Zen and those book-burning Nazis.'[21] Brasch wrote that Hamilton's attack was 'A sour brew concocted of envy and spite. It will do great harm to Hamilton ... and some to *Mate*, which is a pity. I hope you won't attempt to answer it in public ... it's beneath your notice. But such things hurt, I know, and I feel for you.'[22]

The Hamilton 'review' was an extraordinary diatribe. In addition, Maurice heard ridiculous rumours that he had bribed Victor Gollancz, seduced reviewers like Stevie Smith and even written the anonymous *Times Literary Supplement* review himself. The problem, Maurice later concluded, was that he had not, 'belonged to any recognised … literary coterie; I hadn't sat for years at the feet of those who had suffered for art in the antipodean wasteland'.[23] More than a decade would pass before Maurice learned of the actual motivations behind the Hamilton review and Dudding's role, although Dudding hinted at it when he tried to smooth things over. 'I hope one day we can clear things up … If I've done wrong, I'm sorry, as I know you would be if you felt that you were in the wrong at all.'[24]

The *Landfall* review went some way to settle Maurice's outrage and deepening paranoia. It was not entirely complimentary but a balanced and thoughtful critique. Ray Copland, who was to become a professor of English at Canterbury University, began by saying that the stories were 'so good in so many ways that it is a delight to read them. One is struck almost at once with the range of the author's sympathies and understanding.' But he pointed to times when the 'human actuality' is marred by some of the stories' 'social ciphering'.[25]

This was encouraging but Maurice's confidence took another knock when a review by Auckland university lecturer Bill Pearson appeared in the new current affairs journal *Comment*. Pearson's intention was clear from the outset: 'After all the éclat it is necessary to pass a cool eye over Mr Shadbolt's achievement, to see it not as some sudden exotic, blooming for a summer on London bookstands, but as a work that has some relationship to New Zealand and is to be measured in the light of the New Zealand writing that London has not heard of'. Pearson found very little of value in *The New Zealanders*: 'even in the best stories … there is a certain arbitrariness of theme and a lack of direction'. After dismembering the stories on the academic operating table, Pearson wrote: 'One cannot avoid the suspicion that Mr Shadbolt wanted to impress the English that he was not one of them, but of a sturdy independent race that had long cut itself free; and at the same time wanted to impress the locals with his travels, his snippets from foreign phrase-books, his understanding of the big world where things are happening'. This was so far from Maurice's process of writing and of how the stories were published, that it betrayed both rancour on Pearson's behalf and ignorance of the realities of life for a professional author. Pearson did think that Maurice had a 'very good ear for dialogue' and that there was a 'great deal of good material' in the stories; but it was 'not used to best effect'. Among other things, Maurice had to 'learn to be humble towards his subject-matter'.[26] There were a number of points in Pearson's review of which Maurice could take good note: such as his penchant for 'fruity passages' and the use of inexact and dramatic verbiage. But they were encased in such sour condescension that they served only to make Pearson an enemy for life. Pearson's astringent style of reviewing severely damaged his relationships with other writers such as Maurice Duggan, M.K. Joseph and Noel Hilliard, to the point where eventually he gave it up.

Jim Baxter, loyal as ever, wrote to the *Listener* of the review in *Comment*, 'as a notable example of New Zealanders' resentment of overseas success'.[27] Pearson's biographer wrote: 'There is no doubt that Pearson's review was affected by his sense of frustration that a writer like Shadbolt, whose work demonstrated, in his opinion, clear weaknesses, should succeed so easily while his own efforts languished.'[28] Pearson also had met Maurice once at a Wellington party in the mid-1950s and 'wasn't much impressed; he struck me as a vain and boastful young man'.[29] He had described Maurice's review of Maurice Duggan's *Immanuel's Land*[30] as 'log rolling'. From the outset he had been disinclined to view *The New Zealanders* with much sympathy.

So Maurice believed he had become the victim of an élite who were envious of a success which had not been achieved through the right kind of literary apprenticeship and approval from his elders. They were all male, living in a society where public expressions of male achievement were expected to be self-effacing, conforming to a kind of understatement that had its paradigm in Ed Hillary's 'We knocked the bugger off' after he had made the first ascent of Everest: a shrug of the shoulders and 'Really, it was nothing'. Even members of the literary élite did not like blowhards, especially if they threatened their own estimation of themselves and did not conform in this most conforming of village societies.

Bill Pearson thought Maurice 'vain and boastful' and Fleur Adcock that he was 'full of himself'. It was the kind of behaviour that only the most generous could tolerate for long and Maurice seemed unaware of the effect of this on anyone inclined to be an adversary. He bruited his success not only in correspondence. He had also made sure that the laudatory London reviews were forwarded to New Zealand news outlets. On his arrival home he gave interviews to newspapers, magazines and radio stations, to anyone who would listen. Today, relentless marketing of a book, and authorial self-promotion, are not only usual but required. The more 'misery memoir', personal disability or treasured children that can be brought out to attract media attention the better. In 1960 New Zealand, this kind of behaviour promoted envy and enemies.

Maurice was the first New Zealand writer to effectively use the media to promote both his books and his persona as an author. As an individual, he was careless, even unaware, of the effect of all this on his contemporaries, but as a professional writer he knew what he was doing. A decade later, novelist and colleague David Ballantyne would write: 'It seems a fact of modern publishing … that writers must shout to be heard. Neglect is easy to come by. Just keep your mouth shut.'[31]

Maurice soon secured a kind of revenge. Bill Pearson had been working for some years on his novel *Coal Flat* which had been repeatedly turned down by publishers. In August 1960, the editor for Whitcombe & Tombs, David Lawson, asked to see it. Pearson had still not heard back when, passing through Wellington around Christmas, he unexpectedly met Maurice in the company of Jim Baxter. He made his 'explanations' with regard to his review of *The New Zealanders*. 'I said this is not an apology but an explanation of why I adopted that tone. [Maurice] listened but didn't say a word.'[32] A month later Lawson turned down *Coal Flat* for being too long and unsuccessfully realised.[33] Pearson was furious because, by then, he knew the manuscript had gone out to a Wellington reader and that Maurice had also read it and made unfavourable comments that he assumed had influenced Lawson's decision. In October 1961, after denials all round, Maurice finally apologised and confessed to Pearson: 'While still in a pretty bitter mood, I chanced upon a copy of your novel, and slung about a few wild remarks … the truth is that I was doing exactly what I felt you did in that review: judging an imaginary man, and not the work.'[34] Pearson doubted his sincerity.

Apart from Jim Baxter, the only person to whom he could openly express his feelings was on the other side of the world. He wrote to Kevin Ireland that while he liked Wellington — 'It has a character; it is compact; it has a pleasant European flavour' — returning to New Zealand had been a 'sharp jolt'. 'Inhabiting these islands is something akin to being cast adrift with a directionless raft-load of humanity: humanity in this circumstance can be rather frightening.' He deplored the 'bitchiness of the literary scene' and 'From a social, literary and cultural point of view we inhabit a slum here'. As he began to wrestle with his novel, he knew he was 'engaged, perhaps for life, in an obsessional love-hate affair with a strange fact of life and history called New Zealand. Of course one will probably never make sense of it — but one must <u>try</u>, all along the way, one must <u>deny</u>, all along the way, the impossibility of doing it.'[35] New Zealand still had, for him, the 'fascination of a strange, unexplored land.'[36]

The *National Geographic* journeys with Brian Brake became an invigorating distraction, and when he returned to Te Marua at the beginning of April there was the distraction and anxiety of the impending birth of his and Gill's first child. 'One builds up to an emotional climax … and then drowns in anti-climax' because, ten days after the due date of 18 April, 'There's not even a bloody sign, or faint glimmer, of <u>anything</u> happening.'[37] A week later he could write to Kevin Ireland, 'Well — it's happened!' Son Sean Francis was born at Lower Hutt Hospital on 4 May 'after protracted negotiations with his mother'. Maurice had taken a speeding taxi ride to the hospital, escorted by a traffic cop, in response to a doctor's call that the welfare of both child and mother was uncertain. But when he arrived he found Gill well after a Caesarean and his son sleeping peacefully. 'You realise suddenly … that this is what you are meant for; until you've had a child, committed yourself, you can't truly claim membership of the human race'. In his euphoria, he wrote, 'the world flowers like a revelation, its colours palpably different. You're a stranger suddenly, and the mystery is singing around you.'[38] On this occasion at least his purple prose could be forgiven.

Jim Baxter had also written a purple poem in anticipation:

Cicadas drumming
For the march of your exhausted manic friends
Bugle as well for your first child's coming
He (or it might be she) will step down
From the womb's fondling night to a world where three
white ducks sail towards their placid ends.[39]

More practically, mother Vi and his 11 year-old sister Julia travelled down from Auckland to assist Gill during the first post-natal weeks.

Maurice was distracted from negative local criticism of *The New Zealanders* by the reassuring news that it had been picked up by the Italian publisher of *Dr Zhivago*, Feltrinelli, Fischer Verlag in West Germany and the new Atheneum Books in New York, all offering useful advances. Simon 'Mike' Bessie of Atheneum had been attracted to the book by the publication of 'The Strangers' in the *New Yorker*. Livia Gollancz has written Maurice that her father felt it 'enormously important' to maintain the *New Yorker* connection, although he might be 'horrified' by their cuts to his story. She offered her congratulations on his 'ascent into the New Yorker galaxy'.[40] Maurice tried hard but he never had a story accepted by them again.

Auckland might have been full of literary enemies but Wellington seemed full of literary friends. He had been nominated by Charles Brasch, and accepted, as a member of the literary society PEN which was then largely a Wellington affair.[41] He made new contacts at PEN meetings, resumed friendships with the Baxters, the Cooks and Moss Gee and sought out those with whom he guessed he would have something in common. In particular, he warmed to 'tall and amiable' Ian Cross, author of *The God Boy*, who was back from holding the first Burns Fellowship in Dunedin and now worked in Wellington as a journalist. Cross and Maurice had much in common with their journalistic backgrounds and distrust of academia. For Maurice, Cross was a 'lifesaving touchstone'.[42] Cross said, 'We got along well instantly. You couldn't help it with Maurice, he was kind, gentle … near angelic on the surface but under that was a pulsating ambition to do things.'[43]

Maurice described Cross as 'conventional in character and dress, often to be seen as a vociferous rugby fan … As an everyday bloke, in short' which he thought infuriated Cross's detractors.[44] Like Maurice, Cross had also been attacked by the literary élite for publishing a novel successfully overseas without the approved literary credentials. Maurice introduced Cross to the 'first literary group' he had ever met. At Parsons book and coffee shop on Lambton Quay they joined the likes of Jim Baxter, poet Anton Vogt, fiction writer Phillip Wilson, Katherine Mansfield biographer Antony Alpers and, when in town, political scientist and cultural commentator Bob Chapman from the University of Auckland.*

Another who sometimes joined the group was Renato 'Michael' Amato, an Italian who had escaped the ruins and political chaos of post-war Italy and arrived in New Zealand in 1954. He had begun to write in Italy but abandoned his literary ambitions along with his past and became an itinerant labourer and travelling salesman: until he met and married Scots-English immigrant Sheena McAdam and joined her at Victoria University as a mature student of thirty-one in 1959. A year later he was president of Victoria's literary society and approached Maurice for a story for its annual literary journal. He also wanted help with his own stories after Sheena discovered his past manuscripts and pushed him to begin writing again: this time in English, which seemed risky to Maurice despite the examples of Nabokov and Conrad. Bob Chapman, as critic, noted that of writers published in university magazines he was the 'one adult in an adolescent generation'.[45] Maurice and Michael's friendship and collaboration were to prove fruitful and controversial.

A royalty cheque from Gollancz allowed Maurice to buy a secondhand Ford Prefect without too much rust. It gave them increased mobility after

---

*Louis Johnson had moved to Napier to a job as sub-editor on the *Hawke's Bay Herald Tribune*.

months of relying on local buses and trains to travel into Wellington, making it easier for Maurice and Gill to attend social and literary events with baby Sean. From this time, Ian Cross remembers Gill as 'motherly and forgiving', a summary of what Gill had always been for Maurice. Together, they attended Wellington's progressive Unity theatre for readings of plays such as Jim Baxter's *The Wide Open Cage*. Later they were accompanied by 24-year-old Unity member and writer Marilyn Duckworth to readings of Osborne and Wesker plays they had already seen in London. Her first novel *A Gap in the Spectrum* had appeared the previous year. Maurice was attempting to finish yet another play and invited Duckworth out to Te Marua to read and comment on the draft. Duckworth found Gill 'washing baby Sean's nappies in the kitchen wash-house' while on the other side of the stream Maurice worked in his 'comfortable study at a desk pinned with cuttings' and with the poem written for them by Baxter.

By now, Maurice had settled on his image as an author: a thick mop of black hair, lightly trimmed; currently fashionable spectacles above a thick black moustache that turned down at the corners of his mouth; and, more often than a cigarette in hand, a pipe that was to become part of his apparatus until the end.

Unhappy in her own marriage, Duckworth thought the Te Marua 'setting was idyllically romantic and envied Maurice and Gill, particularly their happy relationship, carelessly burping at each other'.[46] Duckworth was Fleur Adcock's younger sister and Maurice saw her as a 'lean, elegant novelist, as cool in prose as her sister in verse',[47] and in need of support in a critical world that condescended to 'Mrs Duckworth, authoress', a housewife who wrote at the kitchen table.

As 1960 wore on Maurice continued to struggle with his novel. 'I was perhaps too anxious to prove that my first book was no accident.'[48] By November he had almost completed a second draft: 'It's generally a botch, a mess of mixed intentions, but it might be possible for publication.'[49]

Although new friendships had eased the stresses of returning to New Zealand, he sometimes wondered if that had been a 'misguided move. Perhaps I should have been better off in London, with those opening doors, after all.'[50] Despite Marilyn Duckworth's envy of their 'happy' marriage, Gill had also begun to resent how her life had become governed entirely by motherhood and the needs of Maurice's work, and how the isolation of Te Marua prevented her from following her own journalistic career. Yet the arrival of Sean had been a joy for them both. On their way to see poet Denis Glover and his wife Kura at Paekakariki, they 'christened Sean with seawater from a wild ocean beach. The ceremony may have been makeshift, but with spray on our faces and foaming sea at our feet it didn't lack majesty.'[51]

Glover listened to Maurice's complaints about the local critical reception of *The New Zealanders* and shrewdly asked if Frank Sargeson had been getting at him. In his pugnacious and invigorating way, he then stated that 'writing should be a capital offence. Writers could have the choice of rope, axe or firing squad. But no possibility of reprieve … so only those who really need to write would risk it.'[52] Maurice had been warned.

Just before Christmas, Maurice and Gill packed up their belongings at Te Marua before driving north to Waihi to present Frank and Vi with their first grandchild; twelve-year-old, 'long-legged' Julia with her first nephew; and Maurice's favourite Uncle Joe with his first great-nephew. At New Year, they drove north to stay with the Mitcalfes at Ahipara and the keepers of the Cape Reinga lighthouse where Maurice again cogitated on the meaning of life in New Zealand and his role in it.

From Waihi on the way back, they went to see author and teacher Sylvia Ashton-Warner near Tauranga. Ashton-Warner had achieved enormous success and an international reputation with her novel *Spinster* and the film version starring Shirley MacLaine. Maurice found Ashton-Warner extravagant, making a dramatic entrance in a flimsy gown and with a glass of champagne. She announced that ever since publishing *Spinster* she had been waiting for another New Zealand writer to call: 'Summers come and summers go. But no one ever comes … Until today. You shall always be my very special friend.'[53] Maurice found that her paranoia about local literary criticism exceeded his own, to the point where she said she had decided her future books would be published only in the United States and Europe. As they drove back to their own uncertain future in Wellington, Maurice and Gill wondered what *they* might do with all the money Ashton-Warner had earned from her success.

CHAPTER 17

THREESOMES

Back in Wellington, they rented the downstairs flat in Nigel and Julie Cook's house at 88 Glenmore Street, across the road from the Botanic Garden. Gill got a job to pay for it, reporting and writing columns for *Truth*, while Maurice stayed at home with his novel and baby Sean. This arrangement proved too optimistic. After a time 'changing nappies, preparing his food, walking him in the gardens and averaging no more than three lines a day, I sensed lunacy looming'.[1] Lunacy was averted when fiction rather than reality absorbed his attention and Sean scalded himself and ended up in hospital.

Ever motherly to both, Gill accepted Maurice's need for morning peace and quiet and Sean's need of reliable day care. Helpfully, Marilyn Duckworth, just up the hill on Northland Road, offered to have Sean in the mornings while Maurice wrote. She had two young girls of her own and another infant would be no bother. There was optimism in this arrangement, too. Duckworth had begun to suffer from narcolepsy, yet to be diagnosed, and sometimes fell asleep during the day, waking to find her children absent, even playing on the pavement outside the local shops.

Gill also seemed unaware of the signals between Maurice and their babysitter. They had enjoyed each other's company and laughter at an Alistair Campbell party and on an evening without Gill at Ian Cross's listening to a radio reading of James Thurber's story 'The Night the Bed Fell'. After that, Maurice drove Duckworth home but via the Mexicalli coffee lounge where they 'held hands and knew what was happening'.[2] Duckworth's marriage had become loveless, her husband accusing her of having an 'unnatural need for affection'. Despite what Duckworth had seen at Te Marua, Maurice told her of his depression at the state of his own. Later he would rationalise that the widening gulf between him and Gill was down to his desire to live in a remote corner of the Far North, writing in isolation, and her need for the city, with its social life and the stimulation of weekly journalism. He was the country boy out of step with the city girl. The cup of coffee and literary gossip Maurice and Duckworth shared when he arrived to pick up Sean each day deepened their connection. She imagined that Gill was encouraging her closeness to Maurice.

Duckworth took the final step. She rang Maurice one morning to say she had a problem. Not with Sean, who was asleep, not with her children who were away with their grandmother, but a serious problem nevertheless and he had to come over. When he arrived, 'What she said was rather sensational. "I think I'm dying" … weak in the knees we sank to the floor'.[3] For Duckworth it was a 'huge relief, lancing an intolerable pressure'. It was as if they had 'known each other at least one time before' and '"Committing adultery" felt so inevitable, a necessary rite of passage, like learning to walk'. It was a release from the stresses of her unhappy marriage; but it was also 'opening a floodgate to let in dangerous tides of true feeling'.[4] If there was relief, there would also be a cost; but infatuation does not care.

Duckworth had been awarded the 1961 Scholarship in Letters for working on her second novel, *A Barbarous Tongue*. When she received the £500 in June she took off, with the approval of her husband, for the anonymity of Hamilton to work without interruption on her manuscript. It was difficult to leave her girls to the care of her in-laws but 'Even my doctor had told me I needed to do something about dividing my domestic pressures from my career pressures'.[5] The only other person who knew where she had gone was Maurice who planned a different kind of therapy. With the excuse of needing to visit his Uncle Joe in Auckland, he drove up to Hamilton, picked up Duckworth and took her to a motel in Orewa which he booked under the name 'Will Faulkner'. They spent an 'idyllic week, walking on the deserted beach looking for driftwood, devouring huge omelettes and black pudding'.[6] They made love and talked, two writers together swapping and claiming metaphors and storylines — 'That's mine, not yours, I thought of it first!'. Maurice was not keen on Duckworth's writing, thinking it lacked social and historical significance and she thought his had too much, too many words as he pursued the white whale of the 'Great New Zealand Novel'.

They swapped family stories. Maurice enlarged on his testicle operation as a sixteen-year-old into a yarn that he had been born with none and had transplants, arranged by his Aunt Sis, from a murderer hanged at Mount Eden. Duckworth took this is a test of her gullibility; it was merely one hyperbole among many yarns as even he had begun to be 'appalled by the fluency of the untruths I was learning to tell'.[7] Or perhaps by the ease with which he hid the truth until it suited him to tell. On the last day of their Orewa idyll, Maurice 'bombed' Duckworth with the news that Gill was pregnant again. She was stunned and tried not think about Gill, wept when he rang her from Hamilton on his way home to see if she was all right after they had agreed their affair was over.

After another married Maurice — Duggan — made overtures to Duckworth, she wondered, 'Did writers subscribe to a different set of moral rules?'[8] Or was their behaviour part of an 'artistic temperament', the popular term used to justify male writers and artists breaking the 'moral rules' because their art demanded it. Avant garde, they were leading the way in examining the human condition and forging new rules. They were artists as heroes, narcissists entitled to whatever they needed; and some women were attracted to the excitement, the energy and the anarchy this engendered. Maurice told Duckworth that he needed both a 'Mimi and a Musetta' in his life,[9] a romantic lover and a loving domestic partner. Maurice left his Mimi and her frozen hand in Auckland and returned to his loving and pregnant Musetta in Wellington.

'Through a particularly black and hopeless Wellington winter I tried to get some control over my life and work again. As I writer I was, it seemed, sinking without trace … I was rapidly becoming another of those promising writers whose first and only books rise like tombstones above their premature graves. As a person I didn't seem of much use either to society or, more important, to those nearest me.'[10] At the end of March he had sent off the third draft of his novel, with the titillating title of 'The Coral and the Nude', to Richmond Towers and Benson, the literary agents he had engaged before leaving London. In May they reported that Gollancz had turned it down. 'We were all enormously impressed by the quality of your writing, but think you don't quite master the form chosen.'[11] Maurice had been half-expecting this but the outlook was now bleak and he began to think he should give up trying to make a living from words alone and look for a well-paid job in journalism, broadcasting, advertising or public relations. Ian Cross had opted for the last with Feltex after mixed success with his own three novels, putting his growing family ahead of an uncertain literary career.

It was Cross who threw Maurice something of a lifeline when he rang at the end of March to announce that Australian novelist Patrick White was in Wellington and an evening had been arranged for him. Maurice was almost speechless in the presence of the author of *The Tree of Man* and *Voss*, taken aback when White said he been enjoying *The New Zealanders*. He told Maurice he was a 'spellbinder' and wanted to know more about him. Maurice discovered that his own paranoia about literary critics paled beside White's vituperative denunciation of Australian writers and reviewers. White told Maurice that Gollancz was not the right publisher for him and his own, Eyre and Spottiswoode, would be much more suitable. He would write and suggest they take him on and, if he was ever in Sydney, Maurice should dine with him. Cross suggested that White's interest was more than literary. A couple of Maurice's stories had sympathetic homosexual characters and White probably thought Maurice was of that persuasion, too. Yet White did write to Eyre and Spottiswoode on Maurice's behalf and his novel did go to them. The coral and the nude were turned down again: 'It was, it turned out, utterly unpublishable.'[12] He confessed to Kevin Ireland that he would not have persisted with it but for the Literary Fund grant. A couple of years later he burned it 'without ceremony'.[13]

Maurice encouraged Ireland to complete his own novel. He had escaped to London from Sofia with his wife Donna in May 1960 after negotiating a bureaucratic paper trail that required sixteen stamped and certificated permissions, even including a signed declaration that books had been returned to the university library. Ireland was not to return to New Zealand for fifteen years and his London flats often became the temporary domicile for peripatetic New Zealand writers and friends. Currently Moss Gee, Carl Freeman — who had joined the Communist Party — and painter Michael Illingworth were within his orbit. Maurice was always eager for Ireland's news and Gill reported on any success by expatriate friends in *Truth*, such as Illingworth's first exhibition at Soho's Gallery One where Ireland had taken over John Kasmin's job.

Occasionally, Maurice expressed a yearning for London and one night he 'suffered some nostalgia' when they met a cousin of Gill's who was mate on an English ship in Wellington, 'drinking Watney's, smoking Players, listening to Fings Ain't Wot They Used to be. But we're not all that isolated here — Stravinsky is coming out to conduct the National Orchestra,'[14] there was now television every night, Bergman and Fellini films to enjoy.

In July 1961, Ireland reported that Moss Gee would be staying on in England until his money ran out and was accompanying Donna and he on a trip to Spain. Gee's 'vision of a grimmer future is to be floating to and fro between the Shadbolts, the Cooks and the Irelands for all eternity'.[15] Gee spent much time with Ireland, at the theatre, having meals, watching football or evenings with friends at the pub. Gee found it remarkable that in London one could spend a Sunday evening in pubs with mixed company. There was still six o'clock closing in New Zealand, male-only public bars and no Sunday opening. There had been one change. Maurice told Ireland: 'You can now buy wine in restaurants legally — at this rate of progress we'll have late closing by 2000 AD'.[16]

Before he left London, Maurice and Gill had tried to place Gee's novel 'The Petition' with Gollancz and then left the manuscript in the hands of Michael Illingworth when it was turned down. After Gee placed two stories with Hutchinson in 1961 they asked to see this novel and, after much revision and editing, published it as *The Big Season* the following year. Maurice read it in one sitting and told Ireland, 'I'm most impressed … it's solid and tenacious (like Moss himself) and I can only think of one or two better novels from this part of the world.'[17] Its critical reception in New Zealand was mixed with an especially harsh review in *Landfall*. Maurice leapt to Gee's defence, vowing to stop buying *Landfall* and having his own books sent for review. He became particularly vituperative after Ireland passed on that Charles Brasch had commented in a letter to him that publishing *The New Zealanders* had done Maurice a disservice: 'But why the hell shouldn't you get a kick in the guts Maurie? Didn't you write a book, you poor bastard? Even your friends can't resist.'[18]

This all fed into his deepening enmity towards the literati, a 'bitter collection of freaks and frustrates … All up each other. All playing a game called "New Zealand literature".'[19] Most of Maurice's feelings were vented in aerogrammes to Ireland and other friends overseas but, as Ireland demonstrated, word would trickle out. For Moss Gee a safer deposit for opinion was in letters to his mother. What would Maurice have thought had he been told of Gee's comments to her about *The New Zealanders*? It had not impressed him. He liked some of the stories but 'There's a faint phoniness about it all, a faint flavour of literariness in the relationships of his characters, and I'm afraid he's not really sensitive to language'. It was 'terribly imprecise at times and his dialogue theatrical'.[20] These were later judged to 'remain consistent themes in the critical assessment of Shadbolt's work'.[21] Or received truths.

Karl Stead was more open. Maurice praised a published story by Stead who replied: 'I am enjoying this moment of harmony between us; principally because our temperaments are so different that I'm sure we are destined to clash again in the future, as we tended at times in London. But if the clashes are productive on both sides, then they're worth the bother.'[22] It was a pre-emptive response. Stead had just given one of Auckland University's 1960 Winter Lectures whose content Maurice would not read until it was published at the end of the following year in the collection *Distance Looks Our Way*. Stead's lecture looked at the response of writers, principally poets, to New Zealand's cultural remoteness from Europe and questions of place and identity. Although it was essentially a tribute to the work of Allen Curnow, one section dealt with the contrasting fictional approaches to the question of New Zealand identity through characters with a foot in both worlds. Stead contrasted Maurice's 'The

Woman's Story' with Frank Sargeson's 'The Making of a New Zealander'. He wrote: 'In trying to assert an identity for New Zealand independent of the outside world, Mr Shadbolt has been driven to the very worst kinds of cliché'. The elements in 'The Woman's Story' were present in the Sargeson 'but because Sargeson is not concerned to romanticise people or scene, they are differently and more convincingly disposed'.[23] It was an unsubtle parallel with Stead's 'K of Henderson' letter to the *Listener* in 1955. Maurice wrote to Stead, challenging his interpretation but Stead brushed it off as 'A lecture is a lecture — one gives them all the time. This one got caught, so to speak. It's like a candid camera shot' but, 'As a lecture, I seem to remember it all went off brilliantly'.[24] If Maurice was careless or unaware of the effect on others of his boasting and self-publicity, Stead seemed equally unaware or careless of the effect of his public dissections of others' work. Stead's response to Maurice was confident and friendly, even disarming, as he invited Maurice and Gill to stay if they needed a bed in Auckland over Christmas.

With the collapse of his novel, Maurice turned seriously to short stories again. A fillip had been winning £100 for his story 'Ben's Land' in the 1961 Wellington Festival literary competition. 'The Room', which he had told Kevin Ireland was 'taking his heart's blood' two years before, was complete and eventually accepted by Charles Brasch for *Landfall*'s spring 1962 edition.[25] It was his last story to be published there, keeping his word to boycott *Landfall* after the cruel review of Gee's *The Big Season*.

By September money was running short and Maurice undertook arduous shiftwork in a bakery. Earning any income from writing rested chiefly on the outcome of *National Geographic* projects. The *Geographic* had accepted Brian Brake's pitch to undertake stories on China. His 'Monsoon' photographic essay, which appeared in *Life*, *Queen* and *Paris Match*, had made him a hot property internationally and Brake had enlisted Maurice as his writer, after their collaboration on the New Zealand story and with Maurice's experience in China in 1957. Maurice spent weeks researching Chinese history and culture in preparation for the project in anticipation of a fat fee, but it was finally abandoned when visas were not forthcoming.

The enthusiasm with which the *Geographic* received Maurice's New Zealand story ensured him a commission for a Western Samoa feature instead. This was to be relatively short, twenty pages compared to the forty-eight devoted to New Zealand but marked Western Samoa's independence with the theme 'The Pacific's Newest Nation'. *Geographic* would not bring Brian Brake from India for the 'comparatively few' extra pictures they needed and a staff photographer was sent to fill the gaps.[26] Brake was 'pissed off' at this, 'as mad as mad can be' and would do no more work for them until he had it out with the *Geographic* editor. One 'blessing' was that Brake would get back his New Zealand pictures once their feature had appeared in the April 1962 issue and then he could 'start work on the book' they were planning together.[27]

Maurice planned to be away in Samoa for four weeks from 10 December. Gill was now heavily pregnant with their second child and he had to be back in good time for the due date in mid-January. About a month before his departure Maurice and Gill shifted from 88 Glenmore Street to 3 Fairview Crescent in Kelburn. They needed more space and privacy for their enlarging family as life at Glenmore Street had become an unending parade of parties, disruptions, new friends and changing tenants in the upstairs flat. In May, Maurice wrote, 'Fleur Adcock is up from Dunedin, and Marilyn D. had a party for her last Saturday which finished in a coffee bar at six in the morning.' Adcock's 'current man is Albert Wendt, a Samoan friend of mine — not a bad writer either.'[28] Wendt was a 21-year-old history student at Victoria University. He had become a regular visitor to the Shadbolts who encouraged his early writing and invited him to parties with other writers such as James K. Baxter, Alistair Campbell, Peter Bland — and now Adcock. Itinerant tenants were Jean Watson and Barry Crump whose first book, *A Good Keen Man*, had become a bestseller. Published in late 1960, by May 1961 Maurice could tell Kevin Ireland that '18,000 copies of G.K.M. have now been printed … the words "a good keen man" have gone securely into the language.'[29] A month later Crump and Watson moved into the upstairs flat. Maurice had just turned twenty-nine: 'Can you imagine? What a bloody age … Jean comes down here during the day to look after Sean Francis. This will enable both Barry and I to write. They also eat in our flat.'[30] Crump and Watson had 'aweing appetites. They consumed at least a dozen eggs and a pound of bacon every morning; our kitchen reeked of their breakfast fryups.'[31]

Maurice knew that Ireland would be interested to hear of Crump's progress because he had been largely responsible for his start as writer. After listening to the young deer culler's pub yarns in the late 1950s, Ireland had given him novels to read and tutored him in narrative style. Maurice told Ireland: 'You know, you should take on a job as a literary coach. First, Shadbolt; then Crump; now Gee. Perhaps Moss, Barry and I should put together a collection of stories and dedicate it to Ireland.'[32] Maurice's own contribution to the Crump phenomenon had been writing out the contract for 'G.K.M.' pro bono. He regularly asked after Ireland's own novel, which never saw the light of day, and was assisting (along with Crump) the publication of his first poetry collection which was finally issued as *Face to Face* by Pegasus Press in Christchurch in 1963.

Barry Crump published a second book, *Hang on a Minute Mate*, in 1961 and by late 1962 the combined sales of both his titles were approaching 100,000, an unprecedented New Zealand publishing phenomenon. Crump could not handle the fame and money. Maurice related to Ireland the drama that unfolded in the new year: 'Fleur came up from Dunedin to spend a week adulterating with Duggan. But Barry dived in before Duggan arrived. This was at a Nigel and Julie party. Next day Duggan arrived, and there was another party at John Cole's … Climaxed by minor chair throwing in the kitchen. Duggan called Fleur "a camp-follower of an anecdotal ape." So things went. Duggan flew back to Auckland, Jean sought refuge with the Cooks. Everyone thought it would weather out. Then Barry took off for Dunedin — to spend three weeks "rooting and writing". I've feared the worst for Barry for some time now … He's burning himself out … he's like a high-wire walker wondering when he's going to fall … He's not eating, but living on drink and drugs. A couple of weeks ago he swallowed ether and was carried off to hospital.'[33]

Soon after this, Adcock married Crump in Dunedin and went up Central Otago for the honeymoon, trailed by female student 'camp-followers'. Crump's erratic and violent behaviour meant the marriage did not last long. On return to Wellington in March they were settled for a while, Crump writing his third book long-hand and Adcock typing it up. Maurice discussed the preface that Crump was writing for Ireland's *Face to Face*. Soon afterwards Crump took off and went bush again with Jean Watson. Adcock had ended up in Wellington Hospital with a bruised face and what was long-related to be a broken arm. Maurice picked her up from hospital and Gill took her in at Fairview Crescent. The injury was, in fact, a dislocated elbow that she had sustained when, after a row with Crump at a party, she had left to go home and jumped over a fence, not knowing 'there was a big drop on the other side'. Until she learned to cope with one arm, Gill looked after her, brought Adcock 'scrambled eggs and toast chopped up small so that I could eat it and helped me do up my bra.'[34]

Crump's 'impulse towards self-destruction is pretty clear to all of us,' Maurice wrote. 'But the tragedy is all the greater because of all the other people he's destroying. Jean too … Now he's sent Fleur off in a downward spiral.'[35] Adcock was perhaps also a party to Crump's self-destruction in a marriage of opposites that was doomed to fail. Crump applied physical violence, Adcock the cool, intellectual kind. As Nigel and Julie Cook stood by, Adcock 'destroyed' Crump in an attack on his writing and character that was so withering he was reduced to tears and Julie Cook asked her to leave the house.[36]

Moving to the Fairview Crescent house, with its eponymous outlook towards Rongotai and Cook Strait one way and over Wellington Harbour to the

Hutt Valley the other, was also not without incident. Gill put their new car out of commission in an accident, and sub-letting their lower flat to a newly married couple produced farce. On the night before the wedding the bridegroom, Max, was arrested '(when drunk and climbing into someone else's car and using his fists), was married in custody, and taken off to goal for a month'.[37]

CHAPTER 18

SUMMER FIRES

In Western Samoa, rather than stay at Aggie Grey's Hotel, host to the likes of Dorothy Lamour, Marlon Brando and Gary Cooper, Maurice took up Albert Wendt's invitation to stay with him and his father's family. Henry Wendt was a Samoan plumber and importer whose home, just back from the Apia waterfront, consisted of two semi-European-style houses and a traditional Samoan fale around a courtyard. 'Here lives his 86-year-old mother and any relatives who choose to stay with him in town.'[1] Henry Wendt was a matai, or chief, who travelled from time to time to the distant village where most of his aiga lived to advise on family matters and to settle disputes.

The name Wendt revealed the part-German heritage of the 'aiga, or family, derived from Germany's colonial rule in the years before World War I. One of the least glorious parts of New Zealand's Pacific history saw its 'invasion' of Western Samoa in August 1914, at the behest of the British government to undertake this 'great and urgent Imperial service'. Lax New Zealand quarantine governance saw the spread of the Spanish 'flu in 1918 which killed more than 8000 of Samoa's 38,000 population. Suppression of dissent, sometimes violent, by New Zealand administrators under both League of Nations and United Nations trusteeships generated rising demands for self-determination which finally brought Western Samoa independence on New Year's Day 1962.

Albert Wendt helped Maurice with a stepladder so that he could see over the fence to view the handover ceremony on the main marae. In another inglorious incident, New Zealand Prime Minister Keith Holyoake 'made use of proceedings to refresh himself with an especially deep sleep. No one dared tap his shoulder and tell him that Samoa had become the Pacific's first Polynesian state while he slumbered. If Samoans were offended, they were too polite to show it.'[2]

Wendt accompanied Maurice on a bus journey through villages east of Apia where children noisily flagged down the driver to wait while their parents finished their domestic work before climbing aboard. Chatter on the bus stopped when Wendt told the passengers Maurice was a *tusitala*, a storyteller. Storytellers were revered figures, weavers of dreams, and they were apprehensive they might appear in Maurice's. Robert Louis Stevenson was the first, and greatest, *palagi* (European) to be accorded the title of *tusitala* and Maurice made a pilgrimage to his grave on Mount Vaea.

Their bus travelled through villages, coconut and banana plantations and beside golden beaches. Maurice's *National Geographic* article told of a tropical Pacific paradise full of welcoming people (and beautiful young women) that owed more to the *palagi* imagination, and the 'romance' of *National Geographic*, than everyday reality.[3] The future was bright, he wrote, for the Samoans in their new-found freedom and he concluded by saying to Wendt that the way of life was so seductive, it would be easy for him to just get off the bus and live in his own *fale* by the sea (among beautiful young women, no doubt). Wendt responded, 'I thought you weren't here to find paradise … ' 'You're getting the *papalagi* disease!'[4]

Maurice's reveries in paradise were cut short by a cable that told him Gill was in maternity hospital and another Caesarean was likely. A friendly diplomat found him a seat on an RNZAF flight back to Wellington on 7 January. In the meantime mother Vi and sister Julia had travelled down to be on hand again. But it was a false alarm; like first-born Sean, Brendan was slow in coming and did not appear until 1 February. In naming their sons, Gill and Maurice had an inclination to the Celtic and the inspiration of Irish playwrights.*

Gill had now finished with *Truth* and without her salary Maurice began regular book reviewing for the *Listener* to supplement the *National Geographic* payments which were the basis for his income in 1962. He managed to persuade the *Geographic* into a commission for a bigger new nation story, Malaysia, which he would undertake towards the end of the year.

Brian Brake was not best pleased with the way the *Geographic* had laid out 'New Zealand: Gift of the Sea', a title which Maurice had conjured up from the Maori Tiritiri o te Moana.** Maurice wrote that this is what early Maori called New Zealand but the term relates not so much to New Zealand as a whole but the Southern Alps. When Brake saw the spread he 'simply blew up'

---

*Sean O'Casey and Brendan Behan.
**Strictly, 'the sharing of the sea'.

and told them 'not to ask for my services again'. He had been annoyed about the Samoan assignment but the layout and picture choice for 'Gift of the Sea' was 'just too much'. He was interested to know of New Zealand readers' reactions and hoped some would write to the *Geographic* and 'criticise shots of natives cooking in hot pools'. Unwittingly he added, 'that really made my blood boil'.[5]

Most New Zealanders were delighted and excited by the unprecedented 48-page feature on New Zealand by one of the world's top photographers, and a Kiwi at that, and its 'brilliant young writer' as the *Geographic* described Maurice. In the heyday of the illustrated international magazine, of transparency film Kodachrome II, when photographers and writers went to corners of the 'globe' where film and television had yet to reach, *National Geographic* could be found in every library, almost every dentist or doctor's waiting room; some households had bound volumes of the magazine. There were three million subscribers[6] around the world: Brake and Shadbolt had put New Zealand on the map.[7]

In the style favoured by the *Geographic*, Maurice founded his text on his and Gill's personal travel story and decision to return home from London so that their first child could be born a New Zealander. He then took the reader on the journey he and Brian Brake had made to capture the country that had '"something of everything" — of Switzerland, of Norway, of England, of America and, above all, a large slice of Polynesia'.[8] In romantic prose, he made it a story of homecoming, rediscovery and a decision to stay. Many New Zealanders sought reassurance about themselves and their country from overseas — in the so-called 'cultural cringe' — and were warmed by the sense of pride generated by Maurice's story and Brake's showcasing photographs. Maurice now became known to hundreds of thousands of New Zealanders, not only those who read fiction.

The wide readership of the feature provided the launching platform for the book to come. In April Brake wrote from Hong Kong that he would get on to this once he had his 'Monsoon' volume and its associated international exhibition out of the way, and he would fly down to New Zealand to take more pictures. By June his schedule had become so hectic with Asian assignments that he did not think he would make it before the end of the year. He was thinking of a 100-page book with about a quarter of that text and it would be best if he did a layout first and then fly down to fill in any gaps. Brake dismissed Maurice's concern that there were a lot of picture books on the market: 'Ours will be much more expensive, and I hope better … I'll let you know my selection so that you can start thinking along text lines and how we can "play" the whole thing.'[9]

David Lawson, publisher at Whitcombe & Tombs, had already expressed interest in the project and in May was enthusiastic about the book Maurice had already finished, a new collection of nine short stories under the peculiar title of 'Seek the Green Inn'. Maurice had completed this in early April and it had already been accepted by Eyre and Spottiswoode. His agents had gone past Gollancz with the recommendation of Patrick White and Lawson had now instructed Whitcombe's London office to go after New Zealand rights. He thought the manuscript 'very fine and deserves an even better reception than *The New Zealanders*. In this one you really come to grips with ... what it is to be a New Zealander.'[10]

Maurice told Kevin Ireland that he had pruned down his final selection from seventeen stories he had worked on since 1959, dropping those with an overseas setting which were perhaps 'weaker'. 'I love fitting stories together, planning a book and imposing a unity on a collection ... It might also mean I am a frustrated novelist (which Dave Ballantyne maintains I am) rather than a story-writer pure.' As if to confirm that judgement, he told Ireland that since the story collection was finished he had been making 'notes' for a novel, 13,000 words worth, that spanned forty years from 1919 with two families involved over two generations. 'It's a novel I've had in mind for years. In fact at least three or four stories — THE STRANGERS and AFTER THE DEPRESSION for two — were, in a way, preliminary sketches.'[11] With the confidence of a contract for his new collection, later titled *Summer Fires and Winter Country*, he applied for the Burns Fellowship and heard in mid-September he had been successful. Soon afterwards he set off on his *National Geographic* Malaysian assignment in the knowledge that he had secured a good income for the next eighteen months and could devote a year of that to purely literary work.

Maurice wrote that he pushed himself to finish the new collection to the point where his 'health cracked'. He was 'hit by violent attacks of colitis for six months' (and intermittently over the following years). It seemed an age since the success of *The New Zealanders*, 'years of change, doubt, disappointment and confusion. So it seemed now or never'[12] to prove that he was more than a one-hit wonder and his critics were wrong. For Maurice, *Summer Fires and Winter Country* would, for years, remain his 'most satisfying book, even if not my best, because I knew then I could and should go on telling the tales I most wanted to tell; that I could survive, regardless.'[13]

In putting together the collection, 'Besides working towards a greater degree of formal control, I wanted to make my stories function in that territory, faintly mapped, between the New Zealand of romantic dream and utopian expectation and the New Zealand of gritty provincial detail; in that territory, rather than on one side or the other, lay the truth about the country'.[14] Maurice, the country boy to the age of fifteen and then an uncomfortable city dweller for the next fifteen, was well-positioned as a writer to explore the 'territory' of discomfort, confusion and inner conflict of pakeha, mostly middle-class, who continued to struggle with where they belonged. He was charting the 'limitations, the lack of choice and the rigidity that then hedged the lives of his fellow countrymen and women'.[15] The stories were also a way of working out where he belonged himself, to 'make sense of New Zealand'. Beneath his declared ambition was an undeclared, and perhaps unconscious, attempt to understand more personal territory, the stresses created by his need for the emotional and practical securities of marriage and the impulse to be free of its sense of entrapment.

In most of the *Summer Fires* stories, women are agents of conflict in triangular relationships where one party, usually male, is either irreparably damaged or dies in implicit suicide. An analysis written thirty years later, and with knowledge of Maurice's later turbulent relationships, suggested that his 'hazy, incomplete image of womanhood emerges through the impact of women characters on the hero, rather than through any inner life of their own. The woman's acts of betrayal, infidelity, or rejection generate in the hero violence, illness, or self-destruction — emotions which effectively draw him further away from some obscure, sexual mystery which he fears to confront … by implication the women who initiate the male protagonist into the knowledge of death, destruction and failure are rarely capable of redemption.'[16]

The *Summer Fires* stories were also criticised for narrating mainly the experience of white male pakeha with their ambivalent attitude towards the land, in contrast to Maori as the natural inhabitants who were portrayed often as easygoing and only occasionally discontented. Yet Maurice was simply drawing from his own first-hand knowledge of the conformist society of the 1940s and 1950s with its emotionally constipated male culture, its constricting effect on women and the few ways in which they learned to fight back. His knowledge of Maori was not an imagined ideal but the way he knew them in his youth. Maurice later wrote that in many of his stories he 'tried to ensure that a whisper or two of these antipodean lives, stunted by time and place, remained on the human record. We were of a generation that grew up in a country no longer quite a colony but not yet a nation.'[17] The book is dedicated to his parents and 'for Joseph Kearon'.

To some critics, Maurice's *Summer Fires* stories did not advance much beyond the work of earlier writers such as Frank Sargeson and Roderick Finlayson, and lacked the psychological insight that might have made them new. The difference, at the time, was that those writers were little known to the general public while Maurice was becoming well known and his stories, no matter how flawed, spoke to them. In later years, he was thanked by an individual for 'making sense of his past. Which is all I need to know. Literature is more than language, or it is nothing at all.'[18]

The stories remain windows into a vanished society. Fifteen years after the publication of *Summer Fires*, Maurice wrote that in re-reading the stories he seemed to be 'revisiting a lost, innocent land … I could never write these stories now: I am glad I wrote them when I did.'[19] Literary judges at the time were also glad. 'Ben's Land' had won the Wellington Festival prize, 'The Room' was taken by Charles Brasch for the September 1962 issue of *Landfall* and 'Homecoming' won the prestigious 1963 Katherine Mansfield Short Story Award.

A more expansive critical view of *Summer Fires* was that 'In their portrayal of Maori-pakeha relations, their embracing of feminist perspectives, and their treatment of such issues as abortion, incest, and homosexuality, the stories … display an awareness of aspects of New Zealand society that few were then willing to confront.'[20] *Summer Fires* was less uneven than *The New Zealanders* with only two real failures: the disjointed, melodramatic 'There was a Mountain' and 'Winter Country', heavy on dialectical dialogue with an unlikely denouement.[21]

The first part of 'Ben's Land' was what is now described as 'creative non-fiction'. It was Maurice's first clear use of Shadbolt family history that was to be a recurring preoccupation over the next thirty years. The narrator tells of four generations of his own and Uncle Ben's family, drawn from pioneering stock on the land but who have become dispersed into the cities. Uncle Ben, unhappy with his suburban lot, buys a few acres of poor farmland, drawn by nostalgia for his ancestors' pioneering past, and leaves his family in an attempt to make sense of his life. He fails in the attempt, returns to the city, and dies in a drunken fall at his waterfront work. Years later, the narrator tries to find the land with Uncle Ben's old hut. He also fails: 'I might have still found it there, somewhere, if I had looked. I suppose I didn't look only because I was afraid I might not find it.'[22]

'The Room' is a successful, if symbolic, story in which parents on the farm represent a pioneering tradition that has declined into provincial conservatism while their children Margaret and Sonny represent the pioneers of the new world in the city. Margaret dies in the attempt from a failed abortion and Sonny begins to find his way through understanding what happened to her and the shocking realisation of their almost incestuous relationship. Sonny is a 'figure of social and historical transition, and he is well depicted as such, an authentic historical type.'[23]

'Summer Fires' is a coming of age story that parallels the modernising change in a coastal settlement with the growing awareness of the young male narrator into the ways of adult relationships. It concludes: 'I began to understand how, if you go after one thing, you're always liable to finish up with something else altogether; I'd never understood before how dangerous people were to one another'. The narrator echoes that of Ian Cross's *The God Boy* and the story's 'Jim' is drawn from the character of Eric Lee-Johnson.

Whereas 'Ben's Land' dealt with an older generation in a nostalgic return to the land, 'Neither Profit nor Salvation' reflected the contemporary urge to abandon the stresses of city life for a country idyll. A woman with two failed marriages, accompanied by a younger homeless woman, leaves her comfortable city flat and round of parties for a rundown orchard by a northern bay. They grow closer as they regenerate the fruit trees and make pottery. All is well until the older woman's ineffectual second husband turns up to claim 'conjugal rights'. This serpent in Eden impregnates the younger woman but then is driven out and drowns in a foolhardy attempt to reach an offshore island. The story was ahead of its time in forecasting migration of the city's young to country communes in the late 1960s and 1970s and even more so in its presentiment of successful lesbian families. 'There would have to be clothes, a cot. And of course both she and Merlyn would have to learn a great deal about children … Yet she was confident that, together, they would make a good job of it.'[24]

The local Maori community plays a role in 'Neither Profit nor Salvation' but in the three remaining stories pakeha-Maori relationships are the central themes. The original version of 'The Wind and the Spray' had been rejected by Charles Brasch who said it should have been titled 'The Negative New Zealander'. In the revised version it reworks themes common to most of the *Summer Fires* stories. Mark leaves the family farm to make a life in the city but returns to take it over when his parents die. He leaves behind Susan, a fiancée he does not love and with a pregnancy he is not responsible for, and falls in love with Huia with whom he does father a child. The ensuing conflicts and consequences leave Mark with nowhere to go. Symbolically, the farm overlooks a dangerous bar on which immigrant sailing ships had foundered with heavy loss of life. Below decks, 'Already coffined, denied sight of their promised land, they would not even have had, at that last moment, the wind and the spray in their faces.'[25] Mark dies as he steers his frail launch into the monstrous breaking waves.

There are echoes of the earlier 'The Strangers' in 'The People Before' which strongly contrasts the difference between Maori and pakeha relationships to the land. In relying again on family history, the story is strongly reminiscent of Maurice's Grandfather Ernest's experience of breaking in the land up the Whanganui River, prospering for a while before the hardships of the Depression. A party of Maori arrive from the coast, carrying a frail old man in a litter who wants to die on Craggy Hill, his turangawaewae on the land that once belonged to his people. The practical pakeha farmer understands nothing of the spiritual meaning of it all, and is outraged when the party leaves, saying they have left the old man behind. A search for a body finds nothing and the Maori travellers tell police the old man simply disappeared into the bush. But he would always be up there somewhere. After this, the farmer 'lost all taste for the farm. It seemed the land itself had heaped some final indignity upon him, made a fool of him.' He sold up. The land and the spiritual power of 'the people before' had rejected him.

The prizewinning 'The Homecoming' was a story salvaged from his doomed novel. Pakeha journalist Eve returns home from London to find herself out of place in the city but begins to feel at home again when she goes back to her parents' farm in the Hokianga. But of her school age friends only Sarah Arapata lives nearby with muscular Muru who had been almost good enough to play for the All Blacks. Eve is appalled at the squalor Sarah is now living in. Earlier, she had gone through training college and married a city pakeha who showed her off but who spoke Maori better than she. With Muru, Sarah could be herself. Eve's attitude towards Maori was mixed. She had imagined them as 'closer to nature, children of earth, less tampered with by civilization'. But were they? What was it about Muru who angrily declared real ownership of the land, 'freakish in his passion and strength'?[26] In a situation possibly drawn from John Osborne's *Look Back In Anger*, Eve persuades Sarah to leave Muru, to go back to a 'better' life in the city and then replaces her, to use Muru in finding her own place on the land. As she began washing dishes in the squalid kitchen, Muru 'just stood there smiling, filling the doorway'. Maurice later thought that the militant Muru was a harbinger of radical city Maori of the 1970s, but there is also a hint of Jake Heke to come in Alan Duff's *Once Were Warriors* (1990).

'For months I have been roaming tin-and-rubber-rich Malaya, teeming Singapore, and their wild, romantic neighbours, Sarawak and North Borneo … Prime Minister Tunku Abdul Rahman … of Malaya described these far-flung lands to me as "a crescent of freedom".'[27] Maurice was away from home for more than three months travelling through the disparate countries of the incipient Federation of Malaysia, coping with colitis in tropical heat and challenging culinary excitements in order to write an article that would satisfy

America's need to read of the success of Democracy in its endless fight against Communism. Almost certainly there was a heavy editorial hand in the end to his article about four separate ex-British colonies coming together under one-government rule, although he must have written its outline. 'In a world haunted by the threat of nuclear destruction, their endeavour has special significance. Future historians might mark it as the beginning of one of the most decisive experiments in man's history ... Can people of so many races, so many beliefs, find a true harmony? ... The answer affects us all. Because Malaysia is not simply a test for Asians ... It is a test for the human race itself.'[28] Singapore's Lee Kuan Yew told Maurice, 'Together we can survive. Divided we can only perish'. Less than two years later Singapore was expelled from the federation over political differences and Lee took the island on its own spectacular course of independent development.

During his long absence, Maurice wrote aerogrammes to Gill about twice a week, telling her of his intestinal woes alongside encounters with ethnically diverse people in various exotic locations. 'I suffered through the jungles of Sarawak, staggered through the bogs of Borneo and bounced sickeningly about the Sulu Sea in a boat filled with a terrifying team of Gurkhas on anti-pirate patrol.'[29]

In 9000 miles of travelling he went from the 'gleaming dusk' of Kuala Lumpur to folk-dancing Khota Baru; from Singapore's 'teeming maze' to a Dayak longhouse in Sarawak. Here, in the *Geographic* article, Maurice is pictured in short-sleeved shirt and shorts waiting for a glass to be filled with rice wine. Just the thing for colitis.

The stay-at-home Mum kept Maurice up to date with the condition of his children. Gill wrote: 'You'll be relieved to hear that Brendy was crawling up on all fours all round the place and as chirpy as a little cricket before he went to bed. There is no sign of a temperature. [If] he continues to improve like this he'll be fine tomorrow. Sean has been off food again today but I have sneaked a couple of eggs into him through bottles.'[30]

Of friends, the Bollingers were 'very well' and Con had applied for a job on the Public Service Journal but there was currently a 'witch hunt' in the PSA and 'he thinks his background etc ... will go against him'. It was 'wonderful' to see Pat and Gil Hanly when they passed through, on their way to hang his pictures in a Christchurch gallery. 'There's an added beauty to Gill's [sic] face, somehow; Pat is more wiry and nuggety and alive than I've ever seen him ... They suggest we go and park in their front garden when we go through at Christmas time.'[31]

Gill had cleaned and polished the car, and she had been taking advice from

Ian Cross's wife Tui about preparing and packing for the Burns Fellowship and Dunedin. Maurice should not worry about rushing home to help with this. She thought it 'very important' he had a break at her mother's place in Sydney on the way home 'even if you sleep the whole time you are there. I'd suggest you had a couple of days of just sleeping and swimming.'[32] There was nothing about her own condition. Implicitly, she was fine and too busy to think about it anyway.

Maurice did stop in Sydney on the way home and visited Patrick White and his companion Manoly Lascaris on their small farm. When Maurice related his adventures in Borneo White told him the world did not need another Joseph Conrad; the best narratives were in one's own backyard. But this was not news.

On arriving home in the New Year of 1963, Maurie still needed a 'rest after the ravages of Asia.'[33] It remains unknown whether or not these 'ravages' included any sexual adventures but given the length of time he was away and his natural proclivities, it seems likely. Resuming family life, he 'grabbed up Gillian and the children' and drove north to Ninety Mile Beach. In a rented caravan he laboured each morning at an upbeat narrative for *National Geographic* before taking Sean and Brendan to the beach. 'We gathered toheroa and tuatua with Maori neighbours and netted flounder with Barry Mitcalfe and other locals. For a time it seemed I might daydream there forever.'[34] And hoping, in vain, that sun, sea and sand might cure his colitis.

CHAPTER 19

FULL OF THE WARM SOUTH

Almost six months had passed since he had engaged in any kind of fiction writing and *National Geographic* journalism was no help in moving him into a literary frame of mind as they packed up again in mid-January and made the 1100-mile journey south to Dunedin. The house that had been arranged for them at 69 Union Street was cold and 'derelict' with, for two-and-a-half-year-old Sean, a disconcerting hole in the lavatory floor.

They were met by English lecturer Bob Robertson and Dennis McEldowney whom Maurice had first befriended when they both lived in Upper Hutt in 1960. McEldowney had been born a 'blue baby', suffering from Tetralogy of Fallot, defects of the heart ventricles which had left him an invalid for all his childhood and youth. Blue babies usually died young but McEldowney survived until, at the age of twenty-four, modern open-heart surgery allowed him to become partially mobile. During his earlier confined years he had honed his skills as an essayist and in 1957 published an account of his early years and operation, *The World Regained*, which won PEN's Hubert Church Memorial Prize for Prose.[1] More advanced surgery in 1960 meant he could lead a relatively normal life and he was about to take up his first job as a clerk at Dunedin's School of Physical Education.

McEldowney told Maurice and Gill that staff in the English Department were relieved they were arriving as a family. Hosting the first Burns Fellow Ian Cross and his family had been a pleasure but the three subsequent fellows had caused problems. The second, Maurice Duggan, had left his wife behind in Auckland and openly enjoyed his affair with Fleur Adcock. (Adcock was about to divorce Barry Crump and return to England, which became her permanent domicile). The third Burns Fellow, John Caselberg, with whom Maurice had shared the *Landfall* 10th anniversary award six years before, had reputedly 'smashed furniture at a faculty function and left lecturers and professors fretful of social gatherings for some time'.[2] The fourth fellow, who was still in Dunedin after his tenure the year before, was R.A.K. 'Ron' Mason, whom Allen Curnow had described as New Zealand's 'first wholly original, unmistakably gifted poet' and whose work Maurice much admired. But he was now in his 'creative twilight'. He had suffered deep depression, during which he had allegedly made sexual advances to a female student, and was taken to hospital for psychiatric care. Staff hoped Maurice's stay would not prove so dramatic.

The study for Burns fellows was an upstairs room, once a children's bedroom, in a two-storey villa in Leith Street only a ten-minute walk from the Union Street house. There was a full-sized typewriter, unlimited amounts of stationery, access to the university library and morning teas with English Department staff of whom Bob Robertson was something of his champion. But before Maurice could think about engaging in a new fiction project, he was under pressure to finish the 'New Zealand book' for Whitcombe & Tombs. He had scarcely settled in when a letter arrived from Brian Brake in Hong Kong saying that he was leaving for Tokyo to show the book's layout to printers whose favourable quote had delighted publisher David Lawson. The book had expanded to over 140 pages, a two-to-one mix of black and white to colour photographs and 40 pages of text which Maurice could not properly draft until the makeup had been finalised. Brake planned to fly to New Zealand at the beginning of March when he would obtain Lawson's final decisions on the print run and content so that 'we could get down to final quotes and the like that will have to be part of the picture lay-out'. Brake was taking an innovative approach to the book which would see a creative linking text between picture sequences.

Brake was so sure of his standing that he also told Maurice 'I think I'll have to see Prime Minister [Keith Holyoake] so that we can get the book duty free'.[3] There were various tax issues affecting book production and earnings. Maurice had written to Holyoake the year before, following the impact of his *National Geographic* article, about the unfair system which saw a local author's royalties taxed in both the overseas country of publication and in New Zealand. It was a letter of enlightened self-interest. In July, Holyoake responded positively, promising that the government would 'examine the whole matter very carefully with a view to introducing suitable legislation'.[4] But the government was more concerned with taxes on patent royalties and copyrights they were losing to the British and not authors' piffling overseas earnings. Nevertheless, Maurice kept his name before the prime minister by ensuring that a copy of *Summer Fires and Winter Country* was sent to Holyoake and a copy of the New Zealand book later that year. Of more concern for New Zealand writers having their books published in London was their receipt of only 5 per cent of the export receipts on copies sold in New Zealand, usually the majority, and often under the imprint of Whitcombe & Tombs. David Lawson was sympathetic to the complaints of Maurice and other writers under his imprint but was able to make little headway with management.

Over 'one frantic & sleepless weekend' Brake and Maurice decided on the final structure of their book and agreed the best title was simply *National Geographic's — New Zealand Gift of the Sea*. As news of it spread, there were warnings that its concept was 'far too arty'[5] for the New Zealand market. But Whitcombe's were more optimistic, conscious of the connection the reading public would make with the *Geographic* article and Brake's fame as a photographer. They ordered a print run of 15,000. The royalty on the book was 15 per cent and Brake, given the dominance of his photographs and all his design and printing legwork, wrote to Maurice saying this should be split 10 per cent for himself and 5 per cent to Maurice for a text which, in the end, amounted to no more than thirty pages.[6]

Although Maurice used elements of his *National Geographic* text for *Gift of the Sea*, the tone and narrative were different, less of a personal journey of rediscovery and more of a paean to a country with unique landscape qualities and human attributes (although not without criticism of the damage done by pioneer farmers and miners). A significant part of his text is given over to the discovery and settlement by Maori and the special qualities of their culture. But the sequence of photographs of Maori and its linking text leads essentially to a celebration of their resilience and adaptation and embrace of the modern world. In this respect and others Maurice and Brake were, of course, reflecting pakeha beliefs, myths and sometimes realities, of their time. New Zealand, with a population of only two and half million, was still seen as a land for migrants. Maurice wrote of the growing number of settlers from Polynesia but 'Asian immigration, to our national disgrace, has been severely and sometimes cruelly restricted. We still prefer third-rate immigrants from Europe to first-rate people from Asia.'[7] This was a comment on the notorious poll taxes on Chinese immigrants until the 1940s but was probably also reflective of Brake's experience of living and working in Asia. Grandly, Maurice declared New Zealand could easily support a population of twenty million.

Gift of the Sea now portrays a kind of lost paradise: of a damaged but still uncrowded natural environment, with people living in equality and harmony and with a 'physical freedom unmatched in the world'. Not only Maori but pakeha outside the cities, too, the 'spiritual descendants of the pioneers', had become '*tangata whenua* — men of the land … Men as native as the kiwi'. Most of the narrative was glowing and infused with myth but it also reminds us of what was soon to disappear. 'The paradox of the Kiwi is that he is a self-proclaimed individualist who lives in one of the world's most collective societies … it's possible to be rich but not very rich. It's also possible to be poor, but not very poor … Equality, in New Zealand, has meant equality of opportunity, an instinctive detestation of privilege.'[8]

Inspirational quotes from poets such as Allen Curnow, A.R.D. Fairburn, Charles Brasch and James K. Baxter studded a book that celebrated New Zealand and New Zealanders in a way never seen before. In company with Brian Brake, Maurice again was presenting his public with what they wanted to hear and see. Unsurprisingly, the Prime Minister's Department ordered 300 copies for use as official gifts and for its embassies.

Maurice found it difficult to settle down to fiction with the distractions of *Gift of the Sea*. The 'frantic' weekend with Brake had created tensions between them over how the book should be 'played'. As Brake's comments regarding *National Geographic* reveal, he had a short fuse if layout and picture choice did not accord with his views. Maurice would have struggled with Brake over space and placing for his text. Publisher David Lawson had to mediate and Maurice credited him for keeping the partnership together.[9] Apart from the stresses with *Gift*, he had proofs of *Summer Fires* to deal with and also the *Geographic*'s editorial requirements for the Malaysian story.

Maurice had 'mixed feelings' about Dunedin, too, in a year of unusually cold and unsettled weather. 'Its smug and synthetic Scottishness tended to madden me. But the old Victorian buildings were genuine. I wished its citizens would see themselves as inhabiting one of the new world's most distinctive cities, one which matched pioneer aspiration' rather than claiming to be the 'Edinburgh of the South'.[10] A generation later they began to do so.

A month after arriving, there was the unwelcome distraction of a Royal Tour. Dennis McEldowney wrote, 'To the Shadbolts for lunch, to a sardonic Maurice and a would-be-monarchist-if-she-weren't-married-to-Morry-Gill'. With Gill and the boys, McEldowney stood in the rain to glimpse the Queen while Maurice, 'true to his principles, went in the other direction, to the English Department'.[11]

There were also the distractions of family life and new friends. Visiting American academic Gordon Fisher and family lived next door, McEldowney was a regular visitor and the Shadbolts spent time with Adolf Diegel and family. German by birth, senior lecturer Diegel had just arrived in Dunedin from the USA to establish Otago University's first degree course in business organisation and management. Adolf Diegel was seen as a 'character', living with his family on an eighty-acre Mount Cargill farm. The Diegels planted trees, ran chooks and had 'two dogs, two cats, two goats, and two donkeys: all pairs except the cats, of which, being canny, they did not get a pair, but instead two females.'[12] They also had two boys to match the Shadbolt pair, the families were university newcomers and they went on fishing and shellfish collecting excursions together.

These trips were made in a brand-new Holden EJ station wagon which Maurice had bought soon after arriving. Its cost was about £850, something he could not have afforded from his Burns Fellowship salary of £1250 for the year. It was also not possible in 1963 to walk into a showroom and buy a new car without 'overseas funds'. *National Geographic* had provided these. Maurice was well aware of the compromises he had to make if he and his family were to live from his earnings as a writer, and buy new cars. Dennis McEldowney, as an author, told his colleagues at the Physical Education School it was not possible to earn a living from writing to which they said, "'Maurice Shadbolt rides around in a great big Holden station wagon." So I have to rephrase my answer to, "*I* can't make a living from writing." Maurice said, "You should say: 'I don't sell my soul.'"[13]

In evenings and at the weekends there was theatre at the Globe and parties and sometimes theatre and parties together. The Shadbolts met perennial student and up-and-coming playwright Michael Noonan whose short play, 'The Rattle', Charles Brasch compared to 'King Lear'. DNTV-2 television had recently arrived in Dunedin and sometimes they would visit neighbours with TV sets to watch programmes. Noonan sometimes read the news bulletins but Maurice was more taken by attractive 25-year-old continuity announcer Barbara Magner who found herself invited to a Union Street party. This proved hazardous with holes in the floor to catch her heels and Sean deliberately riding his scooter into the guests' legs.

Then there were the regular distractions of out-of-town visitors. Maurice and Gill paid for mother Vi and fourteen year-old sister Julia to come down from Waiheke Island, the latest Shadbolt parents' abode, to stay for a few weeks during the summer school holidays and partake of barbecued pig on the Diegel farm. Gill's mother came over from Sydney. Albert Wendt flew down from Auckland in the winter when he had his first introduction to snow on Mount Cargill and wrote a poem 'The First Snowman' for Sean and Brendan.

Maurice also persuaded Uncle Joe Kearon to travel down from Auckland on his only trip to the South Island and took him on a winter family holiday to Arrowtown and Queenstown.

Maurice sat in his Leith Street writing room and worked hard to pick up the threads of the big multi-generational novel he had sketched out the year before. It was not coming easily. 'Perhaps it was the atmosphere of the campus. The Burns fellowship is an extremely worthy institution; and my project … seemed extremely worthy too.'[14] Maurice may have also felt the glooming presence of Charles Brasch, who came down from his dark and book-filled flat on Heriot Row to edit *Landfall* in a room above the University Book Shop not far away. The pair were now on uncertain terms after the Gee review and, as others found, Brasch was not an easy man to know. His literary judgements did not favour John A. Lee's novel *Children of the Poor*, based on his desperate Dunedin childhood, and which Maurice considered one of the few 1930s novels of lasting worth. According to Maurice, Brasch 'failed to talk of Lee without a wrinkling of nose.'[15] But, after all, as Dennis McEldowney noted, 'Charles Brasch is Charles Brasch.'[16] As chief benefactor of the Burns fellowship which paid Maurice's bills, 'It was not for me to grumble.'[17]

In the Leith Street English Department house, Maurice was constantly aware of the coming and going of students. He was not disturbed by staff but Bob Robertson prevailed on him to attend a lecture he gave on Maurice's 'After the Depression'. Incognito, Maurice kept his head down at the back of the room as Robertson said, '"A homeless and footsore man, woman and child wandering a dusty road … What does this say to you? What does it remind you of?" Now that Bob mentioned it, the beleaguered threesome of my story might be seen as the Holy Family. That was daunting.'[18] In a late-life swipe at what he still considered the stultifying effect of academia on creative writing, Maurice concluded that if he had not failed English at university he would never have written the story.

Nevertheless, in those first months in Dunedin he felt obliged to read and re-read many New Zealand novels and short stories so that he could 'discuss that fiction called "New Zealand literature" reasonably and intelligently with staff and students on campus.'[19] It was a necessary preparation for the address he gave on New Zealand writing at the university's arts festival in August. His audience was mainly the 'university literati, beat types nearly all, black bearded and grubby … perhaps they were overawed by one as aged and respected as Maurice, but what it amounted to was Maurice saying to them, "Rebel, damn you!" and their saying to him, "Why?"'.[20] The next day, the *Otago Daily Times* reported him as saying his work had been mostly influenced by Barry Crump and prison escaper George Wilder, when he had actually said 'that he regards both as hopeful signs, showing that New Zealanders have not lost the capacity to create genuine folk heroes.'[21]

Maurice was concerned about the stores of myth and history, Maori and pakeha, that were not found in the local house of literature. In a subsequent article for the *Otago Daily Times* he attacked the New Zealand 'man alone' myth that had grown from John Mulgan's novel as 'not a popular myth, but a critical myth — a literary artifact [that] begins and ends with critics who discuss New Zealand writing as if it exists in a vacuum'. For the man alone was a figure that could be found in the short story throughout western literature. As for Barry Crump it was plain that he was the 'image of what most New Zealanders would like themselves to be. He stands for what we are losing as the frontier society passes away. But Crump the myth is also Crump the creator of the myth.'[22]

By then, Maurice had put aside the painfully wrought 20,000 words of his big novel but agreed to allow a 4000-word extract to be included in the 1963 Otago student literary review. He prefaced this by saying it was from the 'first rough draft' of a novel he had 'tentatively titled SEARCH FOR TIM LIVINGSTONE', and all the main characters had been drawn from earlier published stories, principally from *The New Zealanders*. William Morrison, he wrote, was from 'After the Depression'; Ian Morrison from 'End of Season'; Tim Livingstone from 'The Paua Gatherers'; and Ned Livingstone was the father in 'The Strangers'.[23] Only the Livingstones appeared in the review extract which was the basis for chapters one, three and five for the big novel that would, years later, be published as *Strangers and Journeys*.

Maurice wrote occasionally to James K. Baxter who had given up School Publications and was working as a postie in Wellington. A letter from Maurice telling of his difficulties with the big novel sparked a sequence of thirteen poems written in September and October and dedicated to Maurice when they were published as *Pig Island Letters* in 1966. The first begins:

> The gap you speak of — yes, I find it so,
> The menopause of the mind, I think of it
> As a little death, practising for the greater,
> For the undertaker who won't have read
> Your stories or my verse ...

and concludes ...

> ... In the Otago storms

> Carrying spray to salt the landward farms
> The wind is a drunkard. Whoever can listen
> Long enough will write again.[24]

After their publication, Maurice told Baxter he had learned those four lines 'like a chant, a mental talisman'. For the 'Pig Island' poems 'seemed greater consolation that I deserved: I was bleeding from too many self-inflicted wounds and pitying myself into the bargain'.[25]

Always one for the power of symbols, on mid-winter's day and the day *Summer Fires and Winter Country* was published in London, Maurice now turned to 'something irreverent, possibly so I could feel my own man again', away from the world of NZ Lit and university and into the landscapes of Crump and Wilder. Gill began to hear him whistling as he walked back to Union Street after a day's work. With the family saga put away in a drawer and 'With no premeditation at all, I sat at my Burns desk and began composing a playful pastiche of some New Zealand writing, partly as an oblique exercise in criticism, partly to put some of my more irritant preoccupations into permanent storage, and so escape my year as a responsible citizen intact'.[26] Maurice liked to think of himself as an outsider but there was a root of conservatism in his upbringing, of what was right and proper, that he would never escape.

Dunedin's *Evening Star* reported that 'the launching party' for Maurice's *Summer Fires and Winter Country* at the University Bookshop was the 'first of its kind in Dunedin'. David Lawson, Bob Robertson and Charles Brasch spoke in praise of the book and Maurice praised Lawson and UBS manager John Griffiths who had 'both done a lot for New Zealand writers'.[27] A photograph showed Lawson with his wife and the Shadbolts brandishing cigarettes, Gill elegant with cigarette holder, necklace, ear-rings, a new hair-do and a stylish shawl-like jacket. Dennis McEldowney thought the launch a 'succession of incoherent conversations' and went on to the Shadbolts' where 'bearded Dr Diegel stood guard over a carton of his home brew, the smoke was thick, conversation even more incoherent …'[28]

Reviews of *Summer Fires* in England had been fewer than for *The New Zealanders* but largely favourable. In New Zealand, David Hall in the *Listener* described it as a 'triumph, exhibiting a sureness and maturity … Shadbolt writing at the top of his bent, shows himself superbly a master of this form.'[29] In *Landfall*, H. Winston Rhodes had reservations. At the time, Rhodes was an associate professor of English at Canterbury University. A socialist activist all his life, he had helped found *Tomorrow* in the 1930s, which published Frank Sargeson's first stories, and was currently editor of the left-wing *NZ Monthly*

Review. Rhodes saw Maurice as a writer with an 'enviable assortment of gifts' who knew 'exactly what he wanted to do and did it with energy and skill, able at all times to command and hold the attention of his readers'. Rhodes continued, almost uncannily: 'All art is based on illusion, but there is a difference between artfulness and art, and it is disconcerting to most readers if they become uneasily aware that they have been victims of a clever conjuring trick'. He accused Maurice of creating a myth of New Zealanders as an 'uprooted people wistfully looking back to the romantic past of the tillers of the soil, the early pioneers, the ancestral breakers-in of the country'. Despite all his writerly skills, Maurice relied 'too heavily on the ambiguities that result from a type of narrative impressionism, and in his impatience to achieve intensity and dramatic excitement the subtleties of human relationships are slurred and the exploration of human motives and sensibility is sacrificed'.[30]

Maurice may well have smiled at the conjuring reference; acknowledged the mythic reference with 'all story is myth' and that was what he had been writing about after all; but would have been reluctant to admit that psychological insight was not one of his strong points.

Jim Baxter wrote in 'Pig Island Letters':

> Thank you for your letter. I read your book
> Five days ago: it has the slow
> Imperceptible wingbeat of the hawk
> Above the dry scrublands. The kill is there
> In the Maori riverbed below
> Where bones glitter …[31]

Moss Gee wrote to say that he thought 'Homecoming' and 'The Room' made a 'complete authoritative statement about life in N.Z.' and that his writing 'looks unwaveringly at the painful facts of loneliness & lost illusion, lost innocence'.[32] Gee was now living in Rotorua, working in a dental records office and in a problematic relationship with Hera Smith. He was unhappy not only in his personal life but about lack of progress with his writing in what was becoming a wasted year. His first novel *The Big Season* had sold over 3000 copies which he thought poor and saw Maurice as always the bigger achiever.

Maurice and Kevin Ireland continued to express concern about Moss Gee's welfare. After Gee left London in 1962, Ireland wrote: 'Poor old Maurice Gough Gee is on the high seas at this moment not knowing what he wants to do or where he wants to be'.[33] In June 1963, Maurice reported that he had received a desperate and moody letter from Gee and urged Ireland to write to him. Gee was in a job that could be done by an office girl and unable to write. 'He's in another terrible situation … [one] that might send Moss round the bend.'[34] Gee finally decided that the way out was to apply for the 1964 Burns Fellowship. At the end of September, after he heard that he had received it, Maurice sent him a congratulatory telegram and was relieved, as Ireland and all Gee's friends were, when he responded that he was 'feeling alive again, literary-wise, for the first time in over a year'.[35]

By then Maurice's new picaresque novel had 'become more than a joke; I had to decide how and whether to push it through … I could, if I let the manuscript drift, become bored with it.'[36] But again there were major distractions. David Lawson sent tickets for an October Book Week Party in Wellington which would double as a launch for *Gift of the Sea* and with a possible presentation to Prime Minister Holyoake. The publicity programme for *Gift* was extensive: window slashes, display cards, general advertising and 'biggest — or most expensive — of all, a twenty-second filmed TV commercial that will be shown on all channels in prime time. The cost!'[37] In 1963, the promotional tag, 'As seen on TV!' had an enormous marketing impact. The first shipment had scarcely arrived at the beginning of October when Lawson ordered another 6000.

Then Maurice heard he had to be in Wellington at the same time to receive the Katherine Mansfield Short Story Award for 'Homecoming'. The function at Government House was formal and sedate with the Governor-General, Sir Bernard Fergusson, presiding. Fergusson was a published writer and had read the judges' comments on the entries. Before presenting the award, he noted that many of the stories dealt with Maori-European themes or had Maori characters but where, he asked the assembly of about a hundred, were the Maori among them? None. 'I think New Zealanders should ask themselves why', he said.[38] Maori still had no presence in the literary world, or at such exalted cultural gatherings. But there was another presence that the psychic Maurice was certain of: a woman dressed and coiffured as Katherine Mansfield sitting on the stage. When he later mentioned this to an organiser of the event, considering it inappropriate, she strongly denied any such person had been present. Years later, in conversation with the academic who was judge of the 1963 award, he said he had seen her, too.[39] Shades of Grandmother Ada.

In Wellington, Maurice stayed with Renato and Sheena Amato in Kelburn. 'We argued, as usual, into the early hours of morning. And for some reason I began telling him about the [new] novel'. Maurice did not usually talk about work in progress but he was in two minds about continuing with it and valued the views of this 'sympathetically critical friend'. Amato thought the 'idea splendid, and urged me to continue … Talking to Renato helped to clarify the theme in my mind — crystallise the book.'[40] It also prompted a determination that, before the end of the Burns year, he would escape from the confining and distracting atmosphere of family and university life in Dunedin in order to finish the novel. Using the 100 guineas Mansfield prize money, Maurice bought a 'month of total isolation,'[41] in a cabin at Queenstown, above Lake Wakatipu,[42] with the Remarkable range huge and misty beyond. With no distraction, I wrote from five in the morning until nine at night; and slipped with no effort into the skin of the novel's youthful narrator, to the point where his takeover seemed total. It was almost natural, then, that I should make undisguised appearance within the narrative to remonstrate with the character about the form the novel seemed to be taking.'[43] Although the method was not new in the history of literature, Maurice was writing metafiction in the years before the term had been academically coined.

While he was away, Gill had been given a break when the Diegels took her and the boys up to their farm for a few days. She had been uncertain of going because Adolf Diegel was 'fanatically tidy' and Gill was aware of her reputation for relaxed and sometimes chaotic methods of housekeeping and child-rearing.

Maurice returned to Dunedin with his draft; the children's recitation of a nursery rhyme on their earlier family trip to Queenstown had given him its title. Maurice's self-questioning main character and his family were called Flinders, rhyming with 'Little Polly Flinders' who 'sat among the cinders'. The alliteration appealed and fitted with the metaphor of fiery events being reduced to cinders but were not yet ashes in the mind. So he had his title, *Among the Cinders*.

Maurice arrived back in Dunedin on 18 November just before Dennis McEldowney left for Auckland. Maurice was 'elated', McEldowney wrote. 'One thing the Burns year has taught him is that he can't write so much every day at a desk; trying to had nearly convinced him he'd lost his creative power.' But in Queenstown 'he got on so far, enjoyed it so much, wrote so well, that he's on top of the world. I suppose reaction will set in, but in the meantime it's great for the family.'[44] A comment which suggests that it had been not so great, especially for Gill, when his writing had faltered.

In writing *Among the Cinders* Maurice drew spontaneously on his own youth in Te Kuiti ('Te Ika'), his later attachments to localities in the Far North, his literary friends and enemies but, above all, his own family. The sixteen year-old narrator, Nick Flinders, has a fairly ineffective father called Frank and although his mother is called Beryl, her fussing and protective behaviour towards her son is clearly drawn from experience. In particular, mother Beryl flusters about to protect him from the attentions of Grandfather Hubert Flinders. Hubert is the spitting image of Grandfather Ernest Shadbolt, from his West Auckland house and section to his golf ball collection and betting, from his use of kindling to discipline children to his bent for litigation, to his relationship with Grandmother Ada whose shade would now be content that Maurice had finally begun writing about the Shadbolts.

Although Maurice said that he started out to write a novel that was a playful pastiche of some contemporary New Zealand writing, and the narrative approach owes something to *The God Boy*, this became secondary to a sometimes rollicking, often humorous, picaresque yarn of a grandfather seeking to rediscover his past with a grandson who is seeking to escape his present.

Nick goes hunting in the bush with his Maori mate Sam Waikai whom he had earlier saved from drowning. High among the limestone crags of Te Ika, Nick finds a cave filled with human bones. He tells Sam to have a look, in order to give him a fright after Sam had scared him earlier. But Nick had not allowed for the power of tapu and Sam backs out of the cave in a hurry, falls headlong down a cliff and is killed. Nick breaks a leg trying to reach him but, when he is eventually rescued, insists that Sam had died trying to save him.

Feeling responsible for Sam's death, Nick later remains in seclusion at home, pampered by his mother, refuses to go back to school and will not meet Sam's mother. Nick's older brother Derek, a balding Auckland literary academic — a scarcely concealed characterisation of C.K. Stead — broaches to his shocked parents that Nick's depression might be down to a homosexual friendship between Nick and Sam. Then Grandfather Hubert turns up from Auckland in a blast of fresh air. 'His voice sounded like rusty old iron. "I been waiting two months to see the young bugger. All I get told is he's sick. He probably is too. Sick with woman's fuss and doctor's bullshit. If this keeps up he'll probably be good for nothing but the knacker's yard. Now, where is he?"'[45] Hubert is sent away but Nick soon absconds and hitchhikes north to join him.

At the West Auckland property, Nick argues with Hubert, listens to family stories from frail Grandmother Flinders and deals with brother Derek who tries to persuade him to go home. Derek is consistently portrayed as an unworldly and pretentious intellectual who wrote a poem for Hubert which began, 'You who shared the land's eager rape/ Opening valleys like thighs …' Hubert's response was to tell Nick that Derek was '"Just a plain nut case. Beyond help, son. Anyone who starts seeing valleys like thighs is beyond human help …"'[46]

The main event of Nick's stay, however, was his encounter with a girl from his Te Ika school. He tries to escape her attentions to him as the hero with his picture in the paper and taunts him with sexual overtures. Nick reacts violently and they struggle, tumbling through undergrowth until he 'only biffed her once more, just to show who was boss again, and then I got down to some fairly interesting close stuff … But I must admit that, in teaching her a lesson, I learned quite a bit myself'[47] and, just as important, made Derek with his homosexual theories 'look a fool'. This was the first of Nick's sexual learning experiences that, in the writing, also revealed something of the sexual mores of the time and perhaps of the author.

Soon afterwards, Hubert disguises the death of Grandmother Flinders in the night and insists that he and Nick go off on 'that trip' he had been talking about. They pack all they need in sugar bags, take axe, rifle and gum spear and head off, hitch-hiking north. First, Hubert takes Nick to a derelict homestead where he says, '"That's where we began. You too. And don't forget it"'. There is another beach, another girl, Sally, who is more than a match for him in their physical/sexual encounter.

Hubert and Nick leave in a hurry when they hear the police are looking for them. Hubert fears they have found dead Grandma Flinders, Nick that the Te Ika girl has reported him for rape. They hole up for a while with a hermit 'bloody Dally' on a desolate worked-out gum field. From there they take off for the Coromandel, looking for gold, and leave there when they are recognised. After five days trekking through the bush with horses, they reach the place where Hubert had his first farm. Finally he '"found a place that hasn't bloody changed"'. But it is too late. Hubert goes down with pneumonia and Nick is apprehended when he goes for supplies in the local town; not for any crime but because they had been listed as missing persons with the suggestion that Hubert has abducted Nick. Reconciliations completed, Hubert is taken in by Mrs Waikai.

Derek turns up with his fiancée who turns out to be Sally from the Far North beach and Nick attends their engagement party in Auckland which is attended by a group of recognisable literary figures of the time such as Ian Cross and James K. Baxter. In a piece of metafiction,[48] Nick meets author Maurice Shadbolt whom he engages to write the story of his accident and journey before brother Derek steals it. The novel ends with Nick returning to the site of Sam's death, mulling over memories of the past year. 'Sometimes it seems to me they all made some kind of sense; sometimes it didn't. Finally I decided they must add up to something.'[49]

Among the Cinders adds up to an essentially New Zealand *Bildungsroman* that was to prove immensely popular. The ancillary theme of Maurice's feud with C.K. Stead and the literati may continue to amuse those in the literary know.[50] The novel rambles here and there, is rough around the edges, reflecting the almost inspirational speed with which it was drafted as well as the character of a sixteen-year-old lad from Te Kuiti. For Maurice, 'If anything ever soared out of despair, he did — even to the point of being born on Dunedin's midwinter day.'[51] Building on the themes of earlier stories such as 'Ben's Land' and 'Summer Fires', Nick Flinders' journey of self-discovery even now allows us to discover that other country of the 1950s.

Maurice's days in Queenstown were not completely preoccupied with five to nine writing. He had returned from Wellington agitated and 'finding writers in Wellington agitated, about Mr Hanan's Indecent Publications Act'.[52] Until that time novels such as Nabokov's *Lolita* or the eighteenth century's *Fanny Hill* had been deemed indecent largely on the judgement of Customs Department officials.[53] The new act proposed to formalise judgement on whether or not a publication was indecent by establishing a tribunal of legal and literary experts to judge books (and films) according to set criteria. Many writers strongly objected to any kind of formal censorship system, especially since the draft bill, bizarrely, included a Clause 15 covering unpublished manuscripts. John Reece Cole, secretary of PEN, was caught in the middle of the crossfire between those on the PEN executive committee firmly opposing the bill, such as Ian Cross, and others such as Monte Holcroft, who thought it was a step leading towards a more liberal censorship regime, provided Clause 15 was excluded and the tribunal's decisions were openly announced. A PEN statement along those lines was approved by the executive.

    Cross wrote to Maurice just before he left for Queenstown, criticising Reece Cole, saying that poet Allen Curnow had resigned from PEN and 'My idea is this: why not form another writers' association?[54] … The move would shake the fleas out of the literary blanket. The Group wouldn't have to agree on much, except opposition to censorship.'[55] Kevin Ireland wrote to say that there had been a 'lot in the Guardian about it … What nasty sides there are to our official character — just at a time when the pressure is being taken off practically everywhere else in the world we go back to the Star Chamber.'[56] In 1960, the seminal Lady Chatterley trial in London had greatly relaxed censorship approaches to allegedly indecent publications and both New Zealand and Australia were well behind in acknowledging this ground-breaking precedent. In November, Maurice finally wrote in outrage to John Reece Cole, resigning from PEN stating, 'That a writers' organisation should even passively lend support to a positively bad law, in the belief that anything is better than an indifferently bad law, is in itself beyond belief', as was the executive's intolerance of opposition to its public statements.[57]

Maurice's and others' opposition to the bill was steeped in outrage and even a touch of hysteria. The NZ Council for Civil Liberties, Library Association, Booksellers Association and others supported the introduction of the bill provided there was transparency surrounding a tribunal's decisions. Dennis McEldowney took a commonsensical view. He agreed with Maurice 'in principle but suspect in practice it will be tamer than it seems: that it puts up an illiberal facade. I may be wrong about this, and complacent.'[58] But he was right. The law came into effect on 1 January 1964 minus the controversial Clause 15 and provided for publication of the tribunal's decisions. These sometimes proved controversial, such as the absurd requirement that audiences be segregated to view the 1967 movie of James Joyce's *Ulysses*; but enlightened when the tribunal allowed free circulation of *The Little Red Schoolbook* in 1972. More often than not it found, and its successor continues to find, the right balance between liberality and control of the gratuitously obscene and vicious.

Maurice and Gill with the boys, and joined by fifteen-year-old Julia, left Dunedin in the first week of January 1964 and drove north to catch the inter-island ferry at Lyttelton. He decided to make his first side excursion to Akaroa Harbour and look over ancestral Shadbolt sites. The Shadbolt pub at Duvauchelle, now called Hotel des Pêcheurs, was still there and Ben Shadbolt's homestead was in the final stages of decline. He found overgrown Shadbolt graves on a hilltop above the hamlet, Ben's gravestone inscribed 'esteemed by all who knew him'. Maurice's ancestors had already given lore to some of his stories and lately *Among the Cinders*; but he doubted then he had the stamina for anything more substantial. After this 'first sip of a piquant family past, I looked ahead. The future was in need of thought too.'[59]

CHAPTER 20

AT THE EDGE OF THE SKY

On their way north, they stayed with Michael (Renato) and Sheena Amato who argued that their future lay there, close to them. 'Chain-smoking Michael kept me up till 2 a.m. (with a bottle of whisky) in a last-ditch attempt to persuade me of Wellington's virtues.'[1] Maurice felt Michael was a kind of literary blood brother; they had agreed that whoever died first was free to make use of the life and work of the other. Even this could not persuade Maurice to return to a city carrying too much past emotional baggage.

On arrival in Auckland, they first stayed for a day or two with Uncle Joe Kearon in Henderson. He had retired on meagre savings until his pension arrived. He seemed to have become resigned to the fact there 'could now be no more to his life: no wife, no children and friends few … Just this austere dwelling … and soon the undertaker. My grief undiminished, I attempted to behave as the affectionate son he should have had.'[2]

On Waiheke Island, they stayed with Frank, Vi and Julia and celebrated Brendan's second birthday. But what next? They had the Holden, and household goods in storage, but Maurice had no employment or commissions lined up. Gill was sanguine, happy enough with their current gypsy lifestyle, an 'earth mother' content to roam barefoot on the beach with the boys. And she went along with Maurice's decision that they should try and stay in Auckland where he might pick up some newspaper work and be close to family. 'I had grown tired of being itinerant: I had to settle somewhere.'[3] Auckland city rents, however, were punishing and it seemed a better bet to buy. Maurice knew that sales of *Gift of the Sea* had been phenomenal and he would receive enough in royalties for a substantial deposit on a house. But where?

He drove out west to territory familiar to the Shadbolt family and in his work as editor of the *Waitakere Gazette*. He explored the rough roads that ran down the spurs of the Waitakeres, and was attracted to houses planted in the green 'bird-filled bushland' of Titirangi. Gill came over with the boys from Waiheke and the one local land agent led them down, down to the last narrow no-exit road of the peninsula, overlooking the Muddy Creek estuary of the Manukau Harbour. Appropriately, the road was called Arapito, the way to the end, and below it, among fern trees, lay a modest, two-bedroomed Californian bungalow on a steep quarter-acre section. It had no number: at thirty years old it had been the first house built along the road. On closer inspection, Maurice saw it had a basement he could use as a workplace. 'It was reasonably private among bush & above a rocky shore. It had the advantage of semi-rural isolation along with proximity to the city. Almost too good to be true.'[4] He walked down a steep track to the shoreline, four-year-old Sean racing ahead. There was a small beach overhung by pohutukawa in bloom. '"Look at all this, Dad"', Sean cried and Brendan rushed past them into the water. 'It was the boys' endorsement which decided the issue.'[5]

The headland was known to the tangata whenua, Te Kawerau a Maki, as Tokoroa. The name referred to the wide range of the tides when, at springs especially, the sea was transformed into vast mudflats. There is more than one translation of Titirangi but Maurice preferred the most romantic, The Edge of the Sky.

While they waited for settlement on the Arapito Road house the Shadbolts went to the Far North again and rented a place in Ahipara. In a caravan for an office Maurice finished the final draft of *Among the Cinders* and posted it to London. Afternoons were for fishing and digging for tuatua; Maori neighbours often dropped off bags of crayfish or paua. The diet and Uncle Joe's recipe of a good sherry at last cured his colitis. Exploring the dunes kept the boys busy and regular visitors made for convivial evenings. One who stayed the longest was itinerant London novelist Colin McInnes who had achieved success with a 1950's trilogy centred on youth and black immigrant culture in run-down Notting Hill. Maurice had known him during his London sojourn but McInnes was now out of fashion, the butt of literary critics in tune with the Swinging Sixties. He was on commission to write a book on Australia and New Zealand but, in an alcoholic haze, tinkered with a novel. McInnes sought some kind of redemptive paradise in the Far North even in 1976, the year of his early death, when he wrote to Maurice asking to find him a haven on Ninety Mile Beach.

Crisis loomed as the Shadbolts' golden summer drew to an end. Publisher David Lawson had told Maurice that on 1 April he would receive a £1700 half share of *Gift of the Sea* royalties earned to 31 December. On this assumption Maurice had arranged to pay cash of £1450 on the Arapito Road house and raise a mortgage of £2250 to meet the asking price of £3700. Then Lawson advised him the royalty split on the first printing would be two-thirds to Brian Brake and one-third to Maurice, meaning he would receive only £1200. Brake had spelt out the arrangement to Maurice a year before but he now declared neither he nor Gill knew nothing about it and the contract vaguely stated the 15 per cent royalty would be shared. It seems Maurice was being disingenuous but he appealed to Brake for a 50/50 split and to postpone the one-third, two-thirds split until the third printing which had now been ordered. With only ten days to go to the settlement date, he asked Brake simply to cable him 'OK', otherwise it meant 'doing the house cold and my present (£100) deposit on the house too. This is fairly critical with the family at present homeless, and winter coming on.'[6] Brake could hardly say 'No'.

Gill wrote to the Amatos about the Arapito house and at the end of March, Michael Amato replied, commenting on Maurice's idea of building a writing studio lower on the section. He found it difficult to imagine Maurice 'hammering and sawing to build his "den" ... The only complaint I have, personally, is that you "betrayed" this pretty city [Wellington]: shame on you.' Referring to Monte Holcroft's recent *Listener* editorial defending the Literary Fund's decision not to subsidise Louis Johnson's 1964 *NZ Poetry Yearbook* because of allegedly offensive content, he was not necessarily on the side of '"the poets"' or even Maurice. 'I don't think Monte was unethical: I like mud-throwing at personalities. Take Colin McInnes, for instance. What did you think of him? I took him for a pansified prima donna and I hoped somebody would come out and say so.'[7]

A couple of weeks later, Maurice and Gill were still at Ahipara when Sheena Amato rang. Michael had just dropped dead from a cerebral haemorrhage, at the age of thirty-five. Maurice felt 'It was as if some personal prop had been ripped away. His irony had sustained me ... Without him, I might never have gone on to finish the novel on which so much of my life now seemed to depend.'[8] He went for a long walk on the beach, finding the news difficult to process. Surely it was all a mistake. But it was real: Sheena had asked what she should do with Michael's work, and all that Maurice could answer for the time being was, 'keep it safe'.

But his association with Michael and Sheena still had a long way to run. Ian Cross had been on the phone to Amato only hours before his death: 'And I'm sure that Michael will have left something of himself with Ian, just as he has left something of himself with me, which is some small consolation.'[9] With

Cross, Maurice began to prepare a collection of Amato's stories for publication. The last lines of his last uncompleted story, 'A Walk into the Shadows' read: 'It is a beautiful hill; it is a beautiful day, but it is again as it has always been. I am so short of time.'[10]

Charles Brasch asked Maurice to write a short valedictory note about Amato to accompany one of his stories in the upcoming June issue of *Landfall*. Maurice wished to talk with Sheena Amato first but she did not visit the Shadbolts in Auckland as expected and when he did send the required note to Brasch he told Maurice he was holding it over until September to go along with another writer's obituary of Amato. Using it out of context ignited Maurice's smouldering resentment of *Landfall*'s role as the arbiter of what was good in New Zealand literature and Brasch as its mandarin editor. He could hardly have been more insulting, or self-revealing: 'I like and admire Charles Brasch the man; I have enormous respect … for Charles Brasch the poet. But I don't see why I should have to be interested in a pompous, idiotic and semi-literate magazine which Charles Brasch happens, in an amateurish sort of way, to edit any more, say, than I should have to be interested in the advertising copy which Maurice Duggan happens to write. We all have our bad moments — take my work for Geographic for example; I don't delude myself about it …'[11] He wrote that Brasch was unprofessional, *Landfall* was irrelevant to the new generation of writers, reflected the New Zealand of the 1930s and that the only people who valued it were in university English departments or libraries. Maurice's note on Amato was eventually used, but it was his last contribution to *Landfall* before Brasch's departure as editor in 1967 and his death in 1973.

In his explosion of bile against an icon of the literati, Maurice showed himself to be more 'pompous, idiotic and semi-literate' than Brasch. The letter delivered elements of genuine grievance and valid criticism but beneath a mantle of hubris and mock humility. It was Maurice at his worst and 'Maurice' it increasingly now had to be. For he believed his growing success and stature required him to be taken more seriously than the loose familiarity of the childhood moniker 'Maurie' among friends and colleagues allowed. Until Maurice Duggan's death in 1974, there was a joke among literary people that to be a successful fiction writer in New Zealand one had to be called 'Maurice'. Duggan's death and Moss Gee's self-effacement meant that Shadbolt soon saw himself as the chief Maurice.

The Waitakere Ranges including Titirangi had been heavily milled in the nineteenth century and then cleared in part for orcharding, horticulture and wine-growing. Access was poor, along narrow, winding roads that saw little sealing until after World War II, and many of which Maurice's Uncle Joe had been engaged in maintaining. The first bush reserve was set aside in the 1890s and more added as the ranges became important as the site for dams supplying gravity-fed water to Auckland city. Its citizens also began to look to the Waitakeres for recreation and construction of the Scenic Drive was begun in 1913; but this attracted little traffic until it was extended in the 1930s. By then there was the 'Hotel Titirangi. Ideal Mountain Guest House 700 feet above sea level' with hot and cold water in all rooms.[12] Although subdivisions had been surveyed after World War I, sections were slow to sell. Titirangi was no commuter suburb and at the end of World War II it harboured just a 'sprinkling of raffish cottages, the hideaway homes of society's casualties and the weekend baches of city dwellers'. In 1957, it was seen as a 'sylvan slum' and even twenty years later 'West Auckland as a place to live does not attract the rich in any number … no tradition exists of old and mellow suburbs established by earlier generations of the well-to-do'.[13]

For Maurice, Titirangi's 'reputation as a hangout for those involved in the arts and crafts'[14] was not fully deserved. There were potters among the kauri, some photographers and a handful of 'respectable' painters lived there from time to time, but few writers and no fiction authors except him. Soon after settling in Titirangi he attended a literary function in Auckland where he felt 'preening poets and prosing academics' used him as a literary 'dartboard'. He withdrew from this 'republic of letters' to the relative isolation of his new home. There he could practise a kind of inner emigration to a place where there was more stimulation and generosity in the company of those painters and potters. This had become Maurice's lifelong default position, his defence against the 'darts' of a hostile literary world. Yet his lifelong problem remained that, although he was under no illusions about his mercenary journalism, as he told Charles Brasch, he also wished to be taken seriously in the 'republic of letters'. Repeatedly, he would claim that he was just a storyteller and that the 'house of literature' had many rooms, but this masked a deep-seated need to be seen as a literary master in the penthouse. He never came to terms with the reality that academic critics in particular trade in received truths and do not anoint authors who slum it. In any case, on the Certificate of Title for the Arapito Road house, where previous owners described themselves as 'motor radiator repairer' and 'carrier', Maurice described himself as 'journalist', perhaps the only kind of writer in the 1960s whom lawyers believed could sustain a mortgage.

There were two writers out west with whom Maurice became close and who were non-threatening and supportive as older mentors. Maurice had met forty-year-old Dick Scott during the time of his involvement with the *People's*

Voice and the 1951 waterfront strike which became the subject of Scott's first book *151 Days*. Although he abandoned the Communist Party at about the same time as Maurice, Scott continued to follow a more radical path in his writing. In 1954 he published *The Parihaka Story* through a socialist press but his 1975 book *Ask that Mountain: The Story of Parihaka* became more widely known, went into numerous printings and was responsible for effectively revealing the passive resistance movement of Te Whiti o Rongomai and exposing the iniquities of the government invasion of Parihaka. Scott, also an accomplished local historian, had been living with his family in Titirangi for a couple of years and Maurice counted his comment that it was a great place for kids as one of the prompts for him to look for a home there. Scott was a 'thoroughgoing romantic, with the anecdotal knack of turning trivial incident into wild adventure'.[15] Scott was not so complimentary. On returning home one day he found two figures perched on the ridge of his two-storey house. Visiting Barry Mitcalfe had 'somehow enlisted the normally timorous Maurice Shadbolt to join him — the same Shadbolt who, driving me to Wellington, had seemed to brake at the shadow of every second power pole'.[16]

Maurice wrote that one Auckland writer 'who didn't feel me a threat and welcomed me with arms wide, was the essayist and art historian Eric McCormick'[17] who lived in Green Bay with his sister Myra. At fifty-eight, McCormick was old enough to be Maurice's father. In the late 1930s he had helped shape the programme and become editor for the New Zealand Centennial publications. He had earned an MA Honours degree from the University of New Zealand with a thesis on New Zealand literature when it was a subject never taught at university. He followed this with an MLitt from Cambridge on the same topic. Although always determined to be a writer, McCormick's first publication was the centennial book *Letters and Art in New Zealand*. His judgements in both fields were astutely impartial and the book's influence endured for decades. Following World War II, McCormick had produced a series of notable biographies, in particular seminal works on expatriate Dunedin painter Frances Hodgkins. When Maurice arrived in Titirangi, McCormick was completing a stint as editor of publications for Auckland University, foundation work for the Auckland University Press for which another of Maurice's close scholarly friends, Dennis McEldowney, was soon to become its first full-time editor. 'McCormick, a wise, witty and generous man, soon made me feel at home.'[18] Although neither Scott nor McCormick were creative writers in the 'usual much-abused sense, both seemed to possess much more liveliness of imagination and insight than most New Zealand novelists or poets I had known'.[19]

Closer to hand, 'Arapito Road was then a leaf-fringed lane of faulty hearts and furtive hermits. If a pensioner backed his car into a ditch, I was invariably summoned to help heave it back on the road.'[20] There was the recluse from kauri logging times who lived in a one-room shack without power, phone or piped water and who raised a flag each morning to let neighbours know he was still alive. And the retired champion harness-racing driver who lived in a house besieged by possums and who treated his wife so badly she ran off with a tattooed seaman causing a neighbourhood scandal that resonated for decades.

Tony Atwool, then in his seventies, became Maurice's best pensioner friend despite his serious heart condition and his weekly excursions to the cemetery to 'get used to the idea'. Atwool had been getting used to the idea since his twenties when he had been an aviator with the Royal Flying Corps in France. His wife, whom Maurice never saw, had become a 'madwoman out of a Brontë fiction' who rarely left her bed, read religious tracts and whose voice could sometimes be heard 'drifting shrilly through the trees' from their 'sunless cottage cloaked with greenery'.[21] To escape his stressful domestic life and for Maurice to enjoy an 'antidote to literary stress', Atwool often took him fishing in his motor launch. On one occasion, they pulled in so many snapper that the haul 'didn't allow Tony time to talk or me to light my pipe'. But when they had finished, Atwool's thoughts turned again to death. What did Maurice think lay beyond? Given Maurice's propensity for the psychic it seems unlikely that he simply quoted Socrates: that either one would meet up with old friends after death or simply enjoy a long refreshing sleep; although refreshing for what remained unanswered. A few years later, Tony Atwool found out.

Maurice told the probably apocryphal story that at the moment he first turned the key to the front door of the Arapito Road house, a postie arrived with a telegram from his London agents congratulating him on *Among the Cinders*. This was soon followed by Eyre & Spottiswoode's acceptance and, in July, news that David Lawson was taking 4000 copies under the Whitcombe & Tombs imprint. Then it was taken by Atheneum in New York with a large advance on royalties and who later contracted to publish an American edition of *Summer Fires and Winter Country*. With the continued sales success of *Gift of the Sea*, Maurice could now 'afford, it seemed, to relax; and try finding myself as a writer again. I was most unsure of myself as a novelist. *Among the Cinders* still seemed very much a private joke which had incidentally become public; less a novel than an apology for not writing one. Or, more specifically, for not writing the novel people expected of me.' Several years later he was able to count 1964 as 'quite the happiest and most relaxed year of my writing life', and a year when his 'marriage regained a certain stability'.[22] What had caused instability is unclear except, perhaps, for Maurice's disapproval of Gill's housekeeping deficiencies and her need to find some escape from her isolated domestic life with two small boys by keeping her hand in with articles for *Truth*, and later taking part in afternoon TV chat shows. Maurice had his separate writing space in the block-walled, concrete-floored study under the house. A curved bar left behind by the previous owners served as a shelf for books and papers while he tapped away on his Olivetti portable at a simple work table. For young Sean, the morning sound of typing and the rising odour of the Erinmore pipe tobacco that Maurice most favoured were the imprints of his first years at Titirangi.

Maurice and Gill re-established their friendship with Pat and Gil Hanly who had returned to New Zealand in 1962. Hanly had taken up a position teaching drawing at the University of Auckland's School of Architecture. Struck by the bright, almost shattering light on a Torbay beach after his time in Europe, Hanly had been working on a series of paintings grouped as 'Figures in Light' that portrayed the condition of a 'nation sitting around on its bum doing nothing'.[23] At Hanly's exhibition of these paintings, Maurice met other painters in the increasingly active Auckland art scene, in particular Colin McCahon whose paintings Maurice had first seen on the walls of Charles Brasch's flat in Dunedin. McCahon had been in Auckland since 1953, where he had been working at the Auckland City Art Gallery, and was about to take up a post as a lecturer at the Elam School of Fine Arts. He lived not far away on Otitori Bay Road.

As Maurice settled to writing again, he continued tinkering with 'Search for Tim Livingstone', the novel he thought others expected of him, but was finding it difficult to manage. Yet he felt his 'time of love affairs — short stories — was running out with my youth; that if ever I was to test my talent it had to be in the novel'.[24] In a move that would act as a bridge between the youthful and the mature and provide more direction for 'Search for Tim Livingstone', he began work on a sequence of three novellas. Under the influence of his new artist friend Colin McCahon, he 'conceived the idea of a new book in tryptich form. While the central panel, or story, would take the burden of this book … the side panels, or stories, would have their separate light and shade off towards the centre.'[25]

Maurice worked at his painterly project through the winter and spring, applying the final brush strokes in the late summer of 1965. The underlying drift or light of the triptych is the condition of artists and writers in the 1950s and 1960s. The first 'panel', 'The Voyagers' tells the story of two boys growing up together in a 'King Country town'. The first-person and unnamed narrator relates how his mate Mike goes on to Auckland and university in the 1950s and attempts a career as a painter. The narrator is perplexed and uncertain of Mike's rebellion against the oppressive, conformist society around him. "'There's something missing here", he complained. "Something missing altogether. Something that wasn't plugged in properly'". The conservative narrator suggests, "'Perhaps we don't need to plug in …'" "'There you are,' he said angrily. 'That's what I mean. You don't take me seriously.'"[26]

Like many frustrated young artists of the time, Mike thought his only chance of redemption was to leave the country and go to Europe. "'If Christ himself was born here,' he once said sourly, "he'd have to go overseas first, to get okayed. Otherwise we wouldn't know whether we had the genuine article.'"[27] Mike leaves Auckland abruptly as call-up crew on a merchant ship. In clumsy metaphor, the narrator then makes a failed attempt to sail off in a stolen yacht with Mike's ex-girlfriend whom he then goes on to marry and settle down as a lawyer in that 'King Country town'. They hear little of Mike for five years save for reports of one successful exhibition in London. When he returns, the narrator remembers Mike's additional sour words about a returning Christ: "'[H]e'd never go short on a congregation once he got back. It really wouldn't matter whether he was the genuine article or not. So long as someone said so over there.'" Mike would be safe. More than sixty years later, even in a globalised world, it remains a truth that continues to resonate.

The central 'panel', about three times the size of the other two, and the real novella, gave its title to the eventual book *The Presence of Music*. When he wrote it, he had 'Search for Tim Livingstone' very much in mind and 'wanted to convince' himself that it 'could still be written'.[28] Maurice later tried to disavow that the novella, with its first-person narrator becoming successful in London with a first novel, was autobiographical, while claiming that 'no memory is really trifling for the writer; all memories are trapped in his treasure chest, riches for future disposal'.[29] Yet from the start we can tell that Te Makutu is Te Kuiti, confirmed by his admission that 'This wasn't the first or last time that my thoughts travelled back to Te Makutu. The place never quite vanished from my life.'[30] Aptly, Te Makutu means 'The Spell' or 'Incantation'. Many autobiographical themes, events and places can be detected in the novella, such as a detailed description of the Tite Street basement flat in Chelsea and Ibiza with its ex-pats. Maurice conjured fiction from life and increasingly the two became interchangeable. The narrator admits, 'There must be a limit to the amount of self-knowledge we can bear'.

Substantially, 'The Presence of Music' was an attempt by Maurice to make sense of his search for meaning in his life and writing; to achieve some kind of artistic and personal maturity, especially sexual maturity. There are half a dozen explicit sexual encounters involving the narrator in the novella and 'The Voyagers'. None are satisfactory, even the one occasion he has sex with the idealised Linda who ultimately remains beyond emotional reach; he must settle for the wifely Frances. The failure of the novella was expressed, perhaps unconsciously by Maurice, when one of his women characters says of the narrator: 'He should compose music or paint pictures, anything to say how he feels, but not write a book. His people aren't individuals, they're just variations on a theme — in words instead of in colour or music.'[31]

Colin McCahon had told Maurice that the central panel was always the most important part of a triptych. So *The Presence of Music* as a 'painting' proved a failure when the second panel, 'Figures in Light' far outshone it. Maurice admitted an autobiographical source for this, not from life experience but from a life imagined: one that might have been had he grown up with the older sister who had been stillborn eighteen months before his own birth. Better than in the other 'panels', sister Ruth epitomises the role and place of the artist in a society where many New Zealanders are 'an itinerant people always pulling themselves up to see how deep their roots have grown'. She finds a place to stand as both mother and sister for her younger brother in a motherless family. A 'serene light flows in and out of our childhood, leaving no shadows' but 'Like summer, childhood had an end, even if we might later warm ourselves with the memory.'[32] Maurice described the story as the 'purging of a fantasy, the laying of a ghost', and realised that it was the 'most near to perfect story I was ever likely to write in my life.'[33] Knowing that, he did not tackle another short story until the very end of his writing career.

CHAPTER 21

HOT COALS

Maurice's 'happy and relaxed' first year in Titirangi was marred by unpleasant echoes from his time in the Soviet Union. In May, along with a number of other writers, he received a copy of New Zealand short stories in Russian translation, as acknowledgment of the inclusion of 'After the Depression'. Maurice had attempted to put together an anthology of New Zealand stories for a Moscow publishing house when he was in London, but gave up when it became clear no payment would be forthcoming and there was potential for copyright abuse. A few years later, trade union official Murray Gittos, a minor socialist writer with work published only in *The People's Voice* and his own Unity Artists *Fernfire* magazine, visited the Soviet Union and published a pamphlet about his time there.[1] He also met with a Moscow publisher and agreed to put together an anthology of politically correct New Zealand short stories with some assistance from Dunedin writer O.E. 'Ted' Middleton. The outrage of local writers on receipt of their free copies led to a scandal feature in *Truth*. Writers had 'neither given permission for the works to be published nor had any idea that the material was in Russian hands. None has been paid a rouble.'[2] The book's introduction stated that the writers included were 'advocates of the class struggle in New Zealand, fighters against the racial discrimination that was a "problem of considerable difficulty"'. Gittos had six stories included, Middleton three and an unknown writer who had travelled with Gittos, four, while Moss Gee and others were absent. Several protesting writers were quoted, Maurice saying that the '"people who handled the deal at this end are scabs in the old trade-union sense. The taking of authors' work without permission is theft. They are double-scabs in that they are misrepresenting New Zealand to the Russians".'[3] Gittos brushed off the complaints but soon disappeared from the literary scene.

Ted Middleton took exception to being described as a 'double scab' and told others that Maurice had engineered the *Truth* article, perhaps through Gill. Maurice wrote to him: 'My dear Ted, as you grow older you may learn that the way to discredit another writer is not to invent malicious stories, but simply to write better than that writer.'[4] He had told the *Truth* reporter Middleton was an innocent party and agreed that the article was a badly-written disaster. But he could not understand why Middleton still thought the anthology a 'good thing' when it slandered New Zealand, excluded some of its best writers and did nothing to help the situation of East European writers 'who struggle so bravely against the political distortions of foreign literatures which this anthology represents'. Maurice suggested that Middleton, in spreading rumour rather than going public on the issue, was having 'some trouble' with his conscience. The furore subsided but Maurice had made an enemy for life; of someone who, despite the Soviet suppression of the Hungarian uprising and the recent impact of Alexandr Solzhenitsyn's novel *One Day in the Life of Ivan Denisovich* — which revealed the horror of the 'Gulag Archipelago' — continued to espouse the Soviet socialist dream.

Middleton was not Maurice's only enemy, known or unknown. In the journal he had now begun to keep on an irregular basis, he wrote: 'Informed last night … that I had a lot of enemies. Depressed as always when I hear this kind of thing … it has almost destroyed me twice before, & I ought to be getting stronger. Must I always be vulnerable? … So I withdraw more & more,'[5] retreating with his pipe to corners at parties, pushing away the signals of depression. Maurice clung to those friends who bore him no animus. There was Dick Scott with his endless yarns; Colin McCahon: 'Watch him grope (physically) for words when talking. One wants — at that moment of hesitation — to put a paint brush into his anguished fingers';[6] and above all Eric McCormick: 'He is at home in the world, he has never been one of those frustrated solitaries so familiar. Or let's be blunter — like a Sargeson. And he has the gift of sympathy. God knows how rare that is among literary people.'[7]

While Maurice wrestled with his literary demons, Gill wrestled with the demands of two active small boys and the social isolation, although she did have the Holden for shopping and travelling further afield. A bus service, terminating not far away at the bottom of South Titirangi Road, allowed visitors to come and go, especially Maurice's parents and sister Julia who had now shifted from Waiheke Island to be closer at hand on Titirangi's Woodlands Park Road. Vi came round often to help with the children and Julia found Gill trendy with her penchant for yoghurt, cigarettes smoked in a long holder, and dressed in colourful muumus. Casual visitors in hot summer weather might find Gill wearing nothing at all, brown, lean and statuesque amid the chaos of unwashed dishes, overflowing rubbish bins and floors littered with toys and books.

On 19 November, Gill picked up Dennis McEldowney from the Auckland bus terminal and took him home before they all went out to Piha to paddle in the surf and collect mussels. In the evening Maurice drove him over to the McCormicks in Green Bay where Charles 'Mike' Doyle joined them to enlarge on the literary gossip. McEldowney 'had always thought of the Auckland University English Department as a nest of singing birds, but it sounds more like a snake pit'. They talked about the impact of bad reviews and reviewers. 'Maurice said there was one he would punch on the nose if he met him in the street. I said the most upsetting kind of bad review was the one you agreed with. Charles concurred but not Maurice. Had it not happened to him? He said the worst kind was the one that attributed to you views you did not hold.' Through his bedroom window at Arapito Road, McEldowney could see 'through ponga to moonlight on the Manukau, impossibly romantic, like a not-so-good Shadbolt story'.[8]

Money was not much of a problem for the first year or two at Titirangi. Good royalty cheques arrived at intervals and Gill had her own income stream from *Truth* articles and, until it was capitalised to help with the mortgage, her Family Benefit. Although Gill's relaxed and casual approach to life caused Maurice to describe her as living in the 'timeless world of the daft', she acted efficiently as his secretary in correspondence with agents and publishers when he was away. She never wavered in her belief in his work — 'I am so glad you think Maurice such a fine writer. I have had this belief for quite some time now' — and always regretted the times when it became necessary for him to put aside his fiction and undertake 'heartbreaking, grinding journalism' to make ends meet.[9]

Making ends meet promised to become more difficult when, during another family holiday at Ahipara in the New Year of 1965, Gill discovered she was expecting again. Tests during an increasingly difficult pregnancy revealed by mid-year that she was due to have twins. Maurice told Kevin Ireland, 'It's knocked us a bit sideways, as this house hasn't room for two more children. However the site is so attractive that I don't think we'd want to part with this place.'[10] An extra room would have to be added.

Another unexpected turn in family life was the unannounced arrival of Maurice's eighteen-year-old cousin Tim. Tim Shadbolt's mother had remarried after the death of his father in the 1952 FAA 'plane crash but Tim's stepfather turned out to be a 'deeply disturbed Czechoslovakian refugee'[11] whom they eventually suspected had been a Nazi collaborator. Tim, his mother and two brothers 'did a runner' and 'moved into a shack out in the country' from where he continued going to school; until social welfare officers found them and said 'the boys had either to be adopted by their family or sent to a home'. Tim had heard about Maurice, tracked him down and, on his motorbike, 'just sort of turned up on his doorstep'. It must have been a 'bit of a shock for Maurice' to see this bikie turn up but he was 'really good'.

Maurice and Gill had no room for him at Arapito Road but they arranged for Tim and his beloved motorbike to stay in the garage at Frank and Vi's place. He did gardening work for old-age pensioners with Frank who 'was always listening to the races and I always seemed to be doing most of the work but I was still a very thankful lodger'. He was even more thankful for the proximity of sixteen-year-old Julia. They took a shine to each other, too much of a shine and, when Maurice caught them *in flagrante*, he was banished to board and study at Rutherford High School with Aunt Sis (mostly) and Maurice picking up the fees. 'This saved me in a way because I could finish the sixth form and get my UE.'[12] He went on to the University of Auckland in 1966 and his career of protest and politics.

Maurice finished *The Presence of Music* and sent it off to London at the end of the summer. Then he turned to Opo, 'That summer of the dolphin' which 'had plagued me as raw material for a novel year after year, but with no real response' because the actual story was 'perfect in itself'[13] and left little room for the imagination. To solve that problem, he decided to transplant the dolphin from the Hokianga and 1956 to the Hauraki Gulf and 1965. He was also prompted to make a start because, to his alarm, Patrick White had thought about writing the Opo story in an Australian setting. But the manuscript gained no momentum as the anti-Vietnam War protests and campaign began to gather him in. 'The war was a weight in my gut which I couldn't shift … Why, at such a time, was I trying to write? What relevance had a dolphin anyway?'[14]

Barry Mitcalfe, who was now lecturing at Wellington Teachers' Training College, 'with next to no political past, and pushed by his Wellington students, had become de facto leader of the protest movement'.[15] He pressed Maurice to set up an Auckland anti-Vietnam War committee but after a couple of preliminary meetings, Maurice backed out in favour of others better equipped at bringing together the different factions. He took part in marches, deputations and public meetings but became appalled as former 'comrades of the left' spouted their tired Stalinist propaganda.

As the New Zealand government moved towards a decision on whether or not to send troops to South Vietnam, Maurice diverted his energies into letters to the editor, especially the *Auckland Star* where he became engaged in an exchange with the bellicose president of the Auckland Returned Services Association. The *Star* editorialised against the Vietnam War but Maurice was encouraged to keep up his letters because readers were responding to those more than the paper's editorials. In the *Star*, on the eve of the government's decision, Maurice denounced President Johnson for his failure to negotiate with everyone except the 'people he is actually fighting', the Viet Cong. He argued that New Zealand had no obligations under either the ANZUS or SEATO treaties to send troops. 'To start saying an uncritical yes to the U.S. because we are tired of saying an uncritical yes to Britain is not national maturity but infancy in a new guise.'[16]

A couple of weeks earlier, Maurice had sent a dense three-page letter to Prime Minister Keith Holyoake. He argued that as a country with greater proximity and responsibilities to south-east Asia than the USA, New Zealand should stay out of the war or, at most, give military support to South Vietnam only under the condition that they seek a United Nations administered ceasefire. One can see him pounding the typewriter as he concluded the letter, 'Is New Zealand up to it? I think it is. I know it is. Can a country as small as New Zealand give a lead to the world? It has before, and it can again. It is in your hands to make my children, and your grandchildren, proud to be New Zealanders. May God and the faith of your fellow-countrymen not fail you.'[17] Holyoake may have detected the desperation of the irreligious calling on the divine but not the pompous tone familiar in his own pronouncements.

On 25 May, the day of decision, a tearful Mitcalfe phoned Maurice in the early hours of the morning imploring him to contact everyone he knew to bombard Parliament with protest telegrams. To no effect because, although there were rumours that the National cabinet had been divided on the issue, Holyoake announced New Zealand would send an artillery battery to support Australian infantry in Vietnam. Maurice received a lengthy reply to his letter in which Holyoake hinted at the pressures he had faced in arriving at the decision. It was revealed after his death that it was the least he had been able get away with under the duress of American demands.

Maurice's public anti-Vietnam War protests and correspondence went on for as long as the war lasted, another ten years. He took Ian Cross to task in the *Listener* when he criticised Maurice and other writers for putting their names to a published petition protesting New Zealand's involvement in the war. Cross had stated that the petition had 'aims which were consonant with the political objectives of the use of violence by North Vietnam and the Vietcong' and defended American 'precision' bombing which had been described elsewhere as 'like the weeding of a garden with a bulldozer'. In a letter to the *Listener* Cross had suggested his 'fellow writers were sheep and purchasers of kit-set indulgences from the devil' and in response Maurice accused his old friend of McCarthyism.[18] There was an element of devil's advocacy in Cross's letters although his views were closer to the conservative political establishment than most other writers. The vigorous public debate between Maurice and Cross was the sparring of friends, not enemies.

Visitors provided a welcome distraction from Vietnam altercations. Louis Johnson, 'Bigger, rounder than ever — & still likeable in his plump pugnacity. Louis is, or has been, the literary missionary par excellence.' But Maurice found himself detached from Johnson's literary talk and it was a relief to drive him back into town to drink with Mike Doyle and Colin McCahon where the conversation turned to more painterly matters. Maurice maintained that the 'singing, celebratory voice' was too rarely heard in New Zealand and McCahon said that he 'celebrated the landscape, the country out of despair. And that, surely, is the true triumph. The triumph, perhaps the only one here.'[19]

That day, 26 March, Maurice came home to a celebratory dinner to mark the American publication of *Among the Cinders* which was also about to go on sale in England and New Zealand. First responses augured well. He heard that a German offer had been made and he received a warm letter from established US novelist Stephen Becker who, in his draft for the jacket blurb for the American edition, had written: '*Among the Cinders* is the funniest, saddest most moving book about a boy-man since Huckleberry Finn … for my money it's a small masterpiece, and I can't believe it's a first novel'.[20] It was the beginning of a lifelong friendship.

Dennis McEldowney enjoyed *Cinders* 'so enormously and so emotionally as to quite disqualify me from making an intellectual judgement, I *hope* it is as good as I think it is. It's such an unexpected book. There are corny or mechanical parts in Shadbolt but he has a vitality of invention and an ability to move emotions, beyond any of our other writers. Both qualities can be dangerous and he doesn't escape the dangers — but I'd rather have them all the same.'[21] But even before local reviews appeared, Maurice picked up on negative reactions that were reflected in Charles Brasch's private comments: 'Parts of it very well & racily told' and 'there's no doubt of Shadbolt's narrative gift'. But some scenes were 'designed for Hollywood, and there are pages that try to out-Crump Crump'. The party episode where 'several real people are brought on is a disaster ... I felt I was being got at, & the whole book seemed a fake.'[22] Sales were not as good as expected. In mid-May he heard from Mike Bessie of Atheneum that US sales had reached 4000, a disappointing result for the large US market. To compound matters, Eyre and Spottiswoode turned down *The Presence of Music*.

By the end of June, the 'Dolphin' manuscript had also 'gone dead' and his journal entry[23] was 'like a note left on a desert trek'. It was too convenient to blame this on the Vietnam War or the pressures he felt from agents and publishers. 'Of course the flop of Cinders is partly to blame. I might have known it wouldn't get across. Nobody had time to read the bloody thing. It was enjoyed but not read.' Depression stains the page.

Maurice impulsively decided to escape his midwinter gloom by taking off for the King Country and elsewhere for ten days. It was short notice for Gill, seven months pregnant with twins and now without a car, but family and friends rallied round. The trip was a chance for the country boy to abandon the city and his tiresome domestic life for the fresh and frosty country air that might ventilate depression; to return to a childhood home that might stir new energies.

The journey would also serve as a trial run for the new book he had contracted with Whitcombe & Tombs. Car ownership had climbed over the previous ten years and motoring holidays were becoming popular. There had been a rapid increase in the number of motels and the first roll-on, roll-off ferry between Wellington and Picton had begun sailing in 1962, stimulating car traffic between north and south. David Lawson of Whitcombe's saw the market for a compact motoring guide to New Zealand and the Shell Oil Company, which had been producing guides to the English counties since the 1930s, quickly agreed to sponsor the project.

Te Kuiti on the first of July: 'Muddy cars, dusty people — Maoris & farmers sitting on sunny side of street ... What is the purpose of such a place? To produce young people for the cities? ... I seemed surrounded by ghosts. Where have they all gone? ... Walked first to King Street house. What soft explosions of memory! Quite overwhelmed by almost forgotten things.' At the river ford he remembered where the 'Maori women washed. Where I first became aware — at six — of the power of memory & beauty. "I shall always remember this", I said to myself. "Always".'[24] His journal entry contained vivid images of the Te Kuiti winter landscape, of places that had informed so much of his writing. It became clear that the way forward, carrying this freight of memory, was a return to the manuscript for 'The Search for Tim Livingstone'. 'When I think of the months wasted before coming back to this? This is what interests me — making sense of my time and place.'[25]

Maurice drove on to Rotorua where he spent a night with Moss Gee and his partner Hera Smith. The relationship was 'going extremely badly and when Maurie came it was running down to our last days together but I was hanging on because we had a child',[26] five year-old Nigel (named for Nigel Cook) to whom Gee was deeply attached. Maurice hoped the future did not 'have too much pain for Moss on this account'.[27] Hera Smith was having what Gee described as a 'strange relationship' with the elderly medical superintendent of Rotorua Hospital.[28] He had a collection of black velvet paintings by the Tahitian artist Edgar Leeteg and, although the old doctor was away, Smith had a key to his house. The three went up to see the paintings, accompanied by a friend of Smith's, 'one of those stunners' whose 'marriage was in a bad way'. Gee watched her and Maurice 'striking sparks off each other' and the two went away to bathe together in the doctor's private mineral pool. Maurice wrote that the woman told him the story of her life, unnecessarily, because he had already written it in his story 'Homecoming' and — of course — she had just read it.[29] Gee remembered that Maurice 'never confessed to anything in the morning but he had a satisfied look'.[30]

Maurice drove north to visit Eric and Elizabeth Lee-Johnson in Waihi and then into the Coromandel on a recce for the Shell Guide. He picked up a copy of the latest *Listener* and read a 'less than favourable review' of *Among the Cinders*. Perhaps worse was the letter from Patrick White that Maurice found on his return home: 'On the whole I didn't feel the novel was up to your stories'. White liked best the landscapes, 'full of that dark, murderous green', thought the last chapter 'beautiful' and, despite others' criticisms, that the entrance of the author at the party a 'good gimmick'. But the 'party characters failed to emerge' and the novel was 'chiefly disappointing because I was irritated by the boy and the grandfather.'[31]

The *Listener* reviewer was Joan Stevens, an associate professor at Victoria University who taught a master's paper in New Zealand literature. Stevens's chief problem with *Among the Cinders* was its 'uncertainty of tone' and stylistic inconsistencies with 'schematised and constructed elements in the book, rather than those springing from organic inner pressures'. Around many of the 'excellent' and authentic episodes was much that was 'contrived or just formally clever'. She wrote that Maurice had relied on a 'number of cliches of New Zealand fiction' such as the 'puzzled young narrator coping with a traumatic experience' (e.g. *The God Boy*); 'the loveable old misfit' (*Tidal Creek*); and the 'casual life of road and camp' (*Hang on a Minute Mate*). Stevens concluded that

Cinders was a 'book that will make readers argue. Much in it is good, much in it is too familiar; much of its cries out for a finer linguistic sensitivity, a greater economy of means.'[32]

The trouble for Maurice was that Stevens 'seemed to know what she was talking about,'[33] confirming Dennis McEldowney's view that the most 'upsetting kind of bad review was the one you agreed with'. But Maurice might have argued that Grandfather Ernest, aka Hubert Flinders, was hardly a cliché, that Barry Crump did not have a copyright on itinerant bushmen and in any case Stevens, like all other reviewers, had missed the point. *Cinders*, from the start, was intended as a playful pastiche of some contemporary New Zealand writing. The problem was it had also become something else and the uncertainty of style and tone reflected that. Maurice conceded to Dennis McEldowney that he 'rather wanted to have my cake and eat it too (so far as the mickey-taking is concerned, and the argument I have with this country) — so I've myself to blame, at least in part.'[34]

In contrast to the po-faced approach to *Cinders* by Stevens, were the comments of veteran *New York Times* reviewer, Orville Prescott: 'Mr. Shadbolt may have written about one of the most commonly described themes in fiction. That's immaterial. There are only a few important subjects for fiction anyway. But to write about adolescence and growing up with both charm and insight into character is a considerable achievement.'[35]

Other local literary reviews echoed or enlarged on Stevens's comments. The *Landfall* reviewer dwelt on the confusion between narrator Nick Flinders and author Maurice Shadbolt. He likened Nick Flinders to Holden Caulfield in J.D. Salinger's *Catcher in the Rye* but 'Holden, though he is limited in the same way as Nick, is generally funnier'.[36] *Among the Cinders* was being dissected within an inch of its life. Maurice was fond of quoting André Gide's statement, 'Please do not understand me too quickly'. But then that is what reviewers do.

The reviewer in *Comment* thought Nick's perambulations with his grandfather was where the novel came alive but scorned the use of the Kiwi vernacular and idiom. Yet Maurice's portrayal of Nick's brother Derek, was a 'most delightful portrait of the local species of University Lecturer/Poet: the type who seek symbolism in sex, inner meaning in superficialities and analogies in anuses.'[37]

The *Comment* reviewer of *Cinders* preferred to be identified only by his initials; probably just as well because everyone in the literary world knew that 'Derek' was a caricature of C.K. Stead. Stead was amicable enough in a letter from London. First, there was the domestic connection between them and Stead responded to Maurice's news of twins with 'We are lagging in the rear' with just one two year-old. But Stead quickly moved on to *Among the Cinders*. He had 'devoured' it in a day and a half, 'reading impatiently through the bits in which D.K.F. did not appear, and then reading rather irritably through the parts where he did' and wondered if the best parts were where he was absent. As one caricatured, he was not the best person to judge but also wondered if the 'slight element of spleen (quite justified, in personal terms no doubt) that crept in, didn't throw the whole thing a little out of balance … The important — and difficult — thing is to keep going isn't it? — whatever the bastards (me, in your case; you, in mine!) say.'[38]

Maurice replied, 'D.K.F.'s solemnity about literature seemed to be mine too; that is I often felt I was satirizing myself. There is something in him of most NZ writers.' The literary party episode grew out of his isolation in Queenstown and he felt he had to 'take the mickey out of others, Crump and Cross, and myself too, to square it up … I justify the bloody thing [book] only on grounds of personal therapy'[39] during his difficult Burns Fellowship year.

Gill went into the new National Women's Hospital in late August as pregnancy complications threatened. Her twins were delivered on 7 September by Caesarean, her third and 'definitely the last' Maurice told Dennis McEldowney which required her to stay in hospital for another month. Maurice kept house for that time 'on top of trying to keep up a normal work routine, and packed Sean off to school in the morning, visited Gill in the afternoon (a 25-mile round trip) and cooked dinner at night, Brendan was away most of the time … though at the end I was looking after him, too.'[40] Sean had started at Titirangi Primary on his fifth birthday in May, a school big enough then to have its own dental clinic. On his first day, 'Dad took me along to the end of the street, helped me buy a bus ticket and said, "See all these other kids, just follow them and you'll get there". That was my introduction to school.'[41] But Sean did well and was soon competing with another student for top spot in his class.

Maurice told McEldowney that the twins had been 'belatedly' named Tui and Daniel and that he and Gill were pleased to have a girl when they had, at first, resigned themselves to a third boy. Maurice wrote later that Tui had been named for the birds feeding on the flowering kowhai trees around the house. 'I wished my tiny daughter sweet with the nectar of the land.'[42] But this was seconded by the pleasure of naming her after Ian Cross's wife, too. Maurice wrote that his twin son was 'named in the hope he dared to be a Daniel'.

The arrival of twins distracted Maurice from serious work on 'Search for Tim Livingstone' and with four children under six to house and feed, he told Kevin Ireland, 'I have reached the stage where I never turn anything down, regardless of the amount of money involved — lecturing, reviewing, broadcasting. The old trap. It's all very well knowing the dangers, another thing to avoid them.'[43] For an author trying to earn a living income from writing alone, it was also disheartening to find that UK royalties for *Among the Cinders* had been almost cut in half because the tax agreement between the UK and New Zealand had been suspended. The derogatory comment used by some literary critics of Maurice's work has been 'he was really just a journalist', but most often by those with salaries attached to academic tenure or bureaucratic pay scales. For them, writers should commit to the penurious dedication of a Frank Sargeson or a Janet Frame in order to cut the literary mustard.

During 1965, Maurice averaged one book review a month, mostly for the *Listener*, but sometimes for Sydney's *The Bulletin*. The review he published there of Frank Sargeson's *Collected Stories* shook Sargeson's hand while he directed a well-aimed knee to the groin. He wrote that Sargeson's dedication to living as a writer in New Zealand 'made him a local legend … a place usually reserved for major writers elsewhere'. At sixty-two, he was the 'grand old man of New Zealand letters' but his output had been 'modest to an extreme'. In a short 'patronising' preface, E.M. Forster had said 'Sargeson knows heaps about New Zealand including its Maoris.' 'In fact', Maurice wrote, 'the essential rather open quality of New Zealand life has eluded him altogether and [he] writes almost not at all about Maoris'. He gave Sargeson credit for his 'quite breathtaking artistry in the use of New Zealand vernacular' and quoted Louis Johnson as saying 'New Zealand prose literature begins with Frank Sargeson rather than Katherine Mansfield, because he sought the spirit and essence of our own language as the real means of discovering ourselves'. Maurice added that 'Perhaps the greatest tribute one can pay is to say it is impossible to imagine literature in New Zealand without him'. But this was faint praise when preceded by, 'that his talent is in essence minor is evident on comparison with, say, the novelists Ian Cross or Janet Frame'.[44]

Maurice's review was against the tide of the largely favourable notices of the Sargeson collection. His motives were hardly pure, for he had recently learned, from writer John Reece Cole, that Sargeson had encouraged C.K. Stead to write the notorious 'K. of Henderson' letter to the *Listener* in 1955. Worse, that Sargeson had also incited Ian Hamilton to write his destructive review of *The New Zealanders*, and pressured Robin Dudding to publish it in *Mate* in 1960. It was payback time. But in writing the *Bulletin* review Maurice was seen as committing a kind of heresy, and entrenched the positions of his literary enemies.

At mid-year, Maurice was taken to task by admirers of the Soviet Union for his *Listener* review of *Dissonant Voices in Soviet Literature*, accusing him of being a fellow traveller of the anthology's 'literary cold war warrior' editors. But Maurice exposed the partiality of his critics, concluding that 'They can't even see that one cannot criticize as unrepresentative of Soviet literature an anthology which does not set out to be representative.'[45]

More troubling was his *Listener* review of a collection of short stories, *The Brigadier and the Golf Widow*, by John Cheever, an American writer he admired. 'What distinguishes his voice is not just the wholeness of his vision, but his rare sense of the magic and wonder of the world: something almost vanished from literature.' But he also added, 'By now contemporary literature must be overweighted with homosexual disgust and jeering at life; it is surely time for a little heterosexual celebration to right the balance.'[46] This statement may have been aimed at Frank Sargeson as well as others like Charles Brasch and W.H. Pearson. It may also have unconsciously expressed something latent or suppressed in Maurice's own sexuality. It certainly offended Eric McCormick who wrote to the *Listener*: 'You may describe a writer as inaccurate or sentimental or tasteless and support the charge with quotations. But while the law of this and other countries remains in its present state, if you describe a male writer as homosexual and cite the evidence, you expose him to the risk of criminal proceeding'. Maurice would have been aware of his friend's 'closet' homosexuality for, when McCormick sent a copy to Maurice, he added the note, 'As you realise it was not easy to write the letter. I sent it because the issue involved — in this case verbal and critical more than moral — seems to me so important that it should be publicly rather than privately discussed … perhaps we shall be able to talk it over more fully. I hope so.'[47] They did discuss it and the pair remained friends until the end. In his *Listener* response to McCormick's letter, Maurice averred that a review's brevity 'inevitably leaves a margin for misunderstanding' and lamented the state of a New Zealand society which sent 'people to prison because of their strictly private lives' and 'Must we retreat to the quaint position of calling a spade a large trowel?'.[48] The later irony to this episode was that Cheever's bisexuality was revealed only after his death in 1982.

Maurice found he could not turn down the lucrative offer of a commission to write one segment of a drama touted as New Zealand's first full-length television play. The four parts of the play corresponded to the seasons and Maurice's segment involved the story of a young girl in autumn adapted from his story 'Summer Fires'. He completed this but the other three writers 'came up with scripts impossible to film or no script at all'. Despite his protests, the New Zealand Broadcasting Corporation (NZBC) decided to film Maurice's script as a fifteen-minute one-off play, directed by an Italian who could not read English:'When a character was accused … of having cold feet, the director instructed the actor to look down at his feet and shiver … Nothing good could come of this. Nothing did. My first and last entanglement with television drama ended there.'[49] It was eventually screened on a Friday (late shopping) night in October.

Maurice had promised Sheena Amato that he would write a foreword to the collection of Michael's stories which Whitcombe & Tombs had accepted for publication provided a publishing grant from the State Literary Fund was forthcoming. The first manuscript Sheena put together was rejected by the Fund. 'The reason, quite transparently, was that the sexual frankness of some of the stories offended the committee's more conservative members.'[50] David Lawson at Whitcombe's still wanted to go ahead and asked Maurice and Ian Cross to edit the collection so that the Fund could be approached again. They removed weaker stories from the collection ('including one obviously offensive story') and, after direct representation to the Fund committee by Cross, it agreed to subsidise the book which was published in 1967 as *The Full Circle of the Travelling Cuckoo*.

During his two stays in Wellington for the television project Maurice spent a week going through Amato's manuscripts and papers with Sheena in order to write his 4000-word introduction. Together, they discovered that, as a sixteen-year-old in northern Italy, Amato had been recruited into the notorious 'Black Brigade', a ruthless counter-partisan group Mussolini formed after the fall of Rome. But Amato had been rescued, redeemed, by an allied officer early in 1945 who persuaded the youngster to change sides — and saved his life.

Cross thought Maurice's introduction 'in many respects, the best thing in the book … Will the reader, swept through the introduction by the authority and feeling of Maurice Shadbolt begin the stories expecting more than they deliver? Does your biography say some things better than Michael's stories do?'[51] Sheena Amato's response to the introduction tells why:'I thought it was excellent even if you felt it was fictionalised. There was nothing else you could have done. Who could have found out the truth at this stage? It has amazed me how you have made all the bits and pieces I gave you and the things you gleaned from his own writing into such a lucid whole.'[52] Sheena and Maurice had worked through Amato's papers, 'sometimes in harmony, often in discord' and 'In spite of my best intentions it soon began to seem that a novel, rather than a memoir, was in the making. I asked Sheena how she felt about that prospect' and she told him that, after publication of Amato's collection he was, 'welcome to his life'.[53] Maurice's introduction was a kind of synopsis for what was to come.

Maurice ended 1965 deep in doubt. He admitted to Karl Stead, 'Earlier in the year I had every reason to hope that I might quit fiction. Now I catch myself out making a statement like that. Quite incurable … I've never felt entirely committed to writing, and there was a certain perverse relief in the idea that it might be all over soon.'[54] He confided to his journal, 'I thought I might be able to work out just what kind of writer I am. Still uncertain & still most unconvinced I have any talent at all. A measure of instinctive craftsmanship, a certain feeling for form … I would also like to think … that there is, in my work, something not to be found in the work of other writers here or elsewhere. Perhaps a small thing, but something all the same: something that justifies my existence. To see my country clear & plain is not a parochial concern: it can be universal too.'[55]

This last journal entry for the year became confessional. 'Why must one always balance betrayal of self against the betrayal of other human beings? And when — O Christ, when — do I grow up? Let it be soon.

'I know myself, I think. But God knows that doesn't help much either. It certainly doesn't help make me more honest in human relationships. Just more acutely aware of dishonesty. The one totally unforgivable sin in human relations: to involve another … person wholly, without involving oneself.

'Where does truth begin, deception end? Sometimes I actually do believe in what I appear to be — to others. And then …

'Can I really afford to grow any colder on life — without, finally, hurting & perhaps maiming those around me? … I've never had sufficient capacity for life: such a coward in personal affairs.'[56] There was no mention of love.

CHAPTER 22

COMING APART

There was good news in the new year of 1966: Cassell in London accepted *The Presence of Music* for publication the following year. Otherwise, it had been 'An arid summer with hack-work, which in the end leaves me mindless.'[1] To compile the *Shell Guide*, Maurice had been researching, travelling and writing hard to earn his advance and expenses. This was still not enough, as virtually sole breadwinner, to support the demands of the enlarged family. He continued to punch out almost weekly book reviews and could not afford to turn down a *National Geographic* commission to write an article on the Cook Islands. He was desperate to buy himself time to write fiction again but, more pressingly, four children and two adults into two bedrooms would not go. Money was needed urgently to enlarge the house. With plans drawn up by his old friend, architect Nigel Cook, who had moved to Auckland, Gill capitalised her Family Benefit to augment the cost of an extension which was to sit 'precariously above our old garage. No earthquakes please.'[2]

After the 'first peaceful year or two at Titirangi' Maurice felt he was 'once more losing control of my personal life. That is, when I had time to spare my personal life a glance.' Gill was 'once again impatient with the isolation my work, and four children, imposed on her'.[3] The house in the Titirangi bush with a romantic view of the Manukau provided the ambience and seclusion that Maurice needed for his writing; but, over the almost forty years he was there, it also proved to be the location for recurring domestic conflict and disillusion.

Gill may well have been 'impatient' with her situation. It takes little imagination to understand how much stress and exhaustion was caused her by the incessant demands of four yelling infants, the nappy-squalor, the accumulating household dirt and debris; all of this exacerbated by distance from friends and family, from shops and local community services; and with the constant underlying anxiety of an uncertain income. No matter how much Maurice may have described what he was doing as 'hack-work', and resented the need for it, it also meant he was often not there when family crises occurred. The help of family and friends for Gill could only partially ameliorate this. Yet, during his absences, she continued to look after his essential mail and contacts, to consider his wellbeing.

Maurice undertook the *Shell Guide to New Zealand* because it promised to be a steady earner over many years, contributing towards a base income. Although he travelled to most of the regions at times during 1966 and 1967, he also relied a good deal on material he had gathered on his *Gift of the Sea* travels with Brian Brake. The heavily illustrated[4] 300-plus page hardback was put together on a matrix of twelve regional sections and four on the main centres, following a general introduction. Maurice wrote an environmental and historical essay for each section, followed by 'Books for Further Reading' and a selective Gazetteer with thumbnail place descriptions.[5] Sites worth visiting were printed in bold, along with pithy advice. In Kawakawa, for example, travellers should 'Avoid railway trains in main street'. Maurice's accumulation of information for the *Shell Guide* did have its 'incidental rewards — in forcing [sic] me to history I didn't know. Amassed tremendous amount of knowledge about Maori wars which could be useful one day.'[6]

In May, Maurice flew into Rarotonga in a rackety DC-3 that was later to crash in Samoa, killing three on board. To Maurice, it seemed a small miracle that the pilot found the place at all. 'Take a map and jab a pin into the heart of the Pacific south of the Equator, and with very good luck your pinprick might demolish one of the 15 tiny islands … Scattered thinly over 13 degrees of latitude … they're easy to lose.'[7] This was the start of his article 'or at least some wallpaper prose to plaster between *Geographic*'s photographs.'[8]

While he waited for the *Geographic*'s photographer, Bill Allard, to arrive Maurice lodged at the 'South Sea sleazy' Rarotonga Hotel. This was a kind of boarding house for pakeha New Zealand expatriate bureaucrats helping to run the government of a tiny nation of 20,000 people which had been granted internal self-government only the year before. Many of the expats seemed preoccupied with booze and sex with local girls in their down time. When Bill Allard turned up, Maurice thought him an 'uncouth Midwesterner', an 'inexperienced and incautious traveller' who 'found the sexual electricity of the place dizzying', and who soon had a Rarotongan dancer for a companion. Maurice became friendly with the teacher and guitarist-coach for a local dance team who told him that it was 'hard to be earnest, to study, to think about life, when all around are people who only want to laugh, dance, sing and be happy'. This was 'dangerous stuff. This was what frangipani did, and moonlight through the ironwood trees'. This 'stuff' could not be part of his *Geographic* 'wallpaper' but it was what the 'many-scented shore' could do to a 'reasonably level-headed writer in a week'.[9] Maurice wrote about the preoccupation with sex of others on Rarotonga but not his own, which was to leave him with an unpleasant 'South Sea sleazy' souvenir.

Maurice and Allard circled Rarotonga, visiting villages and schools, orange and coconut plantations, gathering copy and photographs for another romantic *Geographic* feature. Then they went on a 2000-kilometre return trip on the seven-knot chugging, 200-ton island trader *Akatere* to Manihiki, Arahanga and Penrhyn in the north where they snorkelled and swam with pearl and crab divers and curious sharks. The islands' diminishing population was not down to the latter but the steady migration of people to the bright lights of Auckland. Locals lamented that soon only the very young and the very old would be left.[10]

On return to the capital Avarua, Maurice found himself involved in a political scandal. Before he went north, the owner of the Rarotonga Hotel had shown him a letter he said he had found in the waste basket of the Honourable Julian Dashwood, a 67-year-old English ex-trade store manager who was now the only European in the Cook Islands cabinet led by premier Albert Henry. Henry had decided that the Cook Island economy could not grow from oranges and coconuts alone and, with the aid of a New York international stamp dealer, set about producing limited edition stamps for the world philately market. It was a clever move and was to finance up to 20 per cent of the Cook Islands budget. But the letter — which Allard photographed as evidence — showed that Dashwood and Henry were doing a deal with an Australian stamp and coin broker that would line their own pockets. 'It was all there in black and white, so shameless that I couldn't believe [it] ... Julian Dashwood and Albert Henry were a slimy pair of swindlers.'[11] At the Avarua wharf Maurice and Allard were met by policemen and held as witnesses to a felony: the theft of Dashwood's letter by the hotel manager. The heat had gone on Dashwood who took the rap for the dubious stamp deal and resigned from cabinet. Avoiding prosecution himself, Albert Henry then blamed all the Europeans involved in the scandal, including Maurice, and had them leave Rarotonga forthwith.[12] Maurice was happy enough to oblige as he had come down with food poisoning.

In a sequel, the *New Zealand Monthly Review*, in an article about the scandal, said that Maurice had been party to a conspiracy against the Cook Islands government. He demanded a correction be printed that stated he did not 'photograph certain documents used to embarrass, discredit or intimidate that government'.[13] He settled for this because although, 'I suppose the logical thing, in the circumstances, would be for me to consult my lawyer ... a recent illness makes visits to the city something of an effort for me'.[14] His bout of food poisoning had disguised the symptoms of hepatitis. Maurice never identified which strain but his almost certain sexual philandering in the Cook Islands points to hepatitis B.

Hepatitis afflicted Maurice for months after his return from the Cook Islands and was followed by pneumonia at the end of the year. He had energy only to complete the *Geographic* article, scratch out some words for the *Shell Guide* and fiddle with a few more pages of 'Search for Tim Livingstone'. The hepatitis left him confined to Titirangi, 'weak, teetotal and entirely anti-social ... The compensation was that I grew very close to my family and my own obscure and scruffy patch of earth.'[15] His children would remember that there were two Maurices: the one who was never there, on assignment or shut away in his writing studio; and the one who, otherwise, was there for them as a loving and devoted father. As Sean and Brendan grew older, he would take them camping and sometimes on his research trips. There was fishing, almost daily when he was at home, using the dinghy drawn up at the bottom of the section to set nets for mullet and flounder; or scouring the mudflats together for pipi and cockles when the tide was out. The boys also helped him with an extensive vegetable garden, an activity rooted in his Te Kuiti childhood.

After he submitted his Cook Islands story, *National Geographic* asked him to write the Polynesian section of a book on the South Pacific with Olaf Ruhen, who would cover Melanesia. Still barely recovered, the prospect of travelling far and wide did not appeal, but the work and money was too tempting. He undertook research for the project in the new year of 1967 and then spent most of the next four months among the islands. He told Kevin Ireland soon afterwards that 'for once I didn't enjoy the travel, though naturally no one ever believes this; how could one possibly _not_ enjoy the Society Islands, Tonga etc ... ? The fact is I bloody well can.'[16] Constantly on the move, living out of a suitcase in seedy hotels. Still unwell, casual sex had lost some of its charm. Maurice did enjoy revisiting Samoa because Gill was able to accompany him, the children cared for by mother Vi, and they stayed with the Wendts in Apia.

The Samoa trip was one attempt to hold the marriage together. Maurice had also come to accept that Gill's needs, both physical and mental, had to be met somehow. He purchased another small car so that she would never be without transport while he was on the road, and initially supported her efforts to edit and publish an early childhood magazine with journalist Sue

Vaassen called *Child*. This included progressive articles, stories and reviews aimed at parents, educators, researchers and bureaucrats engaged with pre-school education at playcentres and kindergartens. The first of ten monthly or bimonthly issues appeared in November 1967. Dependent on both subscriptions and advertising, its size had diminished from twenty-four pages to sixteen by the time the last issue appeared in December 1968. For Maurice, this 'ill-fated business enterprise, which seemed to offer her prospect of a fresh career, invaded the home and before long all domestic peace was gone'.[17] The constant phone calls and house visits involved with the magazine's production became a chronic source of contention and frustration for him.

As Maurice worked hard to complete his text for the South Pacific book, the publication of *The Presence of Music* provided some relief. It had been taken seriously on its March publication in the UK. Christopher Wordsworth in the *Guardian* wrote that 'Mr Shadbolt has been compared with Patrick White: he can powerfully evoke the *manes* of place. His characters cast long shadows. They bluster around like rejected suitors among the ghosts of the Polynesian past, possessed by the land, unable to possess it.'[18]

The anonymous reviewer in the *Times Literary Supplement* had space to analyse the book more closely. He understood that the stories dealt with the isolated plight of the provincial (or colonial) artist whose strength 'is that if he stays at home to exploit it ... cannot escape from his philistine fellows and perhaps perishes of refinement'. Maurice evoked 'with success the various atmospheres in and out of which his restless and mobile countrymen incessantly move' but 'his splinters of the European scene are observed from the surface, the pyrites of brilliant reporting'. The main failure was that the 'commonsense' first person narrators of the three stories were indistinguishable, all speaking with the same voice and sometimes revealed themselves 'on one page as highly intelligent and as very imperceptive on the next. To the exacting reader whom Mr. Shadbolt deserves and challenges, this sort of implausibility is troubling.'[19]

At home, David Hall in the *Listener* wrote: 'It is heartening to find Maurice Shadbolt resuming the assured mastery of his two volumes of short stories, lost momentarily in his fumbling novel [*Among the Cinders*] ... All three of these stories add to his stature and stand with the best of his work'.[20] There was no review in *Landfall*. By now, Charles Brasch had given up as editor and anointed Robin Dudding his successor. This did not lessen Maurice's antipathy to the journal; the memory of the Hamilton review in Dudding's *Mate* still festered. Sticking to his vow, Maurice instructed his publisher not to send *Landfall* a copy for review.

At the beginning of October, Maurice heard that his 'near perfect story',

'Figures in Light', had won him the Bank of New Zealand Katherine Mansfield Short Story Award for the second time. He then believed the 'rules of the award were revised to ensure that I didn't win it a third or fourth time'.[21] But this was a minor change in the wider world changing around him. He told Kevin Ireland: 'You wouldn't know the country any more. Dollars and cents and 10 o'clock closing; and unemployed again.* We're starting to standardise, homogenise, or something. For good and ill. What worries me is that the NZ I knew, grew up in, is soon going to seem quite unreal; I mightn't be able to write about it without bulky footnotes.' Europe and Britain with its drift towards the Common Market were beginning to seem irrelevant. 'The Pacific has grown around us at last — and for both those opposing and defending the war in Vietnam.' There had been a 'fantastic Polynesian migration' into Auckland, 'a cranky, unpredictable city — yet I literally couldn't bear, now, to live anywhere else. New Zealand had to have a city, sooner or later, and it had to be Auckland (Wellington having successfully passed itself off as reasonable imitation in our day).' 'It was a good place to be young.'[22] Maurice had been down to Christchurch to give the opening address at the Universities Arts Festival and found the south like the country he once knew, 'perfectly preserved, a museum piece … South Islanders are literally a lost tribe now, the Ngati Mamoe all over again, only 700,000 of them against 2 million North Islanders. And it's good to know the place is there, a line of retreat.'[23]

As the world changed around him, Maurice decided it was too late to change himself. A few years later he was to write: 'By this time, I had no real alternative to my life as a writer … There was no going back to, say, routine journalism or film work. There was just the problem of hanging on to what I had; and what I could do best … write fiction.'[24] At the time, he saw 'A simultaneous happening … I can't ever go back on my independence now. My marriage has gone too far along the road. Gill wants and needs her own life. Now she can have it.'[25]

Gill accompanied Maurice to Wellington for the Mansfield award and they visited Sheena Amato who was making plans to leave New Zealand after the publication of Michael's *The Full Circle of the Travelling Cuckoo* in November. After their visit, she wrote to him, 'When I saw you both I suddenly felt incomplete as if I had no right to be there without Michael … Perhaps I felt a little bitter. You always seem to have the things we long for — literary

---

*On 10 July 1967 New Zealand changed to decimal currency. In a late September referendum almost 64% voted to change the licensing laws. A 30% drop in the wool price had prompted both unemployment and inflation to rise.

success, a family — and to appreciate them so little.' Maurice had spoken to her privately, told her he was planning to leave Gill and suggested they could get together. She told him, 'There can never be anything. I said goodbye at the airport … For me Gill will always be someone unique. She has helped you become what you are. You have four children, your loyalties lie elsewhere. If Gill has changed then this is your sin but I do not believe she has changed.' It was not that she had no feelings for him. There were letters, words in her head that she could not say when he was there. 'You can't know then what I think or what I feel? (Shades of luv!).' He still had her friendship, 'all that I can give in the circumstances'.[26]

Maurice returned to Auckland, determined to separate from Gill and the family in order to resume work on 'Search' and the dolphin novel. He saw the move as a parallel to his shift to Queenstown and the writing of *Among the Cinders* in 1963. But he was now in a different, more damaging, emotional climate. His Uncle Joe Kearon had suffered a couple of heart attacks and no sooner had Maurice shifted to a borrowed bach at Bucklands Beach — on the opposite side of Auckland to Titirangi — than the expected telephone call came. 'Just a week ago we talked. It was all right then, almost … Perhaps he knew. But I wish he had known that he was a touchstone in my life. If only I could have told him, instead of stuttering.' Too late. 'It was his rejecting me not long before the end which hurt … I thought I would always be there, that he thought that too, & in the end found I was — had been — fooling myself.' Could it have been any different? Could he have told Joe how much he owed him? Joe had gone too soon at only sixty years old. Too soon, too late. 'Joe — would you, can you, listen?'[27] A mooring in Maurice's life had been severed, a crucial prompt to his conscience had gone.

Maurice's departure from Titirangi for Bucklands Beach and then his preoccupation with Joe's death and funeral emphasised for Gill the widening separation between them, his willingness to neglect the family for the sake of his own work and life. In mute protest, she left Arapito Road with the twins one day and did not come back. For a week Maurice and friends searched for her, until she was discovered at Joe's empty house in Henderson. Her protest did nothing but openly declare the rift between them.

Amid this domestic turmoil, Maurice was unable to come to grips again with the family relationship stories that underpinned his big 'Search' novel and he turned instead to the shorter, imaginative distractions of dolphin fiction. Over the Christmas-New year period he completed the first draft and then abandoned Auckland to take Sean, nearing eight years old and Brendan, almost six, on a camping trip to the Bay of Islands. 'We pitched pup-tents on the edge of a horseshoe beach. Large fish cruised transparent sea; we pursued them excitably with rod and spear. Yachts glided on a glimmering horizon.'

But the return home to Titirangi 'killed the lingering exhilaration of that holiday ... a loud and smoky party was in progress ... The twins were distressed, soon the boys too. The music was deafening, punctuated by stamping feet. Long-haired strangers scrutinised us as if we were strangers. Perhaps we were.'[28]

He was a stranger at least to the new Hippie culture that had erupted in San Francisco the year before; to the dope/pot/hash/marijuana that laced the smoke in his living room; to the psychedelia celebrated in the Beatles' latest album, *Sgt Pepper's Lonely Hearts Club Band*. Gill had heard the call of US psychiatrist and counter-culture leader Timothy Leary to 'Tune in, turn on, and drop out', and decided to let her hair down in a world that seemed to be collapsing around her. Maurice kicked the strangers out but 'It was plain that 1968 would be the last of my fifteen years of marriage'.

CHAPTER 23

WILD COLONIAL BOYS

A couple of months later, Maurice papered over the cracks when he told sister Julia that, 'Gill is well, and the kids too. The twins are so sweet I feel it's a shame they have to grow up.'[1] He wrote to her about what she was due from Uncle Joe's estate for which he and brother Peter, now back in Auckland, were trustees. The three of them and mother Vi had inherited $1261 each (worth about $20,000 today) and was welcome news for nineteen-year-old Julia who was now in Dunedin with her new husband, Ian Hass. He was in his fifth year of medical studies and she was in her second full year at Otago University, studying to be a teacher.

Maurice also told Julia that he was about to attend a 'Vietnam conference' in Wellington. This was the four-day 'Peace, Power and Politics in Asia' Conference ring-mastered by Alister Taylor, later publisher of Tim Shadbolt's *Bullshit and Jellybeans*, and the New Zealand editions of *The Little Red Schoolbook* and *The Whole Earth Catalogue*. Using highly effective public relations and propaganda techniques, Taylor marshalled media interest in a conference that was intended to counter the meeting of SEATO leaders in Wellington to discuss future plans for the Vietnam War in the face of the recent Viet Cong Tet Offensive. Maurice was one of 1300 people registered for the conference and he was one of the scheduled speakers alongside overseas luminaries Krishna Menon and Conor Cruise O'Brien and local speakers such as future cabinet minister Michael Bassett and newly arrived Otago University political scientist Jim Flynn. More than 3000 of the general public attended, too. Midway through O'Brien's speech news broke that US President Lyndon Johnson had cancelled the bombing of North Vietnam and would not be standing for president again in the November election. This caused great jubilation: now the war would soon be over and there was a sense that the conference had somehow swayed his decision. 'Certainly the prepared speeches had to be hastily rewritten. I trashed mine and took a long walk through the Wellington of my youth,'[2] cogitating on his future. The war would last another seven years and the chief effect of the conference had been to energise the peace movement and, later, the anti-nuclear campaign which led to New Zealand's exit from ANZUS. At the time, it strengthened Prime Minister Keith Holyoake's hand in arguing not to commit more troops to a lost American cause.

In 1967, Maurice had become involved in a different kind of cause: the artistic needs of two notorious criminals held under maximum security. In June, during a literary luncheon arranged to promote *The Presence of Music*, Maurice jokingly remarked that, apart from Sir Edmund Hillary, New Zealand could lay claim to one other true national hero, prison escaper George Wilder. At a time when movie westerns were still popular, Wilder had become a folk hero in his role as an outlaw twice outwitting pursuing police posses. He had been convicted first for shop-breaking and theft of Jaguar cars in 1962. Part way through a four-year sentence, Wilder scaled the ten-metre high wall of New Plymouth prison and took off across country. For two months he evaded police capture, driving through barricades, out-swimming police dogs, making getaways by dinghy and horse. Recaptured, he was sent to the fortress of Auckland's Mount Eden Prison but escaped again, using the proverbial knotted sheets. This time he was out for almost six months and his folk-hero status became established. To survive, he broke into unoccupied baches, made himself at home but cleaned up after him and left notes of apology. There were regular newspaper and radio reports and when people heard he might be in their area, food and clothing were left out. The Howard Morrison Quartet recorded a hit single, 'George, the Wild(er) New Zealand Boy'. James K. Baxter and Mike Doyle wrote poems about him. Wilder was finally caught again near Taupo and returned to Mount Eden but made one more escape in February 1964, this time with a sawn-off shotgun. Holed up with others in a Mount Eden house, he surrendered to the Armed Offenders Squad after a few hours.

Maurice's jocular remarks about Wilder were reported in the *Auckland Star* and a few days later he received a phone call from a prison visitor, 'Grace', who told him that 'George' was most upset about what Maurice had said: he was going through a bad time and joking about him did not help. Maurice was mortified as he realised that Wilder was 'more than a plaything of a long-winded novelist looking for a lively theme; that there was a vulnerable human being confined in a joyless maximum security cell …'[3] When Grace told Maurice that Wilder was an aspiring artist but prison officials would not allow him paint and brushes, only pencils and crayons, Maurice's mortification turned to anger and he agreed to visit Wilder and do what he could to help. He became a regular visitor, talked about the books Wilder read and the books he was converting to Braille for the blind. Wilder declared he had 'churned out about 10 cwt of Braille over the last few years'.[4] Maurice promised to get him paints and brushes but made no headway with obdurate prison managers who also lied about prisoners' access to exercise and sunlight. In any case, they explained the situation would become rather better in 1968 when the new maximum security prison was opened at Paremoremo. This was already being dubbed the 'George Wilder Rest Home'.

In August, Maurice travelled down to Christchurch to give the opening address at the Universities Students Arts Festival. His theme was the difficulties faced by writers and artists in New Zealand and he used by way of metaphor the difficulty George Wilder had in obtaining permission to paint in prison. Maurice was surprised this met with so much applause, but he should not have been. Here was the nation's folk-hero being denied creative rights. A press reporter made hay with Maurice's remarks and headlines followed. 'This was the next best thing to a new escape.' The *Sunday Times* dug deeper, supposing that Maurice was collecting material for a Wilder novel. But for Maurice 'fact had erased fiction. How create a fictional, possibly comic Wilder when I saw the real thing weekly?'[5] (At least not yet). Wilder was not best pleased: '"Ace escaper..." National hero ... Arrrr ... You've got no idea how hard all that crap makes it for me in hear [sic] ... I realize it was not youre [sic] wording, but see how those germs have to flower it up and twist it!'[6] But the newspaper stories so embarrassed prison authorities that Wilder got his paints and brushes; and so did his cell neighbour Ron Jorgensen who now declared he also had talent as an artist.

Jorgensen was a 'different kettle of criminal' from Wilder. He had been sentenced to life imprisonment for his role in the 'Bassett Road machine-gun murders' of December 1963. Two men had been shot with a .45 calibre submachine gun in a dispute at an illicit Remuera sly grog and drug house frequented by many in the Auckland criminal community. Jorgensen claimed he had not committed the murders and deserved no more than a five-year sentence as an accomplice after the fact. Now he joined Wilder in developing a prison painting career. 'Their subject matter was in keeping with their characters. George painted wistful landscapes', perhaps inspired by his cross-country escapes, while 'Ron painted boxers and bullfighters'.[7] Both were competent at still life and Maurice encouraged both Colin McCahon and Garth Tapper to visit the prisoners and give them some tuition.

Maurice also encouraged Wilder to write down his story, no holds barred, to put down the truth and not what he thought people wanted to hear. Wilder took him at his word and delivered a hand-written manuscript that not only listed all the crimes for which he had been convicted but also scores for which he had not. 'The list went on and on. In the wrong hands the narrative might have meant another hundred convictions, possibly a longer prison term.'[8] After telling Wilder that his tale was interesting, if a tad too literal, Maurice burned the incriminating manuscript in his backyard incinerator.

Paints and brushes sorted, Maurice then became involved in trying to spring both crims from prison, legally. In June 1968, Maurice 'went to see Ron Jorgensen in jail. A little hipped-up [sic] in anticipation of his trial. Have been working with Peter Williams[9] to prepare his case'[10] of defamation against the *Sunday Times* for a story they published on Jorgensen. If that had succeeded it might have provided a lever with which to challenge his murder conviction. Maurice spent three days at the trial, appearing as a witness for Jorgensen, but to no avail. Jorgensen continued to paint. He gave friends many of his paintings and scorned criticism. He wrote to Maurice, 'I paint, sketch & so on to please me … [censored] anyone else that dislikes my work — it keeps me occupied & that's all I care about it & what friends I happen to give a painting to.'[11] He gave Maurice and Gill paintings for Christmas that year. Ron Jorgensen spent another fifteen years in gaol before being released on parole. In 1984 his car was found at the bottom of a cliff near his home in Kaikoura but with no body. What happened to him remains a mystery.

George Wilder's fate was kinder. Maurice recorded that when he was in Wellington, for the Peace, Power and Politics Conference, he went to see the Secretary for Justice, Dr John Robson, about Wilder's situation. During the 1960s, in concert with Minister of Justice Ralph Hanan, Robson was responsible for many reforms in law, including penal policy, and was receptive to Maurice's plea that Wilder be released from maximum security into a more open prison environment. Maurice assured Robson he could persuade Wilder to give his word not to escape again. Using a go-between, Maurice sent Wilder a note telling him that if he was released from maximum security, and then escaped again, Robson's planned penal reforms would be placed in jeopardy. 'I need an undertaking that you won't attempt to escape again. Give me the undertaking and I can argue your case with confidence.'[12] Wilder promised, was transferred from Mount Eden and a year later paroled.

Soon after his release he went to visit Maurice: 'I took him down to the beach and he looked at sand and rock as if he had never seen it before; he plucked green leaves as if he was going to eat them ... He likes the idea of taking up craft work, in a Titirangi bach, but is still dizzy with freedom.'[13] Not so dizzy that he and Maurice could not talk about writing a book together and Maurice put the idea to popular Wellington publishers A.H.& A.W. Reed. They quickly offered a contract but Maurice was cautious, not certain if the planned format, of he and Wilder writing complementary chapters, would work. He replied that they had 'decided to write experimental chapters — around the first of the famous escapes ... I would write the official story, using newspaper and perhaps police sources, while he tells it like it was.'[14] It would not be a life; Wilder could perhaps write that later.

But Wilder fell in with bad company and six months later he was trapped with a stolen car in a police sting. He took off into the bush again in Henderson and the police called on Maurice to see if he had dropped by. Wilder was recaptured and Maurice went to court again, testifying to the criminal peer pressures Wilder had been under and relating how Wilder had said he might be better off in goal anyway. It did not help. Wilder went back to prison with added time. By now Maurice had had enough. 'It was too much for me. I never meddled as deeply in crime's realm again.'[15]

But he was not quite done. Wilder was paroled again three years later and called in to see Maurice as he tried to evade pursuing reporters. He stayed a night and had breakfast with Eric McCormick, who had also been a faithful prison visitor, before heading south to a new, crime-free life in the Wairarapa. Maurice always maintained the Wilder saga was the best book he never wrote but, as every good agent tells their authors, 'Never throw anything away', whether manuscripts or notes. Wilder would one day appear in a novel Maurice had not yet dreamed of.

CHAPTER 24

SWIMMING WITH DOLPHINS

Amid the deepening chaos of his domestic life, the distractions of the anti-Vietnam movement, and dealing with the Wilder and Jorgensen cases, Maurice managed to complete a final draft, almost, of *This Summer's Dolphin* in April 1968. Soon afterwards, he sent back the final proofs for *The Shell Guide to New Zealand* which was published at the end of the year. During the second half of the year he also drafted more than 200 manuscript pages of 'The Search for Tim Livingstone'. The problems surrounding its structure and characters filled many pages of his journal. By manuscript page 437 he records: 'Think I have control of the third part of Search. Cross fingers.'[1]

He also allowed himself to be distracted by writing letters to the editor, taking on reviews, interviews and just … views. An interview appeared in the current affairs journal *The New Zealander* in July which shocked even close friends and colleagues such as Maurice Gee. Charles Brasch discovered that Maurice had written the 'interview' himself. 'That makes it worse. It becomes harder & harder to smile.'[2] Perhaps Brasch should have smiled. It was essentially a satire of a serious literary interview. 'Q: How do you feel at this stage of your life? A: I feel 36 years old. Q: Is that supposed to have some significance? A: Yes. It feels better than 35.' He then elaborates on all those New Zealand writers who died around that age, and how he had early decided he should not start writing seriously until he was forty and mature; now he was getting close. Of all his non-literary work, the imaginary interviewer asks, what 'was of the greatest value in literary terms? A: Being a professional magician … conjuring as a thing of craft, has a great deal to do with the art of fiction.' He then enlarges on his friendship with painters because there was 'no competitive thing. Besides, New

Zealand writers — in total — aren't a particularly pretty collection. Q: Oh? A: I could be harsh and say pouting, primping prima donnas. Popcorn Prousts and hairless Hemingways. In total that is. They seem to lack all conviction.' He then pointed out that, of all the writers who had signed the anti-Vietnam War petition, he alone had been left to counter the opposing views of Ian Cross in a *Listener* correspondence that had become acrimonious, despite their friendship. In the balance of the 'interview' he 'discusses' his writing and books, taking time to defend *Among the Cinders*. 'Q: So what are you writing now? A: I'm trying to kill off the social realist novel with the longest, most boring book ever written in New Zealand. A labour of love, or hate, I'm not sure which.' The 'interview' ends with 'Q: But you're committed to your craft? A: I'm looking for a way out. I've only four more years after all. And I'm still looking round. The whole thing becomes more and more mysterious.'[3] The 'interview' reflected Maurice's fractured sense of himself as a writer, the knowledge that he was conjuring something from a top hat of disparate skills while wondering why he was on the stage at all and thinking that, in the end, it did not add up to much. 'Q: When do writers become important to a society? A: When they're put in jail. The only real test. We're light years away.'

Maurice's engagement in the letters pages of newspapers, and especially the *New Zealand Listener*, with such causes as the anti-Vietnam War movement, literary censorship and penal reform were evidence of his belief that writers should take a lead on social and political issues, reinforced by his experience in the Soviet Union and Eastern Europe.[4] His contempt for those writers who did not was real: for him, few measured up to the task other than Jim Baxter and Karl Stead. The 'interview' was a piece of facetious polemic aimed at the small intellectual audience who read *The New Zealander*, especially those he knew would be most offended. When larger audiences were to be addressed his role as social commentator demanded serious intent.

Maurice's sympathies for the disadvantaged place of Maori in society were rooted in his Te Kuiti childhood but enlarged during his sojourns at Ahipara and in the Hokianga, as well as his travels, research and writing for *National Geographic*, *Gift of the Sea* and the *Shell Guide*. Maori characters were important figures in his fiction, such as Tui in 'The Strangers' and Sam Waikai in *Among the Cinders*. Maurice's travels throughout the South Pacific expanded his understanding of the wider Polynesian world and, as he wrote Kevin Ireland in October 1967, New Zealand was becoming a Pacific nation, not an antipodean outpost of Europe. In a *New Zealand Women's Weekly* interview published that same month he emphasised the necessity of including Polynesian (that is, Maori) culture and experience in the education system.[5] Maurice's views were not original: Sylvia Ashton-Warner, for example, had explored the subject in her books a decade before. But Maurice's increasing public profile as a writer engaged with social issues ensured they would have some influence.

On 23 May 1968, Maurice attended the second anniversary of the coronation of the Maori Queen Te Atairangikaahu at Ngaruawahia. On his return, the new editor of the *Listener*, Alexander MacLeod, asked him to write an opinion piece under the banner of a new column, 'In My View'. Maurice wrote that the most moving part of the two-day celebration was 'seeing Pakeha faces, sometimes by the dozen, among the parties of Maoris welcomed on to the [Turangawaewae] marae. It was possible, at such times, to glimpse our national ideal of "two races and one people", however far short of that ideal present reality falls.' He went on to write that 'we have hardly begun, officially, to acknowledge that we have not just one but two living cultures'. Later, 'Are we ever going to have Maori taught in our schools? Are we ever going to encourage the Maori in the arts — and not just in crafts suitable for exploitation by the tourist industry? And are we Pakeha to continue murdering the place-names of Polynesia?'[6] Maurice's question about the arts would have been encouraged by meeting artist Selwyn Muru for the first time at Ngaruawahia: 'We got drunk together, & after two days felt I'd known him ten years'.[7]

By June, the *Shell Guide* was 'away at last. Down to the dust jacket. Well.'[8] He had persuaded Whitcombe & Tombs to showcase the work of leading New Zealand artists in the guide. Colin McCahon produced paintings for the jacket and the southern regional title pages and there were title page paintings by Garth Tapper, Juliet Peter and Doris Lusk.

With the guide finished, he went down to Rotorua for a few days with the manuscript of *This Summer's Dolphin* 'rather in hope of finding major reasons for revision. But didn't. Plenty of minor changes to make the text stronger. But that was about it.'[9] He sent the completed manuscript off to his London agent and to Michael Earl, managing director of Cassell Publishers in Auckland.

This Summer's Dolphin was a short novel, about 65,000 words, and was essentially an imaginative reconstruction of the Opo story. The dolphin became, oddly, Motu (island) and the location a Hauraki Gulf island, Motutangi (rather obviously 'funeral island') resembling Waiheke; the time is established as contemporary. The first chapter reveals that Maurice's compilation of the *Shell Guide* during the same period he was writing *This Summer's Dolphin* fatally bled into the novel with its faux non-fiction descriptions of Motutangi: 'Culture. The island has two moving-picture houses, also used as dance halls in summer, and an estimated eight hundred television sets.'[10] Charles Brasch later commented, 'I was very nearly put off by the opening section of this book, in which he describes his island, in almost tourist brochure terms.'[11] In the larger first section, Maurice established the atmosphere of life on the island and the characters and relationships of several disparate couples and individuals; Ben Blackwood the writer acted as surrogate for the author. They are all unable to relate satisfactorily to each other or to outsiders. Maurice described Motutangi as a 'sanctuary for life's walking wounded. No one lives long [there] without more than sufficient reason … Though the characters were taken from other places at other times it is true that I did observe the unhappiness described …'[12]

After the dolphin arrives with a local fisherman and his boat, its artless play with people in the water 'seemed to offer forgiveness for all', spiritual redemption, the chance of miracles. As more and more people travel to the island to interact with Motu, the beaches become populated in a festive community of instant friends. The halt and the lame are taken into the sea to touch Motu, to be healed in semi-religious ritual. Then Motu disappears and seachers find no trace of him. Inevitably, the dolphin has been shot by a disaffected local. The fisherman who attracted Motu in the first place finds him wedged among rocks in an isolated bay. 'Perhaps I ought to forget finding this, he thinks, and leave them, back there, with their wild wishes and foolish fancies, with something.'[13]

Early in 1968, Maurice received a fan letter from a 28-year-old New Plymouth artist, Michael Smither. Smither had been working on a stained-glassed window for Wellington's Victoria University chapel when he cracked the glass by placing a heater too close. 'I was very upset & annoyed. I went to the chaplains library & read a book of short stories by Maurice NZers I think & was very impressed & somehow calmed by his writing.'[14] Smither wrote him a note of appreciation and a few months later they met at a gallery opening in Auckland. 'Michael did much for my morale. We found many things in common. We had both been given a rough ride by New Zealand's critical mafia … I wished New Zealand to leap off the page; he wanted to paint it down to the last pebble.'[15] Maurice had seen Smither's 'religious paintings … which feature figures half in and half out of the water'.[16] When the question of a dust jacket image for *Dolphin* came up, Maurice intuitively sent a copy of the manuscript to Smither who responded with enthusiasm and began working on several ideas. Maurice wrote, 'I'm glad the subject appeals to you, & it seems my instinct was right. When I read your letter I had a sudden grand vision of a whole dolphin series emerging!' If it did, he thought an exhibition could be organised at the Barry Lett Gallery to coincide with the book launch, 'And thus give Auckland a genuine happening'. To his knowledge this kind of event had not occurred in New Zealand before.[17]

After unsuccessfully finding an episode from the novel that would yield the right subject, Smither 'decided to settle for the emblematic approach … underneath all the complications and happenings that surrounded the [Opo] episode the "legend come to life" aspect came through very strongly'. Smither's cover choice was 'very simply a painting of the boy in your manuscript steadying a child on the back of a dolphin & supporting the dolphin with his other hand'.[18] Both Maurice and the publishers were delighted. Smither travelled up to Auckland to stay with Maurice and discuss plans. Afterwards, Maurice wrote, 'That evening with McCahon was very interesting — the one concerned with your exhibition. He really got a lot out of it & is quite a partisan of yours.'[19] By now, Maurice had a McCahon koru for his letterhead and a number designated to the Arapito Road house: 35.

Maurice and Smither quickly became good friends. Smither was close enough emotionally yet far enough away in age and physical distance to Maurice, for him to feel easy about filling letters with angst over his writing and the chaos of his private life. 'I've never written the books I wanted to write — not once', because of the pressure of others' expectations. 'All I've published are scraps — evidence of my intention, & not much more. No point in fooling myself.' He was speaking to Smither's condition as an artist, too, when he wrote that he did not want to think about the 'final cost of it all — to the individual & and to all unfortunate enough to be involved with him. Ideally, perhaps, he should be castrated — this bloody marriage & children — at the first sign of talent'.[20]

For Michael Smither, painting the jacket picture set him off in the 'new direction of exploring the whole inter-species intelligence thing'.[21] At new year, with Maurice and eight-year-old Sean, he travelled to Mount Maunganui to swim with and draw Marineland's dolphins. Smither donned scuba gear so that he could sit at the bottom of the pool and make pencil drawings on a piece of painted hardboard. Maurice and Sean jumped in with the dolphins, too, and 'There was no doubt which human was their favourite. For a few bewitching minutes the classical tales about boys and dolphins came to life.'[22] The dolphins looked at what Smither was drawing and he made connections with them which he found 'quite spooky'. They had intended swimming with the dolphins for a day but stayed for three. Smither went home with thirty drawings and material enough for six paintings for the June exhibition and for the door to Maurice's study. Maurice suspected that Smither's exhibition images 'might overshadow my novel. Art had never known the like since classical times.'[23]

CHAPTER 25

BUTTERCUP FIELDS FOREVER

Swimming with dolphins was an escape at a time when Maurice and Gill's marriage was lurching towards final collapse. Before Christmas, he confessed to Smither: 'Gill & I have been feuding for nearly two bloody years about her magazine, which invaded & demoralized an until then pleasant household. Impossible — for the kids; and for me (particularly since I am obliged to work at home). It just went on — and on — till I could take no more. In September, with months of advance warnings, I quit & left. Nothing else to be done if I was to survive — I can't live in a permanent atmosphere of feud, let alone work in it, though Gill seemed happy to.' Gill's emotional support had shifted to their four young children; her spare energies towards the magazine which she hoped would bring in extra income to supplement the family budget. She had little left over for being mother and cheerleader to Maurice. Pathetically, he told Smither it was the second time he had 'been hurt & demoralized like this. I really have to rethink the whole thing.'[1]

Maurice shifted to Jeff Scholes's potters commune high in the Waitakere hills. He told the children he would not be far away and spent time with them two or three afternoons a week. But on his first day away from home they 'seemed on the far side of the moon; I was sick with grief'.[2] Scholes hoped that Maurice's presence would assist his own writing ambitions and Maurice found a room and a desk in the large, rambling old house with its view of distant Auckland. The monastic atmosphere and rhythmic patterns of the potters' work stimulated a return to working on 'The Search for Tim Livingstone'. But it began to 'wobble' out of control like a misshapen pot on a wheel. Its problems caused him to descend into a 'state of profound spiritual, mental, & physical exhaustion … A mistake to try anything of size. I see that now. I'm a magpie by nature & an effort of substance is beyond me.'[3] In November he put 'Search' aside yet again for another distractingly different project, a novel drawn from Michael Amato's life and work. He worked himself 'almost shitless' and had 50,000 words written by mid-January.

There were visitors to the commune in the evenings: musicians, potters and the occasional writer, but Maurice and Scholes sometimes escaped from their isolation by driving down to the city bright lights with its parties, movies, gallery openings and musical evenings. One weekend he helped Colin McCahon hang a new exhibition. 'He had gone back to the landscapes of his youth, to Otago rendered in cold and monotone colours. None of the written proclamations which distinguished much of his work; no religion … Was Colin viewing death from close quarters? I was not sure we were good for each other.'[4]

On one of his nights in town, Maurice met a petite blonde nurse, Beverly Richards, recently separated from her husband in England. She was attracted by the famous author, the stories of his troubles and his loneliness among the potters in the hills. He was clearly attracted to her, there was an implicit invitation, and one day she turned up at the commune with the makings of a picnic and a bottle of wine. They went off to the beach. 'Surf roared up an empty shore; spray drifted high. Sunset was as splendid.'[5] Cue violins crescendo and … fadeout.

They rented a flat together in Parnell and Richards created an 'oasis' for Maurice, in a 'wild world which exhausts me' and allowed him to make good progress on the new novel. 'For that, & for many other reasons, I'll always be in debt to B. She has never demanded because she understands how little I have to give.'[6] One of the practical 'reasons' was that Richards regularly received money in the mail from a rich, old admirer in England whose life she had saved after he suffered a cardiac arrest: this helped with the rent and groceries. Perhaps her lack of demands was also underpinned by her admirer's unrelenting pursuit, which had earlier resulted in the end of her English marriage. He still wanted her to return, to marry his son (with visiting rights), big house and car included. It was tempting.

Maurice had to leave his oasis and novel in late January 1969 to earn some money of his own, travelling the country with a *National Geographic* photographer for a feature on the Maori. They 'zig-zagged down country, visiting locations of Maori legend, hunting with Maori bushmen, meeting with Maori fishermen, interviewing and photographing tribesmen both illustrious and humble'.[7] 'Very rewarding & fresh experience. Average 800 miles a week. Hell.'[8]

At Tikitiki, on the banks of the Waiapu River near East Cape, he 'stumbled' across New Zealand's greatest carver, Pineamine Taiapa, a 68-year-old Ngati Porou artistic genius responsible for the carvings of about 100 whare whakairo, meeting houses, across the North Island, including the centennial house at Waitangi. For Maurice, it was an introduction to a part of the Maori world he had not fully understood. Taiapa's life had been spent in rescuing ancient Maori traditions in carving, to preserve whakapapa, spirituality and legend in wood, and to pass on skills. Each whare whakaraio 'functioned as a giant book of life, love and death, a treasure house of heroic traditions and mighty forebears.'[9] Taiapa's story was a revelation that Maurice broadcast widely, through articles for the *Listener, Reader's Digest*, and elsewhere.[10] Maurice had seemed to find a friend for life, for Taiapa 'not only explained what his life had been about. More marvellously, he helped me understand what mine was.' He began to see that his 'mission' as a writer was similar to Taiapa's as a carver. For ten years he had been creating his own whare whakarairo, the 'meeting place of *my* tribe' in the shape of his stories and novels, culminating in the unfinished 'Search for Tim Livingstone'. 'Though slow in discovering it, I was a tribesman too, a Polynesian pale in colour.'[11]

Maurice and Taiapa stayed in touch. After his visit to Tikitiki, Taiapa wrote to thank him for books Maurice had sent: 'Your visit has stirred quite a ripple along the Waiapu river causeway … I have received the usual jolt from the elders, by such remarks as, "giving away news of our way of life, our history, our heritage, our culture and such-like, we forbid you … to invite … to inform … strangers". I thrive on these conditions. I invite all and sundry to my house; it is my way of human contact outside my community, I need this to guide me in the present day needs of my community.'[12] Pine Taiapa ignored the strictures of his elders and guided groups of university students, 80 per cent pakeha, on to Ngati Porou marae to absorb and learn about Te Reo and Te Ao Maori.

In the *Listener*, Maurice wrote about meeting Taiapa and the neglect of Maori culture and artistry: 'Must we go on talking of the arts as something for which we need an import licence? … the existence of the Maori meeting house, its development as an art form, gives the lie. When we attempt to take stock of the arts … we should first count our assets. And the Maori meeting house must head that list.'[13] Taiapa wrote to Maurice how his 'frank and challenging article' had given him and his wife 'pleasure and a warm feeling for what you have written so glowingly of my small effort in helping the Maori of yesterday to feel with emotion & pride his background, history and tradition'. He thought the article would stimulate interest in carved meeting houses, but he was not so optimistic about younger Maori whom he felt lacked 'dignity and grace on the marae, inadequate in technique and speech … unemotional during a tangi', even poor hosts with visitors to marae. He was now engaged in writing down the genealogies, songs, stories and proverbs he had memorised as a child early in the century and eventually depicted in his carvings.[14]

While Maurice was away on his *National Geographic* assignment Gill, recognising Maurice's frustration at having to set aside fiction to pursue money-making commissions, conjured up an ameliorating gift as a gesture of reconciliation. The curved wooden bar in his study beneath the house where he stored his manuscripts was crude and needed attention. Gill lit on the idea of having Colin McCahon give it an original coat of paint. He came down, painted Ninety Mile Beach in swathes of blue and yellow on the bar and inscribed 'Ahipara' beneath a pale dune. At the bottom left corner he quoted a Japanese Buddhist text from the twelfth century: 'As there is a constant flow of light we are born into a pure land', and in larger capitals along bottom right, 'BUTTERCUP FIELDS FOREVER', a reference to the seminal Beatles' psychedelic rock song 'Strawberry Fields Forever'. But when Maurice visited home he was 'absolutely furious' with Gill for 'letting anyone into his study'.[15] Or was he just furious that Gill had inspired McCahon to produce such a striking piece of art amid the discarded pages of his failing novel manuscripts? The image of a true artist sheltering the scribblings of a journeyman? Maurice later told Michael Smither how McCahon had 'done a marvellous mural along the bar in my workplace'.[16]

Maurice's reaction to Gill's gesture signalled the beginning of the end. In late March he flew south to visit the Muttonbird Islands on his *Geographic* journey, as Rakiura Maori prepared for the annual harvest of mutton-bird chicks. From Invercargill he called home to check on the children. 'Brendan answered. He told me that the house was full of unfamiliar people. There was din in the background, the 1960s still in full swing. Brendan had to shout to make himself understood. "Dad," he asked "why aren't you here?"'[17] Maurice promptly flew back to Auckland and was met by Beverly Richards who 'valiantly' helped out in the chaotic days that followed but who soon saw that staying with Maurice meant unbearable stress and money problems. Sensibly, she chose the security of life with her English admirer; within a month she was gone.

Maurice told Michael Smither that Gill had 'deserted' the house and children when he returned and that he was helped first by Richards and then by his mother. But his version of events, as with anyone's, was at least partly self-serving. To cope with four young children on her own, Gill had combined forces with friend Cushla Stones and her children. Cushla was the wife of sculptor Tony Stones who, like Maurice, had also left the family home in Titirangi to live with another woman. Gill and Cushla took turns caring for the small tribe of children, sometimes at the Stones house in Henderson, sometimes at Arapito Road, where they had a great time 'running all over the property, swimming and carrying on'.[18] Sometimes, kids' afternoons turned into evening parties; sometimes Cushla's Maori friend Arthur came to help and Gill got to know his young mate Johnny Springhall; sometimes …

When Maurice returned from Invercargill, he was likely told by his mother to start taking responsibility for the situation; he went home and ejected Gill and Cushla Stones from the house. Crockery was smashed and Maurice threatened to demolish Cushla's car with an axe. With the women banished, Maurice occupied the moral high ground and told the children that all their mother's disgraceful goings-on were now over. His father Frank came to tell the children that their mother had 'run off with a Maori boy' and he had asked her to come home but she would not.[19] Maurice told Michael Smither, 'I have really abandoned hope for Gill … She is allowed access to the children under the separation agreement … and I took them to the flat where she is resident. Flat? A horror. A hippie pad at best. I should do something to help her, should have, but I have enough on my hands with the kids.'[20]

Months later, Maurice wrote to Gill's mother in Sydney to explain what had happened. In 1967, when Minnie Heming last visited Titirangi, he had fallen out with her over how to manage his children. She 'butted heads' with Maurice 'quite badly and … he demanded she never come again'.[21] Now he decided she needed to hear the full horror story concerning her daughter. 'The reason Gill does not have custody of her children — and I'm sorry if this comes as a shock to you — is because of her liaison with a young Maori, half her age, who has a criminal record and is or has been a drug addict; and also because of her persistent association with criminals and drug addicts which, in Auckland, brought her to police attention.' He went on to say that he had flown back from Invercargill in April because he heard that the children were 'on the verge of being picked up by the Child Welfare Department … The house was flea-ridden and disease-stricken. Not one of the children was well … They were filthy — it took me a week to scrub them clean.'[22] The situation was now so bad that he might have to put the twins in a home. He admitted he had not been faultless in his marriage but neglected to explain why he had not taken responsibility much earlier for the condition of his house and children. The shock of this letter may have had some bearing on Mrs Heming's death at the age of barely seventy only four months later. Gill was unable to attend her funeral.

(Top) Maurice in his A-frame study at Te Marua, 1960.
(Above) Brian Brake and Maurice on the road for *National Geographic*, 1960.

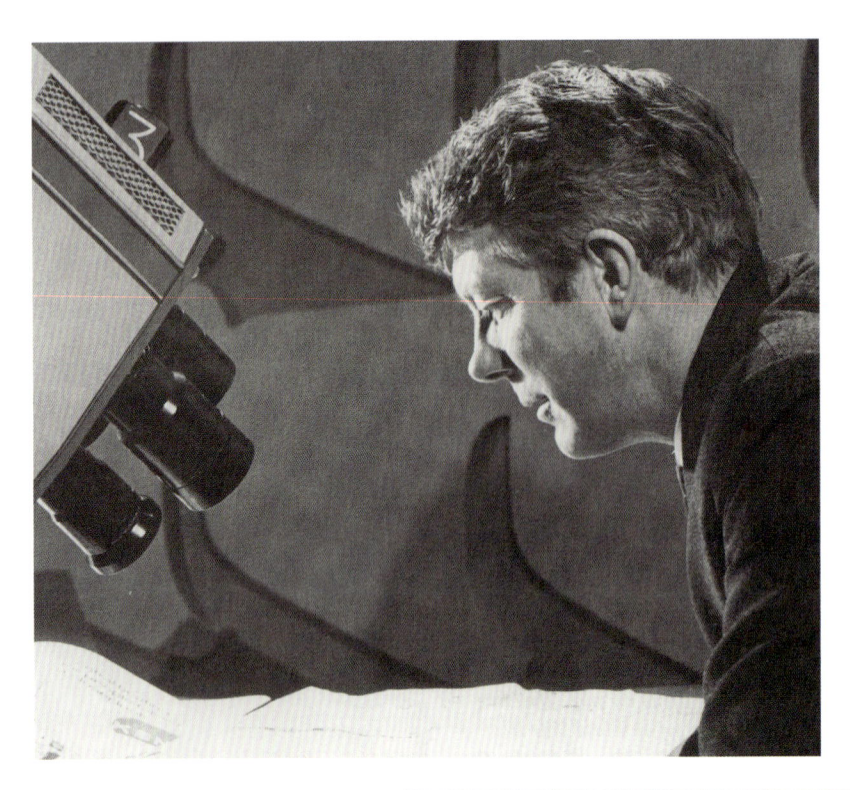

(Above) Ian Cross on TV-1's 'Column Comment' media programme, mid-1960s.
(Right) Gill with her mother Minnie 'Bunty' Heming, Sean and baby Brendan, February 1962.

(Above) Frank Sargeson in his bach, 1964. JOHN REECE-COLE, ATL 1/2-022683-F. (Right) Maurice Duggan when Burns Fellow in Dunedin, 1960. ZELDA LOUISE PHOTOGRAPH: S09-188H, P2009-015/1-001, HOCKEN COLLECTIONS, UNIVERSITY OF OTAGO.

(Above) Maurice on a Pacific assignment, possibly Samoa 1962. (Right) Maurice in Dayak long house, Borneo, 1962.

Dennis McEldowney on Dunedin beach with Gill and boys, 1963.

Uncle Joe with Sean at Thurlby Domain, Arrowtown, winter 1963.

(Above) Julia with Sean and Brendan outside the old Shadbolt homestead at Duvauchelle, Banks Peninsula, New Year 1964.
(Left) Sean and Brendan outside Arapito Road house, 1964.

(Above left) Shadbolt family after birth of twins Tui and Daniel in 1965. Joe and Frank (top); Sean, Julia and Gill (centre); Vi and Brendan (bottom).
(Above right) Maurice working in basement of Arapito Road, 1966. RAYMOND BARLIN.
(Left) Pat and Gil Hanly at their Epsom home, 1968. MARTI FRIEDLANDER, TE PAPA TONGAREWA COLLECTIONS.

George Wilder apprehended.

Party at Garth Tapper's, Titirangi: L-R: Maurice, Lois McIvor, Colin McCahon, Anne and Garth Tapper.

(Above left) Renato Amato.
(Above) Eric McCormick.
(Left) Michael Smither painting the dolphin door of the basement at Arapito Road, 1969.

(Above) 'Buttercup fields forever.' The McCahon bar in Maurice's study. (Right) Marilyn Duckworth, Wellington, 1969. COURTESY M. DUCKWORTH.

(Above) Barbara Magner and
Maurice at Piha, 1971.
(Left) Barbara Magner with Tui
and Daniel at Piha, 1972.

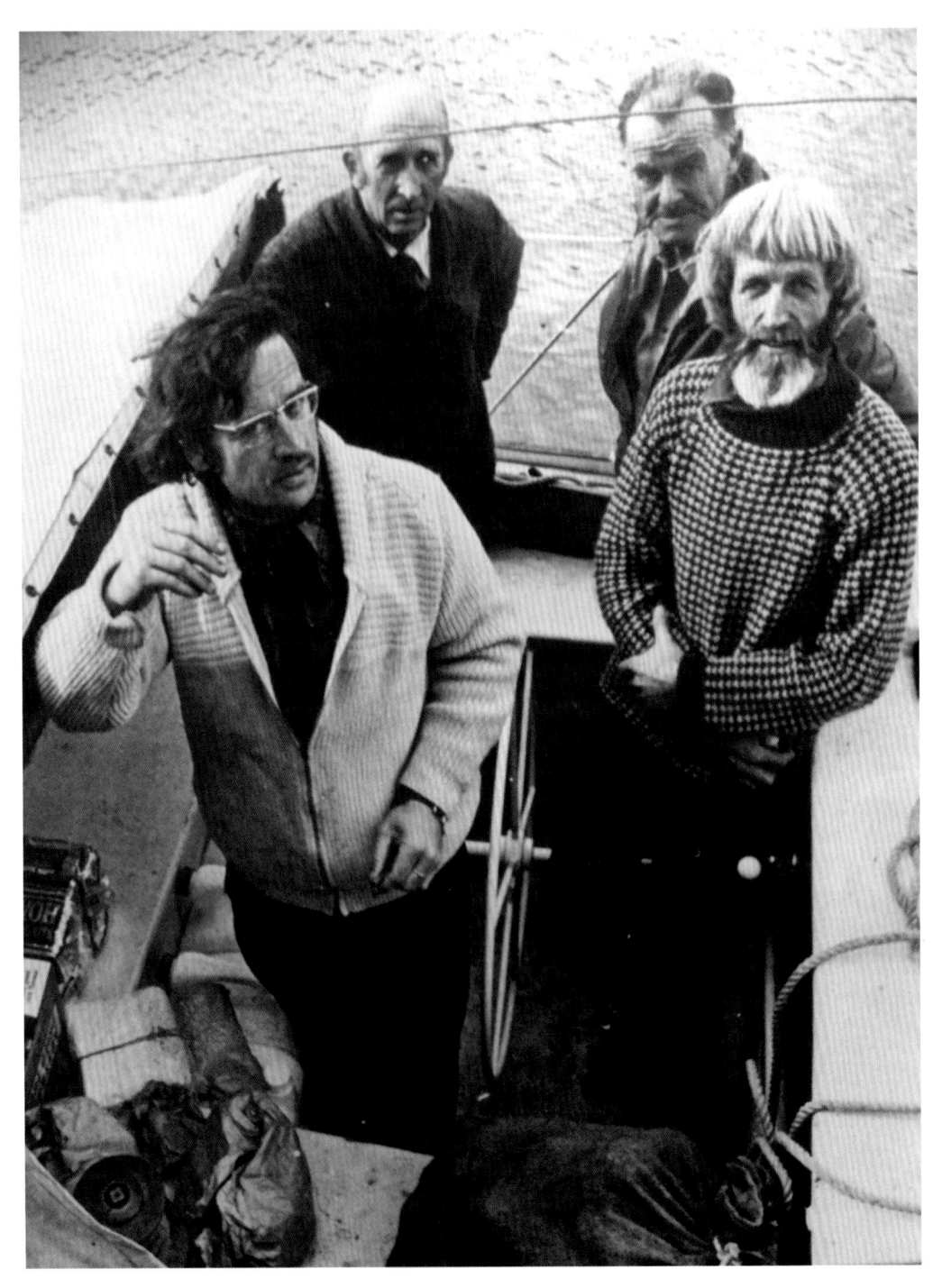

Maurice on the *Tamure* before setting sail for Mururoa, 1972. Others L-R: skipper Jim Sharp, radio operator Jack Harker and navigator Jim Cottier.

James K. Baxter witnessed the separation agreement after he failed to effect a reconciliation. Maurice had seen little of him in the preceding years. Baxter had been the Burns Fellow at Otago University for two years. Then, arising from his conversion to Catholicism, he had been working for the Dunedin Catholic Education Office in 1968 when he experienced a 'revelation' that he should go to Jerusalem (Hiruharama) on the Whanganui River and establish a community where people would live without money or books, work on the land and worship God.

Before going there he arrived in Auckland in April 1969, long-haired, barefoot, clothes in tatters, nothing in his possession but a Bible, and set up a drop-in centre for drug addicts in Grafton among a cluster of squats. It was here that Maurice found Gill. He was not impressed with his old friend Jim's attempts to establish a drugs version of Alcoholics Anonymous. The 'crash-pads, where Jim played barefoot and bearded guru, were to spawn drug dealers as deadly as any in the business. Gillian, with the best of intentions was now on the margin of Jim's hazardous enterprise. I judged it no place for a wife and mother.' Maurice wished that Baxter 'would give his own children half the affection he bestowed on his junkies. Was this fair? Possibly not. The decade was making me a dour conservative.'[23] Apart from ministering to addicts, Baxter wrote poems, ballads and articles and spoke publicly, preaching against the ills of society and the iniquities inflicted on the poor and disadvantaged. In August he adopted the Maori version of his first name, Hemi, and departed for Jerusalem to fulfil his vision.

To compound the chaos, Sean crashed his bike into a Shell petrol tanker soon after his ninth birthday and was lucky to survive with just a broken leg. This complicated the family trip to Rotorua during the May school holidays. It was first planned as a time for reconciliation, but with Gill absent, the days were punctuated by rows between Maurice and his parents about Gill and his relationship with Beverly Richards. Maurice accused his mother of encouraging him to marry Gill in the first place and Vi regretted taking care of the children at Arapito Road when he should have worked harder to keep the marriage together.

Back in Titirangi, Maurice tried to return to work; he had written little since January amid the family upheaval. He told Michael Smither: 'The house needs a woman … a domestic centre' but was surprised at his own efficiency, having the children dressed and breakfasted, and cleaning chores complete by 8.30 a.m. 'If I'd been told I could do this a month ago I'd have replied that it was insane. And this house is now something better than the slum it has been for the past three or four years.'[24] Neighbours had been sympathetic and helpful, especially with babysitting, although he still had to arrange this for Smither's visit to Auckland for the book launch and exhibition opening.

This Summer's Dolphin was launched on 16 June by Eric McCormick 'with a wry, witty speech'. Both books and paintings were sold. 'As usual I had a sense of loss, the kind which comes when a book has wandered off alone into the world. But this time there was worse to worry me. My unkempt existence, for example. My children too. I was a character in another novelist's novel.'[25] Or his own.

Books always wander off into the hands of strangers who may or may not be sympathetic to their fate. Reviews of *Dolphin* appeared promptly in England and New York where the novel had been published simultaneously. Vernon Scannell in the *Sunday Times* thought it 'fresh and refreshing, a truly original allegory of the constant human hunger for more than purely physical sustenance'.[26] The reviewer for the *Times Literary Supplement* was more circumspect. The dolphin had 'shaken the human kaleidoscope for a moment into a pattern of hope and promise: but only to reveal what our own natures are too unregenerate to allow'. Maurice had been wise not to spell out the symbolism but his 'style echoes [Patrick] White's to the point of unconscious parody'.[27] White himself thought *Dolphin* was Maurice's 'best book' although he had thought the novel form was not his metier after reading *Among the Cinders*. 'Now you have been clever in composing this one as a kind of mosaic.'[28] Yet, for Martin Levin in the *New York Times Book Review*, 'this novel is not Mr. Shadbolt at his best'. It was a disappointment after *Among the Cinders*, which was a 'beautifully controlled study of youth and age', 'something quite marvelous concocted out of a bit of humanity and the New Zealand climate'.[29]

These four differing reviews of the same novel, two by-lined, one anonymous and one private, vividly illustrate how the reception of a book by critics will vary according to their predilections, expectations and personal agenda. Yet both leading reviews of *Dolphin* in New Zealand were almost entirely laudatory. In the *Listener*, Maurice's old socialist friend Conrad Bollinger decided that the novel owed less to Patrick White than to the nineteenth century novels of Dickens and Eliot, 'stiff with inexplicit symbolism yet shaped into a conventionally satisfying story that holds the interest by arousing and suspending the expectations.'[30] Although R.A.Copland in *Landfall* found some of the novel's relationships more worked out than others, the novel was 'rich and suggestive, written with a happy command of language and ideas, an urbane, witty ironical work that sets him at an eminence with but in sharp distinction from, the best writers we have ever had in this country'.[31]

Good reviews did not translate into more than average sales; *Dolphin* was a failure in both the UK and USA and Maurice was deeply disappointed at its fate in the new Wattie Book of the Year Awards. Suffering from 'bloody bronchitis' he had to leave the ceremony and dinner soon after the three place-getters were announced. 'Just as well I didn't stay, because I might have been overcome with grief by the fact that 'This Summer's Dolphin' came nowhere while the 'Shell Guide' (a much lesser piece of work) got an award [second].'[32] Fiction did not appear in the Wattie Awards until 1972, and soon afterwards he would have no reason to complain. In the meantime he had to be content with receiving the Buckland Literary Award for *Dolphin*, worth $305.11.

CHAPTER 26

A SELF-CONFESSED ADULTERER

By November 1968, Marilyn Duckworth's second marriage was collapsing and she wrote a story for the *Listener*, 'Among Strangers,'[1] which included a 'sort of SOS to Maurice in case he was still out there'. She inserted clues that only he would recognise from their times together nearly seven years before.[2] They had not communicated or seen each other since. In May 1969, Maurice heard that Duckworth's fourth novel, *Over the Fence Is Out*, would be published later in the year and wrote to say it was good to see her writing again; he referred to her *Listener* story with its clues and said he had experienced a vivid dream in which they had been together again. He sent news of the children and his domestic problems, saying, 'A girlfriend of mine now in England [Beverly Richards] ... will probably come back and take charge of the household for me as secretary-housekeeper'.[3] Duckworth replied secretly, to avoid her husband's surveillance, pouring out her woes. She was already booked for a short business trip to Auckland and wanted to see him: 'If nothing else I needed a friend who was ready to listen to what I had been going through "among strangers".'[4]

Maurice described her visit as 'part of some delirium, some hallucination. I spent seven years denying you — to myself, to other people — pretending you meant nothing in my life (even while knowing that my love for you then had nearly blasted me apart, literally, and that I spent the next two or three years in a state of paralysis ...) I know I would have been a much better person in the end, certainly a much better writer, if I hadn't spent those years denying you.'[5] His prize-winning short story, 'Figures in Light', with its suggestion of an incestuous relationship between brother and sister, had really been about them. Their meeting was the collision of two people in desperate domestic circumstances passionately reaching out to each other for love and emotional security, to find some kind of meaning and order in their messy lives. Logic, money or practicalities did not come into it: they had to come together, eight young children between them or not. It was, Maurice wrote, 'Something out of a bloody bad novel. To touch the heart of all romantics.'[6]

Soon after the launch of *This Summer's Dolphin*, Maurice prevailed on his mother to look after the children while he drove down to Wellington to pick up Duckworth and her children; Michael Smither shared the driving to New Plymouth, Dick Scott from there. Scott owed him one. At that time, one of the few ways to achieve a quick divorce was to go through the charade of staged adultery: and earlier in the year Maurice and Beverly Richards had witnessed Scott in bed with his wife-to-be and with the relieved co-operation of her current husband.

Duckworth met Maurice at Ian and Tui Cross's house in Wadestown where she told him a lawyer had just advised her she could well lose her children if she went to Auckland with him. A night of talking and lovemaking did not alter that fact. For luck, Scott gave her a silver shoe off his wedding cake and drove Maurice back home. Within hours, Duckworth was issued with a divorce petition. When she moved out of the family home with her children she was issued with another to make them wards of court. In 1969, laws governing marriage and divorce were still heavily weighted in favour of the husband. Yet despite the formidable legal obstacles, Maurice and Duckworth still tried to find a way through.

Maurice had written to Beverly Richards, putting off her possible return, saying he would soon be together with Duckworth. In the thick of daily correspondence and frequent toll calls to her, he now presented himself as being placed in an invidious position for the care of his children. Taking charge of the crisis, Duckworth's mother, Irene Adcock, lodged daughter and children in her Mount Victoria house and then flew to Auckland to look after Maurice and family. He told Michael Smither she 'gives me both a breathing space and a chance to unite the children again — though the twins have been only two doors away and often home'. His 'prospective mother-in-law' would be with him for a 'few weeks or a couple of months until we see what happens — if Marilyn can't make it up here, because of legal snarls, she will help me make some permanent housekeeping arrangement for the two years of celibacy'.[7]

This 'celibacy' was entirely figurative. Although many may never be identified, Maurice was rarely short of sexual partners, temporary, medium or long-term. But finding a 'permanent housekeeping' partner, wife or no, was more difficult. He had been looked after by his mother until the age of twenty-one, by Gill for the fifteen years following and it was her failure in the housekeeping department that had precipitated the final separation. His mother had since filled in; Mrs Adcock would do for a while but then what? He could not ask Beverly Richards again. Yet, even before the Wellington drama, he told Michael Smither he had 'found a woman who can help out, from the beginning of July, with the housekeeping'.[8] She would now be needed because Irene Adcock had to shift from Arapito Road: her presence with Maurice would further complicate Marilyn Duckworth's divorce and child custody proceedings. To ostensibly confirm a legal distance between himself and Duckworth, Maurice went through the fiction that he was shifting with his family to Rarotonga. He seems to have considered more seriously a move to Samoa when he wrote to Albert Wendt for advice on how he might 'fulfil a long-held ambition — to spend a couple of years up in the islands … It would be a good break for the kids, who have had a pretty rough time.'[9] Wendt offered to help but Maurice was disingenuous. At the time he wrote to Wendt he was already organising a move to Wellington and the 'woman who can help out' had been with him for a couple of months.

Maurice first met Barbara Magner in 1963 when he held the Burns Fellowship and she was working for radio and DNTV-2 in Dunedin. Magner was one of the first broadcasters to address New Zealand audiences in a natural, non-BBC acculturated accent and her vivacious personality soon made her a popular presenter. Her lively public image belied her tough early life. Born into a dairy-farming family in Te Kowhai near Hamilton in 1937, her Irish father, a notable horseman, died from motor neurone disease when she was only twelve, and in her early twenties she nursed her mother through terminal cancer. Magner began work as a receptionist at Waikato Hospital but also took to the Hamilton stage. She credited her acting and performing talent to the natural Blarney-born storytelling and oratory skills of her father. After her mother's death she shifted to a receptionist job with the NZBC in Auckland and then trained as a radio announcer. Her transfer south was prompted by her need to follow the doctor and aviation enthusiast she had first met at Waikato Hospital. They were married at Dunedin's Wains Hotel in 1962.

This marriage did not last and in 1964 Magner moved back to Auckland to host an evening radio show with 1ZB. In 1966 she became one of the founding members of AKTV-2's TV magazine programme *Town and Around*; this was produced separately in the four main centres until national network television began in 1969. Broadcasting was still run by a staid government bureaucracy yet, despite this, Magner displayed a 'cheeky sense of humour' and her 'raucous laugh helped break the mould of serious BBC-style presenters'. She said that 'Television was so stiff and starch' she became bored and enlivened local TV screens with such moments as riding with the Hawkes Bay Hunt and dancing over Auckland Domain to deliver milk bottles to the steps of the museum. 'Television could be used for fun things, tons of things, whatever anybody wanted.'[10] The bureaucrats were unimpressed it seems, because she was removed from *Town and Around* at the end of 1967 and transferred to more sober announcing roles.

Magner continued to be involved with documentary production and it was her programme on sculptor Pine Taiapa that attracted Maurice's attention in May 1969. He bought her a drink one evening in town, while his parents babysat, and this quickly led to an invitation to visit Titirangi for the weekend. 'The children loved the pretty television lady Dad had brought home: she struck all the right notes on family picnics and trips to the beach. Above all she was funny, which Dad hadn't been for too long.'[11]

After James K. Baxter left Auckland, Gill moved to the Aro Valley in Wellington with Johnny Springhall and picked up work as a postie. Now Maurice planned to follow her, putting out that it was to give his marriage a last chance, and for the sake of the children, but it was chiefly to place himself closer to Marilyn Duckworth. 'Every day Maurice was coming up with new ideas of how we could beat the legal system and get together without my losing the children.'[12] He made a clandestine trip down to discuss options with her and their friends such as Nigel and Julie Cook. Gill visited Duckworth, too: 'Our friendship had survived, despite everything. She was in favour of Maurice and my getting together and offered to write an affidavit for my lawyer if it would help.'[13]

The correspondence and phone calls became frantic and frustrating, swinging between hope and despair. Maurice said that the letters they had written must have amounted to the equivalent of two novels. Amid the confused roil of words, Duckworth wrote: 'You said years ago you and I would be hopeless together because we both needed a nursemaid. Well I don't need a nursemaid. Do you? Because that's not going to be my role in life.'[14]

He now admitted to Duckworth that he already had a 'nursemaid', at least for the children. To Maurice it seemed irrelevant that he had Barbara Magner in his bed, because he was still desperate to be with her: their 'brother-sister' relationship was just as important as any sex. 'You see, we are under the same skin.'[15] In the contemporary world of gender politics, it was more acceptable for men to sleep around than women; for a male writer or artist it amounted almost to an entitlement. So when Duckworth admitted she had slept with an old friend, too, thinking this would help salve Maurice's conscience, he took umbrage. She spent weeks mending the rift while, at the same time, learning to accept Barbara Magner. She wrote to him: 'Julie [Cook] says you must check every night that Barbara has taken her pill. She knows Barbara wants a child very much.'[16] Gill, Marilyn, Barbara: all preoccupied with Maurice's emotional, sexual and domestic needs. From her new home near Oxford, Beverly Richards also wrote to 'My Darling Maurice', recalling the 'most beautiful summer' she had ever had. 'You know I loved you passionately — you know it was an unusual, precious and very rare love — could it have lasted … Could I maintain my youthfulness and optimism against your serious pessimism?'[17] Gill had given up, and been cast aside. But the others continued to be drawn not only to his professed love and desire, meant for each of them alone in a very special way; but also to the vulnerabilities he displayed. The 'artistic temperament' that needed nursing lest he fall into depression or illness; the need to be relieved of domestic obligations so that he could focus on his all-important work. Even with Duckworth, he saw his work as more important than hers.

Late in the year, Maurice came to an arrangement with Wellington writer Phillip Wilson to rent his house in Bank Road, Northland. Wilson, an older author of short stories and novels which had been met with an indifferent reception, had been part of Maurice's literary scene in his earlier Wellington days and an occasional but devoted correspondent. Maurice was able to find a tenant for 35 Arapito Road on a year's lease at $18 a week and persuaded Wilson to agree to a similar rent, reasonable since Wilson would share the house with him, now that his wife and daughters had travelled to England. Maurice said Duckworth, now in a flat not far away, would be taking care of the twins — the quashing of the wards of court petition had made this possible — while Sean and Brendan would not be much trouble. At one point he even considered Gill moving into Duckworth's house to help. But Gill told her she would 'never be able to cope with the demands of M's standards' and Maurice reverted to his view of her as an unsuitable mother. Gill could be more relaxed with Johnny Springhall: 'He knows when I'm tired and just takes over … he knows when I'm depressed and jokes me out of it'.[18]

Maurice packed up and shifted from Titirangi with the children and Barbara Magner at the end of December. He had not allowed Gill to spend Christmas with them. Duckworth prepared the Bank Road house for them but Magner stayed only a few days and then 'reluctantly' left Maurice to her and went off on a South Island holiday. Before he departed Arapito Road, Maurice already knew it would not work. He wrote in his journal, 'I would like to think I will never live another year like this one … I am less & less convinced of the value of my work — what do all those words, over 15 years, add up to? A paper-chase; a hunt for meaning; and I am left weakened, no nearer truth — & a grip on life — than when I began ... I can't see Wellington doing much for me — not really ... I have a feeling that Marilyn & I, out of separate & profound unhappiness, have pursued a will of the wisp — we are seven years too late.'[19]

Maurice's next journal entry was written less than three months later, also in Titirangi: 'How good to be back again, with the children, & how happy Barbara has made me ... All the uncertainties which fogged and confused me, at the beginning, have flown out the window ... The less said about the past two months in Wellington the better.'[20]

They had been depressing: 'The same places. The same hopelessness. The same hunted feeling'. Duckworth recounted that 'there was no time for romance and very little for passion'. Maurice co-opted family members to help with the children: parents Vi and Frank rented a flat in Lyall Bay while indomitable Aunt Sis took charge for a couple of weeks as part of a tour of relatives. Gill never gave up trying to gain access to the children, driving up and down Bank Road, accosting Maurice and Phillip Wilson, desperately trying to 'rescue the twins and assert her motherly rights'.[21] Maurice tried to prevent her and became furious when Duckworth often sneaked Gill into her house to see them. Sean and Brendan were unsettled in their new school. Then, 'When we went en masse to Ian Cross's* for lunch and the children ran riot around the barbecue pit Ian turned his eyes up and shook his head at us despairingly'.[22]

Barbara Magner returned to Wellington in late January and moved in with Maurice at Bank Road. After travelling to Christchurch in the new year, Magner had written to him and prepared the way: 'I wanted to say such a lot of things to you before I left but was overcome by my anxiety for the children and you and the pawn-like situation I found myself in'. And 'Thank you for being so sexually aware and open ... Thank you for being gentle when my Magner "crankiness" got out of hand and thank you too for allowing me to show my love to your children. Thank you for wanting to have a baby with me even though the practical disadvantages dismay you.' She hoped she would soon be able to fulfil her deep maternal instincts but 'if we can't work anything out, I want you to know I spent the happiest time of my life with you'.[23]

Maurice continued to make it difficult for Gill to see the children, so

---

*By this time, Ian Cross was the public relations manager for carpet manufacturer Feltex NZ. Under his influence Feltex sponsored the national television awards from 1970 to 1985. For the first awards, Maurice was judge of the arts/drama category and appeared on screen complete with hired evening dress, bow tie and his now trademark pipe.

she engaged activist family lawyer Shirley Smith to act on her behalf. He told Smith there had been no problem with access, only where Gill took the children when they were in her care and he repeated his description of Gill living in criminal circumstances. Already, at the beginning of February, he was planning to return to Auckland with Magner and, by this time, Gill was living at Winchester Street in Kaiwharawhara where she was to remain for many years. In response to Maurice's accusations, she told Smith that the people the children saw at her flat in Auckland were 'students, teachers musicians Maoris!' She said that Maurice had also told the children she 'got too sick and tired with looking after them and this was one of the reasons I left. I have said yes, I was sick but that there were a few other things that worried me.'[24]

Smith tore into Maurice about his own associations with a 'convicted murderer' (Ron Jorgensen), and a 'persistent prison escaper' (George Wilder). 'How does one define a prostitute these days? and assuming that one has pinned the butterfly down, how does one compare her with an adulteress, particularly in the plural? with yourself as a self-confessed adulterer thrown in for added effect? Nice questions for the court.'[25]

When Gill arrived at Bank Road on the morning of Saturday, 28 February, at a prearranged time to see the children, they with Maurice and Barbara Magner were gone. She found a handwritten letter to her headed 'Saturday 7 a.m.'. His excuse for the hasty departure was that the evening before he had located a 'suitable house in Auckland so we are setting off to see it while it is still available'. This was immediately contradicted by the statement that 'Everything has been flat panic for the past three days', almost certainly since he had received Shirley Smith's letter. Gill had been talking with Maurice about seven-year-old Brendan living with her, something she felt he wanted. Maurice now wrote this was evidence she was trying to split the family, to 'attempt setting your own children against each other'. The letter ended with declarations that the children would always be first in his life, that he was willing to give up all for them and was 'determined to bring up my children alone.'[26]

Maurice had given a little more warning to Duckworth. He rang the day before to explain he had to go back to Auckland with Magner for the sake of the children; but he still loved her, there *would* be a future together and he felt 'sick' at leaving her there. Duckworth was not surprised but 'dropped the phone back in its cradle as if it had exploded in my hand.'[27]

Both Gill and Duckworth had been abandoned, shut out. But, a month later, Phillip Wilson, who had witnessed a great deal, wrote to Maurice, 'I much admired the courageous way you fought your way out of the most awful situation anybody could land in, & my feeling for your human qualities was enormously increased ... I think you've done what was right to do & have made the only possible decision in the circumstances.'[28]

Maurice wrote to Kevin Ireland that Wellington had been 'predictably perhaps' a disaster. 'But not a fatal one; I feel as if I have nine lives. I must have, to have survived the past year. If I get through this one too I should live to be a hundred.'[29]

Despite all the disruption, distraction and emotional turmoil, Maurice had completed his novel based on the life of Renato 'Michael' Amato, a distraction in itself from completing the manuscript for 'The Search for Tim Livingstone'. Its 85,000 words turned out to be not just fictionalised biography but also fictionalised autobiography in which he became a character in one of his own stories. Amato became Pietro Fratta, his wife Sheena was Faith, and Maurice's alter ego, Frank Firth. Titled *An Ear of the Dragon*, after an Italian legend of bravery, the novel skilfully alternates between two storylines. First, Fratta's wartime experiences as a teenager engaged in counter- and then pro-partisan fighting; then his youthful start as a writer in Italy, followed by his life and writing in New Zealand after immigration in the 1950s. The story is closely based on Maurice's biographical introduction to Amato's *The Full Circle of the Travelling Cuckoo* but enlarged with material and detail that could only have been derived from the manuscripts that Amato left behind. The second storyline tells of Firth's developing relationship with Fratta and with Faith, especially after Fratta's equally premature death from a brain haemorrhage. It is scarcely disguised memoir, even to the point of using detail from letters and meetings with Sheena Amato. Uncomfortably so with a description of fellatio between Faith and Frank. Sheena had said, according to Maurice, he was 'welcome' to Michael Amato's life after publication of *Travelling Cuckoo* but — her own? Or had the fellatio been a fantasy unfulfilled?

Through the persona of Frank Firth, the novel frequently became a confessional of Maurice's current condition as a writer. 'Frank contrived a prose to discover a country ... his first success was swift enough to excite his interest ... he created landscapes which he then populated with schemers and dreamers, actually himself in diverse disguise ... the loves and despairs and hopes of these people grew tiny, lost in the land'. (p.31). 'He might be able to fool others but not himself. Outside, indeed, he still presented a plausible front; inside he found himself incredible. And the more incredible for persisting. For he finished a new book, perhaps out of habit, and began another.' (p.83). In reflecting Frank's/his engagement with Faith/Sheena over using the dead Pietro/Renato's manuscripts, she says, '"It's just your attitude. Your attitude,

Frank. As though he's just raw material'". (p.211). Later Faith/Sheena begins to think that Pietro/Renato should be left alone and he responds, "'You're making me feel like a grave robber'". (p.268).

Frank's wife, Sarah, is portrayed as unfeeling and unsympathetic and can be seen, to an extent, as reflecting Maurice's current attitudes towards Gill. 'She grew impatient with motherhood, with domesticity. She pointed out to Frank that she had sacrificed her own life, her own interests, her own career, to his … Frank should look happier about this, look more like a success, and above all be more grateful.' (p.106). There are strong arguments between them about Frank's feelings for Faith which might easily reflect arguments about Maurice's feelings for Duckworth. But did Sarah's suicide attempt with sleeping pills reflect an actual event at Arapito Road?

Faux memoir or not, *An Ear of the Dragon* is an accomplished novel but, like *This Summer's Dolphin*, it could have been better if Maurice had devoted more time to its writing and revision. Of *Dolphin*, Patrick White had commented that he 'could have given it greater <u>depth</u>, perhaps because you were writing too quickly so as not to lose sight of the whole while fitting all the parts together'.[30] Like *Dolphin*, too, *Dragon* shows the lack of a stringent editor who would have surely cut its first page of purple prose, tightened sections of the narrative and tempered Maurice's stylistic tics.[31]

When Cassell UK accepted *Dragon* for publication, an editor wrote to Maurice: 'I found it extraordinarily complete and convincing — especially Pietro's pilgrimage to war and the effect on him of the schizophrenic state of Italy, which must have been very difficult for a non-Italian to write'. Perhaps the Cassell editor suspected the origins of the manuscript when, concerned about the danger of potential libel action, he sought assurance that none of the characters were based 'on any real person'.[32] Maurice explained the book's provenance and reassured Cassell but agreed to some minor changes. In particular, the character of famed American writer Missouri West and Pietro Fratta's encounter with him in Rome, when West attempted to seduce him, was based closely on Renato Amato's encounter with Tennessee Williams who 'feigned an interest in his writing as a preliminary to unsuccessfully attempting to cart him off to bed'.[33] 'Missouri' was indeed 'West' of Tennessee but too close for comfort and it was changed to the safer 'Elliot'.

Until the Arapito Road house became available at the end of the year, Maurice found another Titirangi house to rent on Boylan Road. It was closer to Titirangi Primary School where Sean and Brendan could resume studying after the break in Wellington and where the twins could start when they turned five in September. There was a measure of domestic peace after the dramas of the previous year. He told Kevin Ireland: 'Barbara & I, after some ups and downs, have settled down very well together; and she is marvellous with the children.'[34] A puppy and a kitten had been added to the household.

That winter, Maurice took the boys tramping in the Waitakeres and they also discovered rugby league. He became their team's enthusiastic coach and drove them to senior club games and international matches on the weekends. Their hero was centre Roger Bailey who played thirty tests for New Zealand and also captained the Kiwis. When he was dropped from the national team, Brendan cooked a batch of pancakes and, after a Sunday club game, sprinted across Carlaw Park to hand his hero a paper bag of soggy tribute. The boys became good enough to tour Queensland with a schools team the following year.

From time to time, Maurice and Magner managed the occasional party and visitors enlivened a life 'less monastic than domestic'. Carl Freeman, whom he had not seen for a decade, was 'most congenial company, after all this time'.[35] English author Anthony Burgess, notorious for his novel *A Clockwork Orange*, about to be made into a movie by Stanley Kubrick, was on his way to address an Arts Council conference in Wellington when he was brought out to Titirangi by David Ballantyne. Maurice enjoyed his company, until three in the morning, but his sponsors did not. In Wellington, Burgess told the conference that state-sponsored arts bodies only funded the '*appearance* of culture … art in an emasculated form. Real culture was subversive and dangerous. Museum culture such as opera and ballet' served governments best. Politicians and bureaucrats were not amused at being lectured with the truth.[36]

Maurice's income streams were limited, although rent from the Arapito Road house offset that for Boylan Road. Maurice's *National Geographic* article on the Maori did not appear and he was not commissioned by the magazine again, for reasons unknown, but it is possible he allowed some political polemic to colour his writing. A grant from the State Literary Fund helped and there were royalties from book sales, especially the *Shell Guide*.

His novels had not done well in the United States. *Among the Cinders* had sold, for the USA, a disappointing 4000-5000 copies and *This Summer's Dolphin* only 3000. With these figures no doubt in mind, Mike Bessie of Atheneum decided not to take *An Ear of the Dragon*. Although he found the novel beautifully written, he could not engage with the characters: 'It seemed to me a book that had been carefully planned and skilfully written but somehow the spark of life either was not there or didn't ignite.'[37] Despite this disappointment, modest future riches seemed in store when Maurice heard that the German edition of *Among the Cinders*, published in March, sold 20,000 hardback copies in the first six months and book club and paperback rights had been sold on for another 120,000.[38]

Maurice wrote to Ian Cross in April: 'I think my days as fiction-writer probably near an end [...] after thirteen years of it ... I think I've done my dash'. Since Cross had given up fiction himself, Maurice knew he would understand his dilemma. Perhaps he should 'just settle for a life of unsupplemented income, and perhaps dabble fictionally for mental recreation [...] survival as a writer isn't possible in New Zealand, unless one is a bachelor, a housewife, or retired'.[39] Soon after this plea for sympathy, he received a newspaper clipping of a Sydney interview with Anthony Burgess who described him, provocatively, as the 'most promising writer he had met in Australia and New Zealand' and the only one 'unafraid of experiment'.[40] Maurice put this down to Burgess's attempt to wind up the Australians but it did little to settle his endless ambivalence about his work.

As an editing project for Cassell New Zealand, Maurice had been compiling an anthology of New Zealand prose and poetry from the period 1950 to 1970. It was a belated echo of the anthology he and Kevin Ireland had tried to put together fourteen years before. Maurice approached forty-six writers across the country and assembled a collection of fifty short stories and poems under the title of 'All Things Sweet and Harsh'. When he sent in his preliminary selection he told Cassell that he wanted to 'represent the writers active in New Zealand now. This means, sometimes, selecting relatively weak work to represent an important writer (Joy Cowley's The Moth is an example). Or selecting work to represent a certain trend of writing (Crump and Mitcalfe, for example, represent the folk-yarn) [...] in doing this I cannot use literary excellence alone as a yardstick.'[41] Whether or not the publisher disagreed with this approach, or his proposal that the contributors be paid on a royalty basis, is not clear but, like the first anthology, it never saw the light of day. Disappointment over this and the eventual sales disappointment of An Ear of the Dragon led to the end of Maurice's association with Cassell.

By May, the way was clear enough for him to resume work on 'The Search for Tim Livingstone'. He told Michael Smither, who was now in Dunedin holding the Frances Hodgkins Fellowship at the University of Otago, that he had been 'working at it on and off every winter for the past eight years. When I started it, the end was to be in 1959. Now it ends in 1969. It may be 1979 by the time I finish.'[42] On a page attached to his journal,[43] he kept a note of the months he had worked on it and which page of the manuscript he had reached; the only year missing is the catastrophic 1969. The first entry is June 1962 to page 80. When he had last worked on it in November 1968 he had reached page 626. On 2 November 1970 he wrote again to Smither, 'on a momentous date for me (perhaps?) — this morning I came, or staggered, to the end of the first draft of my "big" novel, 750 pages ... next year I'll have to think about rewriting & completing it'.[44] This in itself would be an immense task when revision and rewriting entailed days of physical work in just retyping the manuscript.

By July, Gill had a new journalism job with the Post Office. She had seen little of her children since February and a week-long trip to Auckland for her work presented an opportunity. Gill sent Maurice a telegram on Friday 10 July and received an answer which stated the children would not be available. Increasingly anxious to see them, she took the Tuesday afternoon off work and went to catch the boys as they left school. Gill took them to a teacher friend's home, buying cakes on the way, and had an impromptu party. When she took them home, Gill attempted to help bathe Daniel but Maurice would not allow her. He told her she 'was no longer welcome in the house and that my going there interrupted the functioning of the household — "and unlike any house you ever ran IT FUNCTIONS"'.[45] Gill was able to see the children again for only a few hours before she flew back to Wellington.

Within a week she received three letters from Maurice, his mother Vi and father Frank, all deploring her visit and urging her not to upset the children again. In an extraordinary diatribe, Maurice wrote, 'If your intention last week was to toy sadistically with the children you so long neglected and then deserted, to demoralize their young minds and divide their loyalties, to inflict upset and unhappiness upon them at home and school and play centre, and to leave general turmoil in your wake, then it may gratify you to know that your visit to Auckland was a splendid success'. He forbade her to come anywhere near the house again and praised the motherly care of Barbara Magner who had given the children 'so much love and energy' and he could not afford Gill driving her out of the house in 'frustration and despair'.[46] Later, he would accuse Gill of elbowing Magner aside and telling her to 'fuck off'.

In Auckland, Gill had encountered Vi Shadbolt in the street and phoned to talk with Frank afterwards. The day before she left, both wrote to her. Frank told her he had found the children 'very miserable and unhappy which always happens after you pay them a visit'. Maurice was under stress financially, too, and 'What will happen if you keep hanging around Barbara will get sick of it and walk out'. If that happened, he and Vi would be unable to take over the children and since Gill was unable also, and housekeepers were expensive, 'Morrie would have no course but to put them in a home'.[47]

Vi Shadbolt supported Frank. 'Every time you visit the children you leave them bewildered and unhappy. Last time Tui cried all one day for you.' Sean seemed detached and 'lives in a world of his own' but Brendan and the twins 'miss you very much'. Consequently, 'it puts a big strain on Barbara'. Vi described the children as nice and likeable but they had been brought up in the 'vital years of their lives with no control whatever' so that she and 'subsequent housekeepers' had the hard work of 'letting them try to understand how other people feel & that the uncontrollable tempers & tantrums that Daniel & Tui used to put on would get them nowhere'. The situation had improved but they were 'still emotionally disturbed & that is why at night they talk or cry in their sleep'.[48] Vi considered the best solution was fewer visits from Gill; but some material help from her in the way of clothes would not be amiss.

Gill had begun to discuss access to the children with lawyer Shirley Smith in April but Smith had advised caution because Maurice could argue she was living in an 'immoral menage' with 'Maori Johnny' Springhall. But after the barrage of Shadbolt letters Gill asked Smith to proceed. Referring to his letter of 22 July, Smith wrote Maurice that he appeared to 'intend to break off all relations, direct or indirect' with Gill and therefore she would have no option but to 'approach the court to determine terms of access'.[49]

In a closely typed, three-page reply Maurice brought all his powers of creative writing into an account which cast Gill as a feckless, immoral and foul-mouthed mother. Under her care, the children had suffered illnesses 'associated with lack of elementary hygiene and uncleanliness in the household'. On her last visit Gill had stated 'succinctly "I intend getting you in the shit in whatever way I fucking can" — again in front of the children'. He portrayed himself as a martyred father (and struggling author) in straitened means endeavouring to bring up his children in decent and responsible circumstances. He declared that he was 'wholly a prisoner of the circumstances Mrs Shadbolt has fashioned; and I seem personally powerless to change the present situation … unless I were to behave with reckless disregard for the interests of my children'.[50]

Shirley Smith told Gill that she had exerted great self-control in replying to this letter, simply telling Maurice that steps should now be taken to arrange formal access for Gill. Through Smith, Gill attempted to see the children again on a weekend in September but Maurice replied they were all booked up with birthday parties and rugby league games and he was no longer prepared to have Gill visit. When she arrived in Auckland, Maurice told her seeing the children was impossible. Gill told Smith that the discussion left her 'utterly bereft, shaken and weepy … I find it impossible to communicate with Maurice and I simply crack up. It still takes hours to get over this. It results in a kind of switched-off, trance-like feeling where all I want to do is lie down and sleep.'[51] A younger friend interceded and persuaded Maurice to let her take the children to see Gill in a Titirangi café before she returned to Wellington.

Gill had admitted to Smith that housework was something 'which I hate, loathe and detest'[52] and even those supportive of her were often appalled at the dirty, messy and unhygienic state of her household. What Vi Shadbolt described as 'no control' over her children probably reflected the kind of open, freewheeling life Gill had experienced as child, as well as a belief in the 'play way' of learning for young children. Add the stress of coping with four young children in a damp house in the 'sylvan slum' of Titirangi, plus the escape offered by marijuana, and a chaotic scenario is complete. Maurice's promiscuity and inability to cope with the overall domestic scene did not obscure his essentially conservative attitudes towards parental roles.

During the closing months of 1970 exchanges between Smith and Maurice's lawyer established that Gill could visit the children at weekends on or close to their birthdays and she would be able to take them all on holiday during the last week of January. A pattern had been established but it would not always be followed with good will. By now the separation agreement Maurice and Gill signed in May 1969 had matured into divorce proceedings.

In November, Maurice told Michael Smither, 'I've been planting the garden furiously around at the old place in preparation for return — peppers, gherkins, aubergines, courgettes, silver beet, pumpkins, celery & tomatoes. It often seems much more satisfying than writing'. Despite his protestations to Shirley Smith, his financial resources had improved to the point where he had also involved himself 'in a property deal with my parents on an adjoining property — an idyllic half-acre above the sea, with a two-bedroom cottage … where I may … eventually build.' He had also bought himself a 'decent sort of boat (13ft) for $80'.[53]

'"We must never leave Arapito Road again"', Brendan said when the family returned in the first week of 1971. 'For adults as well as children the place oozed safety; we were no longer gypsies.'[54] The boys took to the water with their Christmas canoe or in Maurice's new boat and Barbara Magner set about cleaning and redecorating the house with new year vigour as she began transforming herself from 'housekeeper' to wife and mother to her own child, expected in August.

In Wellington, a young poet gave a copy of a poem he had written for James K. Baxter to 'Gill and Johnney — love, SAM' [Hunt].

On the skyline of the Kaiwhara hills,
Gill, a mother to the kids on pills
Keeps open house, sends you her love.
For Johnney too, who may forget to leave
For work some mornings in the woolstore
Sits drinking in the sun outside the door
[...]
My friends at Kaiwhara and I
Observe in this old house against the sky ...
The Fall. Whatever. The sun on the sea.
Too much of this good life, I'll go dry![55]

CHAPTER 27

PERFECT AND IMPERFECT

Maurice tried to work but at first was 'trapped in a trauma composed of shifting house, renovations, diverse domestic distractions, revisions of lifestyle, legal settlements, and school holidays. Plus long grass everywhere, creeping wilderness and thick summer heat.'[1] This was his excuse for not replying more promptly to an offer he could not refuse. In early December, Frank Devine, the new editor-in-chief for the Australian and New Zealand edition of *Reader's Digest*, had lunched with Maurice in Auckland. From the evidence of his articles for *National Geographic*, Devine thought he would be an ideal contributor to the magazine which, with 120 million readers, had the highest circulation in the world. He told Maurice, 'It is hard to find first-rate professional writers in our corner of the Pacific, so think of yourself as a literary El Dorado.'[2] Devine knew that flattery and wit would get him everywhere with writers scornful or distrustful of the conservative, homogenous style of the *Digest*. They could be parlayed with the line, 'Our attitude is that a writer is a holy man and his product a sacred artifact'[3] — along with the promise of fat cheques. A large, ebullient professional himself, New Zealander Devine had begun work on the *Marlborough Express* and gone on to a career with West Australian newspapers and as a foreign correspondent before joining the *Digest* where he was to remain for fifteen years.

Devine worked his worship of the writer into an explanation of the realities of *Digest* journalism. 'The first, and possibly major, hurdle a writer has to get over when he launches himself into the Wonderful World of the Digest is his own uneasiness, as the father of things composed in solitude, with the tumult of committee journalism … The scar tissue you have acquired from your association with National Geographic should help.'[4] Stories had to have a plot line, subjects should be of 'lasting interest' and be enlivened by anecdotes, personalised if possible. It was best if the story ideas came from the writer's own enthusiasms. Deep research was expected and articles of up to 6000 words which would then be 'digested' to no more than 1500 by the 'committee' editing process. 'I hope you will remember that all the meddlers are searching for the perfect way to tell a story'. It was hard to be certain how devoted to the *Digest* creed Devine was. Ever the good company man, his flamboyance was sometimes tinged with cynicism. But for their willingness to swallow their literary pride, writers were rewarded by all expenses paid and $US1500 (worth about $NZ2200) for each accepted story, a phenomenal amount when the average New Zealand yearly income was only two to three times that. There was an element of philanthropy in Devine's approach: 'I was charmed by This Summer's Dolphin. I hope that many half-years of Digest writing will buy you many more half-years of doing, as they say, your own thing.'[5] But Devine's concern was not overly altruistic. For each Australian-New Zealand edition story he published that was later used by other *Digest* editions, he received a monetary credit which enhanced his ability to purchase other stories, as well as his own editorial reputation.

Maurice was a little anxious about the personalised anecdote requirement but replied: 'I don't think you will find me a too difficult a contributor; I like to imagine that I reserve my literary conceits, of which I have more than a few, for my fiction. For the rest, I'm a tradesman in the marketplace, producing as professionally tailored a product as I can. Perhaps not a perfect way to live, but my way.'[6] Not perfect but rewarding. Over the following decade Maurice would average three *Digest* stories a year for both local and international editions. The first, unsurprisingly, was about Opo.

At the time he first wrote to Devine, Maurice was interviewed for a sober, sometimes self-deprecating, article for the short-lived *Affairs Magazine*. 'I like to have two things working for me. One is a private myth, which I want to work out to a conclusion. Something personally felt quite deeply. And the other is a public myth, if you like. And between these two things at work in the book there is, or should be, a tension or spark which illuminates both. But most of the time I just take a story and see what it says to me. In writing I discover what I am saying.'[7] The real tension for Maurice lay in the 'private myth' of himself as writer and the recurring reality of being a 'tradesman in the marketplace'.

On being asked about the role of the writer in society he did not think a writer's voice carried much weight in New Zealand and 'this is partly the writer's failure. It's also partly because we're a new country. A writer's voice in the United States has a … better chance of influencing people.' In Eastern

Europe and Russia a 'writer is a dangerous man ... Perhaps the only real test of a writer's importance is whether he's worth putting in jail.' He was not in New Zealand. He thought the novel would survive so long as the personal voice was valued. 'I see myself and other New Zealand writers as so much manuka scrub waiting for a kauri tree to grow. And when a major writer appears in New Zealand, then we'll be able to talk about having New Zealand literature.'[8] But he admitted he did not follow local literary activity with any regularity. It was part of his self-imposed isolation, both physical at Titirangi and emotionally from a hostile literary world.

Yet, in an essay for *Encyclopaedia Britannica* on Australian and New Zealand literature, completed in August, he was able to outline the nineteenth century precursors to the native-born writers of the twentieth in a wide-ranging and critically orthodox manner. He singled out Patrick White whose novels 'use Australia unforgettably as a battleground for the human spirit'; and Janet Frame as 'by general consent the most remarkable so far' amongst New Zealand fiction writers 'with a large and sometimes discomforting literary talent.'[9]

Maurice was to use his long autobiographical essay, 'Life & Litters', completed the year before, in several publication forms such as for the *Islands* 'Beginnings' essay in 1981 and for his entry in the *Contemporary Authors Autobiography* Series in 1986. But parts never saw the light of publication day, such as his conclusion that 'It seems I have flung out my books, like bottled messages, merely telling where I am, in the course of a voyage which admits of no satisfying destination. Lost somewhere in those books, images, messages, is not just what I am; but also what I might otherwise have been.'[10] Perhaps he later realised this was one piece of self-dramatisation too far.

In talking about the tension between private and public myths for *Affairs Magazine*, 'The Search for Tim Livingstone' was probably at the forefront of Maurice's mind. He worked hard at the revision from February 1971, 'revise to P.120', until 'July 23 to P.742 (old manuscript) AND THE END !!!'.[11] Most of his journal entries were preoccupied with the revision. His feelings ranged from concern about problems of structure, length and character to conviction that he had pulled it off. 'It was never meant to be the great New Zealand novel — & probably isn't — but it has become a storehouse for so much of what I feel and know about this country' (14 March). Before the sheer labour and difficulty of revising such a big book kicked in, he was overcome by euphoria. 'This manuscript, more than anything I've written, probably defines my passage upon the earth, and might be the one thing I am fleetingly remembered by.' (7 February). 'It is a story for the ages, or it is nothing — it has the quality of a national or racial myth; its own luminous glow. At times I can hardly believe it. It doesn't matter, really, whether I ever write anything again.' (16 March). It was the feeling of triumph, of disbelief, that every author feels at completing a major work; that nothing like it will be possible again. After two full years of labour, spread over a tumultuous nine-year 'pregnancy', he had finished the construction of a literary 'storehouse'.

The novel, now re-titled *Strangers and Journeys*, was split into three relatively equal parts of around 70,000 words each, titled 'Fathers', 'Fathers and Sons' and 'Sons', with a final part, 'Fathers', of about half that length. Maurice wrote in his journal (14 March) that 'Everything I have ever written, until now, has been a rehearsal for this book'. It was a kind of compendium of his past writing, even touching on being an omnibus edition, when short stories such as 'After the Depression' and 'The Strangers' were included in scarcely modified form. Characters, themes and situations were drawn and modified from many other short stories, as far back as 'End of Season' and 'Sing Again Tomorrow'; as well as novels and novellas, especially *Among the Cinders* and *The Presence of Music*. The latter had been, in many ways, a training run for the second part of *Strangers and Journeys*.

The first part, 'Fathers', is a powerful, at times brutal, story of two men returning from World War I: Ned Livingstone to break in a farm from unforgiving King Country bush and scrub; and Bill Freeman to fight the socialist cause on the streets of Auckland. They are two strong and archetypal inter-war characters which have achieved a permanent place in New Zealand literature.

Part Two, 'Fathers and Sons' tells of their sons, Tim Livingstone and Ian Freeman, growing up in Te Ika (Te Kuiti) and dealing with the demands of their fathers before escaping to the big smoke of Auckland. Tim develops a self-loathing relationship in his career as an artist while Ian develops a desultory career in journalism, on the edge of socialist politics and in the shadow of his famous radical father. They cross paths intermittently in an uneasy, often antagonistic relationship.

This is probably where the novel should have concluded, as a substantial story of generational change, with the sons beginning to find their way in a new post-war world. But from this point Maurice's ambition had overcome his skills and experience as a novelist. He had intended finishing the novel near the time he began writing it in 1963. The distractions of other work, and his chaotic personal life, meant that he failed to draw the necessary line under it. *Strangers and Journeys* had then ballooned out to a rambling saga in which he tried to fit almost everyone he knew and almost all the major events he had been involved with until the end of the 1960s. In the second half of the novel, for example, there is the 1951 waterfront strike and the Queen Street march to match the events of 1932; and the Bassett Road machine gun murders of 1963 with a composite Jorgensen-Wilder character. Tim Livingstone is a mix of Colin McCahon and Michael Illingworth; only the names have been changed for John Kasmin and Gordon Dryden; Ian Freeman is Maurice's pale alter ego. There is a satisfying conclusion, a circularity to the overall story, and there are some memorable observations. In a neat paraphrase of Muriwhenua chief Nopera Pana-kareao's comment on the Treaty of Waitangi, tough pioneer father Ned Livingstone and wayward painter son Tim are compared as one having the 'substance of the land, the other the shadow'.[12]

But the way there is through thickets of dialogue and irritating digressions with unnecessary minor characters. This inadequately processed material may have proved fruitful for a second novel written at a greater distance from his subject matter. It was the first clear evidence that Maurice did not have what Ernest Hemingway regarded as 'The most essential gift for a good writer — a built-in, shockproof, shit detector'.[13] But then Hemingway and other American writers of his time, such as F. Scott Fitzgerald and Thomas Wolfe, also had the guidance and 'shit detector' of a great editor, Max Perkins of New York publisher Scribner's. With Wolfe, for example, Perkins managed to edit out 90,000 words from his first massive novel to make it a publishing success. But there was no-one in New Zealand, or anyone elsewhere interested in New Zealand writing, capable of giving Maurice's huge manuscript the criticism and cutting that it needed.

So who would publish this quarter-million word novel? Was it the 'Great New Zealand Novel' the world had been waiting for, New Zealand's answer to Patrick White's *The Tree of Man*? Or, after his disjointed and sporadic attacks on the project, would it be judged that the parts did not add up to a whole?

Maurice was 'contemplating a split with my old agents, publisher etc — I feel I'm getting nowhere with them'[14] and turned to the local branch of Hodder & Stoughton. The Auckland editor, Neil Robinson, 'an old friend, ex-journalist and book reviewer' was by the end of September 'red-eyed and ragingly enthusiastic about the manuscript … and is dispatching it this week to his firm's London readers'.[15] He sent a carbon copy to his greatest American fan, novelist Stephen Becker. They had yet to meet in person but had established a warm relationship by correspondence and, after Maurice's break with Atheneum, Becker agreed to try other New York publishers.

Even before the good confirming news arrived from London, just sending the manuscript away had the effect of removing the burden of its dead weight upon all the creative ideas it had suppressed. The week after it went, he wrote,

'I'm trying to keep my imagination on a tight rein … I don't want to go riding off wildly in a new direction yet.'[16] But only a month later, he made a 'Summary of possible future novels:-

1./ Titirangi novel
2./ Rarotonga novel
3./ Te Kooti novel
4./ George W.[ilder] novel
5./ Thriller based on anonymous man in anonymous cell'.

He had first referred to a 'Te Kooti/Maori War' idea in an August journal entry but by November this and the 'George W. novels appear to have slipped away.'[17]

The completion of *Strangers and Journeys* was made possible by a year of domestic harmony: 'Without Barbara I might never have had the guts to pull it off'.[18] His journal is sprinkled with his delight at being with Magner 'who becomes more extraordinary a person the longer I know her'. (3 February). 'Barbara is managing her pregnancy amazingly' (3 July), and when their daughter, Brigid, was born on 9 August, 'B. has never looked more beautiful as she lay there with the baby in her arms'. (26 August). 1971 was a year in which 'B & I can both take much satisfaction'. (16 December).

Maurice did not want Gill upsetting his new domestic bliss and work routine at 35 Arapito Road and, although he formally agreed to her taking the boys and twins away for holidays to Taupo in January and Kawhia in May, their handover had to be away from the house. He insisted on meeting up at Lynn Mall shopping centre instead. This became a regular drop-off point and, if Gill was late, he would leave the children there with their baggage on the pavement. Young Tui was never sure whether Maurice simply abandoned them or went off and parked at a distance to observe them until he saw Gill had arrived. At the end of each trip she returned the children to Lynn Mall or to the home of Pat and Gil Hanly in Epsom. Gil Hanly recalls Gill's deep distress and misery, and sometimes the children's, at having to separate.

In a report to Shirley Smith, Gill referred to the likely increased stress at Arapito Road when a fifth child arrived on the scene. As divorce approached, Gill was concerned about the fate of the children should anything happen to Maurice. 'What if he does go mad — as he has been threatening to do for so many years? Can they come to me in Wellington? What if he dies? Can they come to me in Wellington? Is there any way we can be certain of this?'[19]

Maurice continued to be maddened by his chronic dilemma. 'Perhaps at the very moment I am convinced again that I <u>can</u> write, I find myself losing grip on life again. And those who mean most to me in this world. Should I try to cut my losses, write myself off as a person, and see if I can make something of myself yet as a writer?' Or the reverse. 'It may be that I'm too damaged either way to make an effective or useful choice. God knows.'[20] Later, 'All I have ever asked of life is peace, & some security — so I can get on with my work ... I cannot even finish this entry because of my daughter's commotion. Yet without my children I am nothing.'[21] Even so, he was glad of Gill taking the children in the holidays, so that he and Barbara could travel to the Far North and Hokianga in January and to New Plymouth in May to visit the Smithers.

Maurice's doubts about his work were not alleviated by the reactions to *An Ear of the Dragon*. The novel was published in London in March but received little attention. The *Guardian* included it at the end of a joint review with five other new novels. 'Mr Shadbolt takes an intense unleavened view of life and of the shortcomings of his native land [...] Urgency gets lost in earnestness.'[22]

When it was published in New Zealand in June, Maurice was cheered by David Ballantyne's laudatory comments. He described Maurice as an 'assured professional who knows exactly what he's doing and how best to carry it through. His new novel is splendid. It has strengths that lift it above the general run of fiction. To be sure, certain of those strengths reflect the romantic in Shadbolt and seem a trifle old-fashioned.' Ballantyne saw the parallels with Renato Amato's life and work but it remained a 'book of considerable power'.[23]

Two months later, in the *Listener*, Wellington academic James Bertram made clear the provenance of *An Ear of the Dragon*: 'it is a fictional account of the abrupt, confused, and tragically shortened life of the late Renato Amato'. And the New Zealand writer, Frank Firth, was 'all too frank a chronicler, too forthright a consoler' of widow Faith. Bertram thought that anyone who 'came upon this novel unforewarned would find its structure ingenious, its narrative line exciting and compelling, and the conclusion in its own way sourly convincing'. Yet, in a 'work that owes so much not just to another man's life but also to his writing, some clearer acknowledgment of debt other than a cryptic dedication was surely called for. For my own part, I could wish that Mr Shadbolt had invented a good deal more freely, or that what seems to be invented left a cleaner taste in the mouth.'[24]

Maurice wrote to Bertram to justify his fictional treatment of Amato's life, on the grounds that even in his biographical note to Amato's *The Full Circle of the Travelling Cuckoo* much was supposition based on scanty resources and that Sheena Amato had described this as the best piece of fiction he had written. He said he had fulfilled a promise to Amato to write about his life and had planned to include an explanatory note in *Dragon* but then thought it would be too confusing for readers and, because it would matter only to a handful of people, he had taken a 'calculated risk'. He also wrote that the Fratta character was based as much on other exiled writers he had met as much as Amato, and that Frank Firth was an amalgam of New Zealand writers, too.[25]

In reply, Bertram cut through Maurice's long-winded excuses, taking the moral high ground. 'Once Pietro is identified as Amato, you become Frank, and as Chekhov wrote, "a wife is a wife". What you do with your own fictional analogue is your own affair; but the women might well have different ideas. On the face of things, two living women, if they felt so disposed, would have fair enough grounds for libel actions.' Bertram disposed of Maurice's other arguments: for example, how was anyone to know that his earlier biographical introduction had been largely fiction? 'You took a "calculated risk": these are the biggest risks of all. Somewhere … there was bound to be a reaction […] I didn't like either the procedure or tone of The Dragon, and had to say so.'[26]

Bertram's Victoria University colleague, Joan Stevens, who had astringently reviewed *Among the Cinders* in 1965, expressed similar views on National Radio and literary hackles were raised across the country, culminating with a curious 'non-review' in *Landfall*. K.O. Arvidson, lecturing at the University of the South Pacific, sent a three-page letter (longer than a usual review) explaining why he could *not* review *An Ear of the Dragon*. This was principally on the grounds of the book's provenance, bordering on plagiarism, and how it would be differently appraised depending on whether or not the reviewer was in the know about Amato and Shadbolt. 'As a result I find it impossible to adopt an ordinary detachment in my critical approach to it.' Arvidson also found fault with the 'New Zealand Artist syndrome' embodied in the character of Frank Firth. He thought that an 'author who proposes nationalistic implications for his work is making a proposal which at the very least is inartistic'.[27]

For the following issue, Eric McCormick wrote to point out that Arvidson had, in fact, reviewed the novel by 'indirect means and portentous hints in a prose stiff with modish jargon' which included his 'incomprehensible remarks on the "New Zealand Artist syndrome"'. Arvidson was allowed to reply to this in the same issue with the lame observation that McCormick had called *Dragon* a work of fiction which he felt could not be applied to the book 'without qualification'.[28] Fifty years on, in the era of 'creative non-fiction', this seems an arcane argument. But *Dragon* would have weathered the squalls in the halls of academe if Maurice had, after all, included a note explaining the novel's provenance. As it was, the lofty chastisements of Bertram and Stevens killed it stone dead both in the marketplace and on prospective prize lists. Yet it remains, as David Ballantyne accurately commented, a novel of 'considerable power'.

On 16 December, Maurice wrote in his journal: 'Divorced on Monday, pallbearer at my Uncle Arthur's funeral on Tuesday, and married again tomorrow [Friday]'. His father Frank had been 'very broken up' at the sudden death of his younger brother: 'he had been with Arthur until a minute or two before his fatal collapse'. They had been together, making a go of it on the Coromandel goldfields nearly forty years before, the source of little Maurie's first childhood memories. For Maurice, Arthur was 'always a loner' existing in 'some of my stories — Ben's Land, for example. Rugged, self-mocking & golden-hearted.'[29]

Earlier in the year there had been Maurice's first literary funeral, of R.A.K. 'Ron' Mason who had died in July aged sixty-six and 'survived his poetry by nearly fifty years'. In the funeral crowd there were 'so many familiar faces; one knows many may never be seen again. The men of the thirties are starting to fade, literally.'[30]

Maurice's decree absolute was delivered on 13 December and he and Barbara Magner were married four days later. (Martyn Finlay and Dick Scott were the witnesses.) 'B & I make it at last — it has been a long journey, but we are no longer strangers.'[31] With Gill, it had been a journey of eighteen years but now they were strangers again. 'Two years ago I was as good as finished — and now? I have something like life again, more and more so every day …'[32]

The year was ending in domestic harmony. The vegetable garden was thriving and the fish were jumping. Over the summer, with the help of the boys, he cut and later concreted steps down the steep section, through the bush, to a site he had chosen for a studio where he would, at last, be separate from family alarums and excursions. It would be his 'hideout', a 'sanctuary' where he could construct a writing life within his own personal ecology. As he reached his fortieth birthday, building the studio was the throwing out of a spiritual anchor. Whatever travels he might undertake he would always return; he would never again permanently leave 35 Arapito Road.

The new studio cost $2416. Maurice had good cause to thank Frank Devine and *Reader's Digest* for his economic deliverance when he learned that his London agent had drunk away almost all the royalties he was due from the huge sales of *Among the Cinders* in Germany. In late November he told Devine he 'would very much appreciate' the money he was due for articles he had written on the toheroa and Pine Taiapa to 'survive Christmas among other things.'[33] Maurice complained that Whitcombe & Tombs planned no more reprints of *Gift of the Sea*, after sales of 60,000 copies, and wrote to Brian Brake about whether they should offer it to someone else. Now he could no longer afford to pay the mortgage on the half-acre property next door, despite the $20 a week he received from renting the cottage, and offered it to Brake for $10,000. They had not been in touch for some time but Maurice had heard Brake might be coming back to New Zealand and was looking to live nearby.[34] It was too soon for Brake, who did not return for another five years, and then built a house on Titirangi's Scenic Drive.

Another death and funeral came to seem more significant to Maurice than either the passing of literary luminary Ron Mason or his own Uncle Arthur. In the spring of 1971, he told Michael Smither he was writing the *Reader's Digest* story on Pine Taiapa: 'Tremendous person; a giant among us, unrecognised. When the story of 20th century art is written his name will shine out.'[35] Taiapa had undertaken to carve his first urban whare whakairo, in Henderson, and asked Maurice to drive over to the East Coast to pick him up and take him to the dedication ceremony. Now seventy years old, 'He confessed that he had lately been in a slump, ready to farewell his carving tools and forget' this final building, his 104th. Then a prophetic dream had given him new inspiration. But he wanted Maurice to record the beginnings of the new meeting house because, Taiapa told him, '"You will see this building grow … I will not"'. A few months later, cancer claimed him and Maurice went to Tikitiki to attend his tangi. 'All through a long day muddy cars spilled out mourners arriving to pay tribute to Pine, some from the furthest south …' In retrospect, thirty years later, Maurice decided that it was 'plain to me that as a novelist I remained most in debt to a weathered Maori carver; my business, like his, had been with the tales of my tribe.'[36]

During the first half of 1972, Maurice battled with the frustrations of having to earn a living from journalism and non-fiction, leaving him with no time for new fiction. There were *Reader's Digest* stories on crime writer Ngaio Marsh, jet-boat pioneer Bill Hamilton, landscape artist Rei Hamon. The list of dramatis personae was lengthening but final acceptance of *Digest* articles was never guaranteed and Maurice sought, and obtained, assurance from Frank Devine that there would be a continuity of paid commissioned work.

He also had to undertake the 'dreary' detailed work of revising *The Shell Guide to New Zealand* for a new edition. When he did turn to fiction, it was to the revision of *Strangers and Journeys* which proved more demanding than he expected, involving almost a month of his time, and cutting 20,000 words. By mid-April he was thinking of how he could cut his living expenses — even entertaining the idea (only) of giving up smoking and drinking — to earn the 'right' to spend one week out of four or five 'writing what I want to write. Otherwise I shall be forever postponing — in the interests of the family economy — getting around to fiction again.'[37] A day later, he wrote, 'I wish I hadn't kept pushing exciting ideas for novels to the back of my mind ... it's difficult to quarry back to them through the debris of journalism.'[38]

A trip to the Bay of Islands at new year was refreshing; but partying with artist Fassett Burnett in Russell blew out the drinking and smoking budget. At the end of January Maurice and Barbara visited Michael and poet Elizabeth Smither again in New Plymouth when they discussed a jacket painting for *Strangers and Journeys*. 'Michael is painting wonderfully well and it was good to be in his company for a while'. On the return journey they travelled via Te Kuiti 'where I was tempted to look in on the school jubilee. But in the end, of course, I fled. What should I do with these people of my imagination if they came to life?'[39]

But a trip to Ninety Mile Beach in May with Barbara and Brigid, fishing and digging for tuatua, freed the imagination. 'Ideas for new novel float back & forward.' He had an urge to write something set outside New Zealand, a novel set in Rarotonga perhaps, but then felt that a first-person novel set in Titirangi would 'serve better as vehicle for my own preoccupations. Earth — the clay of the land — the central motif.' It could be a 'book which pulls in men of contemporary New Zealand, of the way we live now.'[40] But he was wary of writing something simply for the sake of turning out another novel. One idea in January that became buried beneath the 'debris of journalism' was a 'big, bawdy, happy book. A historical theme? Pioneers?'[41] It would have to wait half a dozen years to be dug out.

The proofs of *Strangers and Journeys* arrived belatedly at the end of June 1972 when Maurice was given only five days to check more than 600 pages, because of a printers' strike; he felt he went 'almost blind from the effort.'[42] There had also been frustration over Michael Smither's paintings for the jacket. Maurice thought the first he produced 'breathtakingly beautiful — it seems to breathe the things I only made half-articulate in the book.'[43] But the marketing division of Hodder & Stoughton disagreed and wanted something more 'pictorial'. He was mortified at having to ask Smither to try again and said he would buy the first from him, anyway, to 'put on the wall and remind me of the jacket that might have been. Or should have been.'[44] Smither's second offering was accepted by Hodders and Maurice also thought this 'bloody marvellous.'[45]

The occasion of his fortieth birthday on 6 June was darkened by the knowledge that his father had cancer. Looking over his life, he thought, 'All around I seem to have made a fearful hash of my first forty years. It has often been tempting to think otherwise, but there is no harm, & much to be said for, looking truth in the face for a change. The question is what do I do about it? Again & again the alarm bells have sounded to tell me of my inadequacies as a human being; again & again I have evaded the message. And put my head down. Do I listen now? Or can I? Discontent becomes a solid block inside me; the problem is whether I can sculpt something sane from it.'[46]

Gloomy journal entries like these seem to be the punctuation to his continual struggle with depression. Expressions of self-loathing dated back, at least, to his extraordinary letter to Gill from Aberdeen in October 1958. Before and since then he had managed his depressive bouts successfully under the maternal ministrations of Gill, and for a time now with Barbara. But the chaotic turns of the previous four years were taking their psychological toll. Physically, his depressive tendencies manifested themselves in almost continuous aches, pains and illnesses in an overt hypochondria that came to be a mechanism for seeking support and sympathy.

CHAPTER 28

IN THE ZONE

At Ninety Mile Beach in May, Maurice had unexpectedly encountered Barry Mitcalfe. They went fishing together which had, at least partially, healed the rift between them that had occurred over disagreements during the anti-Vietnam War protests of the mid-1960s. The Vietnam War was now into its seventeenth year but US President Richard Nixon had promised American withdrawal if re-elected for a second term and was pursuing a policy of 'detente' with the Communist world, marked by his visit to China, the first by a US president. The election year of 1972 would also prove to be pivotal in New Zealand politics and international affairs. The National government under Keith Holyoake, and now Jack Marshall, was nearing the end of twelve years in office and was running out of energy and ideas. Labour leader Norman Kirk, with considerable oratorical gifts, promised much social renewal and a genuinely New Zealand foreign policy. Britain was about to join the European Economic Community and many New Zealanders wished to finally cut the British apron strings and register an independent stance in world affairs. A withdrawal of New Zealand troops from Vietnam was promised if Labour won the election; but also some kind of action against nuclear testing in the South Pacific.

Dozens of air blasts had been undertaken at Mururoa atoll in the southern Tuamotu archipelago since 1966 by the French military and a New Zealand anti-nuclear protest movement had grown which led to a 10,000 signature petition in 1972. Between April and June, Canadian David McTaggart — later Greenpeace International's first chairman — and two others sailed the 38-foot yacht *Vega*, renamed *Greenpeace III*, from Auckland to Mururoa and provoked an international incident when they sailed into the test zone and were boarded by French commandos. It was the first step leading to New Zealand being declared a nuclear-free zone fifteen years later.

News of *Greenpeace III*'s arrival and arrest inspired the departure of a small fleet of other vessels from New Zealand and Maurice watched the unfolding story on television news. Barry Mitcalfe was prominent in rousing support for this new cause. Just as Maurice was in the midst of his battle with the proofs of *Strangers and Journeys*, Mitcalfe rang and asked if he could drive a Titirangi man with his gear to Tauranga to join another protest yacht. It was impossible, with such a tight deadline for the proofs. Maurice arranged for someone else to do the job but, feeling guilty, rang back later to check if the man had made it. Then he found himself volunteering to crew a protest boat. Mitcalfe said he was not asking that. But 'He was wrong on that score. I found I expected myself to.'[1]

A week before departure, Maurice wrote, 'Perhaps this voyage — the challenge of the thing — will shock my life into sanity & more plausible shape. It is time to risk myself against the madness of the times. I can't always be a passive recorder; sooner or later I must live on my nerve-ends, at an extreme of my function as a human being.'[2] But what about leaving behind a wife and five children? '"If you feel you should go", Barbara said, "then you must. You're free. Other people aren't. Don't worry about me. I'll manage." Yet it wasn't easy for her to say. The easy part was mine.'[3]

In his account of the voyage[4], Maurice set out his disgust for New Zealand's current government, willing to slap the French on the wrists with diplomatic protest notes, carefully worded for fear they would block our butter and lamb exports to the Common Market: 'So we behave like lambs and talk like butter: such protests have become a charade to placate the people of New Zealand.'[5] He and others on the protest yachts would have to do the government's work for them.

Maurice also wrote that he undertook the voyage because he wanted to be able to 'make some account of myself before my grandchildren … to say that, once or twice at least, I tried to stop the madness'. But Maurice was, after all, the famous, even controversial, author who had recently married a much-loved TV personality. His decision to sail was instantly covered by press and radio. 'People — many of them total strangers — were shaking my hand in the street or calling me on the telephone, asking just what they could do to help get the protest boats on the way … to help Barbara and the children in my absence.'[6]

On 15 July, Maurice sailed from Auckland with three others on the 37-foot sloop and ocean racer *Tamure*. Mayor Dove-Myer Robinson gave them the Auckland coat of arms and a New Zealand ensign, and they were waved off by a crowd of hundreds which included Barbara and the children. As they drove away, six year-old Tui asked, 'Has Dad ever been on a sailing boat before?' When casting off, Maurice's colour blindness had made it difficult for him to distinguish which rope he was supposed to handle. It also proved to be a false start. Trouble with the rudder caused them to turn back before they had left the Hauraki Gulf and take the *Tamure* out of the water for a thorough inspection. They finally left on the seventeenth, running before a westerly storm.

The skipper and owner was 59-year-old Jim Sharp, a successful marine engineer of whom Maurice wrote that he was probably undertaking the voyage 'because he thought the world too important to be left to politicians'. Then there was master mariner and navigator, 38-year-old 'bearded and gentle Manxman', Jim Cottier. Maurice thought he voyaged because he was a 'pacifist, and lover of the natural world' and saw New Zealand as a 'country not yet beyond repair or even salvation'. He cooked marvellous vegetarian meals. The fourth crew member was 55-year-old radio operator Jack Harker who had served on the cruiser HMNZS *Leander* during World War II. Harker espoused right-wing politics, endorsed apartheid and the racist view that 'Europeans had a right to rule "the wogs"'. He did not see himself as a protester but someone who had gone along to help out. 'When I observed that this at least implied support of protest against French nuclear testing, Jack replied that he hadn't quite thought that one out yet'.[7] Worse, he refused to send official or news messages on the radio transmitter Radio Hauraki had provided, for fear of government prosecution. He did not tell the rest of the crew this until the *Tamure* was two days on its way, for fear of being left behind. Half the purpose of the voyage was now gone.

To begin, Maurice seemed to be living, as he expected, on his 'nerve-ends'. It was, after all, mid-winter. 'We ran before storms and squalls and huge swells. To make fast time to Mururoa we kept to low (sic: high) latitudes, and picked up driving westerlies. Before long everything was damp: clothes, sleeping bags, pillows. We seemed to become sodden vegetables, feeding the whims of our always crashing craft; it lapped up our energies, draining us dry, just as it fed off wind and wave. In three weeks we had just one bright day to air ourselves, and our belongings.'[8] Equally relentlessly, the four of them talked: about Polynesian navigation, politics, sex, agriculture, religion, art, drugs, sport, whatever passed the wet days and wetter nights. Skipper Sharp suffered from chronic sea-sickness and talked about spending just a few days in the 'danger zone' to fly the flag before returning home via the calmer climes of Rarotonga and Fiji; he would probably sell *Tamure* when he got back.

They never reached Mururoa. After three weeks they heard, faintly, on a transistor radio that the tests had been called off. They changed course for

Tahiti where the nuclear test fleet would soon be moored. On arrival they were threatened with imprisonment if they uttered one word of anti-nuclear protest. Maurice had also been sent news that father Frank's cancer had worsened and daughter Brigid was in hospital with pneumonia. Alarmed, and disgusted with French authoritarianism, Maurice flew home, taking just six hours to cross the ocean that *Tamure* had taken four weeks to navigate. On arrival he found that, although Frank's condition continued to be serious, one-year-old Brigid was recovering. The manager of the local Titirangi supermarket handed him a couple of cold beers: 'he thinks I might have worked up a thirst. He is right. But a thirst for all things familiar and loved.'[9]

Immediately after he returned, Maurice wrote his 6000-word account of the *Tamure* voyage for Barry Mitcalfe's publication *Boy Roel: Voyage to Nowhere*. But then asked for it to be excluded when he learned there would be nothing in the book about McTaggart and the seminal voyage of *Greenpeace III*. Either the publication was too far along in production or Mitcalfe ignored him, because it appeared anyway. The fourteen-page story is an entertaining and honest account, more of the voyagers than the voyage, and is also perhaps, Maurice's most open political document. He attacked both the New Zealand and French governments and took some satisfaction from evidence that the protest voyages had at least stirred Tahitians to protest, too. But French authorities continued to be heavy-handed with the local people and carried on testing bombs at Mururoa regardless.

Maurice's political sympathies, once overtly Communist, had shifted to strong support of the Labour Party. He developed close friendships with local Labour members of Parliament Eddie Isbey (Grey Lynn) and Martyn Finlay (Henderson); as well as leading historian, poet, Auckland University professor (and Labour candidate) Keith Sinclair.[10] There was much rejoicing in the Shadbolt household and among all his friends on the election night of 25 November when Labour were swept into office with more than 48 per cent of the vote. Prime Minister Norman Kirk took the portfolio of Foreign Affairs, placing New Zealand on the world stage by recognising the People's Republic of China, refusing sporting contacts with apartheid South Africa and opposing the French nuclear tests. Martyn Finlay was appointed Attorney-General and Minister of Justice and he immediately took France, along with Australia, to the International Court of Justice. The French ignored the court's ruling that tests should stop so, in June and July 1973, Kirk despatched two navy frigates to Mururoa with a cabinet member on board to bear public witness to French atmospheric tests. This greatly magnified international protests and achieved the success of forcing French tests underground. But France did not cease testing until the Comprehensive Test Ban Treaty came into force in 1996. In the interim, France bombed the *Rainbow Warrior* in Auckland Harbour in 1985, an act of state-sponsored terrorism in retaliation for Greenpeace's continuing anti-nuclear protests. It proved to be a long, 24-year voyage but Maurice *could* tell his grandchildren he had been there at the beginning, to try and 'stop the madness'.

Maurice moved into his new 'bush-bound' studio soon after he arrived home. 'It is most pleasant to sit at this desk with winter sunshine filtering through the ferns.' Yet, 'Such elegant surrounds, after 15 years of writing in scruffy corners, threatens to leave me tongue-tied, but I hope the block will not be substantial'.[11] He could not settle on a new fiction project, wavering still between tackling a Titirangi, Rarotonga or, now, Mururoa novel.

The voyage had been deeply unsettling all round and he needed someone to confide in, someone who would understand. He rang Marilyn Duckworth who was living in Auckland that year with playwright and political commentator Dean Parker. They had coffee at Mission Bay and he told her about the voyage. Duckworth wrote: 'He had thought about me in the force-eight winds. He wasn't happy. He didn't believe Barbara understood marriage and all that it meant. He hadn't been able find any socks that morning.' He seemed distracted: 'Did I exist for him at all in the real world or only in his imagination?'[12] It seems likely Barbara heard of this meeting for, at this time, he wrote, 'Life again — or my life — once again exploding in my face with seasonal predictability'. Before going on to quote the Yeats poem, 'The Choice' in his repetitive wrestle with a man's need to choose between 'perfection of the life, or of the work'.[13] But soon Maurice's wrestle with the conundrums of life and work was, for a time, overwhelmed by sudden loss.

The privations of life in the commune at Jerusalem on the Whanganui River had caused a serious decline in the health of his old friend James K. Baxter, and he had moved to a more supportive commune in Auckland. Maurice met with him on 18 October: 'We embraced, as has been his custom in late years. It was an affectionate meeting, and I am glad of that; it was nearly three years since we had seen each other'. It closed the rift that had occurred because of Baxter's support of Gill in the marriage break-up. In retrospect, Maurice saw something fateful in the meeting, a premonitory farewell.[14] 'He was coming out to see us. All Labour Weekend I waited for the call; we were going to walk along the shore together, under the trees of Titirangi. Instead the call came that he had died over at Hone Tuwhare's'.[15] Baxter had, in fact, suffered a coronary thrombosis in the street and died in the nearby house of a stranger.

On 24 October, Maurice joined Baxter's wife Jacquie and children at the undertakers and 'by 12.30 Jim was on his way to his home marae at Jerusalem. I followed down with Selwyn Muru and a couple of others and caught up with Jim, for the last time, at Taumarunui. We didn't get to Jerusalem until after midnight. Then the vigil, the tangi … in that isolated place, hundreds arriving from nowhere; pakehas of all ages behaving and mourning like Maoris; from ex-crims to university professors.'[16] In an emotional 'Letter to Jim', quoting from Baxter's poem 'Homage to Lost Friends', Maurice wrote that he was there for 'other old cloud riders', too, 'other companion shakers of morning, in my bloody shirt. For Lou [Johnson], in Australia; for Mike [Doyle], in Canada; for Kevin [Ireland], in London; for Al [Wendt], in Samoa.'[17] To Ireland, he wrote, 'If Jim had done no more, it would have been sufficient that he taught us how to cry again. His death, in a way I can't yet explain, was a triumph for all he stood for — aroha, the mingling of Maori and pakeha, the breaking down of all that separates human beings from each other.' For Maurice, 'too few writers were there. Jim had gone out to a wider world than ours. Alistair [Campbell], Bill Oliver, Jack Lasenby, Hone, and [Denis] Glover (drunk). I drove back through the night and went to mass the next day. About six hundred filled St. Pat's.'[18] It was a fraction of those around the country for whom Jim Baxter had become a Christ-like figure among the poor, the lost and the sick.

In his 'Letter to Jim', which he wrote while he was still shedding tears many days after the tangi, Maurice waxed eloquent about the debt he owed Baxter. 'I remember you telling me once, as we raced to catch some bus together, that you wrote because New Zealand was a pain in your gut. And that you liked my work because I shared that pain. Perhaps. All I know now is that you made a triumph of our pain.'[19] With Baxter's death, it seemed as if a key part of the foundations of his writing life had been removed. In an interview with the *Auckland Star* on the publication of *Strangers and Journeys* at the beginning of December, he told of his early debt: 'I met Jim within months of my starting to write seriously. He is virtually the only other writer who read my work in manuscript. Without him I might have muddled around for years … In a very real way, I owe Jim every book I've written. This one, too.'[20]

One of the epigraphs to *Strangers and Journeys* was a line of Baxter's — 'A country made for angels, not for men' — but the dedication was wide-ranging, drawing in all those other friends who had been part of Maurice's creative journey: his father, Kevin Ireland, Barry Mitcalfe, Dick Scott, Eric McCormick, Ian Cross, Colin McCahon and Michael Smither. Barbara Magner was included, too, but not those other women who had contributed most to making the journey possible — his mother and Gill. The women included in the dedications to Maurice's novels may be taken as barometer readings of his current emotional weather.

The novel made an impact for its sheer size — 636 pages; nothing like it had been published in New Zealand before. The jacket blurb mentioned Patrick White, and thus obliquely *The Tree of Man*, while the quotes on the back were all from UK or US publications and drawn mostly from reviews of *The New Zealanders*. None of Maurice's books had since equalled its impact overseas. *Strangers* had been published in England in November and both the success and the limitations of the novel were first noted in reviews in the *Guardian* and *Observer*. Maurice was said to write 'with obvious sensibility, as well as solidity and power' but the novel's structure became diffuse after the first half, 'too big to be artistically governable … a federation of novels?'.[21] Although Maurice had a 'grand design', and tried with a 'Herman Wouk-style laboriousness, to imitate the accidental pattern and global bigness of life', its last 150 pages had a 'dying fall'.[22] But the tone of the reviews was largely warm and even the *Times Literary Supplement*, while pointing out its structural flaws, could conclude: 'The virtue of the book lies in its portrayal of life in a hard land and its oblique but faithful picture of the land itself. It is an attempt at something big. Even if reach exceeds grasp, the bigness remains. This is easily Mr Shadbolt's most considerable work so far.'[23]

David Ballantyne in the *Auckland Star* announced *Strangers and Journeys* as 'This is how it was here' and 'AN ASTONISHINGLY RELEVANT NEW ZEALAND NOVEL', arriving as it did in synch with Labour's election victory.[24] James Bertram in the *Listener* saw the parallels with *The Tree of Man* and clearly identified how key sections of the novel were drawn from Maurice's short stories. In the latter part it was 'chiefly the clever reporter at work; only with the older generation is the imaginative novelist fully engaged'. Maurice was no Patrick White, but in Ned Livingstone he had 'created a monumental and unforgettable ancestral figure, presented with a searing realism White cannot match'. It was unquestionably his 'finest literary achievement so far.'[25]

Maurice wrote an ingratiating letter to Bertram to thank him for his 'sensitive and thoughtful review … Lately I've begun to feel that the people who read me with most care — David Hall, John Reid,[26] Jim Baxter — have been lost before I could thank them decently … Hence this note.' He explained that the origins of *Strangers and Journeys* went back even further than Bertram had noted, to his first *Landfall* stories. Disingenuously, he concluded that perhaps he was, 'after all, just another one-book writer, if in rather rotund disguise. Some time in the years ahead I must try to write another one.'[27]

Conrad Bollinger in the New Zealand *Sunday Times* was as enthusiastic as David Ballantyne but was the only reviewer to point out that, 'Sex tends to be obtrusive and overwhelmingly joyless, though unusually varied (including incest and fellatio)'.[28] A seam of misogyny could now be traced back through almost all of Maurice's work published up to that time.

More extensive analysis was to come in the literary journals with a four-page review in *Landfall*[29] and an insightful six-page thesis-style examination in *Islands*. Michael Volkerling[30] considered the first part of the novel 'perhaps our finest work of historical fiction'. But although Maurice had created the fully realised characters of Bill Freeman and Ned Livingstone and connected their 'lives convincingly with consistent trends in New Zealand's historical and social development', the characters of their sons Ian and Tim failed take on the same 'sort of representative significance' and the introduction of many minor characters served only to confuse. The later parts of *Strangers* shifted to a take on society drawn more from the personal and not as well connected to current social trends, a problem shared by the contemporary works of both Frank Sargeson and Janet Frame in *The Hangover* and *Owls Do Cry*. 'Moreover, the skills of factual reporting are too often substituted for imaginative engagement in the lives of the characters.' Volkerling thought James Bertram had accused Maurice of lack of effort, 'settling for less', but thought it was more a 'lack of *control* … of the materials the author is dealing with and the ability to organize them in terms of some coherent vision'. Yet, in the end, *Strangers and Journeys* should be 'assessed not in relation to its inherent strengths and weaknesses, but rather in terms of the amount of ground it has cleared for other writers to build on.'[31]

The impact of *Strangers and Journeys* was almost physical. It demanded widespread attention and for some it was the long-awaited 'Great New Zealand novel', whatever its flaws. It was a literary Everest climbed, an Olympic race won, even if Maurice had staggered across the line. In 1973, the only year when the Wattie Book Awards winners were all works of fiction, Maurice claimed first prize ahead of Janet Frame's *Daughter Buffalo* and Witi Ihimaera's first book, *Pounamu Pounamu*. Maurice Gee considered *Strangers and Journeys* to be a 'big breakthrough novel', showing what could be done in New Zealand.[32] Time would reveal that the ground it 'cleared' gave him, most of all, the space to build on.

In bringing together all the themes, characters and preoccupations of his past fiction, Maurice was satisfied that *Strangers and Journeys*, 'Whatever its flaws [...] justifies my 40 years. How many can say that?'[33] At forty, the age he had once facetiously nominated as the time he should start writing seriously, he faced a creative crossroads. He had become convinced that his new fiction should deal not with the past but with the present: both the world and community immediately around him and big issues of the world at large. But how much attention had he paid to the constructive criticisms of the best reviewers, embodied in Michael Volkerling's judgments, that although *Strangers* was the country's best historical fiction to date, the novel failed in its imaginative rendering of contemporary society? And would he be able to manage the separation in future between his creative work and the journalism that too often dogged construction and style in his fiction?

The success of *Strangers and Journeys* greatly increased Maurice's reputation and public profile. He was a celebrity, again, and the sexual messages of the book and his past relationships, the gossip that he was 'good in bed', attracted more moths to the flame. Earlier, Maurice had dwelt on Yeats's poem 'The Choice', to signify his wrestle between perfection of the life and perfection of the work. He may also have recalled other lines of Yeats, and wondered if his centre would continue to hold.

POSTSCRIPT

By 1973, where this Volume One of *Life As a Novel* ends, Maurice Shadbolt's writing career had spanned eighteen years. During that time he had produced two collections of short stories, a book of novellas, four novels and two outstanding non-fiction books. All of them achieved international circulation, awards and much critical acclaim. He had reached the age of forty, been married twice and fathered five children; he had also become involved in several affairs, often concurrently. Could his work become even more productive and his life even more complicated?

Volume Two will traverse the last thirty years of Maurice's life during which he published a further six novels, that included much of his best work, as well as an influential play and non-fiction. He also married twice more and involved himself in more affairs. He became New Zealand's most well-known and controversial author: and steadily 'engaged in an intricate dance of death'[1] as he completed his 'life as a novel'.

ACKNOWLEDGEMENTS

Every author of a book of this kind depends heavily on the encouragement and practical support of many others: of any form of creative literature, biography comes closest to being a team effort. That said, the responsibility is entirely mine for the story told here. Maurice Shadbolt may have approved of that term. He always saw himself as a storyteller and in his Author's note to his first memoir, *One of Ben's*, he 'advised that a novelist is at work in these pages'. There is a novelist at work in these pages, too, not with Maurice Shadbolt's licence to creatively embellish but more in the pursuit of narrative, character and motive. Yet, whatever way a writer approaches another's life, it should always be in quest of authenticity. In this respect I should note that although I have used numerous quotes from *One of Ben's* and Shadbolt's later memoir, *From the Edge of the Sky*, they have been chosen as being at least close to an authenticity endorsed by other sources.

There are many people to thank and I should start with Maurice's children: Sean, Brendan, Tui, Daniel and Brigid who have been supportive all along. Sean and Brigid, as his literary executors, have been particularly helpful with my frequent questions.

This book would have been bereft of many insights into Maurice's life and career without the extensive recollections of his lifelong friend Kevin Ireland who has shown an unflagging interest in the project. In 1975, Maurice wrote that Kevin was his 'abiding comfort' in life.

Many thanks to all those who agreed to be interviewed or corresponded with me about Maurice Shadbolt, and who provided me with material, links and advice during both my initial and ongoing research: Fleur Adcock; Bridget Armstrong; Shaun Barnett; Betty Barrell; Rachel Barrowman; Peter Bland;

Tom Brooking; Dean Brewster; Bernard Brown; Martin Cole; Nigel Cook; Ralph Crane; Ian Cross; Gordon Dryden; Marilyn Duckworth; Tom Finlayson; Chris Francis; Carl Freeman; Maurice and Margareta Gee; Murray Gray; Ray Grover; Cherry Hankin; Gil Hanly; Michael Harlow; Julia Hass; Janine Hedley; Rob Heming; Gill Heming-Shadbolt; Lynley Hood; Alan Horsman; Sam Hunt; Lawrence Jones; Rhys Jones; John Kasmin; David Lawson; Graeme Lay; Jim McAloon; Naomi McCleary; Gordon McLauchlan; Owen Marshall; Colin Meads; Marian Minson; Joshua Muir; Robin Munro; National Union of Students press team, London; Bryn Nicholson; Jim O'Halloran (Te Kuiti Historical Society Inc.); Vincent O'Sullivan; Keith Ovenden; *Overland* (Alex Skutenko, Jacinda Woodhead); Alan Owen; Katherine Pawley (Auckland University Library); Catherine Saunders; Dick Scott; Tim Shadbolt; Yvonne Shadbolt; Peter Simpson; Elizabeth Smither; Michael Smither; C.K. Stead; Kay Stead; Rudy Sundes; Stephen Temple; University of Indiana Library; Albert and Sina Wendt; Michal Were (Te Kuiti Genealogy Branch, NZSG); Janet Wilson; Alex Witherow; Russell Young.

For permission to access archived material and to quote or reproduce from this and published material, thanks to: the Hocken Collections, University of Otago Library: Alan Roddick and the estate of Charles Brasch, John Baxter and the estate of James K. Baxter, Catherine Robertson and the estate of Zelda Louise Robertson; Sean Shadbolt and Brigid Magner and the estate of Maurice Shadbolt; Anthony Holcroft and the estate of M.H. Holcroft; Te Papa Tongarewa Collections, Len and Sylvia Bell and the estate of Marti Friedlander, Simon Lee-Johnson and the estate of Eric Lee-Johnson; C.K. Stead; Elizabeth Caffin and the estate of Dennis McEldowney; Helen Sutch; David Ling; Kevin Ireland.

I am immensely grateful to Creative New Zealand for two arts grants, one for research and development and another to assist the book's writing. Thanks, too, to the Henderson House and Arts Residency Trusts for providing the space and time to begin.

Thanks to publisher David Ling for his enthusiastic embrace of the manuscript, to editor Chris O'Brien, David Faulls for design and layout and Diane Lowther for an excellent index.

Last, abiding thanks to my wife Diane Brown for her forbearance and clear-eyed views during the several years (so far) that have been devoted to this project.

In all instances where quotations are used, due acknowledgment is made. In all cases we have made every effort to locate copyright holders and, where that has not been achieved, we shall continue to do so and to seek the necessary permission for any future edition of this work.

BIBLIOGRAPHY

Unpublished sources
Research for this biography began at the end of 2013 and continues. This has involved many recorded or noted interviews across New Zealand, as well as in Australia, England and France. All of Maurice Shadbolt's literary and personal papers are held in the Alexander Turnbull Library (ATL), National Library of New Zealand, Wellington, although some remained in family hands at the time of research. The over-arching accession reference for the ATL Maurice Shadbolt Papers is MS-Group-1280. Individual files are referenced in the footnotes as in the following example: 'MS to M. Palmer, 22 November 1959, ATL MS-Papers-8044-337'. The abbreviation 'MS' for 'Maurice Shadbolt' should not be confused with the ATL reference as in 'MS-Papers'.

During my several visits to the National Library I have been greatly assisted by ATL staff and, although it seems invidious to single out individuals, Jocelyn Chalmers was always helpful in negotiating reference mazes and requests and Linda McGregor continues to be of great assistance at long distance. In Dunedin, I have been able to rely on the swift and expert assistance of staff at both the Hocken Collections, University of Otago Library and the McNab New Zealand Collection of the Dunedin Public Library.

Bibliography of works cited or referred to for this volume.
Amato, Renato, *The full circle of the travelling cuckoo*, Christchurch: Whitcombe & Tombs, 1967.
Anon., 'Maurice Shadbolt: Writer', *Affairs*, February 1971.
Barrowman, Rachel, *Maurice Gee, Life and Work*, Wellington: Victoria University Press, 2015.
Burgess & Treep Architects, *Conservation Plan* for Maurice Shadbolt House and Studio, Going West Trust, September 2013.
Caffin, Elizabeth and Mason, Andrew, *The Deepening Stream, A History of the New Zealand Literary Fund*, Wellington: Victoria University Press, 2015.
Carlyon, Jenny and Morrow, Diana, *Changing Times, New Zealand since 1945*, Auckland:

Auckland University Press, 2013.
Crane, Ralph J. (ed), *Ending the Silences: Critical Essays on the Works of Maurice Shadbolt*, Auckland: Hodder Moa Beckett, 1995.
Crane, Ralph J., Introduction to *Selected Stories, Maurice Shadbolt*, Auckland: David Ling, 1998.
Cross, Ian, *Such Absolute Beginners*, Auckland: David Ling, 2007.
Duckworth, Marilyn, *Camping on the faultline*, Auckland: Vintage, 2000.
Frame, Janet, *An Angel At My Table*, Auckland: Penguin, 1984.
Guyan, Alexander, 'I Believe Writers Should Speak out', *Sunday News*, 16 May 1965.
Gittos, Murray, *A kiwi takes a look: a pen-pusher visits the Soviet Union*, Auckland 1962.
Hamilton, Ian, 'The Amazing Mr Shadbolt,' *Mate 4*, February 1960.
Heming-Shadbolt, Gillian, 'Flames in the Sea of Peace', unpublished MS.
Holcroft, M.H., *Reluctant Editor*, Wellington: A.H. and A.W. Reed, 1969.
Hunt, Sam, *From Bottle Creek*, Wellington: Alister Taylor, 1972.
Ireland, Kevin, *Backwards to Forwards*, Auckland: Vintage, 2002.
Ireland, Kevin, *Beginnings, Islands*, Vol.8, No.1, March 1980.
Ireland, Kevin, *Literary Cartoons*, Auckland: Islands/Hurricane, 1977.
Ireland, Kevin, *Under the Bridge and Over the Moon*, Auckland: Vintage, 1998.
King, Michael, *Frank Sargeson, A Life*, Auckland: Viking, 1995.
King, Michael, 'Sargeson, Frank', Wellington:*Dictionary of New Zealand Biography. Te Ara — the Encyclopedia of New Zealand*.
McEldowney, Dennis, *Full of the Warm South*, Dunedin: John McIndoe, 1983.
Mason, Andrew, 'Holcroft, Montague Harry', Wellington: *Dictionary of NZ Biography, Te Ara — the Encyclopedia of New Zealand*.
Mercer, Erin, *Telling the Real Story, Genre and New Zealand Literature*, Wellington: Victoria University Press, 2017.
Millar, Paul, *No Fretful Sleeper, A Life of Bill Pearson*, Auckland: Auckland University Press, 2010.
Mitcalfe, Barry (ed), *Boy Roel: the Voyage to Nowhere*, Wellington: Alister Taylor, 1972.
Mitcalfe, Barry, *Maori Poetry — The Singing Word*, Wellington: Victoria University Press, 1974.
Montgomerie, Deborah, *The Women's War: New Zealand Women 1939-45*, Auckland: Auckland University Press, 2001.
Pearson, Bill, *Fretful Sleepers and Other Essays*, Auckland: Heinemann, 1974.
Reid, Bryan, *After the Fireworks, A Life of David Ballantyne*, Auckland: Auckland University Press, 2004.
Reid, Tony, 'Dolphins — Man's Kindliest Friends', *NZ Weekly News*, 3 February 1969.
Richards, Ian, *To Bed At Noon, The Life and Art of Maurice Duggan*, Auckland: Auckland University Press, 1997.
Robinson, Roger and Wattie, Nelson (eds), *The Oxford Companion to New Zealand Literature*, Auckland: Oxford University Press, 1998.
Scott, Dick, *A Radical Writer's Life*, Auckland: Reed Books, 2004.
Scott, Dick, *Fire on the Clay, The Pakeha Comes to West Auckland*, Auckland: Southern Cross Books, 1979.
Shadbolt, Tim, *A Mayor of Two Cities*, Auckland: Hodder Moa Beckett, 2008.
Shieff, Sarah (ed), *Letters of Frank Sargeson*, Auckland: Vintage, 2012.
Taylor, Alister (ed), *James K. Baxter 1926-1972, A Memorial Volume*, Martinborough: Alister Taylor, 1972.
Vaassen, Sue, 'Shadbolt Speaks Out', *NZ Women's Weekly*, 23 October 1967.
Various, *Distance Looks Our Way, The Effects of Remoteness on New Zealand*, Winter Lectures 1960, Auckland: Auckland University Press, 1961.
Volkerling, Michael, 'Clearing the ground', *Islands 2*, Spring 1973.
Weir, J.E. (ed), *Collected Poems, James K. Baxter*, Wellington: Victoria University Press, 1979.

Wood, Naomi, *Mrs. Hemingway*, London: Picador, 2014.
Young, Russell, *The Story of Te Kuiti*, Wellington: Winter Productions, 2013.

A Bibliography of Maurice Shadbolt's Writing 1955-1973

This bibliography is largely confined to the biographical period covered by Volume One. It is based on 'A Bibliography of Maurice Shadbolt 1956-1993' compiled by Brigid Shadbolt (Magner) which, in turn, was based on the earlier work of Murray Gadd ('A Bibliography of Maurice Shadbolt, 1956-1980'. *Journal of New Zealand Literature 2* (1984): 75-96). It lists Shadbolt's published work from 1955 to 1973, fiction and non-fiction, including articles for *National Geographic*; as well as his National Film Unit productions. It does not include listings of the seventy-odd book reviews he wrote during this period; articles for *Reader's Digest*; his letters to the editor; interviews given or reviews of his books. A bibliography for the period 1974-2000 will be included in Volume Two. The complete Brigid Shadbolt bibliography 1956-1993 may be accessed at the Alexander Turnbull Library, Wellington, MS-Group-1280, reference MS-Papers-8044-282.

FICTION

Short stories
'Annual Holiday.' *NZ Listener* 10 June 1955: 8-9.
'Twosome.' *Numbers* 4 (October 1955): 10-12.
'On the County.' *NZ Listener* 4 November 1955: 8-10.
'Sing Again Tomorrow.' *Landfall* 36 Vol. 9, No. 4 (December 1955): 288-292.
'And Then There Were Two.' *Numbers* 5 (May 1956): 5-8.
'The Gloves.' *NZ Listener* 21 September 1956: 8-9,30-31.
'End of Season.' *Landfall* 40 Vol. 10, No. 4 (December 1956): 278-317.
'Play the Fife Lowly.' *Landfall* 41 Vol. 11, No. 1 (March 1957): 35-54. (Incl. in *The New Zealanders* 1959).
'The Funniest Thing.' *Arena* 50 (1958): 2-8.
'After the Depression.' *Landfall* 48 Vol. 12, No. 4 (December 1958): 318-322. (Incl. in *The New Zealanders* 1959).
'A Beer for Old Johnny.' *Arena* 51 (1959): 2-7. (In Bulgarian translation 1957).
'The Strangers.' *The New Yorker* 3 October 1959: 38-45. (Original version in *The New Zealanders* 1959).
'Nightfall.' *Spike* (VUW 1961): 87-91.
'The Room.' *Landfall* 63 Vol. 17, No. 4 (September 1963): 215-232. (Incl. in *Summer Fires and Winter Country* 1963).
'Towards a Character: Ned Livingstone.' Otago University Students' Association Review 1963: 6-18. (Excerpt from early draft of *Strangers and Journeys*).

Novels and short story collections
The New Zealanders: A Sequence of Stories. London: Victor Gollancz; Christchurch: Whitcombe & Tombs, 1959; New York: Atheneum, 1961; Milan: Feltrinelli, 1962 as *Le Acque Della Luna* (Waters of the Moon); Hamburg: Hoffman und Campe, 1965 as *Mädchen Fluss und Zweibel — Geschichten aus Neuseeland* (Girl River and Onion — stories from New

Zealand). The book was reissued by Whitcombe & Tombs in 1974 with an introduction by Cherry Hankin and a revised edition with an introduction by the author by David Ling, Auckland in 1993, reprinted 1997. Chinese language edition, Transoxania International, Taipei, 2016.

Summer Fires and Winter Country. London: Eyre & Spottiswoode; Christchurch: Whitcombe & Tombs, 1963; New York: Atheneum, 1966.

Among the Cinders. London: Eyre & Spottiswoode; New York: Atheneum; Christchurch: Whitcombe & Tombs, 1965; Hamburg: Hoffman und Campe, 1970 as *Und er nahm mich bei der Hand* (And he took me by the Hand). The book was reissued by Whitcoulls in 1975 with an introduction by Stephen Becker and a revised edition by Sceptre NZ Auckland in 1993. A Danish edition appeared from Munksgaard of Copenhagen in 1987 as *Mig og min bedstefar* (Me and my grandfather).

The Presence of Music: Three Novellas. London: Cassell, 1967.

This Summer's Dolphin. London: Cassell; New York: Atheneum, 1969; Hamburg: Hoffman und Campe as *Der Sommer des Delphins* (Summer of the Dolphin); Zurich: Buchclub Ex Libris, 1973.

An Ear of the Dragon. London: Cassell, 1971.

Strangers and Journeys. London: Hodder & Stoughton, 1972 and Coronet Books, 1975 ; New York: St Martin's Press, 1973; Auckland: Sceptre NZ, 1990.

NON-FICTION

Books

New Zealand: Gift of the Sea. With photographs by Brian Brake. Christchurch: Whitcombe & Tombs, 1963 and revised edition 1973; Honolulu: East-West Center Press, 1964 (revised); Auckland: Hodder & Stoughton, 1990 (revised).

Isles of the South Pacific. With Olaf Ruhen. Washington DC: National Geographic Society, 1968 and 1971 (revised).

The Shell Guide to New Zealand. Christchurch: Whitcombe & Tombs, 1968, 1973 (revised) and 1976 (revised with photographs by Philip Temple); London: Michael Joseph, 1969 and 1976 (revised edition).

Additionally, Shadbolt memoirs relevant to Volume One:

One of Ben's: A New Zealand Medley. Auckland: David Ling, 1993; (revised edition when sub-title dropped), 1994, reprinted 1999. London: Bloomsbury, 1993 as *One of Ben's: A Tribe Transported.*

At the Edge of the Sky. Auckland: David Ling, 1999.

Contributions to books

'Renato Amato.' *The Full Circle of the Travelling Cuckoo: stories by Renato Amato.* Christchurch: Whitcombe & Tombs, 1967: 7-18. An introductory memoir.

'On New Zealand Literature.' *Encyclopedia Brittanica 10.* Chicago: Encyclopedia Brittanica Inc., 1971: 1231-1232.

'Tamure.' *Boy Roel: Voyage to Nowhere* by Barry Mitcalfe et al. Wellington: Alister Taylor, 1972: 113-126.

'Letter to Jim.' *James K. Baxter 1926-1972: A Memorial Volume,* ed. Alister Taylor. Wellington: Alister Taylor, 1972: 28-40.

Contributions to periodicals

'The Value of the New Zealand Short Story.' *Evening Post* 29 December 1956: 7. As an introduction to review of *Immanuel's Land* by Maurice Duggan.

'China, Russia, Bulgaria, A Journey.' *Landfall* 46, Vol.12, No. 2 (June 1958): 125-144.

'The Quiet American.' *NZ Listener* 8 August 1958: 8. Shadbolt, a Venezuelan poet and an

American writer in Paris.
'John Feeney and the National Film Unit.' *Landfall 47*, Vol. 12, No. 3 (September 1958): 226-232.
'Story of a Book.' *NZ Listener* 14 November 1958: 8. About *Dr Zhivago*.
'Postscript on Pasternak.' *Landfall 49*, Vol.13, No. 1 (March 1959): 81-85.
'Two Views on Dr Zhivago.' *Overland 14* (March 1959): 30-31.
'Tomorrow Might be Better.' *NZ Listener* 17 April 1959: 8-9. Shadbolt and an Italian painter in Majorca.
'From A West-East Notebook.' *Landfall 52*, Vol. 13, No. 4 (December 1959):341-352.
'New Zealand: Gift of the Sea', *National Geographic*, Vol.121, No.4, April 1962.
'Western Samoa — the Pacific's Newest Nation', *National Geographic*, Vol. 122, No.4, October 1962.
'Signposts on the way to a New Zealand literature.' *Otago Daily Times* 24 August 1963: 17.
'In Storied Lands of Malaysia', *National Geographic*, Vol.124, No. 5, November 1963.
'Shadbolt on the Short Story.' *Craccum* 3, August 1964: 8-11.
'Michael (Renato) Amato 1928-1964.' *Landfall 71*, Vol.18, No.3 (September 1964): 250-252.
'Fires Across the Tasman.' *Bulletin* 9 April 1966. Recent New Zealand writing.
'Goodbye Katherine Mansfield — New Zealanders are ready to pension off their old governess.' *Books and Bookmen* February 1967: 17-19. New Zealand literature since K.M.
'A Writer Out of Hiding.' *NZ Listener* 12 July 1967: 19-20. Problems of writing in New Zealand.
'New Zealand's Cook Islands — Paradise in Search of a future', *National Geographic*, Vol. 132, No.2, August 1967.
'In My View', *NZ Listener*, 26 July 1968: 15. Maori and the arts.
'Maurice Shadbolt Interviewed', *The New Zealander*, 30 July 1968, pp 17-20.
'In My View', *NZ Listener*, 15 August 1969:15. Pine Taiapa and Maori carving.
'Literature: Australia and New Zealand', *Encyclopaedia Britannica*, 1971.
"Hermit of Hawera.' *NZ Listener* 12 February 1973: 9. Obituary of Ronald Hugh Morrieson.
'White: Filling the Australian Void.' *NZ Listener* 17 November 1973:11. On the work of Patrick White.
'The Making of a Book.' *Landfall 108*, Vol.27, No.4 (December 1973): 275-289.

Additionally relevant to Volume One:
'Beginnings: the Disobedient Days,' *Islands 31-32*, Vol.8, No.4; Vol. 9, No.1, June 1981.
Contemporary Authors Autobiography Series, Vol. 3, Detroit: Gale 1986.
'Lee-Johnson, Eric Albert', Wellington: *Dictionary of New Zealand Biography. Te Ara — the Encyclopedia of New Zealand*.

Unpublished
'Life & Litters,' April 1970: ATL MS-Papers-8044-175.

Film and TV
'Shark Fishermen.' In *Pictorial Parade 41*, October 1955. National Film Unit. Written, directed and edited.
'Spring Roundup on Molesworth.' *Pictorial Parade 44*, December 1955. National Film Unit. Written, edited and co-directed with Derek Wright.
'Opo and Pelorus Jack.' In *Pictorial Parade 47*, March 1956, National Film Unit. Written, directed and edited.
'Artist in Northland.' A film about Eric Lee-Johnson. In *Pictorial Parade 55*, November 1956, National Film Unit. Co-written, directed and edited.
'Down by the Cool Sea.' Television play adapted by Shadbolt from his story 'Summer Fires.' NZBC-TV 21 October 1966.

NOTES

EPIGRAPH
1   ATL 91-047-16/02. 'Kolenko' is probably Shadbolt's (vodka?) garbled rendition of 'Loukanka', a Bulgarian salami speciality.

PROLOGUE
1   The *Guardian*, 26 October 2004.
2   *A Sort of Conscience, The Wakefields*, Auckland 2002.

CHAPTER 1
1   'Life & Litters', 17 April 1970, p.1. ATL MS-Papers-8044-175.
2   Ibid.
3   'Beginnings: the Disobedient Days,' *Islands* 31-32, Vol.8, No. 4/Vol.9,No.1, June 1981, p.78.
4   *One of Ben's*, Auckland 1994, p.113.
5   Ibid, p. vii.
6   *Islands* 31-32, p.78 and *One of Ben's* p.102.
7   *One of Ben's*, p.100.
8   Julia Hass, pers. comm., 24 August 2015.
9   *One of Ben's*, pp. 26-27. This was paraphrased uncritically, with factual errors, in Michael King's *The Penguin History of New Zealand*, Auckland 2003, pp. 174-175.
10 Ibid, p.31.
11 Ibid, p.36.
12 Ibid, p.48.
13 Ibid, p.54.
14 *A Mayor of Two Cities*, Tim Shadbolt, Auckland, 2008, p.11.
15 *One of Ben's*, p.63.
16 *A Mayor of Two Cities*, pp.12-13.
17 *One of Ben's*, p.56.
18 *Mayor of Two Cities*, p.15.
19 *One of Ben's*, p.58.
20 Ibid, p.61.
21 Ibid, p.60.
22 Yvonne Shadbolt interview, 6 March 2014.

23 *One of Ben's*, p.65.
24 Ibid.
25 Ibid, p.89.
26 Julia Hass, pers. comm., 23 August 2015.
27 Ibid.
28 *One of Ben's* p.90
29 Ibid, p.92.
30 Ibid, p.93.
31 *Islands* 31-32, p.79.
32 *One of Ben's*, p.104.
33 Yvonne Shadbolt interview, 6 March 2014.
34 *One of Ben's*, p.110.
35 *Islands* 31-32, p.86.
36 *One of Ben's*, p.111.

CHAPTER 2
1 *Islands* 31-32, p.79.
2 Ibid, p. 79.
3 *The Story of Te Kuiti*, Wellington 2013, p.36.
4 *One of Ben's*, p.115.
5 Ibid, p.124.
6 Ibid, pp. 117-118.
7 Ibid, p.118.
8 Ibid, p.126.
9 Montgomerie, Deborah, *The Women's War: New Zealand Women 1939-45*, Auckland, 2001. p.131.
10 *King Country Chronicle*, 19 October 1942. ATL MS-Papers-8044-012.
11 *One of Ben's*, pp. 127-129.
12 Ibid, p.128.
13 Ibid, p.115.
14 Ibid, p.133.
15 Ibid, p.143.
16 Pete Ingram to MS, 3 December 1993. ATL MS-Papers-8044-048.
17 'Life & Litters', p.5.
18 *Islands* 31-32, p.88.
19 *One of Ben's*, p.139.
20 Colin Meads, pers. comm., 12 August 2015.
21 Alan Owen, pers. comm., 11 August 2015.
22 Betty Burrell, pers. comm., 10 August 2015.
23 ATL MS-Papers-8044-277
24 *One of Ben's*, p.137.
25 'Life & Litters', 17 April 1970, p.5.
26 Yvonne Shadbolt interview, 6 March 2014.
27 *One of Ben's*, pp. 140-141.
28 Ibid, p.141.
29 Ibid, pp.134-135.
30 Pete Ingram to MS, 3 December 1993.
31 *One of Ben's*, p. 135.
32 Ibid, p.144.
33 *Islands* 31-32, p.88.

CHAPTER 3

1. *One of Ben's*, p.170. Shadbolt's sister Julia has a different take. 'Many of the moves were to rented houses while they looked for a house in the same town' or when 'they bought a house sometimes they thought they would improve their finances by making some sort of profit. Sometimes they moved perhaps to rekindle the old days'. Julia Hass, pers. comm., 1 July 2014.
2. *One of Ben's*, p.146.
3. Ibid, p.147.
4. Ibid.
5. *Islands* 31-32, pp. 88-89.
6. Maurice Gee interview, 4 December 2014.
7. Carl Freeman, pers.comm., 8 October 2015.
8. *One of Ben's*, p.145.
9. Carl Freeman, pers. comm., 5 October 2015.
10. Kevin Ireland interview, 31 December 2013.
11. Kevin Ireland, pers. comm., 11 September 2015.
12. Maurice Gee, pers. comm., 4 October 2015
13. *One of Ben's*, p.146.
14. Frame, Janet, *An Angel At My Table*, Auckland, 1984, p.70.
15. *One of Ben's*, p.148.
16. Ibid, p.149.
17. Ibid, p.150.
18. Ibid, p.151.
19. Ibid, p.86.

CHAPTER 4

1. *Islands* 31-32, p.89.
2. 'Life & Litters', p.8.
3. *One of Ben's*, p.155.
4. *Islands* 31-32, p.90.
5. *One of Ben's*, p.154.
6. *Islands* 31-32, p.90.
7. *One of Ben's*, p.153.
8. Ibid, p.157.
9. 'Life & Litters', p.8.
10. nzhistory.net.nz: *The 1951 waterfront dispute* p.3.
11. 'Life & Litters', p.9.
12. No copy of this issue of *Craccum*, Vol.25, No. 8, can now be found in any New Zealand library. Copies must have been confiscated and destroyed by university authorities or police or both.
13. *One of Ben's*, p.161.
14. Ibid, p.164.
15. Ibid, p.161.
16. Ibid.
17. Maurice Gee interview, 4 December 2014.
18. 'Life & Litters', p.10.
19. Kevin Ireland interview, 31 December 2013.
20. Ibid.
21. Kevin Ireland, pers. comm., 8 March 2014.
22. 'Life & Litters', p.10.
23. *One of Ben's*, p.168.

24 'Life & Litters', p.11.
25 Ibid, p.12
26 *Islands 31-32*, p.93.
27 *One of Ben's*, p.172.
28 Kevin Ireland, eulogy at Maurice Shadbolt's funeral, October 2004.

CHAPTER 5
1 *One of Ben's*, p.177.
2 Ibid.
3 Ibid, p.180.
4 Gillian Heming Shadbolt, 'Flames in the Sea of Peace', unpublished memoir, p.3.
5 'Flames in the Sea of Peace', p.14.
6 Robin Heming, Classic Wallabies, www.rugby.com.au
7 Shadbolt Family Papers
8 Kevin Ireland, pers. comm., 23 October 2015.
9 Shonagh Koea interview, 7 March 2014.
10 *One of Ben's*, p.181.
11 MS to Gill, 17-18 March 1953, Shadbolt family papers.
12 *One of Ben's*, p.183.
13 Ibid, p.185.
14 Ibid, p.186.
15 MS to Gill, n.d. June 1953, Shadbolt family papers.
16 Ibid.
17 *One of Ben's*, p.184.
18 Ibid, p.173.
19 MS to Gill, 21 June 1953, Shadbolt family papers.
20 Kevin Ireland, eulogy at Shadbolt's funeral, October 2004.
21 MS to Gill, n.d. June-July 1953, Shadbolt family papers.
22 Ibid.
23 MS to Gill, n.d. June-July 1953, Shadbolt family papers.
24 Ibid.
25 MS to Gill, n.d. June-July 1953, Shadbolt family papers.
26 Ibid.
27 Ibid.
28 MS to Gill, n.d.October 1953.
29 MS to Gill, n.d.June 1953.
30 *One of Ben's*, p.162.
31 Kevin Ireland, pers.comm., 16 October 2015.
32 Julia Hass interview, 2 April 2014.

CHAPTER 6
1 *Islands 31-32*, June 1981, p.95.
2 *One of Ben's*, p.188.
3 'Life & Litters', p.15.
4 MS —To Whom It May Concern, 17 April 1964, ATL 91-047-16/08. A reference for James Harris.
5 *Islands 31-32*, p.95.
6 Ibid.
7 Ibid.
8 John Kasmin interview, 24 April 2014.
9 Kevin Ireland, eulogy at Shadbolt's funeral, October 2004.

10 *Beginnings*, Kevin Ireland, *Islands*, Vol.8, No.1, March 1980, p.29.
11 Kevin Ireland interview, 31 December 2013.
12 *Islands* 31-32, p.95.
13 MS to Gill, 2 April 1955, Shadbolt family papers.
14 *Islands* 31-32, p.96.

CHAPTER 7
1 Andrew Mason. 'Holcroft, Montague Harry', from the *Dictionary of New Zealand Biography*. Te Ara — the Encyclopedia of New Zealand.
2 *NZ Listener*, 1 July 1955, p.7.
3 Michael King. 'Sargeson, Frank', from the *Dictionary of New Zealand Biography*. Te Ara — the Encyclopedia of New Zealand.
4 Holcroft, M.H., *Reluctant Editor*, Wellington 1969, pp. 35 and 111.
5 Ibid, p.112
6 Ibid, p.113.
7 Ibid, p. 31.
8 Entry for Johnson in *The Oxford Companion to New Zealand Literature*, edited by Roger Robinson and Nelson Wattie, Auckland 1988.
9 *Islands* 31-32, p.96.
10 Maurice Gee to MS, 3 April 1956. ATL 91-047-16/02.

CHAPTER 8
1 *One of Ben's*, p.196.
2 Ibid, p.66.
3 Ibid, p.68.
4 Ibid, p.71.
5 Ibid, p.73.
6 *To Bed At Noon* by Ian Richards, Auckland 1997, p. 206: from interview with MS 29 April 1993.
7 *Islands*, Vol.6, No 3, March 1978, p.323.
8 'Life & Litters', pp 19-20.
9 Kevin Ireland, pers. comm., 17 February 2016.
10 *Islands*, Vol.6, No 3, March 1978, p.323.
11 *Islands* 31-32.
12 *One of Ben's*, p.196.
13 Ibid, p.197.
14 *Islands* 31-32, p.97.
15 *One of Ben's*, p.198.
16 Ibid.
17 *Islands* 31-32, p.97.
18 *One of Ben's*, p.198.
19 NFU *Pictorial Parade No. 47*, March 1956.
20 *One of Ben's*, p.199.
21 *Islands* 31-32, pp. 97-98.
22 Eric Lee-Johnson to MS, 4 April 1957, ATL 91-047-16/02.
23 *One of Ben's*, p.189.
24 Eric Lee-Johnson to MS, 4 April 1957.

CHAPTER 9
1 *Numbers 5*, edited by Baxter, Louis Johnson and Charles Doyle.
2 'Life & Litters', p.21.

3 M.H. Holcroft to MS, 9 April 1956. ATL 91-047-16/02.
4 *NZ Listener*, 21 September 1956, p.8.
5 Charles Brasch to MS, 7 June 1956. ATL 91-047-16/04.
6 Charles Brasch to MS, 2 August 1956. ATL 91-047-16/04.
7 *Landfall 40*, Vol. 10, No 4, December 1956, pp. 278-317.
8 Kevin Ireland to MS, n.d. c. Aug. 1956. ATL 94-180-5/18.
9 Kevin Ireland to MS, 19 September 1956. ATL 94-180-5/18.
10 Kevin Ireland to MS, 4 October 1956. ATL 94-180-5/18.
11 MS to Gill, 26 October 1956, Shadbolt family papers.
12 Gill to MS, 3 November 1956, Shadbolt family papers.
13 Gill to MS, 10 November 1956, Shadbolt family papers.
14 Gill to MS, 3 November 1956.
15 Gill to MS, 10 November 1956.
16 MS to Gill, 6 November 1956, Shadbolt family papers.
17 Maurice Gee to MS, 8 October 1956, ATL 91-047-16/04.
18 Maurice Gee interview, 4 December 2014.
19 *One of Ben's*, p.208.
20 Maurice Gee, pers. comm., 12 May 2016.
21 Maurice Gee interview, 4 December 2014.
22 MS to Frank Sargeson, 21 February 1957, ATL MS-Papers-0432-112.
23 Maurice Gee interview 2014.
24 MS to Frank Sargeson, 21 February 1957.
25 Ibid.
26 *Evening Post*, 29 December 1956.
27 Shared with John Caselberg's 'Eli Eli Lama Sabachtani'.
28 'Life & Litters', p.18.
29 Maurice Gee to MS, 27 August 1956. ATL 91-047-16/04.
30 *Mine Eyes Dazzle* (Alistair Campbell) and *A Splinter of Glass* (Charles Doyle). Both Pegasus Press, Christchurch, 1956.
31 Charles Brasch to MS, 1 January 1957, ATL 91-047-16/02.
32 MS to Frank Sargeson, 30 May 1957, ATL MS-Papers-0432-112.
33 C.K. Stead, pers. comm., 24 May 2016.
34 Maurice Gee to MS, 10 December 1956. ATL 91-047-16/04.
35 *One of Ben's*, p.209.
36 *Islands 31-32*, p.98.
37 'Life & Litters', p.21.
38 Nigel Cook interview, Auckland 15 March 2015. He also saw James K. Baxter and MS as in a 'master-pupil' relationship. MS does acknowledge his debt to Baxter.
39 *One of Ben's*, p. 208, and following quotes.
40 Ibid, p.209.

CHAPTER 10
1 MS to mother 19/6/57, ATL MS-Papers-8044-002.
2 Gill Shadbolt, c. 1/7/57, ATL MS-Papers-8044-001.
3 *One of Ben's*, p.210.
4 Gill c.1/7/57.
5 MS to mother, c. 1/7/57, ATL MS-Papers-8044-001.
6 Gill c.1/7/57.
7 Ibid.
8 MS to mother, c. 1/7/57.
9 *One of Ben's*, pp. 212-214.

10 MS to mother 15 July 1957, ATL MS-Papers-8044-001.
11 Ibid.
12 Ibid.
13 *One of Ben's*, p. 215.
14 Ibid.
15 Ibid, p.216.
16 MS to family, 15 August 1957, ATL MS-Papers-8044-001.
17 Nineteen have now been held since 1947, mostly but not always in Communist countries.
18 Gill to V. Shadbolt, c.13 August 1957, ATL MS-Papers-8044-001.
19 MS to family, 15 August 1957, ATL MS-Papers-8044-001. Readers who wish to see what the opening ceremony was like can view Pathé News footage at https://www.youtube.com/watch?v=MRi6VnXbG34.
20 *Landfall 46*, Vol.12, No.2 (June 1958), p.128.
21 *One of Ben's*, p.220.
22 Ibid, p.221.
23 Ibid, p.222.
24 MS to family, 15 August 1957, ATL MS-Papers-8044-001.
25 *One of Ben's*, p.223.
26 Ibid, p.231.
27 MS and Gill to family, 27 August 1957, ATL MS-Papers-8044-001.
28 Gill to Shadbolt family, 6 September 1957, ATL MS-Papers-8044-001.
29 *One of Ben's*, pp. 235-239.

CHAPTER 11
1   Gill to Shadbolt family, 16 September 1957, ATL MS-Papers-8044-001.
2   Ibid.
3   *One of Ben's*, p. 241.
4   Ibid.
5   MS to family, 14 October 1957, ATL MS-Papers-8044-001.
6   MS to family, 25 September 1957, ATL MS-Papers-8044-001.
7   MS to family, 24 September 1957, ATL MS-Papers-8044-001.
8   Gill to Shadbolt family, 6 October 1957, ATL MS-Papers-8044-001.
9   Gill to Shadbolt family, 25 September 1957.
10 Ibid.
11 *One of Ben's*, p.244.
12 Ibid, p.247.
13 Gill to Shadbolt family, 6 October 1957, ATL MS-Papers-8044-001.
14 MS to mother and family, 14 October 1957, ATL MS-Papers-8044-001.

CHAPTER 12
1   MS to Kevin Ireland, 9 November 1957, ATL MS-Papers-8044-055.
2   Ibid.
3   *One of Ben's*, p.252.
4   Jenny Bojilova to MS, 29 November 1957. ATL MS-Papers-8044-037.
5   Ibid.
6   Jenny Bojilova to MS, 29 November 1957 (2). ATL MS-Papers-8044-037.
7   Gill to Shadbolt family, 28 December 1957, ATL MS-Papers-8044-001.
8   *One of Ben's*, p.265.
9   Jenny Bojilova to MS, 29 November 1957 (2).
10 Kevin Ireland, pers. comm., 14 July 2016.
11 Gill to Shadbolt family, 20 November 1957, ATL MS-Papers-8044-01.

12 Ibid.
13 Ibid.
14 Gill to Shadbolt family, 18 February 1958, ATL MS-Papers-8044-01.
15 Charles Brasch to MS, 13 November 1957, ATL 91-047-16/02.
16 *Landfall 46*, Vol.12,No.2, (June 1958), pp. 125-144.
17 *Landfall 47*, Vol.12, No.3 (September 1958), pp. 226-232.
18 Charles Brasch to MS, 13 November 1957, ATL 91-047-16/02.
19 Gill to Shadbolt family, 27 January 1958, ATL MS-Papers-8044-01.
20 Jenny Bojilova to MS, 29 November 1957 (2).
21 Gill to Shadbolt family, 5 February 1958, ATL MS-Papers-8044-01.
22 *NZ Listener*, 8 August 1958, p.8: 'The Quiet American'.
23 *One of Ben's*, p.261.
24 *Strangers and Journeys*, London and Auckland, 1972, p.13.
25 Maurice Gee to MS, 31 March 1958, ATL 91-047-16/02.
26 Gill to Shadbolt family, 19 February 1958, ATL MS-Papers-8044-01.
27 Gill to Shadbolt family, 24 March 1958, ATL MS-Papers-8044-01.
28 Louis Johnson to MS, 1 April 1958, ATL 91-047-16/02.
29 MS to mother, 28 March 1958, ATL 91-047-17/04.
30 Gill to Shadbolt family, 15 April 1958, ATL MS-Papers-8044-01.
31 Jenny Bojilova to MS, 27 April 1958, ATL MS-Papers-8044-037.
32 MS to family, 7 May 1958, ATL MS-Papers-8044-01.
33 *One of Ben's*, p.265.
34 Jenny Bojilova to MS, 31 May 1958, ATL MS-Papers-8044-037.
35 Jenny Bojilova, 26 May 1958, ATL MS-Papers-8044-037.
36 'Thank You Goodbye' was included in *The New Zealanders*, London 1959.
37 Jenny Bojilova to MS, n.d. June 1958, ATL MS-Papers-8044-037.
38 Jenny Bojilova to Gill Shadbolt, 13 July 1958, Shadbolt family papers.

CHAPTER 13
1 *One of Ben's*, p.277.
2 MS to Gill, 23 July 1958, Shadbolt family papers.
3 MS to Gill, 24 July 1958, Shadbolt family papers.
4 *One of Ben's*, p.277.
5 MS to Gill, 21 October 1958, Shadbolt family papers. Also following quotes.
6 MS to Gill, c. 24 October 1958, Shadbolt family papers, and following quotes.
7 MS to Gill, 27 October 1958, Shadbolt family papers, and following quotes.
8 *One of Ben's*, p.283.
9 MS to Gill, 27 October 1958, Shadbolt family papers, and following quotes.
10 About to be published in *Landfall 48*, Vol.12, No.4, (December 1958).
11 See p.80.
12 *Overland*, March 1959, p.30.
13 C.K. Stead interview, 7 March 2014.
14 Charles Brasch to MS, 19 March 1959, ATL 91-047-16/02.

CHAPTER 14
1 Charles Brasch to MS, 11 January 1959, ATL 91-047-16/02.
2 Copies courtesy C.K. Stead.
3 *The New Zealanders*, p.50.
4 Ibid, p.53.
5 Ibid, p.54.

6 *One of Ben's*, p.283.
7 Hilary Rubinstein to MS, 6 March 1959, ATL 91-047-17/10.
8 'Life & Litters', p.34.
9 C.K. Stead to Frank Sargeson, c.20 March 1959, courtesy C.K. Stead.
10 *The New Zealanders*, pp. 68-69.
11 Ibid, p.72.
12 Charles Brasch to MS, 21 May 1959, ATL 91-047-16/05.
13 MS to Charles Brasch, c. 1 June 1959, ATL MS-Papers-8044-337.
14 MS to C.K. Stead, 22 June 1959, courtesy C.K. Stead.
15 Charles Brasch to MS, 19 March 1959, ATL 91-047-16/02.
16 Gill to family, 31 May 1959, ATL MS-Papers-8044-001.
17 MS to mother, 2 July 1959, ATL MS-Papers-8044-002.
18 MS to C.K. Stead, 22 June 1959, courtesy C.K. Stead.
19 Kevin Ireland, pers. comm., 8 January 2017.
20 Kevin Ireland to MS, 28 March 1957, ATL 94-180-5/18.
21 Kevin Ireland interview, 31 December 2013. Ireland also told MS that Karl Stead was the writer of the 'K of Henderson' letter, believing he was the first with the news. In a strange piece of theatre, MS appeared shocked and unbelieving, saying Stead was now a friend and this could affect their relationship. His expressed ignorance was possibly a deceitful way of explaining away how much time he had been spending with Stead.
22 Ibid. This was the basis for Ireland's first published collection, *Face to Face*, Christchurch 1963.
23 *One of Ben's*, p.289.
24 John Kasmin interview, 24 April 2014.
25 *One of Ben's*, p.290.
26 John Kasmin interview.

CHAPTER 15
1 Gill to family, 26 July 1959, ATL MS-Papers-8044-001.
2 *One of Ben's*, p.291.
3 Steven Murray-Smith to MS, 2 July 1959, ATL 91-047-16/05. *Overland* and the Australian Communist Party parted company over the issue; *Overland* has survived.
4 *One of Ben's*, p.291.
5 Ibid, p.293.
6 MS to Gill, 27 August 1959, ATL 91-047-16/05.
7 MS to Gill, 21 October 1958, Shadbolt family papers.
8 Gill to family, 8 August 1959, ATL MS-Papers-8044-001.
9 MS to Gill, 27 August 1959.
10 *One of Ben's*, p.304.
11 Kevin Ireland, *Backwards to Forwards*, A Memoir, Auckland 2002, p.64.
12 Ibid, p.62.
13 'River, Girl and Onion'.
14 From 'The Literary Man Meets Maurice Shadbolt Again', *Literary Cartoons*, Kevin Ireland, Auckland 1977.
15 MS to Kevin Ireland, 3 October 1959, ATL 91-047-17/08.
16 MS to family, 22 September 1959, ATL MS-Papers-8044-002.
17 Gill to family, 8 August 1959, ATL MS-Papers-8044-001.
18 Shelagh Delaney to Shadbolts, 24 November 1959, ATL 91-047-16/05.
19 Gill to family, 8 August 1959.
20 MS to Frank Sargeson, 12 October 1959, ATL MS-Papers-0432-112.
21 James K. Baxter to MS, 12 October 1959, ATL 91-047-16/01.

22 MS to M. Palmer, 22 November 1959, ATL MS-Papers-8044-337.
23 *One of Ben's*, pp. 308-9.
24 Gill to family, 14 November 1959, ATL MS-Papers-8044-001.
25 A personal note: Pitman was my English teacher at Sloane Grammar School, Chelsea, in 1954-56, before he took to journalism, and encouraged my writing. He asked MS to look out for me in NZ which he eventually did.Pitman died less than ten years later aged only 44.
26 MS to Kevin Ireland, 14 November 1959, ATL 91-047-17/08.
27 *One of Ben's*, p.309.
28 C.K.Stead to MS, 1 November 1959, ATL 91-047-16/05.
29 *NZ Listener*, 20 November 1959, pp. 12-13.
30 'Island Race', Anon. (Noel McLachlan), *Times Literary Supplement*, 27 November 1959, p. 689. NOTE: TLS reviewers at that time were anonymous; half a century later it is possible to discover who they were. Noel McLachlan was an Australian historian and journalist for *The Times*.
31 *One of Ben's*, p.310.

CHAPTER 16
1 'Life & Litters', p.27.
2 *From the Edge of the Sky*, p.24.
3 Ibid, p.25.
4 MS to Kevin Ireland, 1 March 1960, ATL 91-047-17/08.
5 *From the Edge of the Sky*, p.27.
6 Maurice Shadbolt, 'Lee-Johnson, Eric Albert', from the *Dictionary of New Zealand Biography. Te Ara — the Encyclopedia of New Zealand*.
7 Barry Mitcalfe to MS, 26 July 1959, ATL 91-047-16/05.
8 *From the Edge of the Sky*, p.31.
9 Barry Mitcalfe, *Maori Poetry — The Singing Word*, Wellington, 1974.
10 *From the Edge of the Sky*, p.34.
11 MS to Kevin Ireland, 1 March 1960, ATL 91-047-17/08.
12 *Te Ao Hou*, The New World, a magazine for Maori, was published by the Maori Affairs Department from 1952 to 1976.
13 *From the Edge of the Sky*, p.39.
14 Ibid, p.42.
15 Ibid, p.44.
16 Ibid, p.49.
17 Ibid, p.52.
18 Duggan was 10 years older.
19 Fleur Adcock interview, 22 April 2014.
20 Michael King, *Frank Sargeson, A Life*, Auckland 1995, p.234.
21 *Mate 4*, February 1960, pp. 44-48.
22 Charles Brasch to MS, 22 March 1960, ATL 91-047-16/05.
23 'Life & Litters', p.27.
24 Robin Dudding to MS, 11 March 1960, ATL 91-047-16/05.
25 *Landfall 53*, Vol.14, No.1 (March 1960), pp. 87-89.
26 Bill Pearson,'A Mixed Performance', first published in *Comment*, autumn 1960, and later included in *Fretful Sleepers and Other Essays*, Bill Pearson, Auckland 1974, pp. 75-79.
27 W.H. Pearson to Paul Millar, 5 August 1999, quoted in *No Fretful Sleeper, a life of Bill Pearson*, Paul Millar, Auckland 2010, p.259.
28 Millar, p.258.
29 Millar, p.257.

30 See p.90.
31 From the article 'He deserves it; he fought hard' by David Ballantyne in *Zealandia*, November 1971, quoted in *After the Fireworks, A life of David Ballantyne*, Bryan Reid, Auckland 2004, p.172.
32 W.H. Pearson to Paul Millar, 6 December 2001, quoted in *No Fretful Sleeper, a life of Bill Pearson*, p.261.
33 *Coal Flat* was finally published by Paul's Book Arcade, Hamilton in 1963.
34 MS to W.H. Pearson, 17 October 1961, quoted in *No Fretful Sleeper, a life of Bill Pearson*, p.261.
35 MS to Kevin Ireland, 1 March 1960, ATL 91-047-17/08.
36 MS to Kevin Ireland, 2 November 1960, ATL MS-Papers-8044-055.
37 MS to Kevin Ireland, 28 April 1960, ATL MS-Papers-8044-055.
38 MS to Kevin Ireland, 6 May 1960, ATL MS-Papers-8044-055.
39 *From the Edge of the Sky*, p.55.
40 Livia Gollancz to MS, 4 September 1959, ATL 91-047-17/10.
41 International PEN, whose acronym at the time referred to poets, essayists and novelists, was founded in 1921 in London with John Galsworthy as its first president. Its aim was to promote friendship and intellectual co-operation among writers everywhere. The New Zealand PEN Centre was established in 1934. To become a member, an author had to have at least one book published and be nominated and seconded by existing members.
42 'Life & Litters', p.29.
43 Ian Cross interview, 6 February 2014.
44 *From the Edge of the Sky*, p.53.
45 *The Full Circle of the Travelling Cuckoo*, by Renato Amato, Christchurch 1967, Introduction by MS, p.16, footnote.
46 *Camping on the faultline*, A memoir, Marilyn Duckworth, Auckland 2000, pp.125-126.
47 *From the Edge of the Sky*, p.60.
48 'Life & Litters', p.28.
49 MS to Kevin Ireland, 2 November 1960, ATL MS-Papers-8044-055.
50 'Life & Litters', p.30.
51 *From the Edge of the Sky*, p.68.
52 Ibid, p.69.
53 Ibid, p.71.

CHAPTER 17
1 *From the Edge of the Sky*, p.72.
2 *Camping on the faultline*, p. 128.
3 *From the Edge of the Sky*, p.73.
4 *Camping on the faultline*, p. 130.
5 Ibid, p. 132.
6 Ibid, p.133.
7 *From the Edge of the Sky*, p.77.
8 *Camping on the faultline*, p. 141.
9 Marilyn Duckworth interview, 13 January 2014. This refers to the contrasting female characters in Puccini's opera *La Bohème*.
10 'Life & Litters', p.30.
11 Richmond Towers & Benson to MS, 25 May 1961, ATL 91-047-16/07.
12 MS, 'The Making of a Book', *Landfall 108*, Vol. 27, No. 4 (December 1973), p.279.
13 MS to Kevin Ireland, 8 December 1964, ATL MS-Papers-8044-055.
14 MS to Kevin Ireland, 27 July 1961, ATL MS-Papers-8044-055.
15 Kevin Ireland to MS, 13 July 1961, ATL MS-Papers-8044-054.

16 MS to Kevin Ireland, 2 November 1960, ATL MS-Papers-8044-055.
17 MS to Kevin Ireland, 19 July 1961, ATL 91-047-17/08.
18 Kevin Ireland to MS, 26 June 1961, MS-Papers-8044-054.
19 MS to Kevin Ireland, 3 July 1961, ATL MS-Papers-8044-055.
20 Maurice Gee to Lyndahl Gee, 16/23 November 1959, quoted in *Maurice Gee: Life and Work*, Rachel Barrowman, Wellington 2015, p.94.
21 *Maurice Gee: Life and Work*, Rachel Barrowman, Wellington 2015, p.94.
22 C.K. Stead to MS, 5 August 1960, ATL 91-047-16/05.
23 'For the hulk of the world's between', C.K. Stead, in *Distance Looks Our Way*, The Effects of Remoteness on New Zealand, Winter Lectures 1960, Auckland 1961, pp.93-94.
24 C.K. Stead to MS, 28 November 1961, ATL 91-047-16/05.
25 *Landfall 63*, Vol. 16, No. 3 (September 1962), pp. 215-32.
26 Frederick G. Vosburgh to MS, 4 December 1961, ATL 91-047-16/05.
27 Brian Brake to MS, 6 December 1961, ATL 91-047-16/06.
28 MS to Kevin Ireland, 19 May 1961, ATL MS-Papers-8044-055.
29 Ibid.
30 MS to Kevin Ireland, 6 June 1961, ATL MS-Papers-8044-055.
31 *From the Edge of the Sky*, p.78.
32 MS to Kevin Ireland, 22 November 1961, ATL 91-047-17/08.
33 MS to Kevin Ireland, 5 February 1962, ATL 91-047-17/08.
34 Fleur Adcock interview, 22 April 2014.
35 MS to Kevin Ireland, 2 April 1962, ATL 91-047-17/08.
36 Nigel Cook interview, 12 March 2015.
37 MS to Kevin Ireland, 22 November 1961, ATL 91-047-17/08.

CHAPTER 18
1 'Western Samoa — the Pacific's Newest Nation', *National Geographic*, Vol. 122, No.4, October 1962, p.578.
2 *From the Edge of the Sky*, p.87.
3 MS told Kevin Ireland that the article was 'textually predictable'. MS to Kevin Ireland, 19 July 1961, ATL 91-047-17/08.
4 *National Geographic*, October 1962, p.588.
5 Brian Brake to MS, 17 April 1962, ATL 91-047-16/06.
6 In the New Zealand issue the editor noted New Zealand readers' loyalty. In 1961, 'renewals reached an unprecedented 99 percent'.
7 As a bonus, the April 1962 issue also included 'Jet Boats Climb the Colorado River', a feature about New Zealand's Hamilton jet-boats.
8 'New Zealand: Gift of the Sea', *National Geographic*, Vol.121, No.4, April 1962, p.467.
9 Brian Brake to MS, 1 June 1962, ATL 91-047-16/06.
10 David Lawson to MS, 22 May 1962, ATL 91-047-16/02.
11 MS to Kevin Ireland, 19 July 1962, ATL 91-047-17/08.
12 'Life & Litters', p.32.
13 'The Making of a Book', *Landfall 108*, p.237.
14 'Life & Litters,' p. 31.
15 'Realist or Romantic?' by Cherry Hankin, in *Ending the Silences: Critical Essays on the Works of Maurice Shadbolt*, ed. Ralph J. Crane, Auckland 1995, p.45.
16 'Mythological Selves: Women in Shadbolt's Early Works', by Janet Wilson in *Ending the Silences*, p.59.
17 *Contemporary Authors Autobiography Series*, Vol. 3, Detroit c.1986, p.257.
18 Ibid.
19 *Figures in Light*, Selected Stories, Auckland, 1978, p.237.

20 Introduction to *Selected Stories, Maurice Shadbolt*, Selected and Introduced by Ralph Crane, Auckland, 1998, p.14.
21 An interesting anecdote here is that the high country homestead dinner scene contained a 'suspiciously familiar picture of our household customs' according to David McLeod of Grasmere Station where Maurice stayed with Brian Brake in 1960. Quote from *Down From the Tussock Ranges*, David McLeod, Christchurch 1980, p.155.
22 *Summer Fires and Winter Country*, p.33.
23 'Out of the Rut and into the Swamp: The Paradoxical Progress of Maurice Shadbolt', by Lawrence Jones, in *Ending the Silences*, p.14.
24 *Summer Fires and Winter Country*, p.224.
25 Ibid, p.49.
26 Ibid, p.145.
27 'In Storied Lands of Malaysia', by Maurice Shadbolt, *National Geographic*, Vol.124, No. 5, November 1963, p.734.
28 Ibid, p.782.
29 *From the Edge of the Sky*, p.93.
30 Gill Shadbolt to MS, 2 November 1962, ATL MS-Papers-8044-044.
31 Ibid.
32 Ibid.
33 *From the Edge of the Sky*, p.94.
34 Ibid.

CHAPTER 19
1 This was the only national prose award at the time and survives today as the NZ Society of Authors (PEN NZ) award for best first book of prose.
2 *From the Edge of the Sky*, p.98.
3 Brian Brake to MS, 1 February 1963, ATL 91-047-16/07.
4 Keith Holyoake to MS, 20 July 1962, ATL 91-047-16/06.
5 'Life & Litters', p.32.
6 Brian Brake to MS, 1 February 1963, ATL 91-047-16/07.
7 *New Zealand Gift of the Sea*, by Brian Brake and Maurice Shadbolt, Christchurch 1963, p.66.
8 Ibid, pp. 62-63.
9 David Lawson, pers. comm., 6 May 2017.
10 *From the Edge of the Sky*, p.96.
11 Dennis McEldowney, *Full of the Warm South*, Dunedin, 1983, p.21.
12 Ibid, p.43.
13 Ibid, p.34.
14 'Life & Litters', p.33.
15 *From the Edge of the Sky*, p.96.
16 *Full of the Warm South*, p.13.
17 *From the Edge of the Sky*, p. 96.
18 Ibid, p.99.
19 'Life & Litters', p.33.
20 *Full of the Warm South*, p.40.
21 Ibid.
22 'Signposts on the Way Towards a New Zealand Literature', *Otago Daily Times*, 24 August 1963, p.17.
23 'Towards a Character: Ned Livingstone', Otago University Students Association Review 1963, pp.6-18.
24 'Pig Island Letters (to Maurice Shadbolt)', in *Collected Poems, James K. Baxter*, edited by

J.E. Weir, Wellington 1979, p.276.
25 MS to James K. Baxter, 22 October 1966, ATL 91-047-16/08.
26 'Life & Litters', p.33.
27 *Evening Star*, 5 August 1963.
28 *Full of the Warm South*, p.38.
29 *NZ Listener*, 4 October 1963, p.18.
30 H. Winston Rhodes in *Landfall 68*, Vol.17, No.4 (December 1963), pp.389-391.
31 'Pig Island Letters (to Maurice Shadbolt)', p.279.
32 Maurice Gee to MS, 28 August 1963, ATL 91-047-16/03.
33 Kevin Ireland to MS, 7 March 1962, ATL 94-180-5/18.
34 MS to Kevin Ireland, 27 June 1963, ATL 91-047-17/08.
35 Maurice Gee to MS, 1 October 1963, ATL 91-047-16/07.
36 'Life & Litters', p.34.
37 David Lawson to MS, 11 September 1963, ATL 91-047-16/07.
38 *From the Edge of the Sky*, p.101.
39 Ibid, p.102.
40 'Life & Litters', p.35.
41 It seems likely his 'month' was broken by a short return to Dunedin.
42 Mountain View Lodge.
43 'Life & Litters', p.35.
44 *Full of the Warm South*, p.48.
45 *Among the Cinders*, London and Christchurch 1965, p.75.
46 Ibid, p.81.
47 Ibid, p.126.
48 About a decade before the term was coined.
49 *Among the Cinders*, p.301.
50 This section was excluded from later editions of the novel.
51 MS Journal, 26 March 1965, ATL MSX-7036.
52 *Full of the Warm South*, p.45. The Hon. Ralph Hanan was Minister of Justice. Two years earlier he had engineered abolition of the death penalty.
53 I had a copy of *Fanny Hill* removed from an incoming shipment by customs officials in 1964.
54 PEN NZ was essentially a literary and social club but, in the absence of anything resembling a writers' union, found it had to represent writers in all manner of political and commercial issues. There were regular calls for something along the lines of the British Society of Authors from about this time but nothing came about until the early 1990s, on my initiative, which led to the creation of the NZ Society of Authors (PEN NZ) Inc. in 1994.
55 Ian Cross to MS, 15 October 1963, ATL 91-047-16/07.
56 Kevin Ireland to MS, 22 October 1963, ATL 94-180-5/18.
57 MS to John Reece Cole, 11 November 1963, ATL 91-047-16/07.
58 *Full of the Warm South*, p.45.
59 *From the Edge of the Sky*, p.104.

CHAPTER 20
1 *From the Edge of the Sky*, p.104.
2 Ibid, p.105.
3 'Life & Litters', p.35.
4 Ibid.
5 *From the Edge of the Sky*, p.106.
6 MS to Brian Brake, 22 March 1964, ATL 91-047-16/08.

7   Michael Amato to Shadbolts, 27 March 1964, ATL 91-047-16/08.
8   'Life & Litters', p.36.
9   MS to Charles Brasch, 17 July 1964, ATL 91-047-16/08.
10 *The full circle of the travelling cuckoo*, Renato Amato, Christchurch 1967, p.135.
11 MS to Charles Brasch, 22 May 1964, ATL 91-047-16/08.
12 This building still stands on the corner of Titirangi Road and South Titirangi Road.
13 *Fire on the Clay*, The Pakeha Comes to West Auckland, Dick Scott, Auckland 1979, p.173 and p.194.
14 *From the Edge of the Sky*, p.111.
15 'Life & Litters', p.38.
16 *Dick Scott, A Radical Writer's Life*, Auckland 2004, p.207.
17 *From the Edge of the Sky*, p. 112.
18 'Life & Litters', p.38.
19 Ibid.
20 *From the Edge of the Sky*, p. 114.
21 Ibid, pp. 114-115.
22 'Life & Litters', pp.37-38.
23 'Patrick Hanly: a conversation with Hamish Keith', *Art New Zealand 14*, Summer 1979-80.
24 'The Making of a Book', *Landfall 108*, pp.280-281.
25 'Life & Litters', p.37.
26 *The Presence of Music*, London, 1967, p.19.
27 Ibid, p.16.
28 'The Making of a Book', *Landfall 108*, p.286.
29 Ibid.
30 *The Presence of Music*, p.58.
31 Ibid, p. 146.
32 Ibid, pp. 214 and 184.
33 'The Making of a Book', *Landfall 108*, p.288.

CHAPTER 21
1   Murray Gittos, *A kiwi takes a look: a pen-pusher visits the Soviet Union*, Auckland 1962.
2   *NZ Truth*, 9 June 1964, pp.3 and 5.
3   Ibid.
4   MS to O.E. Middleton, 14 September 1964, ATL 91-047-16/08.
5   MS 'Working Journal', 7 April 1965, ATL MSX-7036. MS began keeping this journal on 24 March 1965 on an irregular basis. Henceforth it will be referred to here as 'MS Journal'.
6   MS Journal, 29 March 1965.
7   MS Journal, 27 March 1965.
8   *Full of the Warm South*, p.86.
9   Gill Shadbolt to US agent Monica McCall, 6 May 1966, ATL 91-047-17/11.
10 MS to Kevin Ireland, 29 July 1965, ATL 91-047-17/08.
11 Tim Shadbolt, *Mayor of Two Cities*, Auckland 2008, p.19.
12 Tim Shadbolt interview, 22 January 2015.
13 'Life & Litters', p.39.
14 Ibid, p.40.
15 *From the Edge of the Sky*, p.117.
16 MS to *Auckland Star*, 25 May 1965, ATL 91-047-16/08.
17 MS to Keith Holyoake, 11 May 1965, ATL 91-047-16/08.
18 MS to *NZ Listener*, 3 January 1966. ATL 91-047, Box 18/1.

19 MS Journal, 26 March 1965.
20 Stephen Becker to Mike Bessie, 25 February 1965, ATL 91-047-17/17.
21 *Full of the Warm South*, p.104.
22 Charles Brasch journals, 17 April 1965, Hocken Collections MS-4084/041.
23 MS Journal, 28 June 1965.
24 MS Journal, 1 July 1965.
25 MS Journal, 8 August 1965.
26 Maurice Gee interview, 4 December 2014.
27 MS to Kevin Ireland, 29 July 1965, ATL 91-047-17/08.
28 See *Maurice Gee: Life and Work*, pp.151-2.
29 *From the Edge of the Sky*, p.121.
30 Maurice Gee interview, 4 December 2014.
31 Patrick White to MS, 8 July 1965, ATL 91-047-16/08.
32 *NZ Listener*, 9 July 1965, p.18.
33 *From the Edge of the Sky*, p.121.
34 MS to Dennis McEldowney, 22 October 1965, ATL 91-047-16/08.
35 'Growing Up in New Zealand', Orville Prescott, *New York Times*, 26 March 1965, ATL 91-047-14/07.
36 R.L.P. Jackson review in *Landfall 77*, Vol. 20, No.1 (March 1966), pp.95-97.
37 V.M. review in *Comment 7*, December 1965, pp.38-39.
38 C.K. Stead to MS, 13 December 1965, ATL 91-047-16/08.
39 MS to C.K. Stead, 22 December 1965, ATL 91-047-16/02.
40 MS to Dennis McEldowney, 22 October 1965, ATL 91-047-16/08.
41 Sean Shadbolt interview, 7 January 2014.
42 *From the Edge of the Sky*, p.121.
43 MS to Kevin Ireland, 29 July 1965, ATL 91-047-17/08.
44 'NZ's Grand Old Man', *The Bulletin*, 19 June 1965, pp 53-54.
45 MS to *NZ Listener*, 6 August 1965, p.10.
46 *NZ Listener*, 5 November 1965, p.18.
47 Eric McCormick to *NZ Listener*, 3 November 1965, ATL 91-047, Box 18/1.
48 MS to *NZ Listener*, 3 December 1965, p.11.
49 *From the Edge of the Sky*, p.122.
50 'Life & Litters', p.41.
51 Ian Cross to MS, 16 February 1966, ATL 91-047-16/08.
52 Sheena Amato to MS, 12 March 1966, ATL 91-047-16/08.
53 *From the Edge of the Sky*, p.123.
54 MS to C.K. Stead, 22 December 1965, ATL 91-047-16/02.
55 MS Journal, 26 December 1965.
56 Ibid.

CHAPTER 22
1 MS Journal, 17 February 1966.
2 MS to Kevin Ireland, 28 May 1967, ATL 91-047-17/08.
3 'Life & Litters', p.42.
4 The 100-plus black and white photographs were drawn from a number of sources but with a majority from National Publicity Studios.
5 Maurice also drew on the expertise of friends and area specialists such as Dick Scott (for the Wanganui-Manawatu section), Jim Henderson (Nelson) and Nigel Cook (architecture). John Stacpoole of the NZ Historic Places Trust guided him in his writing about historic sites.
6 MS Journal, 17 February 1966.

7 'New Zealand's Cook Islands — Paradise in Search of a future', *National Geographic*, Vol. 132, No.2, August 1967, p.203.
8 *From the Edge of the Sky*, p.129.
9 Ibid, pp.129-130.
10 The Cook Islands population and migrant situation remains much the same after more than 50 years. Almost three times as many people of Cook Islands descent live in New Zealand than in their home islands.
11 *From the Edge of the Sky*, p.131.
12 Albert Henry was premier of the Cook Islands for 12 years. In 1974 he received a knighthood for his services to the nation but this was forfeit in 1980 after he was convicted of electoral fraud in 1978. He died in 1981.
13 MS to editor *NZ Monthly Review*, 16 September 1966, ATL 91-047-16/08.
14 MS to editor *NZ Monthly Review*, 29 August 1966, ATL 91-047-16/08.
15 MS to Kevin Ireland, 28 May 1967, ATL 91-047-17/08.
16 Ibid.
17 'Life & Litters', p.42.
18 'Philistia down-under', Christopher Wordsworth, *Guardian* 10 March 1967, p.7. ATL 91-047-14/08.
19 'Stay At Home', Anon. (Dan Davin), *Times Literary Supplement*, 23 March 1967, p.235. ATL 91-047-14/08. New Zealand author Davin was academic publisher for Oxford University Press.
20 'The Road Forks', *NZ Listener*, 30 June 1967, pp.20-1.
21 *From the Edge of the Sky*, p.153.
22 MS Journal, 14 October 1967.
23 MS to Kevin Ireland, 6 October 1967. ATL 91-047-17/08.
24 'Life & Litters', p.43.
25 MS Journal, 14 October 1967.
26 Sheena Amato to MS, 12 October 1967, ATL 91-047-16/10.
27 MS Journal, 21 October 1967.
28 *From the Edge of the Sky*, pp.154-156.

CHAPTER 23
1 MS to Julia Shadbolt, 25 March 1968, ATL 91-047-16/10.
2 *From the Edge of the Sky*, p.156.
3 Ibid, p.145.
4 George Wilder to 'Grace', 13 September 1968, ATL 91-047-16/10.
5 *From the Edge of the Sky*, p.148.
6 George Wilder to MS, August 1967, ATL 91-047-16/10.
7 *From the Edge of the Sky*, p.148.
8 Ibid, p.149.
9 The noted defence lawyer and penal reformer who was appointed Queen's Counsel in 1987 and knighted shortly before his death in 2015 aged 80.
10 MS Journal, 23 June 1968.
11 Ron Jorgensen to MS, 29 August 1968, ATL 91-047-16/10.
12 *From the Edge of the Sky*, p.151.
13 MS to Michael Smither, 3 July 1969, Michael Smither Papers.
14 MS to Arnold Wall, 29 July 1969, ATL 91-047-16/11.
15 *From the Edge of the Sky*, p.172.

CHAPTER 24
1 MS Journal, 23 June 1968.

2   Charles Brasch Journal, 21 October 1968, Hocken Collections, MS-4084/044
3   'Maurice Shadbolt Interviewed', *The New Zealander*, 30 July 1968, pp.17-20.
4   'I Believe Writers Should Speak out', Alexander Guyan, *Sunday News*, 16 May 1965, pp.16-17.
5   *NZ Women's Weekly*, Sue Vaassen, 23 October 1967, pp. 35-36.
6   'In My View', *NZ Listener*, 26 July 1968, p.13.
7   MS to Michael Smither, 15 June 1968, Michael Smither Papers.
8   MS Journal, 23 June 1968.
9   Ibid.
10 *This Summer's Dolphin*, p.4.
11 Charles Brasch Journal, 24 March 1971, Hocken Collections, MS-4084/047
12 'Dolphins — Man's Kindliest Friends', Tony Reid, *NZ Weekly News*, 3 February 1969, p.5.
13 *This Summer's Dolphin*, p.166.
14 Michael Smither to Philip Temple, 6 February 2014.
15 *From the Edge of the Sky*, p.160.
16 'Dolphins — Man's Kindliest Friends', p.3.
17 MS to Michael Smither, 15 June 1968, Michael Smither Papers.
18 Michael Smither to MS, 9 June 1968, ATL 91-047-16/10.
19 MS to Michael Smither, 2 December 1968, Michael Smither Papers.
20 MS to Michael Smither, 2 December 1968, Michael Smither Papers.
21 Michael Smither interview, 20 December 2013.
22 *From the Edge of the Sky*, p.163.
23 Ibid.

CHAPTER 25
1   MS to Michael Smither, 12 December 1968, Michael Smither Papers.
2   *From the Edge of the Sky*, p.157.
3   MS Journal, 13 October 1968.
4   *From the Edge of the Sky*, p.161.
5   Ibid.
6   MS Journal, 11 February 1969.
7   *From the Edge of the Sky*, p.165.
8   MS to Michael Smither, 17 March 1969, Michael Smither Papers.
9   *From the Edge of the Sky*, p.165.
10 See *Love & Legend*, Maurice Shadbolt, Auckland 1976, pp.155-164 for the *Reader's Digest* story in book form.
11 *From the Edge of the Sky*, p.165.
12 Pineamine Taiapa to MS, 22 May 1969, ATL 91-047-16/12.
13 'In My View', *NZ Listener*, 15 August 1969, p.15.
14 Pineamine Taiapa to MS, 27 August 1969, ATL 91-047-16/12.
15 Sean Shadbolt interview, 7 January 2014.
16 MS to Michael Smither, 12 May 1969, Michael Smither papers.
17 *From the Edge of the Sky*, p.166. Later, Maurice enlarged this to 'hearing Brendan weep over the phone' (MS to Gill 28 February 1970, ATL MS-Papers-8044-013). Brendan does not now recall the phone call (pers. comm., 1 September 2017).
18 Sean Shadbolt interview, 7 January 2014.
19 Sean Shadbolt, pers. comm., 31 August 2017.
20 MS to Michael Smither, 1 June 1969, Michael Smither papers.
21 Sean Shadbolt interview, 7 January 2014.
22 MS to Mrs H.R. Heming, 15 November 1969, ATL MS-Papers-8044-072.

23 *From the Edge of the Sky*, p.168.
24 MS to Michael Smither, 1 June 1969, Michael Smither papers.
25 *From the Edge of the Sky*, p.167.
26 'Passion at the bedside', Vernon Scannell, *Sunday Times*, 25 May 1969, p.61, ATL 91-047-14/09.
27 'Not Today', Anon. (Dan Davin), *Times Literary Supplement*, 19 June 1969, p.667. ATL 91-047-14/09.
28 Patrick White to MS, 1 February 1970, ATL 91-047-16/02.
29 *New York Times Book Review*, 22 June 1969, ATL 91-047-14/09.
30 'Animal Catalyst', Conrad Bollinger, *NZ Listener*, 1 August 1969, p.25.
31 *Landfall 92*, Vol. 23, No. 4 (December 1969), pp.405-407.
32 MS to Michael Smither, 4 August 1969, Michael Smither papers.

CHAPTER 26
1 *NZ Listener*, 15 November 1968, p.18.
2 *Camping on the Faultline*, p.166.
3 Letter MS to Marilyn Duckworth, quoted in *Camping on the Faultline*, p.171.
4 *Camping on the Faultline*, p.171.
5 Letter MS to Marilyn Duckworth, quoted in *Camping on the Faultline*, pp.171-172.
6 MS to Michael Smither, 3 July 1969, Michael Smither papers.
7 Ibid.
8 MS to Michael Smither, 1 June 1969, Michael Smither papers.
9 MS to Albert Wendt, 23 September 1969, ATL 91-047-16/11.
10 NZ On Screen, Barbara Magner biography, nzonscreen.com
11 *From the Edge of the Sky*, p.167.
12 *Camping on the Faultline*, p.180.
13 Ibid.
14 Quoted in *Camping on the Faultline*, p.183.
15 Ibid, p.184.
16 Quoted ibid, p.184.
17 Beverly Richards to MS, 7 October 1969, ATL 91-047-16/11.
18 *Camping on the Faultline*, p.188.
19 MS Journal, 20 December 1969.
20 MS Journal, 14 March 1970.
21 Janet Wilson, pers. comm., 18 September 2017.
22 *Camping on the Faultline*, pp.186-187.
23 Barbara Magner to MS, 11 January 1970, ATL 91-047-16/11.
24 Gill Shadbolt to Shirley Smith, 19 February 1970, MS-Papers-8044-013.
25 Shirley Smith to MS, 23 February 1970, MS-Papers-8044-013.
26 MS to Gill Shadbolt, 28 February 1970, ATL MS-Papers-8044-013.
27 *Camping on the Faultline*, p.188.
28 Phillip Wilson to MS, 1 April 1970, ATL 91-047-16/11.
29 MS to Kevin Ireland, 24 May 1970, ATL MS-Papers-8044-056.
30 Patrick White to MS, 1 February 1970, ATL 91-047-16/02.
31 Maurice had a chronic habit of dropping the indefinite article. For example, in the first pages of both *Dolphin*, where hills 'echoed with axe', and in *Dragon* where the wind 'left gleam everywhere'.
32 Richard Sharp to MS, 30 June 1970, ATL 91-047-17/09.
33 *Such Absolute Beginners*, Ian Cross, Auckland 2007, p.102.
34 MS to Kevin Ireland, 24 May 1970, ATL MS-Papers-8044-056.
35 Ibid.

36 *From the Edge of the Sky*, p.169. Note: Can confirm this from personal attendance.
37 Simon Michael Bessie to MS, 17 June 1970, ATL 91-047-17/17.
38 The German edition was titled *Und er nahm mich bei der Hand* ('And he took me by the hand').
39 MS to Ian Cross, 22 April 1970, ATL 90-047-17/16.
40 *From the Edge of the Sky*, p.170.
41 MS to Michael Earl, Cassell NZ, 1 April 1970, ATL 91-047-17/09.
42 MS to Michael Smither, 20 July 1970, Michael Smither papers.
43 ATL MS-Papers-8044-175.
44 MS to Michael Smither, 2 November 1970, Michael Smither papers.
45 Gill Shadbolt to Shirley Smith, late July 1970, ATL MS-Papers-8044-013.
46 MS to Gill Shadbolt, 22 July 1970, ATL MS-Papers-8044-013.
47 Frank Shadbolt to Gill Shadbolt, 18 July 1970, ATL MS-Papers-8044-013.
48 Vi Shadbolt to Gill Shadbolt, 18 July 1970, ATL MS-Papers-8044-013.
49 Shirley Smith to MS, 25 August 1970, ATL MS-Papers-8044-013.
50 MS to Shirley Smith, 29 August 1970, ATL MS-Papers-8044-013.
51 Gill Shadbolt to Shirley Smith, 13 September 1970, ATL MS-Papers-8044-013.
52 Ibid.
53 MS to Michael Smither, 2 November 1970, Michael Smither papers.
54 *From the Edge of the Sky*, p.175.
55 'Letter to Jerusalem (2)', Sam Hunt, December 1970, ATL MS-Papers-8044-046.

CHAPTER 27
1   MS to Frank Devine, 20 January 1971, ATL 91-047-18/5.
2   Frank Devine to MS, 16 December 1970, ATL 91-047-18/5.
3   Ibid.
4   Ibid.
5   Ibid.
6   MS to Frank Devine, 20 January 1971.
7   *Affairs Magazine*, February 1971, p.20.
8   Ibid, p.21.
9   'Literature: Australia and New Zealand' manuscript for *Encyclopaedia Britannica*, 24 August 1971, ATL 91-047-16/1ll.
10 'Life & Litters', p.47.
11 ATL MS-Papers-8044-175.
12 *Strangers and Journeys*, p.627.
13 *Paris Review* interview 1958.
14 MS to Kevin Ireland, 26 August 1971, ATL MS-Papers-8044-056.
15 MS to Stephen Becker, 1 October 1971, ATL 91-047-16/13.
16 MS Journal, 10 October 1971.
17 MS Journal, 10 November 1971.
18 MS Journal, 23 July 1971.
19 Gill Shadbolt to Shirley Smith, 1 June 1971, ATL MS-Papers-8044-017.
20 MS Journal, 9 May 1971.
21 MS Journal, 27 August 1971.
22 'Accusing Dreams', Christopher Wordsworth, *Guardian*, 25 March 1971, p.8.
23 'Of war and friendship', *Auckland Star*, 12 June 1971, p.20.
24 *NZ Listener*, 16 August 1971, pp. 48-49.
25 MS to James Bertram, 31 August 1971, ATL 91-047-16/13.
26 James Bertram to MS, 4 September 1971, ATL 91-047-16/13.
27 Correspondence, *Landfall 100*, Vol. 25, No.4 (December 1971), pp. 469-473.

28   Correspondence, *Landfall 101*, Vol.26, No.1 (March 1972), pp. 97-98.
29   MS Journal, 16 December 1971.
30   MS Journal, 3 August 1971.
31   MS Journal, 16 December 1971.
32   MS Journal, 27 December 1971.
33   MS to Frank Devine, 26 November 1971, ATL 91-047-18/5.
34   MS to Brian Brake, 26 November 1971, ATL 91-047-16/13.
35   MS to Michael Smither, 28 October 1971, Michael Smither papers.
36   *From the Edge of the Sky*, pp.176-177.
37   MS Journal, 16 April 1972.
38   MS Journal, 17 April 1972.
39   MS Journal, 31 January 1972.
40   MS Journal, 10 May 1972.
41   MS Journal, 9 January 1972.
42   MS Journal, 2 July 1972.
43   MS to Michael Smither, 16 April 1972, Michael Smither papers.
44   MS to Michael Smither, 20 April 1972, Michael Smither papers. *Note: This painting was eventually used for the jacket of the author's first novel,* The Explorer *(1975), also published by Hodder & Stoughton.*
45   MS to Michael Smither, 19 May 1972, Michael Smither papers.
46   MS Journal, 6 June 1972.

CHAPTER 28
1   *From the Edge of the Sky*, p.179.
2   MS Journal, 10 July 1972.
3   'Tamure', *Boy Roel: Voyage to Nowhere*, Wellington 1972, p.115.
4   Ibid, pp.113-126.
5   Ibid, p.115.
6   Ibid, p.116.
7   Ibid, p.119.
8   Ibid, p.121.
9   Ibid.
10   Sinclair had briefly been the Labour member for Eden in 1969 before late postal votes overturned his election result.
11   MS Journal, 30 August 1972.
12   *Camping on the faultline*, p.218.
13   MS Journal, 6 September 1972.
14   MS to author, pers.comm., 1974.
15   MS to Kevin Ireland, 1 November 1972, ATL 91-047-16/12.
16   Ibid.
17   *James K. Baxter 1926-1972, A Memorial Volume*, Wellington 1972, p.33.
18   MS to Kevin Ireland, 1 November 1972, ATL 91-047-16/12.
19   *James K. Baxter 1926-1972, A Memorial Volume*, p.34.
20   *Auckland Star*, 9 December 1972, p.18.
21   'The Outback and beyond', Norman Shrapnel, *Guardian*, 23 November 1972, p.17.
22   'New Zealand primitive', Russell Davies, *Observer*, 5 November 1972, p.39.
23   'Up under', Anon. (Dan Davin), *Times Literary Supplement*, 15 December 1972, p. 1521.
24   'This is how it was here', David Ballantyne, *Auckland Star*, 9 December 1972, p. 18.
25   'Fathers and sons', James Bertram, *New Zealand Listener*, 11 December 1972, p.50.
26   Both David Hall and John Reid, Auckland University Professor of English, had died in recent times.

27 MS to James Bertram, 4 December 1972, ATL 91-047-16/12.
28 'Shadbolt At last!', Conrad Bollinger, *Sunday Times*, 14 January 1973, p.34.
29 *Landfall 106*, Vol. 27, No. 2 (June 1973), pp.167-71.
30 Volkerling's 1975 PhD thesis topic was 'Images of society in New Zealand writing — an examination of the social concerns of New Zealand writers 1960-1970'. He was director of the QEII Arts Council from 1977 to 1988.
31 'Clearing the ground', Michael Volkerling, *Islands 2*, Spring 1973, pp.319-325.
32 Maurice Gee interview, 4 December 2014.
33 MS Journal, 23 February 1973.

POSTSCRIPT
1 From a 1968 review of Carlos Baker's biography of Ernest Hemingway

INDEX

P1 indicates photographs in the first plates section between pages 112 and 113.
P2 indicates photographs in the second plates section between pages 240 and 241.

Abdul Rahman, Tunku 176
Aberdeen 124–127
Adcock, Fleur 10, 151, 154, 158, 166, 167, 179–180
Adcock, Irene 245
Affairs Magazine 260–261
A.H. & A.W. Reed 230
Ahipara 148–149, 159, 195, 206, 232, 239
All Black tour of South Africa, 1960 135
All-China League of Democratic Youth 96
Allard, Bill 219–220
Alpers, Antony 157
Amato, Renato (Michael) 157, 188–189, 194, 196–197, 237, 265, **P2**
  The Full Circle of the Travelling Cuckoo 197, 216–217, 223, 251, 265
  Maurice's novel, *An Ear of the Dragon* 237, 251–252, 253, 254, 265–267
Amato, Sheena (née McAdam) 157, 188, 194, 196, 197, 216–217, 223–224, 251–252, 265
Among the Cinders (Shadbolt) 11, 188–192, 193, 200, 209–210, 211–213, 214, 232, 242, 253–254, 262, 267
ANZUS 208, 227
Armstrong, Bridget 9-11, 12
Armstrong-Jones, Anthony 151
Arrowtown 151
Arvidson, K.O. 266
Ashton-Warner, Sylvia 159, 233
  Spinster 131, 159
Atheneum, New York 156, 200, 210, 253, 263
Atwool, Tony 200
Auckland 41, 147, 194, 223
  see also Glen Eden, Auckland; Green Bay, Auckland; Oratia, West Auckland; Takapuna, Auckland; Titirangi, Auckland
  Mount Eden Prison 24, 227
  Queen Street riots 18–19, 77, 263
Auckland Education Board 48
Auckland Returned Services Association 208
Auckland Star 208, 227, 277
Auckland University
  English Department 206
  Winter Lectures, 1960 164
  Auckland University College 47, 52
  Labour Club 47
  Socialist Club 49–50, 51
  Students Association 49
Auckland University Press 199
Auckland–Wellington literary disputes 92
Auden, W.H. 127
Australia
  see also Sydney
  Australian and New Zealand literature 100, 261
Australian Communist Party 128, 137

Avondale College 42–45, 47, 51

Babel, Isaac 100
Bacon, Francis 136
Bailey, Roger 253
Ballantyne, David 122, 128, 135, 142, 155, 172, 253, 265, 267, 277
Banks Peninsula 11, 19–22, 24, 25, 53
Barnett, John 69
Barry Lett Gallery 234
Basset Road machine-gun murders 228, 263
Bassett, Michael 226
Baxter, Jacquie 88, 125, 149, 150, 157, 276
Baxter, James K. 71, 75, 76, 87–88, 125, 166, 182, 227, 232, 277, **P1**
   Catholicism and move to Jerusalem (Hiruharama) 241, 247, 276
   death and tangi 275–276
   drop-in centre for drug addicts 241
   friendship with Maurice 84–85, 89, 149, 150, 155, 157, 185–186, 241
   'Homage to Lost Friends' 133, 141, 276
   letter to Listener about Pearson's review of The New Zealanders 154, 155
   Pig Island Letters 185–186, 187
   poem in anticipation of birth of Maurice and Gill's first child 156, 158
   poem written by Sam Hunt 257–258
   praise for The New Zealanders 141–142, 143
   representation in Among the Cinders 191
   The Wide Open Cage 158
Bay of Islands 224–225, 269
Becker, Stephen 209, 263
Bell, Brian 86
Bertram, James 265–266, 277-278
Bessie, Simon (Mike) 156, 210, 253
Biaggini, E.G., The Reading and Writing of English 43
Binney, Don 9
Bistritsa Palace, Bulgaria 108–109, 110, 117, **P1**
Bland, Peter 87, 166
Bojilova, Eugenia (Jenny) 108, 109, 110–111, 115, 117, 119–121, 123, 125, 126, 139, 140, **P1**
Bollinger, Conrad 53, 60, 86, 122, 135, 142, 177, 242, 278, **P1**
Grog's Own Country 53
A Book of New Zealand Verse (Curnow, ed.) 44
The Bookman 141, 143
Borneo **P2**
Botev, Hristo 140
Bowen, Godfrey 150
Bowen, Ivan 150
Boyd, John 135
Brake, Brian 67, 95–96, 114, 149, 150–151, 155–156, 165–166, 180, 181, 268, **P2**
   'Monsoon' 165, 171
   New Zealand: Gift of the Sea (book) 180–182, 188, 194, 196, 200, 219, 267–268
   'New Zealand: Gift of the Sea' (National Geographic article) 170–171
Brasch, Charles 71, 91–92, 129, 182, 183, 201, **P1**
   comments on, and reviews of, Maurice's writing 85, 130, 132, 134, 152, 164, 186, 209–210, 231, 233–234
   homosexuality 215
   Landfall editorship 76, 85, 90, 113–114, 134, 165, 174, 175, 184, 222
   mentoring of Maurice 85, 130, 134, 152
   relationship with Maurice 115, 152, 156–157, 165, 184, 197
Buckland Literary Award 243
Bulgaria 105–109, 110–111, 114, 117, 118, 119, 121, 137, 138, 139
   writers 105, 106, 108, 109
The Bulletin 214
Burgess, Anthony 253, 254
Burnett, Fassett 269
Burns Fellowship see Robert Burns Fellowship

Campaign for Christian Order 34, 35
Campbell, Alistair 91–92, 148, 151, 160, 166, 276
Canton (Guangzhou) 96–97, 111, **P1**
Cape Reinga 149, 159
Capricorn Press 76, 118
Caro, Anthony 136
Cartier-Bresson, Henri 67, 96, 150
Caselberg, John 180

Cassell Publishers, Auckland and London 218, 233, 252, 254
Caxton Press 76
censorship 45, 49, 76, 192–193, 232
Chapman, Bob 157
Cheever, John, *The Brigadier and the Golf Widow* 215
Chesworth, Dennis 132, 135
Child magazine 221–222, 236
China 96–98, 165, 271
Chukovsky, Korney 101, 103
CIA, use of *Dr Zhivago* as anti-Soviet propaganda 128
Cockburn, Claud 127
Cockburn, Jean (Jean Ross) 127, 131
Cole, John Reece 167, 192, 214
Comment 153–154, 212–213
communism 62–63, 64, 97, 105, 127–128, 147, 271
Communist Party 18, 27, 28, 31, 33, 34, 45, 47, 49, 51, 52, 53–54, 66, 93, 94, 163, 199
   The People's Voice 62, 198–199, 204
compulsory military training (CMT) 45, 53
Conrad, Joseph 149, 178
Contemporary Authors Autobiography series 261
Cook, Julie 93, 157, 160, 163, 167, 247, 248
Cook, Nigel 93, 157, 160, 163, 167, 211, 218, 247
Cook Islands 218, 219–221, 246
Copland, Ray 153, 242
Coromandel 211
Cottier, Jim 273, **P2**
Couper, Alistair 124
Cowley, Joy, *The Moth* 254
Craccum 49–50, 66
Cross, Brian 87, 88
Cross, Ian 157, 158, 160, 162, 178, 179, 191, 192, 196–197, 208–209, 213, 214, 232, 245, 254, 276, **P2**
   The God Boy 131, 157, 175, 190, 211
Cross, Tui 178, 213, 245
Crump, Barry 166–167, 179, 184, 185, 186, 209, 212, 213, 254
   A Good Keen Man 166
   Hang on a Minute Mate 167, 211
Curnow, Allen 71, 76, 92, 164, 180, 182, 192

A Book of New Zealand Verse (editor) 44

Dashwood, Julian 220
Davin, Dan 75, 143
Davin, Winifred 143
Delaney, Shelagh 141
   A Taste of Honey 141
Depression, 1930s 18–19, 25, 31, 44, 45, 61, 89, 131
Devine, Frank 259–260, 267, 268
Diegel, Adolf 183, 186, 189
Dissonant Voices in Soviet Literature 215
Distance Looks Our Way 164
Doyle, Charles (Mike) 75, 76, 91, 206, 209, 227, 276
Dryden, Gordon 53, 62, 66, 88, 263, **P1**
Duckworth, Marilyn 158, 166, 246, 275, **P2**
   'Among Strangers' 244
   A Barbarous Tongue 161
   A Gap in the Spectrum 158
   Over the Fence Is Out 244
   relationship with Maurice 160–162, 244–245, 247–249, 250
Dudding, Robin 80–81, 147–148, 152, 153, 214, 222
Duff, Alan, *Once Were Warriors* 176
Duggan, Eileen 44
Duggan, Maurice 74, 75, 79–80, 86, 87, 127, 151–152, 154, 162, 167, 179, 197, **P2**
   Immanuel's Land 90, 154
Dulles, John Foster 103
Dunedin 178, 179–180, 182–187, 189
Duno, Pedro 115, 116, 117
Duvauchelle, Banks Peninsula 20–21, 22, 24, 25, 53, 193, **P2**

An Ear of the Dragon (Shadbolt) 237, 251–252, 253, 254, 265–267
Earl, Michael 233
Ehrenburg, Ilya 100–101, 114
   The Thaw 100
Elizabeth II, Queen 61, 182
Encyclopaedia Britannica 261
England 110–122, 123–124, 126, 128–129, 132, 135–136
Evening Post 69, 88, 90, 124
Eyre & Spottiswood 163, 172, 200, 210

Fairburn, A.R.D. 71, 182
Faulkner, William 59, 161
Federation of Labour 28
Feeney, John 67, 113–114, 135
    'John Feeney and the National Film Unit' (Shadbolt article) 113–115
Feltex national television awards 249
Feltrinelli 156
Fergusson, Sir Bernard 188
Fernfire magazine 204
Finlay, Martyn 267, 274
Finlayson, Roderick 173
    Tidal Creek 211
Fischer Verlag 156
Fisher, Gordon 182
Flynn, Jim 226
Forlong, Michael 114
Forster, E.M. 214
Frame, Janet 44, 74, 76, 123, 214, 261
    Daughter Buffalo 278
    Owls do Cry 74, 131, 278
France, nuclear testing in Pacific 271–275
Frances Hodgkins Fellowship 254
Fraser, Peter 45
Freeman, Carl 45, 47, 49, 50, 59, 63, 101, 163, 253, **P1**
French Farm, Banks Peninsula 19–20
Freyberg, Bernard 46

Gallery One, London 136, 163
Garrett, John **P1**
Gee, Lyndahl 89
Gee, Maurice (Moss) 47, 86, 163, 164, 166, 187–188, 197, 204
    The Big Season 164, 165, 184, 187
    Burns Fellowship 188
    career in writing 93
    friendship with Maurice Shadbolt 43, 50–51, 77, 88–90, 91, 92, 117, 118, 157, 163, 164, 187, 211, 231, **P1**
    Going West 51
Gee, Nigel 211
Georgia 103–104, 110
Gittos, Murray 204–205
Glen Eden, Auckland 18–19, 28, 32, 33, 34, 60, 87, 118, **P1**
Glover, Denis 71, 76, 118, 158–159, 276
Glover, Kura 158
Golden Dawn gold mine, Waikino 18, 27, 148
Golden Dragon café, Auckland 48

Gollancz, Livia 156
Gollancz, Victor 127, 130, 132–133, 134, 137, 141, 142, 149, 153, 157, 162, 163, 172
Gordon, Ian **P1**
Gotz, Sir Leon **P1**
Green Bay, Auckland 24–25, 33, 70
Greenpeace 271–272, 274, 275
Griffiths, John 186
Guardian 12, 222, 265, 277

Haas, Ernst 96
Hall, David 143, 152, 186, 222, 277
Hamilton 89, 161, 162
    1981 Springbok tour protest 37
Hamilton, Bill 68, 268
Hamilton, Ian, hostile review of *The New Zealanders* 148, 152–153, 214
Hamon, Rei 268
Hanly, Gil 9, 123, 177, 201, 264, **P2**
Hanly, Pat 9, 123, 177, 201, 264, **P2**
    'Figures in Light' 201
Harker, Jack 273, **P2**
Harris, James 68
Hass, Ian 226
Hawera 55–56, 59, 60, 63, 65, 77, 89, **P1**
Haytov, Nikolai 139
Heming, Gillian *see* Shadbolt, Gillian Eve Muriel (Gill, née Heming)
Heming, Minnie (Bunty, née Weymouth) 57–58, 63, 66, 95, 178, 183, 240, **P2**
Heming, Ray 56–58
Heming, Robin (Rob) 57–58, 95
Hemingway, Ernest 44, 59, 73, 76, 86, 232, 263
    For Whom the Bell Tolls 36
    'Hills Like White Elephants' 120, 121
    The Sun Also Rises 122
Henry, Albert 220
Hillary, Sir Edmund 61, 154, 227
Hilliard, Noel 52–53, 86, 154
Hockney, David 136
Hodder & Stoughton 263
Hodgkins, Frances 123, 199
Hokianga 82–83, 87, 122, 148, 176
    see also Opononi
Holcroft M.H. 'Monte' 72, 73, 75, 76, 85, 118, 192, 196, **P1**
    feud with Frank Sargeson 73–74, 80
Holland, Sidney 45, 47, 48–49

Holyoake, Keith 169–170, 180–181, 188, 208, 227, 271
Home Guard, Te Kuiti 35
'Home Guard Assistance Corps' 35
homosexuality 91, 163, 174, 215
Hong Kong 95, 96
Howard Morrison Quartet, 'George, the Wild(er) New Zealand Boy' 227
Howes, 'Bully' 36
Hubert Church Memorial Prize for Prose 179
Hungary 93–94, 97, 120, 205
Hunt, Sam 257–258
Hutchinson, Maurice 43

Ibiza 121, 122–123, 124, 202
Ihimaera, Witi, *Pounamu, Pounamu* 278
Illingworth, Michael 163, 263
Indecent Publications Act 1963 192–193
International Union of Students 99
Ireland, Kevin 12, 61, 63, 76, 132, 276, **P1**
  anthology of new New Zealand writing 86–87, 254
  Bulgaria, and marriage to Donna Marinova 137, 138, 139–140, 141, 163
  comments on Maurice's work and ambitions 54, 70–71, 74, 80, 85, 86, 90, 136
  and Crump 166
  and Dudding 147
  Face to Face 166, 167
  friendship with Maurice 12, 51–52, 59, 69, 79, 87, 88, 93, 155
  and Gee 163, 187–188
  letters to and from Maurice 110, 136, 143, 155, 156, 163, 164, 172, 192, 206, 213–214, 221, 223, 232, 251, 253, 276
  in London 135–136, 163
  and Sargeson 80, 90
Isbey, Eddie 274
Isherwood, Christopher 127
  Goodbye to Berlin 127
Islands 81, 261, 278

James, Henry 134
Jenkins, Elizabeth 141
Johnson, Louis 75, 76, 118, 157, 196, 209, 214, 276
Johnson, Lyndon B. 208, 226

Jorgensen, Ron 228–229, 250, 263
Joseph, M.K. 154
Jowsey, Kevin *see* Ireland, Kevin
Joyce, James
  The Dubliners 127
  Ulysses (film) 193

Kasmin, John (Kas) 69–70, 86, 126, 136, 163, 263
Katherine Mansfield Short Story Award 174, 188, 189, 223
'Kavieng Massacre' 58
Kearon, Joseph (Joe, jnr) 18–19, 26, 34, 45, 59, 118, 173, 198, **P1, P2**
  death and estate 224, 226
  importance to Maurice 53–54, 60–62, 65, 147, 159, 161, 194, 224
  politics 18, 34, 53–54, 62, 97, 101, 102, 107
  portrayal in Maurice's writing 73, 131
  retirement 194
  visit to Dunedin, Arrowtown and Queenstown 184, **P2**
Kearon, Joseph (snr, 'Arklow Joe') 18, 26–27, 34, **P1**
Kearon, Louisa (née Morris) 18, 26–27, 33, 60, **P1**
Kearon family 60
KGB, Moscow 102–103, 128
King Country 30–31, 42, 210, 262
  see also Te Kuiti
Kirk, Norman 271, 274
Koea, George 55, 59
Kooning, Willem de 122
Korean War 70
Kruschev, Nikita 93–94, 99, 100, 102, 103, 128

Labour governments 27, 28, 45, 66, 274
Labour Party 27, 28, 36, 49, 271
  Southern Cross newspaper 53
Landfall 44, 70, 72, 76, 77, 80–81, 85, 86, 91, 113–115, 130, 134, 164, 165, 174, 180, 184, 277
  Arvidson's letter about *The Ear of the Dragon* 266
  'China, Russia, Bulgaria. A Journey' (Shadbolt article) 90, 91
  Maurice's resentment and boycott 165, 197, 222
  prose competition 90, 91, 180

review of *Among the Cinders* 212
review of *Strangers and Journeys* 278
review of *Summer Fires and Winter Country* 186–187
review of *The Ear of the Dragon* 265–266
review of *The New Zealanders* 152, 153
review of *This Summer's Dolphin* 242
short story by Amato, and obituaries 197
Lascaris, Manoly 178
Lasenby, Jack 276
Lawson, David 11, 155, 171–172, 180, 181, 182, 186, 188, 195-196, 200, 210, 216
Lee, John A., *Children of the Poor* 184
Lee-Johnson, Elizabeth 148, 211
Lee-Johnson, Eric 82–83, 122, 148, 175, 211, **P1**
Lee Kuan Yew 177
Leeteg, Edgar 211
Left Book Club 32, 33, 127
Levin, Martin 242
Listener *see* New Zealand Listener
Literary Fund 44, 72, 76, 118, 196, 253, **P1**
  Scholarship in Letters 90, 118, 149, 161, 163
literature, New Zealand *see* poetry, New Zealand; writing, New Zealand
The Little Red Schoolbook 193, 226
Little River, Banks Peninsula 21–22
Littlewood, Joan 135
London, Jack 27, 76
  The Scab 49
Lowry, Bob 87, 93
Lusk, Doris 233

MacLeod, Alexander 233
Macmillan, Harold 113
Magner, Barbara 183, 246–247, 248, 249, 250, 253, 255, 256, 257, 264, 267, 269, 270, 272, 273, 275, 276–277, **P2**
Magnum photo agency 67, 96
Malaysia 172, 176–177, 182
Maleter, Pal 120
Mandelstam, Osip 100
Mansfield, Katherine 71, 138, 144, 157, 214
Mao Tse-Tung 97

Maori
  exclusion from 1960 All Black tour of South Africa 135
  Far North 148–149
  Maori–pakeha relationships 133–134, 175–176
  Maurice's *National Geographic* feature 237–238, 239, 253
  Maurice's sympathies for disadvantaged place in society 232–233
  Mitcalfe's translation of waiata and karakia 148–149
  portrayal in 'End of Season' 86
  portrayal in *New Zealand: Gift of the Sea* 181
  portrayal in *Summer Fires and Winter Country* stories 173, 174, 175
  Sargeson writes 'almost not at all about Maoris' 214
  Sir Bernard Fergusson's comments 188
Marinova, Donna 139, 141, 163
Markish, David 102
Markish, Esther 101–102, 110
  The Long Return 102
Markish, Peretz 101–102
Marsh, Ngaio 268
Marshak, Samuil 101, **P1**
Marshall, Jack 271
Martha Mine, Waihi 27–28
Martin, 'Froggy' 43
Mason, R.A.K. (Ron) 180, 267
Matamata 24
Mate 147
  hostile review of *The New Zealanders* 148, 152–153, 214, 222
Mazengarb Report 75–76
McAdam, Sheena *see* Amato, Sheena (née McAdam)
McCahon, Colin 13, 201, 203, 205, 209, 228–229, 233, 235, 237, 263, 276, **P2**
  koru for Maurice's letterhead 235
  painting on bar in Arapito Road house 239, **P2**
McCarthyism 49–50, 62–63, 209
McCormick, Eric 199, 205, 206, 215, 230, 242, 266, 276, **P2**
  Letters and Art in New Zealand 199
McDiarmid, Hugh 140
McEldowney, Dennis 179–180, 182–183, 184, 186, 189, 193, 199, 206, 209, 212, 213, **P2**

The World Regained 179
McInnes, Colin 195
McIvor, Lois **P2**
McTaggart, David 271–272, 274
Meads, Colin 37
media, Maurice's use for self-promotion 154–155
Menon, Krishna 226
metafiction 189, 191
Middleton, O.E. 'Ted' 204, 205
Mirams, Roger 67, 69
Mitcalfe, Barbara 148, 159
Mitcalfe, Barry 148–149, 159, 178, 199, 207, 208, 254, 271, 272, 276
    Boy Roel: Voyage to Nowhere 274
Morrieson, Ronald Hugh 56, 59
Morris family 33–34, 60
Moscow 99–103, **P1**
Mount Possession muster 150–151
Mulgan, John 75
    Man Alone 185
Murray-Smith, Stephen 127, 128, 137
Muru, Selwyn 233, 276
Mururoa atoll 271–275
Muttonbird Islands 239
myths 12
    'all story is myth' 187
    myth of New Zealanders as 'uprooted people wistfully looking back' 187
    New Zealand 'man alone' myth 185
    pakeha 181, 182
    personal mythology 17–18, 149
    private and public myths 260, 261

Nagy, Imre 120
Nanking 98
Nash, Walter 66, 135
National Council of Churches 35
National Film Unit (NFU) 65–66, 67–69, 70, 71, 75, 80, 84, 87, 90, 91, 93, 95, 114
    documentary on Eric Lee-Johnson 82–83
    Inventor in the Mackenzie Country 68
    'John Feeney and the National Film Unit' (Shadbolt article) 114–115
    'Opo the Friendly Dolphin' 81–82
    Pictorial Parade 68, 81, 87
    The Snows of Aorangi 67
National Geographic, Maurice's assignments 11, 149, 150–151, 155–156, 178, 183, 218, 232, 259, **P2**
    Cook Islands 218, 219–221
    feature on the Maori 237–238, 239, 253
    Malaysia 172, 176–177, 182
    Polynesian section of book on South Pacific 221, 222
    Samoa 165–166, 169–171
National governments 45, 48–49, 65, 271
National Orchestra 163
National Union of Students (NUS), London 113, 116, 124, 126, 134
nationalism, literary 76
New Ireland 57, 58
New Plymouth 54, 55, 59
New Statesman 135
New York Times 212
New York Times Book Review 242
New Yorker 137, 141, 149, 156
New Zealand
    see also myths; poetry, New Zealand; writing, New Zealand
    Maurice's views 12, 13, 155, 159, 163, 165, 173, 174, 211, 215, 217, 223, 232
    National Film Unit portrayal 67
    passing of frontier society 185
New Zealand: Gift of the Sea (Shadbolt, with Brian Brake) 11, 180–182, 188, 194, 196, 200, 219, 232, 267–268
'New Zealand Artist syndrome' 266
New Zealand Broadcasting Corporation (NZBC) 216, 246–247
New Zealand Broadcasting Service 72
New Zealand Herald 49, 50, 66
New Zealand Listener 76, 80, 85, 196, 208–209, 232, 244
    'Annual Holiday' and criticism by 'K of Henderson' 72–75, 80, 81, 91, 165, 214
    Maurice's articles 113, 118, 124, 238
    Maurice's book reviewing 170, 214, 215
    Maurice's 'In My View' columns 233, 238
    Maurice's letters 232
    review of *Among the Cinders* 211–212
    review of *Strangers and Journeys* 277–278
    review of *Summer Fires and Winter*

Country 186
  review of *The New Zealanders* 143, 152
  review of *The Presence of Music* 222
  review of *This Summer's Dolphin* 242
New Zealand Literary Fund *see* Literary Fund
New Zealand Monthly Review 186–187, 220–221
New Zealand Players, 'The Solid Gold Cadillac' 88
New Zealand Poetry Yearbook 69, 76, 196
New Zealand Women's Weekly 232
The New Zealander (current affairs journal) 231–232
The New Zealanders (Shadbolt, short story collection) 118, 123–124, 126, 127, 130–136, 162, 185, 234
  Baxter's comments 141–142
  Brasch's comments 152, 164
  Gee's comments 164
  Hamilton's hostile review 148, 152–153, 214
  Mitcalfe's comments 148
  publication 132–133, 138, 139, 140, 141–142
  reviews 142–144, 147, 149, 152, 158–159, 277
  Stead's comments on manuscript 130–131
  titles of sections drawn from Baxter's 'Homage to Lost Friends' 133
Ngati Maniapoto 30, 31
Nicholson, Jane 136
Ninety Mile Beach 178, 195, 239, 269, 271
  see also Ahipara
Nixon, Richard 271
Noonan, Michael 183
  'The Rattle' 183
Norfolk Island 19
nuclear testing in South Pacific 271–275
Numbers 75–76, 77, 84, 86, 106

Oakley, Don **P1**
O'Brien, Conor Cruise 226
Observer 118, 277
Oliver, Bill 276
One of Ben's 17, 26, 35, 103, 108, 112, 138
Opo
  Maurice's novel, *This Summer's Dolphin* 207, 210, 231, 233–235, 242–243, 252, 253, 260
  Maurice's *Reader's Digest* story 260
  'Opo the Friendly Dolphin' (film) 81–82
  Smither's exhibition 234–235, 242
Opononi 79, 81–82
Opononi Gay Dolphin Protection Committee 82
Oratia, West Auckland 41, 42
Osborne, John, *Look Back in Anger* 115
O'Shea, John 67, 69
Otago Daily Times 184, 185
Overland 127–128, 137

Pacific Films 67
Pana-kareao, Nopera 263
Parsons book and coffee shop, Wellington 157
Pasternak, Boris 101, 103
  Dr Zhivago 103, 127–128, 137, 138
Patea Hospital Board 60
'Peace, Power and Politics in Asia' Conference, Wellington 226, 229
Pearson, Bill 153–154, 215
  Coal Flat 155
Pegasus Press 166
Peking (Beijing) 97, 98
PEN New Zealand 118, 142, 157, 179, 192
People's Republic of China 274
The People's Voice 62, 198–199, 204
Perkins, Max 263
Peter, Juliet 233
Pictorial Parade 68, 81, 87
Piha 206, **P2**
Pitman, Robert 142
poetry, New Zealand 71
  see also names of individual poets
  A Book of New Zealand Verse (Curnow, ed.) 44
  New Zealand Poetry Yearbook 69, 76
  Wellington school of poets 76
Poland 138
Pollock, Jackson 122
Popov, Vasil 105, 106, 108, 109, 111, 137-139, 140
Post and Telegraph Department (P&T) 32, 33, 34, 38, 51–52, 148
Prescott, Orville 212
The Presence of Music (Shadbolt, book in triptych form) 201–203, 207, 210,

217, 222–223, 227, 262
Prichard, Katharine Susannah 128
Queenstown 184, 189, 192, 213

Radio Hauraki 273
railways
   main trunk railway 27, 31
   Maurice's employment 48, 49
   support of railway unions for waterside workers, 1951 49
   Te Kuiti railway station 38–39, 40
Rainbow Warrior 275
Reader's Digest 10, 12, 238, 259–260, 267, 268
Reid, John 277
Remmel, Willi 79
Rhodes, H. Winston 186–187
Richards, Beverly 237, 239, 241, 244, 245, 246, 248
Richmond, Towers and Benson 162
Robert Burns Fellowship 130, 151, 157, 172, 178, 179–180, 184, 188, 213, 241, 246
Robertson, Bob 179, 180, 184, 186
Robinson, Dove-Myer 272
Robinson, Neil 263
Robson, John 229
Roddick, Alan 87
Rosenberg, Julius and Ethel 62–63
Ross, Jean 127
Rotorua 66, 187, 211, 233, 241
Royal Court Theatre, London 115, 135
royal tours 21, 61, 182
Rubinstein, Hilary 132–133, 141
rugby
   1981 Springbok tour protest, Hamilton 37
   Maurice's account of learning to play rugby 37
Ruhen, Olaf 221

Sargeson, Frank 73, 74, 75, 81, 86, 132, 152, 173, 186, 205, 214, **P2**
   Collected Stories 214
   encouragement of Stead's 'K of Henderson' letter 92, 214
   feud with Monte Holcroft 73–74, 80
   and Hamilton's hostile review of *The New Zealanders* 214
   The Hangover 278
   homosexuality 215

'I for One' 86
'The Making of a New Zealander' 165
relationship with Maurice 80, 87, 88, 90, 92, 93, 94, 127, 129, 141, 159
Speaking for Ourselves (editor) 44, 86, 87
Scanlan, A.B. 60
Scannell, Vernon 242
Scholes, Jeff 236–237
School Publications 150
Schwimmer, Eric 149
Scott, Dick 198–199, 205, 245, 267, 276
   151 Days 199
   Ask that Mountain: The Story of Parihaka 199
   The Parihaka Story 199
Scott, Nellie 94
Scott, Sid 94
'Search for Tim Livingstone' *see Strangers and Journeys* (Shadbolt)
SEATO 208, 227
Security Intelligence Service (SIS) 66
Seddon, Dick 22
Shadbolt, Ada (née Shaw) 21–22, 23, 24, 26, 46, 47, 50, 70–71, 77, 78, 91, 188, 190, **P1**
Shadbolt, Amelia 21, 22, 24, 25, 53
Shadbolt, Arthur (Bill) 18, 27, 28, 46, 267
Shadbolt, Benjamin (Ben) 19–20, 21, 25, 193, **P1**
Shadbolt, Brendan 183, 194, 213, 236, **P2**
   after Maurice and Gill's separation 239, 240, 248, 249, 250, 255, 256, 264
   Arapito Road, Titirangi 195, 257
   birth and babyhood 170, 177
   family holidays 178, 221, 224–225
   rugby league 253
   Titirangi Primary School 252
Shadbolt, Brigid 264, 269, 274
Shadbolt, Daniel 213, 224, 225, 226, 236, 240, 245, 248, 252, 255, 256, **P2**
Shadbolt, Dick (Seddon) 19, 147
Shadbolt, Donald (Tim) 24, 46, 70, 206
Shadbolt, Elizabeth (née Perham) 19–21
Shadbolt, Ernest Francis 19, 21–25, 45–46, 78, 176, **P1**
   representation in Maurice's fiction 190
   'Shadbolts by Land and Sea' 25
Shadbolt, Francis Clement William (Frank) 18–19, 21, 22, 24, 25–26, 45, 53, 147, 267, 276, **P1**

betting on the races 25, 32, 37, 41, 75, 87
cancer 269, 274
frequent moves 41–42
grandchildren 159, 205, 240, 241, 247, 249, 255, **P2**
marriage 18, 19, 26, 28, 33, 41-42, **P1**
pacifism 32
politics 18, 27, 28, 33, 37, 38, 101, 102, 107
relationship with Doris 33
relationship with Gill 63, 118, 240, 241
representation in Maurice's fiction 131, 189
Te Kuiti 28–29, 32, 33, 34, 35, 36, 37–38, 39–40, **P1**
and Tim Shadbolt 207
Waiheke Island 183, 194
Waihi 27–28, 148
Shadbolt, Gillian Eve Muriel (Gill, née Heming) 74, 79, **P1, P2**
Ahipara, temporary rental 196–197
Arapito Road house 195, 196, 200–201, 205–206, 207, 218–219, 224, 225, 239–240, 257
Baxter's support 241, 247, 275
belief in Maurice's work 64, 84, 206
casual article writing 113, 124, 135, 158
Child magazine editing and publishing 221–222, 236
children 65, 138–139, 148, 149, 158, 162, 166, 171, 189, 194, 201, 205, 206, 210, 213, 224, 236, 239–240, 257 (*see also* Shadbolt, Brendan; Shadbolt, Daniel; Shadbolt, Sean Francis; Shadbolt, Tui)
children, access after separation from Maurice 240, 248, 249–250, 255–257, 264
daily life and finances 88, 118, 205–206, 210, 218–219, 236
divorce from Maurice 257, 264, 267
Dunedin 179, 182–184, 186, 189
Evening Post position 69, 88, 90
gift to Maurice of McCahon painting on bar, Arapito Road 239, **P2**
Hawera 56–59, 63, **P1**
housekeeping 189, 201, 206, 246, 256, 257
letters to and from Maurice 62–64, 71, 87, 123, 124–126, 127, 139, 177–178, 270
London 112–113, 115–118, 119, 122, 123, 126, 128, 131, 135, 139, 140–141
marital tensions 107, 112, 118, 119, 120, 123, 124–126, 135, 160–161, 189, 217–218, 224–225, 236, 252
marriage to Maurice 63–65, 66, 69, 119, 124, 135, 138–139, 158, 201, 221–222, 223–224, 225, 246, 277, **P1**
maternal ministrations to Maurice 65, 107, 119, 158, 160, 270
Maurice's affair with Jenny Bojilova 111–112, 119–121, 123, 125, 126
National Union of Students publicity officer, London 113, 116, 124, 126, 135
relationship with Johnny Springhall 240, 247, 248, 256, 257–258
Samoa trip with Maurice 221
separation from Maurice 224, 225, 236–237, 239–241, 247, 248
Te Marua 149, 150, 157–158
travel to China, Soviet Union, eastern Europe and England, 1957–1959 93–94, 95–136, 137–139, 140–144
Truth journalist 160, 163, 170, 201, 206
Wellington 69, 84, 87–88, 160, 166, 167–168, 177–178, 247, 248–249
Shadbolt, Jack (Dardy) 25, 46
Shadbolt, Johnnie 25, 28–29
Shadbolt, Julia Louise 42, 53, 61, 65, 66, 95, 109, 119, 156, 159, 170, 194, 205–206, 207, 226, **P1, P2**
visit to Akaroa 193
visit to Dunedin 183
Shadbolt, Maurice Francis Richard
awards, prizes and honours
Buckland Literary Award 243
Burns Fellowship 130, 172, 178, 179–180, 184, 213, 246
Katherine Mansfield Short Story Award 174, 188, 189, 223
Landfall prose competition 90, 91, 180

Literary Fund grants 118, 253
Literary Fund Scholarship in
    Letters 149, 163
Wattie Book of the Year
    Awards 243, 278
Wellington Festival literary
    competition 165, 174
Youth Carnival for Peace and
    Friendship prize 52–53
childhood, youth and family
    childhood 17–18, 27–38, **P1**
    conjuror 39, 40, 43, 47, 48, 52
    convict ancestors 19–20, 34
    education 32, 35–37, 42–45, 47,
        48, 50, 52, **P1**
    enduring sense of superstition and
        the supernatural 38
    family background 11, 18–28,
        33–34, 193, 267
    frequent household moves 41–42
    'Home Guard Assistance Corps' 35
    storytelling 36
    Te Kuiti 17, 28–40, 134, 189, 192,
        210–211, 221, 232, **P1**
    youth 39–48
children (see also Shadbolt, Brendan;
Shadbolt, Brigid; Shadbolt, Daniel;
Shadbolt, Sean Francis; Shadbolt, Tui;
and under Shadbolt, Gillian Eve Muriel
(Gill, née Heming))
    custody after separation from
        Gill 240, 241–242, 245, 246,
        247, 248, 249–251, 252–253,
        255–257, 264, 265
editing
    anthology of new New Zealand
        writing 86–87, 254
    anthology of New Zealand
        prose and poetry for Cassell
        N.Z. 254
    New Zealand short stories for
        Russian translation 117
health
    Asian 'flu, 1957 99
    bronchitis 243
    colitis 172, 176, 177, 178
    depression 26, 60, 64, 65, 111,
        116–117, 126, 210, 248, 270
    hepatitis 221
    pneumonia 221
    spinal surgery in London 116,
        117–118, 119, 122, 124
    'tummy upset,' Bulgaria 107
    undescended testicle surgery 42,
        161
homes and daily life
    Ahipara, temporary rental 195–
        196
    Bucklands Beach, borrowed
        bach 224
    car purchases 157–158, 168, 183,
        221
    Dunedin, 69 Union Street 179,
        182–184, 186
    finances 69, 88, 113, 118, 165, 170,
        178, 206, 213–214, 218, 219,
        239, 253–254, 255, 267–269
    London, Chelsea Embankment
        132, **P1**
    London, Ealing flat 112–113,
        116–117, 118
    London, Tite Street flat,
        Chelsea 122, 123–124,
        135–136, 140–141, 202
    need for housekeeper after
        separation from Gill 245–246
    Parnell flat with Beverly
        Richards 237
    Te Marua, 46 Valley Road 149,
        150, 155–156, **P2**
    Titirangi, 35 Arapito Road 9-11,
        195, 196, 198, 200–201,
        218–219, 221, 239, 241–242,
        248, 257, 267, 275, **P2**
    Titirangi, Boylan Road 252–253
    Wellington, 370a The Terrace 69,
        84, 86, 89–90, 91, 93
    Wellington, Bank Road,
        Northland 248–249, 250–251
    Wellington, 3 Fairview Crescent,
        Kelburn 166, 167–168
    Wellington, 88 Glenmore
        Street 160
marriages (see Armstrong, Bridget; Magner,
Barbara; Shadbolt, Gillian Eve Muriel
(Gill, née Heming)) **P1**
occupations
    bakery shiftworker 165
    builder's labourer 52
    casual worker 53
    conjuror 39, 40, 43, 47, 48, 52, **P1**
    journalist 49, 50, 52, 54, 55–56,

59–61, 91, 132, 198, 206, 214, 268–269, 278
National Film Unit documentary maker 65–66, 67–69, 70, 71, 81–83, 84, 87, 90, 91, 93
proofreader of business directories 50
railway worker 48, 49
roadman 59, 60, 61, 75
textile factory worker 93
wool store and labouring 47, 53, 73
personal characteristics
appearance 26
'artistic temperament' 64, 248
claim to inherited psychic powers 70, 188
emotional insecurity and volatility 65, 119, 124–125, 126, 217
inherited characteristics 24, 26, 60
need for securities of marriage 65, 126, 173, 236, 270
uncertainties 65, 217, 269–270
personal interests, beliefs and views
anti-nuclear protests 135, 271–274, **P1**
anti-Vietnam War protests and correspondence 207–209, 226–227, 231, 232, 271
boating 257
inherited beliefs and views 27, 51, 59
painting materials for George Wilder and Ron Jorgensen 227–230, 250
politics and social activism 47–48, 49–50, 52, 53–54, 62–63, 64, 66, 102, 106–107, 124, 232–233, 274
protest about exclusion of Maori from All Black tour, 1960 135
reading 34, 36, 44, 59, 67, 71, 73, 75, 80, 184–185
tramping and walking interests 11, 48, 60, 253, **P1**
views on New Zealand 155, 159, 163, 165, 173, 174, 211, 215, 217, 223, 232
sexual relationships 12–13
affair at Kessingland with young Jewish woman, Pam 125, 126

Barbara Magner 247, 248, 249
Beverly Richards 237, 239, 241, 244, 245, 246, 247
on Cook Islands trip 220, 221
first regular mistress 52
Fleur Adcock 10
Jenny Bojilova 110–111, 115, 117, 119–121, 123, 125, 126, 139, 140
Marilyn Duckworth 160–162, 244–245, 247–249, 250
rarely short of sexual partners 245, 257
search for sexual maturity 202–203
while a student 47, 48
travel overseas
Borneo **P2**
China, Soviet Union, eastern Europe and Britain, 1957–1959 93–94, 95–144, 147, 204, 232, **P1**
Cook Islands 219–221
Dublin 10
Ibiza, 1958 121, 122–123, 124
Malaysia 172, 176–177, 182
South Pacific islands 221, 232, **P2**
Western Samoa 165–166, 169–170, 171, 221–222
writing
advice from retired British army colonel 50
American influences 44, 59
Brasch's guidance 85, 130, 134, 152
in Bulgaria 105, 109, 117
career in writing 11, 13, 90, 93, 149, 223, 254, 280
conviction of becoming a major writer 80, 81, 90, 127, 197, 198
in England 113–114, 116–117
experience of pictorial visualisation a strength 83
first attempts as an adult 47, 52
five-year plan, 1959 143
mission 238
myths 12, 17–18, 149, 185, 187, 260, 261
need for money-making commissions 165, 170, 172, 213–214, 218, 219, 239, 260, 268

Opononi cottage as intended
    retreat 78, 79
painters as subjects 82
PEN membership 156–157
poetry 50, 51, 52, 62, 63–64, 68,
    70–71
portrayal of known people and
    places 73, 90–91, 131, 133,
    134, 171, 174, 176, 189–190,
    192, 202–203, 210–211, 221,
    232, 268
uncertainties 80, 81, 84, 91, 124,
    127, 217, 232, 235, 236–237,
    248–249, 251, 254, 264–265
underlying drive to think fictionally
    not visually 71, 75
use of media for self-
    promotion 154–155
writing: articles, reviews, stories, etc.
  for journals and newspapers 231,
    238 (see also National Geographic,
    Maurice's assignments)
  Affairs Magazine 260–261
  The Bookman 141
  The Bulletin 214
  'China, Russia, Bulgaria. A Journey'
    (article) 114
  comment on Pasternak's Doctor
    Zhivago 127–128, 137
  Druzhba Naradov (The People's
    Friendship), Moscow 101
  Evening Post 69, 90, 124
  Islands 81, 261
  'John Feeney and the National Film
    Unit' (article) 114–115
  Landfall 70, 77, 79, 80–81, 86, 90,
    91, 113–115, 130, 134, 277
  letter criticising Stead's review
    of poetry by Doyle and
    Campbell 91–92
  Literaturnaya Gazeta, Moscow 100
  Moscow News 101
  New Yorker 137, 141, 149, 156
  'New Zealand: Gift of the
    Sea' (article, with Brian
    Brake) 170–171
  New Zealand Listener 72–73, 74,
    75, 80, 81, 85, 113, 118, 124,
    170, 208–209, 214, 215, 232,
    233, 238
  New Zealand Women's Weekly 232
  The New Zealander 231–232
  Numbers 75–76, 77, 84, 86, 106
  Otago Daily Times 185
  Overland 127–128, 137
  The People's Voice 62
  Reader's Digest 10, 238, 259–260,
    267, 268
  report on Seventh World Youth
    Festival 137
  review of Duggan's Immanuel's
    Land 90, 154
  Sunday Times 143
  Times Educational Supplement 137
  'The Value of the N.Z. Short Story'
    (article) 90
writing: daily journalism 91
  New Zealand Herald 49, 50
  Taranaki Daily News 54, 55–56,
    59–60, 61
  Truth 60
  Waitakere Gazette 61, 195
writing: in childhood and youth 34, 37
  'Saved from the Hau-Haus' 37
writing: non-fiction 280
  'Beginnings' (essay for Islands) 81,
    261
  Introduction to Amato's The
    Full Circle of the Travelling
    Cuckoo 216–217, 265
  'Letter to Jim' 276
  'Life & Litters' (autobiographical
    essay) 261
  New Zealand: Gift of the Sea (book,
    with Brian Brake) 11, 180–
    182, 188, 194, 196, 200, 219,
    232, 267–268
  One of Ben's 17, 26, 35, 103, 108,
    112, 138
  planned book with George
    Wilder 230
  Shell Guide to New Zealand 11,
    210, 211, 218, 219, 221, 231,
    232, 233, 243, 253, 268
writing: novels and novellas 11, 55, 61,
    62, 201, 280 (see also Strangers and
    Journeys (Shadbolt))
  Among the Cinders 11, 188–192,
    193, 200, 209–210, 211–213,
    214, 232, 242, 253–254, 262,
    267
  autobiographical novel 59, 68, 71

An Ear of the Dragon 237, 251–252, 253, 254, 265–267
first novel (unpublished) 143, 149, 155, 158, 160, 162, 163
future novel possibilities 264, 269
metafiction 189, 191
The Presence of Music (book in triptych form) 201–203, 207, 210, 217, 222–223, 227, 262
Season of the Jew 12
'tales of my tribe' 238, 268
This Summer's Dolphin 207, 210, 231, 233–235, 242–243, 252, 253, 260
writing: plays 135, 158, 215–216
writing: short stories 61, 62, 70–71, 75, 85–86, 90, 142, 280 (*see also New Zealanders, The* (Shadbolt, short story collection))
   'After the Depression' 127, 131, 133, 172, 184, 185, 204, 262
   'And then there were two' 84
   'Annual Holiday' 72–73, 74–75
   'A Beer for Old Johnny' 106
   'Ben's Land' 165, 174, 192, 267
   'Conversation' 85
   criticism of 'Annual Holiday' by 'K of Henderson' 73, 74–75, 80, 81, 91, 165, 214
   'End of Season' (novella) 85–86, 90, 91, 127, 132, 133, 185, 262
   'Figures in Light' (second 'panel' of triptych *The Presence of Music*) 203, 223, 244–245
   'The Gloves' 85
   'The Homecoming' 174, 176, 187, 188, 211
   'Neither Profit nor Salvation' 175
   'Night of the Chariot' 86, 87, 90, 91, 132–133
   'On the County' 75
   'The Paua Gatherers' 185
   'The People Before' 175–176
   'Play the Fife Lowly' 90, 91, 133
   'The Presence of Music' (central 'panel' of triptych *The Presence of Music*) 202–203
   'The Room' 143, 165, 174–175, 187
   'Sing Again Tomorrow' 70, 77, 86, 133, 262

'The Strangers' 133–134, 137, 141, 149, 156, 172, 185, 262
'Summer Fires' 175, 192, 215
Summer Fires and Winter Country (collection; earlier title, 'Seek the Green Inn') 172–176, 181, 182, 186–187, 200
'Thank You Goodbye' 120–121, 131, 133, 139, 140
'There was a Mountain' 174
'Twosome' 75, 91, 106, 133
'The Voyagers' (first 'panel' of triptych *The Presence of Music*) 201–203
'The Waters of the Moon' 130, 134
'Winter Country' 174
'The Woman's Story' 164–165
Shadbolt, Peter 19, 20, 27, 34, 38, 42, 95, 226, **P1**
Shadbolt, Rod 70
Shadbolt, Sean Francis 177, 179, 183, 194, 236, **P2**
   after Maurice and Gill's separation 240, 248, 249, 255, 256, 264
   Arapito Road, Titirangi 195, 201, 213, 221, 257
   birth and babyhood 156, 158, 160, 161, 166
   family holidays 178, 221, 224–225, 235, 241
   rugby league 253
   Titirangi Primary School 213, 252
Shadbolt, Sis (Renee) 23, 78–79, 81, 87, 207, 249, **P1**
Shadbolt, Stanley 22–23
Shadbolt, Tim 70, 206–207
   Bullshit and Jellybeans 226
Shadbolt, Tui 213, 224, 225, 226, 236, 240, 245, 248, 252, 256, 264, 273, **P2**
Shadbolt, Violet (Vi, née Kearon) 18, 19, 26, 115, 128
   frequent household moves 41–42
   Glen Eden 33, 34, **P1**
   grandchildren 156, 159, 170, 205, 221, 239, 241, 245, 246, 247, 249, 255–256, **P2**
   marriage 18, 19, 26, 33, 41-42. **P1**
   relationship with Gill 63, 107, 119, 255, 256, 257
   relationship with Maurice 27, 43, 45, 48, 52, 65, 119, 239, 240, 241, 246, 277

representation in Maurice's
 fiction 189–190
socialist ideals 35
stillborn daughter 19, 203
Te Kuiti 29, 32–33, 34, 35, 37, 38, 40,
 P1
visit to Dunedin 183
Waiheke Island 183, 194
Waihi 118–119, 147, 148
Shadbolt, Yvonne 27, 38
Shadbolt family 11, 33–34, 38, 53, 63, 64,
 147, 174, **P1**
 convicts 19–20, 34
 representation in Maurice's fiction 22,
  73, 131, 189–190, 193
Shanghai 98
Sharp, Jim 273, **P2**
Shaw, William and Annie 21
The Shell Guide to New Zealand 11, 210,
 211, 218, 219, 221, 231, 232, 233, 243,
 253, 268
Sillitoe, Alan 142–143
Sinclair, Keith 87, 274
 A History of New Zealand 132
Singapore 177
Sister Renee Shadbolt Park, Green Bay,
 Auckland 24
Smith, Hera 187, 211
Smith, Shirley 250, 256, 264
Smith, Stevie 142, 153
Smither, Elizabeth 269
Smither, Michael 13, 234–235, 236, 239,
 240, 241–242, 245, 246, 254, 255, 268,
 269, 276, **P2**
 Frances Hodgkins Fellowship 254
Solzhenitsyn, Alexandr, *One Day in the Life
 of Ivan Denisovich* 205
Somervell's coffee bar, Auckland 48
South Africa, sporting contacts 135, 274
Soviet Union 18, 33, 34, 62–63, 93–94,
 97, 99–104, 105, 147, 204–205, 232
 Maurice's review of *Dissonant Voices in
  Soviet Literature* 215
 writers 100–102, 103, 108, 114,
  127–128, 261
Soviet Writers' Union 101, 102, 103, 114,
 128
Spanish Civil War 78–79
Speaking for Ourselves (Sargeson, ed.) 44,
 86, 87
Springhall, Johnny 240, 247, 248, 256,

 257–258
Stalin, Joseph 62, 93–94, 100, 101, 102,
 103–104, 114, 127–128
Stalin Museum 104
State Literary Fund *see* Literary Fund
Stead, Karl 86, 91–92, 128–129, 132, 134,
 143, 191, 217, 232, **P1**
 Auckland University 1960 Winter
  Lecture 164
 comments on *Among the Cinders* 213
 comments on *The New
  Zealanders* 130–131
 'K of Henderson' letter 73, 74–75, 91,
  93, 128, 165, 214
 The New Poetic 128
 representation in *Among the
  Cinders* 190, 212
Stead, Kay (née Roberts) 92, 128, **P1**
Steinbeck, John 28, 36, 44
Stella, Frank 136
Stevens, Joan 211–212, 266
Stevenson, Robert Louis 170
Stones, Cushla 239–240
Stones, Tony 240
Strangers and Journeys (Shadbolt) 117,
 131, 134, 172, 184, 232, 276–277,
 278–279
 early title, 'Search for Tim
  Livingstone' 185, 201, 202,
  210–211, 213, 224, 236–237, 238,
  251, 254–255, 261–262
 first draft, revisions and proofs 255,
  261–262, 268, 269, 272
 jacket paintings 269
 parts: 'Fathers,' 'Fathers and Sons' and
  'Sons,' with final 'Fathers' 262–263
 re-titled *Strangers and Journeys* 262
 reviews 277–278
Sturm, Terry 86
Sunday Express 142
Sunday Times 143, 228, 229, 242, 278
Surkov, Alexei 103, 114
Sydney 52–53, 57, 58, 66, 95, 163, 178
Szkup, Jerzy 138

Taiapa, Pineamine (Pine) 238–239, 247,
 267, 268
Takapuna, Auckland 51, 74, 79, 80, 86,
 87, 88
Tamure 272–274, **P2**
Tapper, Anne **P2**

Tapper, Garth 228–229, 233, **P2**
Taranaki Daily News 54, 55–56, 59–60, 61
Taranaki Herald 55, 56
Tasmania, Port Arthur prison 19
Taumarunui 12, 22, 23, 276
Taumarunui Hospital Board 23, 24
Tawhiao 30
taxation of royalties 180–181, 214
Taylor, Alister 226
Te Ao Hou 149
Te Atairangikaahu, Te Arikinui 233
Te Kao 149
Te Kooti Rikirangi 30–31
Te Kuiti 17, 28–29, 30–33, 34–40, 134, 189, 192, 202, 210–211, 221, 232, 262, 269
   A&P Winter Show 39
   Home Guard 35
Te Kuiti District High School 36, 42, **P1**
Te Kuiti Primary School 32, **P1**
Te Kuiti railway station 38–39, 40
Te Marua 149, 150, 155–156, **P2**
Te Tokanga-nui-o-noho meeting house 31, 32
television 183
Tempest, Peter 105, 106, 109
Tempest-Yossifova, Brigita 105, 106, 108, 109
Theatre Royal, London 135
This Summer's Dolphin (Shadbolt) 207, 210, 231, 233–235, 242–243, 252, 253, 260
Thomas, Dylan 85
Tikitiki 238, 268
Times Educational Supplement 137
Times Literary Supplement 143, 158, 222, 242, 277
Titirangi, Auckland 195, 197, 198–199, 204, 205, 230, 252, 257, 268, 274, 275
   35 Arapito Road 195, 196, 198, 200–201, 218–219, 221, 239, 241–242, 248, 257, 267, **P2**
   Maurice's idea of setting for novel 264, 269, 275
Tomorrow 186
Tourist and Publicity Department 114
Town and Around 246, 247
Trans-Siberian Railway 93, 98–99
Truth 60, 160, 163, 201, 204, 205
Tuwhare, Hone 53, 275, 276
Unemployed Workers' Movement 18

Unity Artists 204
Unity theatre, Wellington 158
Universities Students Arts Festival 228
Utting, Gerald 50

Vaasen, Sue 221–222
Venezuela 115, 116, 117
Victoria University 157
Vietnam War 207–209, 223, 226–227, 231, 232, 271
Vogt, Anton 157
Volkerling, Michael 278, 279

Waiheke Island 183, 194, 233
Waihi 27–28, 118–119, 126, 132, 147, 148, 149, 159, 211
   'Black Tuesday' strike, 1912 28
Waihi Gold Mining Company 28
Waikai, Bill 32, 40
Waikai family 31, 32
Waikino 18, 27, 148
Waitakere Gazette 61, 195
Waitakere Ranges 11, 42, 60, 197–198, 236–237, 253, **P1**
Walsh, Dave 88, **P1**
waterfront lockout and associated strikes, 1951 48–49, 50, 199, 263
Watson, Jean 166, 167
Wattie Book of the Year Awards 243, 278
The Week 127
Weekly Review 65
Wellington 65, 66, 69–70, 71, 87–88, 156–157, 162–163, 188–189, 192, 193, 196, 223, 227
   see also Te Marua
   3 Fairview Crescent, Kelburn 166, 167–168
   88 Glenmore Street 160
   370a The Terrace 69, 84, 86, 89–90, 91, 93
   Auckland–Wellington literary disputes 92
   Bank Road, Northland 248–249, 250–251
   Gill, after separation from Maurice 247, 248–249
Wellington Festival literary competition 165, 174
Wendt, Albert 166, 169–170, 183, 246, 276
   'The First Snowman' 183

Wendt, Henry 169, 221
Western Samoa 165–166, 169–170, 171, 221–222, 246, **P2**
Whanganui River district 22, 23, 24, 176
Whitcombe & Tombs 11, 142, 155, 171–172, 180, 181, 200, 210, 216, 233, 267–268
White, Patrick 144, 162–163, 172, 178, 211, 222, 242, 252, 261
 The Tree of Man 263, 277
The Whole Earth Catalogue 226
Wilder, George 185, 186, 227–230, 250, 263, 264, **P2**
Williams, Peter 229
Williams, Tennessee 252
Wilson, Colin 142
Wilson, Mabel 36, 37–38
Wilson, Norman 37–38
Wilson, Phillip 75, 118, 157, 248, 249–250
Wolf, Don 47
Wolfe, Thomas 44, 59, 68, 263
Wordsworth, Christopher 222
World Federation of Democratic Youth 99
World Festival of Youth and Students
 Seventh, Vienna, 1959 137
 Sixth, Moscow, 1957 93, 99–101
World War I 101
World War II 34, 35, 38, 46, 48, 57–58, 61, 70, 152
writing, New Zealand
 anthology of short stories in Russian translation 204–205
 Auckland–Wellington literary disputes 92
 autobiographical tradition in fiction 90
 coming of age for fiction 131
 Ireland and Shadbolt's anthology of new New Zealand writing 86–87
 Maurice's address at Otago University arts festival 184–185
 Maurice's article in *Otago Daily Times* 185
 Maurice's essay for *Encyclopaedia Britannica* 261
 Maurice's interview for *Affairs Magazine* 260–261
 Maurice's interview for *Literaturnaya Gazeta*, Moscow 100
 Maurice's role 13
 Maurice's talk in Georgia 104

Speaking for Ourselves (Sargeson, ed.) 44, 86, 87

Yeats, William Butler, 'The Choice' 275, 279
Young, Alex 98
Young People's Club (YPC), Auckland 45, 47, 48, 51, 68, **P1**
Youth Carnival for Peace and Friendship, Sydney 52–53

Zhivkov, Todor 106, 108, 110